WAGNER

VINTAGE
MASTER
MUSICIANS

Other titles in the Vintage Master Musicians series

Bach by Malcolm Boyd
Verdi by Julian Budden

WAGNER

BY

BARRY MILLINGTON

Series edited by

Stanley Sadie

VINTAGE
MASTER
MUSICIANS

VINTAGE BOOKS

A DIVISION OF RANDOM HOUSE

NEW YORK

First Vintage Books Edition, March 1987

Library of Congress Cataloging in Publication Data
Millington, Barry.
    Wagner.
    (The Master musicians series)
    Reprint. Originally published: London: Dent, 1984.
    Bibliography: p.
    Includes index.
    1. Wagner, Richard, 1813–1883. 2. Composers—
Germany—Biography. I. Title. II. Series.
ML410.W1M58 1987   782.1'092'4   [B]   86-40460
ISBN 0-394-75279-1

Manufactured in the United States of America
10   9   8   7   6   5   4   3   2   1

Preface

'Noch eine Wagnerbiographie, wozu?' began the preface of Julius Kapp's biography nearly seventy-five years ago. And the necessity for a new book on Wagner is to this day regularly and rightly questioned. The Master Musicians format offered the opportunity to try something a little different from a conventional biography and/or exegesis of the music. In the present book my purpose has been, in addition to providing a basic life and works, to take a critical look at some of the myths that have adorned Wagner biographies ever since the composer dictated his own fanciful account, to examine their ideological significance, and to air some of the issues and controversies that have developed in recent years. Above all it has been my aim to direct readers towards studies that treat the various aspects (whether or not covered in this book) in a more detailed and authoritative fashion. Leitmotif-naming guides will not be found here, nor even plots (except for the early, lesser-known operas): these can readily be consulted elsewhere. Instead, it is hoped that the fruits yielded by the recent endeavours of musicologists and other writers both in Germany and in this country may be enjoyed by a wider audience.

The new insights into Wagner and his work offered by current musicological, analytical and other source-based studies are bringing about yet another major re-evaluation of the subject. With these as one point of reference, and the cultural and social background of Wagner's Germany as another, I hope to have provided a text that may be of some use at several different levels.

Acknowledgment is due to the Cambridge University Press for permission to quote Mary Whittall's translations of the passages on p. 198 (from Curt von Westernhagen, *Wagner: A Biography*) and p. 160 (from Carl Dahlhaus, *Richard Wagner's Music Dramas*). The three extracts from *Wagner: A Documentary Study*, ed. H. Barth, D. Mack and E. Voss, are reproduced by permission of Thames and

Hudson Ltd. All quotations from *Cosima Wagner's Diaries* are given in Geoffrey Skelton's translation, by permission of William Collins Sons & Co. Ltd. Unless otherwise stated, all remaining translations are my own, but I gratefully acknowledge the invaluable help and advice on such matters from David Britt and Stewart Spencer. For reading parts or all of my manuscript at different stages, I am deeply grateful to Konrad Bund, John Deathridge, Ingrid Grimes, Jeremy Schonfield, Stewart Spencer and Arnold Whittall, each of whom has helped to make it a better and more accurate book. My thanks also to the following, who responded to specific queries: Joachim Bergfeld, Manfred Eger, Alexander Knapp, Paul S. Machlin, Reinhard Strohm, Isolde Vetter and Egon Voss. I am obliged to the authors of the forthcoming *Wagner-Werkverzeichnis* that I have been able to draw on the scholarship that has gone into this mammoth and extremely important undertaking. My final thanks are to Jeremy Spencer for his first-rate photographs and to all those, chief among whom is Pauline Baseley, who have assisted and encouraged me over the last couple of years.

March 1984   B.M.

Full details of works mentioned in footnotes are to be found in the select bibliography.

Preface to the paperback edition (1986)

Recent research has established that Wagner's mother Johanna was not the daughter of Prince Constantin (see p.1) but his mistress. This surprising discovery is recounted in full in Martin Gregor-Dellin, 'Recent Researches on Wagner (His Mother's Secret)', Bayreuth Festival Programme, vol. ii (*Parsifal*), 1985, pp.50–71.

Contents

List of Illustrations

Plates between pages 22 and 23

1 Wagner. Pencil drawing by E.B. Kietz, begun January 1840, completed June 1842. (*BBC Hulton Picture Library*)
2 Minna Wagner. (*BBC Hulton Picture Library*)
3 Mathilde Wesendonck. (*BBC Hulton Picture Library*)
4 Autograph score of *Rule Britannia* Overture. (*Reproduced by permission of the Trustees of the British Library*; photo *Jeremy Spencer*)
5 Barricade at Wilsdruffer Gasse (now Strasse), Dresden, 1849. Lithograph. (*Richard-Wagner-Archiv, Bayreuth*)
6 Wilhelmine Schröder-Devrient. Caricature by Cherrier in *Leipziger Charivari*, 1849. (Photo *Jeremy Spencer*)

Between pages 86 and 87

7 Wagner in Paris, 1860. (*BBC Hulton Picture Library*)
8 Ludwig II of Bavaria. (*Mansell Collection*)
9 Page of composition draft of *Götterdämmerung*. (*BBC Hulton Picture Library*)
10 'Richard Wagner in Heaven'. *Der Floh*, Vienna, 1883. (Photo *Jeremy Spencer*)

Between pages 150 and 151

11 Bayreuth Festspielhaus. *The Graphic*, 12 August 1876. (*BBC Hulton Picture Library*)
12 *Parsifal* bells. (*Richard-Wagner-Archiv, Bayreuth*)
13 Wagner. Portrait by Franz Lenbach. (*BBC Hulton Picture Library*)
14 Palazzo Vendramin, Venice. (*BBC Hulton Picture Library*)
15 *Parsifal* review in the *New York Times*, 25 December 1903.
16 Announcement of 1933 Bayreuth Festival.
17 Cosima Wagner. (*Richard-Wagner-Archiv, Bayreuth*)

Wagner

Line illustrations (all photos Jeremy Spencer)

1

Childhood and adolescence (1813–32)

It is surely no mere coincidence that it should be Wagner of all composers over whose paternity there hangs a question-mark. His works have long since been acknowledged as containing deeply penetrating insights into the human psyche, but Wagner's own character and behaviour provide no less fertile ground for an investigation into psychological motivation. His relationships with women, with friends, with enemies, his attitude to Jews all become clearer and more intelligible – though scarcely more attractive – when seen, as they will be at the appropriate points in this study, in the context of a whole personality.

The question of Wagner's paternity is just the first of many contributory problematic factors that require to be taken account of in any appraisal of his life and work. The issue has been obfuscated by the false assertions of hostile individuals wishing to prove that Wagner was of Jewish descent. That possibility, we now know, can in any event be firmly ruled out, though Wagner himself remained in ignorance of that fact.

He was the ninth child to be born into the family of Carl Friedrich and Johanna Rosine Wagner. Friedrich was a police actuary of some social standing; Johanna (*née* Pätz) was possibly the illegitimate daughter of Prince Constantin of Saxe-Weimar-Eisenach (the brother of the Grand Duke) and a tanner's daughter from Weissenfels. Friedrich was a devotee of the theatre: nor was this mere armchair enthusiasm. He is known to have trodden the boards himself in his spare time, but he derived perhaps even more satisfaction from paying court to young actresses of the day. One in particular, Friederike Wilhelmine Worthon (later Hartwig), an outstandingly attractive young woman in her twenties, took his fancy and Johanna used to joke playfully that she often had to keep meals waiting for him. He claimed to have been delayed by work at the office but when he held up his hands to show his ink-stained fingers they were absolutely clean. Perhaps Johanna's conscious mind

1

suppressed the details of what seems to us the obvious purpose of these after-hours visits to the green room; alternatively, extra-marital affairs may have been regarded as a harmless diversion in the Wagner household. It is a matter for pure speculation, as ultimately is the question of whether another of Friedrich's acquaintances, the actor and painter Ludwig Geyer, ever slept with Johanna while her husband was still alive. We know that Geyer was a close friend of Friedrich (remaining so until the latter died) and that he invited both the Wagners to Teplitz, in Bohemia, to take refuge from the hostilities raging around Leipzig.

For the first years of Richard Wagner's life, 1813–15, gunfire and fighting provided a terrifying backdrop to daily existence as the wars of liberation against Napoleon took their bloody course. During 1813 Napoleon engaged with the Allies (Austria, Prussia and Russia) in a series of battles and it was at Leipzig in October of that year that he was defeated by them in the Battle of the Nations. Leipzig was clearly not a healthy place to be that summer and although Teplitz was probably only marginally safer (the matter is disputed), and in spite of the fact that Friedrich was required to stay on duty, Johanna and presumably the two-month-old Richard made the dangerous trek of a little over 100 miles from Leipzig to Teplitz through enemy-occupied territory. A favourite explanation for this apparently unnecessary journey is that Johanna urgently wished to show the baby to its father. The stay lasted only three weeks, from 21 July to 10 August, because Austria then declared war on Napoleon and all visitors had to leave Bohemia. Geyer, who was with a theatrical troupe, went with them to Dresden; Johanna and child returned to Leipzig, where Richard was belatedly baptized on the 16th.

In the outbreak of typhus that followed the Battle of the Nations Carl Friedrich died (23 November 1813). Geyer brought the widow immediate emotional support and what financial help he was capable of. He took the family into his care even though for a time he could offer assistance only from a distance. The following February Johanna visited him in Dresden and they became engaged; their relationship must have been consummated by late May to early June, if not long before, because a child, Cäcilie, was born to them on 26 February 1815. The marriage took place on 28 August 1814 and the couple moved to Dresden where Geyer was engaged by the Court Theatre. He thus became the father Richard knew until his death in 1821; the boy was called Richard Geyer at school until the age of fourteen, reverting to Wagner some years after Geyer's death.

No firm conclusion can be drawn on the question of Wagner's paternity. There are certainly strong arguments in favour of Geyer's candidature: he was probably lodging with the Wagners the previous summer as usual, he was always particularly attached to Richard, whom he called 'the Cossack', and there is also Johanna's extraordinary visit to Teplitz. On the other hand, he apparently provoked no jealousy in Friedrich, his letters to Johanna of that period and shortly after her husband's death reveal no undue intimacy and there is not a scrap of incontrovertible evidence to prove that Johanna was in any way paying back Friedrich for his late working at the office. Much has been made of physiognomic similarities, but these have been invoked by advocates of both points of view.[1]

The paternity issue would have virtually no significance were it not for the fact that Wagner himself thought he may have been the son of Geyer and – unthinkable though the idea might be to him – there was a suggestion that Geyer had Jewish blood. The effects of this nagging suspicion on him will be discussed later in the context of his anti-semitism. For the time being it is necessary only to record that Geyer has since been proved to be of thoroughly Protestant stock.

As a young child Richard was sickly, so much so that his mother thought he would not survive. He remained pale and slim, with rather too small a body to support his abnormally large head. From either of his putative fathers he may have inherited something of a passion for the theatre. He made an early appearance on stage as an angel, in tights, with wings on his back, taking great pains to achieve what he assumed to be a graceful pose.

At the age of seven he was put into the care of Pastor Christian Wetzel at Possendorf, near Dresden, at which time he had a few piano lessons. Summoned back to Dresden to Geyer's deathbed, he was called on to play two tunes on the piano, a performance which caused Geyer to say to his mother – with what degree of optimism or incredulity we do not know – 'Might he perhaps have a talent for

---

[1] Nothing of substance has emerged on the paternity issue since Newman discussed it in his *Life*. See vols i, pp. 3–18; ii, pp. 608–13; iii, pp. 558–62.

music?'[2] At any rate it had been his intention to 'make something' of the boy, and it was in accordance with this dying wish that Johanna resolved not to encourage any theatrical instincts he might have had, in spite of the fact that his sisters Rosalie, Luise and Klara had been allowed to go on the stage. The difficulties experienced by their mother in bringing up a large family on limited resources did not, Wagner later supposed, encourage in her an excess of maternal tenderness. He could not recollect being much fondled by her. And yet he retained a deep affection for his mother;[3] in later life when speaking of her his voice would soften, and his letters to her, though not regular, overflow with apparently genuine expressions of love and gratitude. The hints in his autobiography of lack of mother love must, however, indicate a real sense of emotional deprivation in his early years. This, coupled with the closeness of war when he was a baby, the economic insecurity of his family's situation, the constant separation and uprooting of parts of the family and uncertainty about his paternity, not to mention his physical frailty and gawkiness, might be thought to be the perfect recipe for an inferiority complex and probably more serious and far-reaching psychological disorders as well.

Little wonder that from his boyhood on he protected himself with his wit and a sharp tongue. At an early age too he proved himself in another direction by acquiring some agility in climbing and being able to perform acrobatic feats. The inflammatory skin complaint (erysipelas) that was to plague him throughout his life began to develop at this time and it was noted that it seemed to be accompanied by fits of depression and irritability; few these days would deny that the malady was psychosomatic in origin. His head-strong, obstinate nature often led to quarrels, but he would deflect violence by means of verbal diplomacy; he was always extremely reluctant to cause physical pain. He had a great affection for animals and knew every dog in the neighbourhood. He would rescue puppies

---

[2] *Mein Leben* (p. 6). There is no independent testimony for this anecdote (discounting Glasenapp) which may be a fiction – of the kind later to be found in abundance – designed to foster the myth of a natural genius brought forth and guided by the forces of destiny.

[3] Notwithstanding the letter of 11 September 1842 to his sister Cäcilie and her husband Eduard Avenarius, in which he complains at length about their mother's parsimony.

from drowning and on one occasion, knowing he couldn't take the creature home, he concealed it in his sister's bed. An incident he never forgot concerned the slaughtering of an ox that he witnessed with some friends. As the axe descended, the boy would have rushed at the butcher had his friends not held him back. For some time after he refused all meat. His fertile imagination transformed articles of furniture into animate beings and even as an older boy he would wake screaming in fear after ghostly dreams. But that did not put him off Weber's *Der Freischütz*, with its supernatural theme; on the contrary he was drawn to this melodramatic representation of horror – appreciation of Weber's artistry was to follow.

Entering the Dresden Kreuzschule on 2 December 1822 he made little headway with those subjects he had no interest in, such as mathematics; even Greek was hedged around with troublesome grammatical rules, though he was gripped by the activities of the mythological heroes. A fellow-pupil suddenly keeled over dead one day, and submissions were invited for commemorative poems. Wagner's was adjudicated the best and duly printed and circulated. His mother was delighted and his destiny as a poet seemed assured.

When he was thirteen the family moved to Prague, where his eldest sister Rosalie, who provided the chief income, had secured a good post at the theatre. Wagner remained in Dresden in order to continue his studies at the Kreuzschule until he was old enough to go to university. Staying with the family of some schoolfriends he came into contact both with a rougher, boyish life-style and with some charming young ladies, whose proximity he enjoyed with a pre-pubescent innocence. A friend joined him when he made the journey, almost entirely on foot, to Prague and back to Dresden. This was only the first of many marathons he blithely undertook throughout his life.

On a school trip to Leipzig in the summer of 1827 he renewed the acquaintance of his scholarly uncle Adolf, took possession of a fair-sized collection of Geyer's books that he had inherited, and developed a great liking for the dress and attitudes of the university students. Finding an excuse to leave the school in Dresden, he moved in with two of his sisters and his mother, now back in Leipzig. He spent much time with his uncle, listening to Greek tragedies and absorbing his free-thinking philosophical outlook. On 21 January 1828 he entered the Nicolaischule, but school studies soon began to be neglected and when it was discovered that he had been writing a quite unsuitable tragedy called *Leubald* – a tale of ghosts, insanity and multiple murders – he was called to account for this appalling waste of his time and talents.

His family were no less disturbed by his first determined attempts to master the art of musical composition. He had long been excited by such sounds as the striking of open fifths on the violin; he had also responded to the music of Weber (*Der Freischütz*) and Beethoven (especially the overture to *Fidelio* and the Seventh Symphony). Now he wanted to set *Leubald* to music such as Beethoven had written for Goethe's *Egmont* and in order to acquire the necessary expertise he borrowed from the library a copy of J.B. Logier's *Thorough-Bass* (possibly also using the same pedagogue's more recently published *System der Musik-Wissenschaft*). When the expected mastery did not materialize first in weeks, then in months, he began to owe the library an ever-increasing sum of money in fines. As the bill mounted, he had no alternative but to divulge both the debt – the first of a lifelong stream of financial embarrassments – and the musical aspiration which had brought it about.

For a short time he was distracted by an infatuation for the beautiful daughter of a Jewish banker, Leah David. He lost her to another and took the blow philosophically. As for his other obsession – acquiring a compositional technique – the family would have liked to deter him from what they thought was simply a passing whim, but since domestic circumstances left him alone in the house for a period, he was free to pursue a course of harmony lessons with a local musician called Christian Gottlieb Müller. Wagner's autobiographical account of these lessons belittles their significance: it may have been true, as he says, that he came to regard his tuition as the working of dry academic exercises, but the lessons lasted for the best part of three years and provided him with a firm grounding in harmonic style.

In return for promising to make a renewed assault on studies at school, Wagner was allowed to continue his harmony lessons. He had no interest in becoming a pianist, but made a piano transcription of Beethoven's Choral Symphony, which was politely rejected for publication by Schott, and also learnt much by copying out scores of composers he admired.

His passion for the music of Beethoven is linked, in his autobiography *Mein Leben* (My Life), with an account of a supposedly formative experience. Wagner tells how the young soprano Wil-

6

helmine Schröder-Devrient, who had already taken Germany by storm with her electrifying performances, came to Leipzig for a guest appearance in *Fidelio*. So enthralled was he by the almost satanic intensity of her portrayal that after the performance he wrote her a note saying that from that day his life had found meaning and that if in time to come she should ever hear his name praised in the world of Art, she might remember that it was she who on that evening had made him what he hereby vowed to become. There is, however, no record of such a performance of *Fidelio* taking place in Leipzig at that time. The most likely explanation is that two memorable theatrical experiences were compressed into one by Wagner.[4] He had a strong psychological need to place himself inside a cultural tradition. His earliest endeavours owed everything to the Greeks, to Shakespeare, Goethe and Beethoven (he even dreamed that he met and spoke with Shakespeare and Beethoven). Much of his subsequent theorizing was designed to show that he was Beethoven's heir, the artist who could bring to fulfilment the great combined artwork that Beethoven had but foreshadowed. Poetic fantasy required there to be a single experience that set him on the course of his composing career; self-esteem demanded that the experience be centred on Beethoven.

School studies still did not progress and at Easter 1830 he eventually left the Nicolaischule. His interest in history was further stimulated by Karl Friedrich Becker's *History of the World*, the proofs for a revised edition of which he was given to read, for a small fee, by his brother-in-law Friedrich Brockhaus. Suddenly the people and events of the Middle Ages and the French Revolution sprang to life in his imagination. All at once history became more than an hour's worth of tedium on the school curriculum: it was about real men and women, heroes and villains, triumphs and disasters. One wonders about the effects of this revelation on the typographical accuracy of Becker's *History*.

Revolution was soon to arrive on his doorstep: the July Revolution in Paris (1830) set off tremors elsewhere in Europe. In Leipzig there was restlessness, even fighting. The university students sang and marched in the streets; a brothel was ransacked, in a riot not of

---

[4] It is surely significant that Wagner's enthusiastic recollections of Schröder-Devrient, recorded in Cosima's Diaries, include five references to her assumption of Bellini's Romeo, and not one to any performance in *Fidelio*.

lust but of righteous indignation. Wagner found himself caught up in the frenzy and woke the following morning as though after a night of alcoholic debauchery, with a tatter of red curtain as his only evidence that it had really happened.

Just how 'revolutionary' the spirit behind these activities was became clear before long. The working class who, unlike the privileged undergraduates, had a deep-rooted grievance against exploitative employers, rose up in defiance, inspired by the general mood of agitation. Now that property was threatened and a social overthrow more than mere idle talk, the forces of the establishment regrouped. Students were commissioned by the authorities to arm themselves and provide protection for the wealthy entrepreneurs at risk, a task they carried out with great zeal.

Wagner enthusiastically joined the undergraduates in this and when the alarm subsided considered how he could most quickly enter their ranks. He enrolled at the Thomasschule in order to be able to matriculate with a nominal attendance there. But after six months his teachers were unconvinced about the genuineness of his desire for education, and the only course open to him was to register as a 'studiosus musicae', which demanded less in the way of matriculation requirements but still entitled him to wear the cap and colours of whichever students' club he chose to join.

He took an active part in the students' boisterous gatherings, and in the duels which inevitably followed, savouring the thrill of danger as much as the quaint codes of behaviour. More than once he received the summons to an appointed place and faced the prospect of serious injury or worse. On one occasion he was saved by the fact that his opponent cut an artery in a previous contest; on another, his would-be adversary was killed in a duel shortly before they were to meet.

Giving himself up to dissipation, he earned the contempt of both his beloved sister Rosalie and his mother. In the feverish excitement of gambling he one night lost all and in a desperate bid to restore his fortunes he staked his mother's pension. Miraculously his luck turned; he won back enough to pay off his debts and was able to return home and supply a happy coda to this operatic little scene by confessing and finding forgiveness.

Early compositions included a fateful Overture in B flat major. His plan to execute the score in red, green and black ink was compromised by the unavailability of green, but it was striking enough for the Kapellmeister of the Leipzig Court Theatre, Heinrich Dorn, to schedule as the opening work for a special charity concert at the theatre. The overture had a novel feature in that after every four-bar melodic phrase a fifth bar was inserted that consisted of nothing but a loud stroke of the timpani on the second beat. Wagner went unannounced and not a little apprehensively to the performance, giving his identity only to the doorman in order to secure a seat at the front. As the piece went on, and the timpanist followed his instructions, the audience's reaction oscillated between astonishment and hilarity. The abrupt ending that he had thought appropriate did nothing to moderate their amazement, and his intense humiliation was compounded by the look the doorman gave him as he fled the theatre.

He attended some lectures at the university and underwent a course of study with a new teacher, Christian Theodor Weinlig, Kantor of St Thomas's, Leipzig (the post formerly held by J.S. Bach). He achieved a degree of fluency in contrapuntal writing and was also set pieces to compose for the piano: first a Sonata in B flat along traditional lines and then a Fantasie in freer style. Various instrumental works date from these years, most notably overtures and a Symphony in C which acknowledged a debt to Beethoven and Mozart, among others. Incompetent performances of Beethoven's Ninth led him to the conclusion – not to be revised until he heard it in Paris several years later – that the work was somehow beyond his comprehension.

Visiting Count Pachta on his estate at Pravonin, near Prague, he became enamoured, as he was expected to, of the Count's attractive daughters. He had already been struck by them when making their acquaintance a few years earlier, but now nineteen and sporting a beard he catapulted into an infatuation with the elder, dark-haired sister, Jenny. She did not return his love and made him aware of the fact in some painful way that he did not elaborate on. A letter to his friend Theodor Apel (16 December 1832) contains a shaft of mature insight: 'My idealizing vision saw in her everything it desired to see, and that was the cause of my misfortune!' His imagination transformed later lovers into paragons; unable to accept them on their terms, he had to recreate them in his own image. Jenny couldn't or wouldn't play the game; the sisters teased him by flirting with aristocratic admirers and he became impatient with their philistinism. He left their home with mixed emotions.

Also in Prague he gave his attention to the writing of a sketch for an opera, with the title *Die Hochzeit* (The Wedding). The drama had reminiscences of his earlier gory epic *Leubald*, but this time he felt there were some subtle touches worthy of a maturing talent. His sister Rosalie, however, took a more critical view and in deference to her judgment he destroyed the manuscript on the spot.

Heinrich Laube.

It was through Rosalie that he met one of the leading Young German writers: Heinrich Laube. This man's sincerity and bluntly expressed sense of justice had an inspiring effect on Wagner, and a favourable review of his symphony by Laube did nothing to diminish the friendship that had sprung up. In January 1833 Wagner left Leipzig to stay in Würzburg with his brother Albert, who held an appointment at the theatre there. The time had come for him to earn his keep.

2

Chorus master and musical director (1833–9)

Albert secured the job of chorus master for Wagner at the theatre in Würzburg and almost immediately he was having to drill the chorus for their parts in Marschner's *Der Vampyr* and Meyerbeer's *Robert le Diable*. For his brother's benefit he wrote the words and music of a florid final section for Aubry's aria 'Wie ein schöner Frühlings-morgen' in *Der Vampyr*. The new ending, with scalic runs and arpeggios, was more of an exhibition piece than the original and his brother was highly pleased. Other works he was responsible for rehearsing included Hérold's *Zampa*, Paër's *Camilla*, Auber's *La muette de Portici* and *Fra Diavolo*, Marschner's *Hans Heiling* and operas by Cherubini, Rossini, Weber and Beethoven. It was while exposed to this repertory that he wrote the music for his first complete opera, *Die Feen* (The Fairies).

One of the chorus sopranos, Therese Ringelmann, came to him regularly for singing lessons, and out of their sessions together developed what Wagner referred to as his first love affair. They met also in the public gardens and at her parents' house, but when matrimony loomed on the horizon he took fright and the affair came to an end. With another good-looking young woman, Friederike Galvani, he also scored something of a success and derived a certain satisfaction from temporarily depriving her oboist lover of her on the occasion of a country wedding. This conquest, he said later, served to boost his self-respect; for the first time he experienced the pleasure that resulted in being accepted, of feeling that he might after all count for something.

At the beginning of 1834 he returned to Leipzig and came again within the orbit of Heinrich Laube. Laube was one of the leading lights of Young Germany, a radical literary and political movement of the 1830s which promoted republican and democratic ideals. Other prominent members of this un-coordinated group included Karl Gutzkow and Ludolf Wienbarg (Heinrich Heine and Ludwig Börne were also inspirational figures) and their prime targets were

11

the social and political conditions of the time, reactionary morality and Catholic mysticism. In aesthetic terms the Young Germans' cult of passion represented emancipation from Classical constraints and strict forms and from the influence of such former idols as Goethe and Mozart, but also, more significantly, from what they regarded as the sentimentally conceived Romanticism of composers like Weber and writers like E.T.A. Hoffmann. A sense of uncertainty among creative artists accompanied the rising national consciousness of Germans; as far as opera was concerned it was considered that in order to realize its true greatness, German art should be prepared to learn from the Italians and French. In Wagner's first published critique, 'German Opera', which appeared in Laube's *Zeitung für die elegante Welt* in June 1834, and in a piece written three years later, *Bellini*, the Italianate capacity for expressiveness, by means of the *bel canto* line, is elevated above the fussy academic tendency of contemporary German composers.

In spite of the liberal nature of Wagner's views in these years, it should not be overlooked that there is a contrary streak present also in his writings and in those of Laube, namely a form of 'benevolent totalitarianism' that derived from Saint-Simonism, a movement active in France *c.* 1829–31.[1] The Saint-Simonists' conception of an 'organic' society, in which individuals surrender themselves wholly and unconditionally to the interests of the wider community, was a product of their elevation of irrationality to a political and artistic principle. In the days before the emergence of a Marxist analysis of society, sincere republican and democratic convictions were often intermingled with reactionary and disturbingly authoritarian doctrines.

While Wagner was in Leipzig Wilhelmine Schröder-Devrient made a guest appearance there as Romeo in Bellini's *I Capuleti e i Montecchi*. Then with his long-standing friend Theodor Apel, a well-to-do young man who aspired to be a poet, he took a holiday in Bohemia. Submitting to hedonistic ideals they indulged themselves with good food, fine wines, bodily comforts and exuberant intel-

---

[1] The concept of 'benevolent totalitarianism' is discussed by Georg G. Iggers, *The Cult of Authority: the Political Philosophy of the Saint-Simonians* (The Hague 1958). See also John Deathridge, *Wagner's 'Rienzi': a reappraisal based on a study of the sketches and drafts*, 25–8, for a discussion of Laube and Saint-Simonism with especial reference to *Rienzi*.

lectual arguments, overheard with alarm by people who passed their hotel window. A creative outlet was found for this sensual, iconoclastic fervour in a prose sketch for a libretto based loosely on Shakespeare's *Measure for Measure*. This second opera, *Das Liebesverbot* (The Ban on Love) was over the next eighteen months elaborated and composed in a markedly different style from that of *Die Feen*, one that reflected the Mediterranean spontaneity and voluptuousness of the subject.

Wagner returned from Bohemia to the news that he had been offered a job as musical director of Heinrich Bethmann's theatre company. The troupe, which performed both drama and opera, was based in Magdeburg but in the summer months it travelled to neighbouring spas. At the end of July (1834) the company was playing in Bad Lauchstädt and Wagner went along to reconnoitre. The place had gone downhill since the time when Goethe and Schiller had been associated with it. Confronted by the dissipated Bethmann, who met him in the street wearing his dressing-gown and night cap, by the toothless skeleton of the theatre attendant, and by the request to prepare a performance of *Don Giovanni* by the following Sunday in spite of the refusal of the visiting orchestra to rehearse on the Saturday, Wagner came to an instant decision: he informed them that he would not be taking the post.

An actor he happened to know from Würzburg undertook to secure overnight accommodation for him and offered to place him in the same lodging as the most charming young lady in town – one of the company's leading actresses, Christine Wilhelmine ('Minna') Planer. The young lady in question by chance met them at the door of the lodging. Wagner was introduced as the new conductor and she made it her business to ensure that the landlady looked after him. Wagner was enchanted by Minna; with her blue eyes and dark wavy hair she was indeed attractive and there was something about her manner – a blend of impulsive affability and dignified poise – that he found irresistible. He immediately took a room and announced that he would conduct *Don Giovanni* on the Sunday after all.

Returning briefly to Leipzig for his luggage he found Laube being harassed by the authorities. A reactionary crackdown on dissident intellectuals was under way and Laube was forced to leave Saxony. Wagner conceived a plan for Laube to be harboured by Apel on his estate in Prussia but Apel was unwilling to risk trouble and refused; shortly after, Laube was arrested and jailed. Laube's fate weighed heavily on Wagner, but he lost no time hurrying back to Bad Lauchstädt and Minna. *Don Giovanni* marked his début as an opera conductor; all went well and he noted with satisfaction that everyone seemed to have confidence in him.

His affection for Minna was undiminished and appeared to be reciprocated. She was three-and-a-half years older than he, approaching her twenty-fifth birthday that summer. A predominant consideration in their relationship must have been the sexual attraction they felt for each other. There can be little doubt that they gave physical expression to this well before their formal engagement. Neither had any scruples about that, though each had their own concept of 'morality', albeit one fashioned by nineteenth-century social and sexual roles: in Minna's case it was tantamount to propriety, respectability beneath the public gaze; in Wagner's it was something more akin to an expectation of loyalty and devotion. Minna's cautious reserve with her many male admirers was undoubtedly the result of the bitter lesson she had learnt at the age of fifteen, when she had been seduced and abandoned by a guards captain, Ernst Rudolph von Einsiedel. Her pregnancy was concealed and the child, Natalie, was brought up as her sister.

But when Minna played hard to get, Wagner was all the more infatuated. There was an impulse deeply rooted in his character to pursue the unattainable. Playful, but in a mature, composed way, Minna answered his need for close company and for the domestic comforts which, true to his era, he imagined ought to be provided by a wife. When one night, having forgotten his key, he made a late-night entry to his room via the window, she did not hesitate to clasp his hand and greet him goodnight. Later that year as he hid in his room suffering from erysipelas, which left his face temporarily disfigured, she visited him regularly and nursed him. When he had all but recovered, save for a rash round his mouth, she delighted him by ignoring it and kissing him.

The Bethmann company moved on to Rudolstadt (Thuringia), Wagner and Minna with it. He was not required to conduct the operas there but that August he set to work on another symphony, in E major (which he abandoned in the middle of the second movement), and the libretto of *Das Liebesverbot*. In October the company returned to Magdeburg, not a moment too soon for Wagner, as he was now able to resume his place on the rostrum on the company's home territory. He rapidly acquired a reputation as a competent and exhilarating conductor, popular with performers and audiences alike.

Flushed with his success at Magdeburg, Wagner pressed on with *Das Liebesverbot* and was able to secure the performance of his friend Apel's play about Christopher Columbus, with his own incidental music. The highlight of the season occurred towards its close when Schröder-Devrient arrived in April (1835) for a series of performances under Wagner. Once again he was stirred by her dramatic portrayals, and so successful was their artistic collaboration that the soprano generously offered to return for an extra benefit concert from which the proceeds would go to Wagner himself. The event was a catastrophe. Wagner spent extravagantly to obtain a reliable and expanded orchestra; for Beethoven's Battle Symphony he laid on doubled and trebled brass and a deafening array of percussion instruments and cannon effects. Confidently too he told his rapidly growing number of creditors that they might come to his hotel the day after the concert for repayment. But not believing that the great Schröder-Devrient would really appear for an unknown provincial conductor, and perhaps also deterred by the higher prices asked, the people of Magdeburg stayed away. Schröder-Devrient arrived, as Wagner never doubted she would, and sang Beethoven's *Adelaide* to a half-empty hall. More humiliation was to follow. The excessive reverberation of the hall, coupled with the massive forces assembled, made Wagner's *Columbus* overture a painful experience for the audience. And when the cannons and muskets let fly in the Battle Symphony the audience took their cue from Schröder-Devrient's hasty exit and left the orchestra playing to a deserted hall. The proceeds from this disastrous evening did not even cover the expenses and Wagner was saved from the irate creditors thronging outside his hotel room only by an enterprising one of their number who, in collusion with Wagner, fended off the others with talk of the young conductor's good connections in Leipzig.

In the summer Wagner undertook a tour of Bohemia and south Germany scouting for talent. Hindered by the incompetent management of the Magdeburg theatre he returned almost empty-handed. But two experiences were stored away in his memory for future occasions. The small Bavarian town of Bayreuth made a favourable impression on him in the warm glow of sunset, while at Nuremberg he witnessed a street brawl whose senseless fury and sudden dissolution were to be portrayed three decades later in *Die Meistersinger von Nürnberg*.

Minna was not at this stage anxious to rush into marriage: she had a career to pursue on the stage and neither of them was earning enough to launch what she would have regarded as a securely founded relationship. Nor was Wagner in a hurry; indeed his feelings towards her were ambivalent, to say the least. But no sooner had she accepted an engagement at the Königstadt Theatre in Berlin than he was pining for her. On the day she left (4 November), he tore off a letter to her: 'Minna, my state of mind can't be described. You are gone and my heart is broken. I am sitting here scarcely in control of my senses and weeping and sobbing like a child. Good God, what shall I do?' Every day from the 4th to the 12th he wrote in a similar vein, shamelessly abasing himself before her, beseeching her to return, promising her marriage, security, anything she wanted. Under this bombardment she caved in and was back in Magdeburg within a fortnight of leaving.

Das Liebesverbot was completed and put on in Magdeburg the following spring (1836). It came off prematurely and the Bethmann company finally yielded to the bankruptcy that had long been threatening. Minna was now offered a contract at another theatre, this time in Königsberg. She accepted in the hope that it might be possible to secure a position there for Wagner too, but in the meantime she went alone. In the period before her departure the couple were drawn together, by adversity, by their sense of uncertainty about the future and by the depressing experience of seeing a man commit suicide before their eyes. He jumped into the river and although he tried to save himself by clutching at a rake held out by another man, he just failed to grasp it and disappeared from view. Then on the day that Minna was leaving, Wagner heard sickening accounts of the death of a criminal who had been publicly executed that morning by being broken on the wheel.

Wagner approached the Königstadt Theatre in Berlin in an attempt to persuade them to stage *Das Liebesverbot*. The promises he was given evaporated into thin air but the trip to Berlin had one positive aspect: a large-scale representation of Spontini's *Fernand Cortez* impressed him and showed him how effective a grand opera with all the trappings could be. From this seed grew *Rienzi*.

As Minna seemed to be taking her time securing the conductor's post for him at Königsberg, he went on there himself to try to settle the matter. He found that although the director of the theatre was well disposed towards him the post was still for the present, albeit temporarily, occupied. While in Königsberg, in July, Wagner sketched out a prose scenario for an opera suitable for treatment in the grand style. He sent it off to Eugène Scribe in Paris, hoping that the famous dramatist and librettist might work it into a text which he, Wagner, could then be commissioned to set to music for the Opéra. *Die hohe Braut* (The Noble Bride) was eventually elaborated into a libretto not by Scribe but by Wagner himself in Dresden; it was offered first to Reissiger and then to Ferdinand Hiller, but was finally set by Jan Bedřich Kittl.[2]

Proximity to Minna began to make Wagner wonder again whether they were ideally matched. In *Mein Leben*, written thirty years later and with at least a degree of detachment, he criticizes her superficiality, her lack of artistic feeling and even her talent for acting. Harsh words, but he seems to have sensed from early on that although she supplied some of the steadiness that he felt to be lacking in himself, she in no way measured up to the extraordinarily high demands he made of a partner, or even a friend. Those demands included total and uncompromising devotion to his art as well as to himself. Minna was unsuited both by temperament and by education to his radical, visionary concept of art. As far as personal devotion was concerned, she had a considerable capacity for loyalty and compassion but at this stage she was not, any more than he, prepared to commit herself exclusively. Indeed, that was the cause of a bitter and violent wrangle between them now in Königsberg. Wagner was angry to find out that Minna had been intimately involved for some time with a man called Schwabe; Minna was equally angry that he should make such an issue out of it. Nevertheless they decided to take the fateful plunge and preparations were made for the marriage. The day before the ceremony they visited the priest, who opened the door to find them squabbling and on the point of separating. They all appreciated the comical aspect of the situation, however, and the wedding went ahead on 24 November 1836. According to the only eye-witness, Minna's daughter Natalie, it was not long before Wagner was daily bullying Minna and reducing her to tears, following up these brutal outbursts by pleading penitently for forgiveness.

[2] For the full history of Wagner's libretto and its setting, see Isolde Vetter, 'Wagner and Kittl', *Wagner*, v (1984), 20–30.

Natalie may well be exaggerating but there is no doubt that Wagner had a fearful temper which he made all too little effort to control.

On 1 April 1837 Wagner was eventually appointed to the musical directorship at the Königsberg Theatre. It was not a happy time for him. The theatre, on the verge of bankruptcy, had to ask its employees to work for no salary for a period. And Minna secretly left him in favour of a merchant called Dietrich. For a man as profoundly insecure as Wagner this was a threat with which he could not cope. He pursued her in a jealous rage, swearing vengeance, but only later tracked her down at her parents' house in Dresden. Dietrich had not accompanied her the whole way. She was not prepared to return immediately with Wagner but agreed to stay with him for a time in lodgings outside Dresden, at Blasewitz. There he read Bulwer-Lytton's novel about the Roman demagogue and last tribune Rienzi, which provided him with the subject and the inspiration for the five-act grand opera he had been wanting to write.

Meanwhile he had concluded a much-desired agreement to become musical director of the theatre in Riga, a Lithuanian town (part of the Russian Empire) colonized by Germans. This he fervently hoped would bring both artistic satisfaction and the material security that he and Minna acknowledged was necessary to provide a firm base for their troubled marriage. But it was alone that he undertook the journey by land and sea, across the Baltic to Riga, arriving there on 21 August. He found the place a cultural backwater, with cramped conditions in the theatre, and little or no willingness on anybody's part to improve matters. When Minna wrote a heartrending letter apologizing for her conduct, Wagner was moved to take the blame himself and invited her to come to Riga and stay with him and her sister Amalie, who had accepted a singing engagement at the theatre.

The following summer, 1838 (not 1837, as often given following *Mein Leben*), he tried his hand at a comic opera based on a tale from *The Arabian Nights*, calling it *Männerlist grösser als Frauenlist, oder Die glückliche Bärenfamilie* (Man's Cunning greater than Woman's, or The Happy Bear Family). He wrote the text and got as far as composing some of the music (it was to be in the form of a Singspiel, with prose dialogue and individual numbers), but abandoned it and concentrated his energies on *Rienzi*, of which he had written the poem and begun the music by August. Wagner clung on to his marriage and his job until in the March of 1839 he found that his contract was not being renewed and that he was therefore in effect being sacked. The former director of the theatre, Karl von Holtei, had not seen eye to eye with Wagner, as well as failing to seduce his wife, and as a parting gift he bound his successor to an agreement that the conductorship would go to Heinrich Dorn, Wagner's old acquaintance who had also been working in Riga as the municipal director of music. Wagner and the new director, who was his ally, were powerless. But the episode only increased his determination to free himself from the petty dealings of provincial theatrical life. Success and fortune, he reasoned, would bring him independence, and these lay within his grasp. Paris, it seemed, was where his destiny lay.

3
Failure in Paris, success in Dresden (1839–47)

With the help of an old Königsberg friend, Abraham Möller, Wagner planned his escape from Riga. It would need to be a clandestine retreat in order to elude his creditors, Möller advised, but he could repay them when he had made his fortune in Paris. As debtors, Wagner's and Minna's passports had been impounded, but Möller's plan obviated that difficulty by means of an illicit crossing of the Russian frontier to an East Prussian port, from where they would journey by sea as stowaways. Möller's coach took them to the frontier and they were led on foot to a suspicious-looking house; it proved to be a smugglers' den. A ditch ran the length of the frontier, which was watched by armed Cossack soldiers. In the few minutes they had while the watch was being relieved, Wagner, Minna and their faithful Newfoundland dog Robber, who had insisted on coming, had to speed down the hill, through the ditch and away out of range of the guards. A single excited bark from the dog might have caused them to be shot on sight. Miraculously all went well and they rejoined Möller at an inn on the Prussian side, exhausted but safe. Their troubles had only begun, however.

They made their way in a small rudimentary conveyance over bumpy roads – in order to avoid Königsberg – and the cart came to grief in a farmyard, keeling over and throwing the two passengers out. Minna was injured and had to take refuge for the night in a nearby peasant's cottage. The owners were 'surly' and 'dirty', Wagner tells us in *Mein Leben*, but he omits to mention that he himself could not have presented a very dignified spectacle as he had been turfed out, on impact, onto a heap of manure. Nor does he mention that Minna was injured so badly that she suffered a miscarriage, an incident which was probably responsible for the fact that the couple were to remain childless throughout their marriage. These details we know only through Natalie, who would have had it straight from her mother; she is not generally the most reliable of witnesses, it is true, but she is the source of some interesting sidelights on the marriage.

Reaching the little Prussian port of Pillau (now Baltiysk, USSR) they had to board their ship furtively before daybreak, haul Robber up the side, and then hide below deck when the boat was given a pre-sailing inspection by officials. They were on a small merchant vessel called the *Thetis* bound for London with a crew of seven. After a week's sailing they had made little progress because of the extreme calm, but then suddenly a violent storm was on them; they suffered sea-sickness and feared worse. Eventually forced to take refuge in a Norwegian fjord they enjoyed a brief respite from stormy weather, going ashore at a small fishing village called Sandwike (actually Sandwiken on the island of Boröya).[1] By the time he came to write *Mein Leben* a quarter of a century later, the experience of this calm after the storm, and of the crew's shouts echoing round the granite walls, had merged in his mind with the creative inspiration for *Der fliegende Holländer*. The sharp rhythm of these shouts began to shape itself into the chorus of the Norwegian sailors, he tells us there, and the opera even began to take on 'a definite poetic and musical colour'. This retrospective cross-fertilization of art and life will be discussed further in the chapter on the *Holländer*. After yet more violent storms they eventually set foot on English soil, though it was several days before they had recovered their health and equilibrium.

Wagner decided to look up Sir George Smart of the Philharmonic Society, to whom he had earlier sent the score of his *Rule Britannia* Overture. Smart was not in London; nor did he have any more luck with Sir Edward Bulwer-Lytton, the author of the novel *Rienzi, the Last of the Tribunes*. It was with his dramatization of this story that Wagner hoped to score a success in Paris, but when he called at the Houses of Parliament to discuss the matter with Bulwer-Lytton he was told that he too was out of town. They crossed the Channel from Gravesend to Boulogne where, by seemingly incredible good fortune, Meyerbeer at that time was. Wagner hurriedly completed the orchestration of the second act of *Rienzi* and visited the reigning monarch of the Paris Opéra to pay his respects. Meyerbeer received him kindly, listened with interest to the libretto as it was read to him, and promised to provide letters of recommendation to Charles Edmond Duponchel, the director of the Opéra, and François Habeneck, the conductor.

[1] See Gunnar Graarud, ' "Sandwike ist's, genau kenn' ich die Bucht!" ', *Bayreuther Festspielführer* (1939), 61–72.

The Paris in which Wagner spent two-and-a-half cheerless years of profound significance for his future development, both social and artistic, was the Paris of the July Monarchy (1830–48) under Louis-Philippe. It was a society in which enormous wealth and power were enjoyed by a bourgeois élite while a middle bourgeoisie shared the underprivileged lot of the peasants and workers. There was little social mobility and it was all but impossible to make headway without either money or connections. Affluent people, on the other hand, could buy favours and good opinions; even if he had wished to, Wagner's poverty shut off that option, and he voiced the frustration and resentment experienced by many. His exigency did not induce him to lust after wealth; on the contrary, he maintained throughout his life an admirable indifference, if not hostility, to money. He firmly believed that it was not associated with the things of real value in life, and he had no respect for it, whether it was his own or someone else's. What roused his indignation was seeing banality and triviality prosper while he was unable even to get a hearing.

Fortune at first seemed to be favouring him when in March 1840 the Théâtre de la Renaissance accepted *Das Liebesverbot* for performance. But only two months later the theatre went bankrupt and was forced to close. In *Mein Leben*, Wagner was to ascribe to 'his friends' the suspicion that Meyerbeer had had intimations of the impending collapse. Certainly in the 1860s Wagner is careful to give little hint of any gratitude for Meyerbeer's endeavours on his behalf during the Paris years. But if he did harbour any such suspicions himself at the time he managed to stifle them. His letters to Meyerbeer continued to display an embarrassingly shameless attitude of obsequiousness: he throws himself at Meyerbeer's feet, calls him 'Master', himself 'your property' and 'your slave', putting his head and hands entirely at the revered one's service. Moreover, a letter to his friend Heinrich Schletter (15 September 1840) states that Meyerbeer's help has given him renewed hope that his dealings with the Opéra will lead to a fruitful conclusion.

In the June of 1840 Wagner had sent a copy of his sketch for a one-act opera based on the Flying Dutchman legend to Meyerbeer in the hope that he would recommend it to the management of the Opéra. (A month earlier he had also sent the sketch to Scribe, with a view to securing his collaboration.) Meyerbeer introduced Wagner to Léon Pillet, the new director of the Opéra, who according to *Mein*

1 Wagner at the age of 29, depicted by his friend Ernst Benedikt Kietz.

2 Minna Wagner, his first wife.

3 Mathilde Wesendonck.

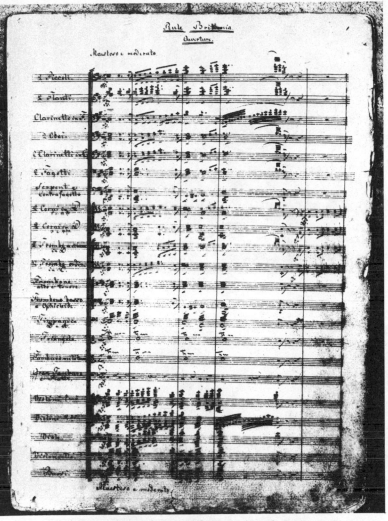

4 First page of the autograph score of Wagner's *Rule Britannia* Overture, written in 1837; note the massive orchestration. Long thought to be lost, the score is safely lodged in the British Library.

5 Barricading the streets of Dresden, 1849.

Madame Schröder-Devrient als stille Beobachterin
der Dresdener Barrikaden.

6 'Madame Schröder-Devrient as silent observer of the Dresden
barricades'. The famous soprano was later to suffer for the sympathy she
expressed with the insurrectionists: for a time she was banned from
Saxony.

Leben eventually persuaded Wagner to sell the story for 500 francs so that it could be made into an opera by one of the composers under contract to him. By this time Wagner had already made his own versification and three numbers of the opera had been written at least a year before (see p. 159). The two librettists given Wagner's sketch by Pillet did not, as frequently stated, use it as the chief source for their own work, *Le Vaisseau fantôme*.[2]

Rienzi was completed in November (1840) but Wagner failed to get a commitment from the Opéra to produce it; he also approached the Dresden Court Theatre and it was eventually accepted by them for performance. To bring in some cash while waiting for his reputation to be made with *Rienzi*, Wagner undertook a considerable amount of work arranging other composers' music for different instrumental combinations and preparing vocal scores of operas. Much but by no means all of this was done for the publisher Maurice Schlesinger and the work was more extensive than has hitherto been recognized.[3] Nor was the labour forced on him by Schlesinger, as Wagner claims in *Mein Leben*: a draft letter in the British Library, published for the first time in 1984, reveals that Wagner himself took the initiative.[4]

In addition to these arrangements of popular operas of the day, such as Donizetti's *La favorite* and Halévy's *La reine de Chypre* and *Le guitarrero*, he wrote a series of reviews for the Dresden *Abend-Zeitung* of musical events in Paris. He deplores the superficial mediocrities after which Parisian society hankers, but praises Halévy, Meyerbeer and Auber who continue to produce worthwhile operas. For Schlesinger's *Gazette musicale* he also wrote three novellas – short stories that contain many indications as to his aesthetics at the time. In *A Pilgrimage to Beethoven*, which describes in a blend of humour and reverence an imaginary visit to the

---

2 See Barry Millington, 'Did Wagner really sell his "Dutchman" story? A re-examination of the Paris transaction', *Wagner*, iv (1983), 114–27. The question can now be answered decisively in the affirmative (see Isolde Vetter's forthcoming article in *Wagner*, vii (1986), though the *Vaisseau fantôme* librettists remain no more indebted to Wagner's scenario. See also under Dietsch in Appendix C.

3 This is made clear in the *Verzeichnis der musikalischen Werke Richard Wagners und ihrer Quellen* by J. Deathridge, M. Geck and E. Voss.

4 See 'Wagner autographs in London', *Wagner*, v (1984), 3–4.

venerated composer, Beethoven is made to outline the future Wagnerian music drama as the continuation of his own work: poetry and
music to be united in a new synthesis; arias, duets and other divisions
to be replaced by the continuous fabric of a drama. Such a projection
is understandable in an aspiring composer seeking, in the midst of an
alien environment, a tradition in which to root himself. The style of
all these Paris writings, which draw heavily on personal experience
for their content, owes much to E.T.A. Hoffmann; they are readable,
often amusing and do not suffer from the turgidity that paralyses
Wagner's later writings.

This was a time of abject poverty for Wagner and Minna: they
pawned their valuables and even sold the tickets; often they did not
know where their next meal was coming from. To save fuel they
confined themselves to one room, the bedroom. The arrangements
he was given to do were so onerous that Wagner left his work table
only to cross the room and go to bed; every fourth day he allowed
himself a walk. This regime was largely responsible for the gastric
and bowel disorders that were to plague him for the rest of his
life.

On 25 October 1840 Minna sent a letter, drafted by Wagner
himself, to Theodor Apel, the affluent friend of his youth, imploring
him to relieve their pecuniary distress. She states that her husband
had had to leave her that very morning for the debtors' prison and
that a concert two weeks hence including his *Rienzi* overture would
have to be cancelled in the absence of Wagner. This has often been
taken as evidence that Wagner spent a period at the end of October
and the beginning of November in prison for the non-payment of
debt, particularly since the first of the four pages of the draft is
lacking – presumed destroyed by Minna or Natalie to remove the
ignominious reference. But the editors of the Collected Letters of
Wagner have adduced powerful evidence[5] to suggest that the threat
of imprisonment did not actually become a reality, that it was
dramatized in order to spur Apel to action: in October and November Wagner was working on *Rienzi* and *A Pilgrimage to Beethoven* and this was more than he could have coped with in prison;
the scheduled concert with the *Rienzi* overture is mentioned nowhere
else and was probably therefore another fiction to persuade Apel; the
small pieces of paper used for the draft of the letter were of the same

[5] Sämtliche Briefe, i, pp. 414–16 (note 1).

kind as those used for other compositions, so that it is insufficient to argue that such scraps were all that was available in prison. Taken individually, these first points are not conclusive. Wagner had completed the actual composition of *Rienzi* by 23 October and in any case greater masterpieces have been written in gaol. If a concert *had* been called off for that reason, it would not be surprising if references to it were similarly lacking in Wagner's autobiographical writings. But there are two final pieces of evidence. On 3 December Wagner wrote to Laube telling him that the last two days had been the most terrible that anyone could experience: with their remaining pennies his friends had averted until the 15th next the blow that would mean immediate and irrevocable distraint and the loss of his personal freedom. Wagner would surely not have written in these terms if he had already just suffered imprisonment. Finally, it appears that the correct date of the letter to Apel is 25 October,[6] not 28 as given on its original publication; but on the 25th Wagner sent his close friend Kietz a note urging him to come round that evening – 'It's important', he added. So he was obviously expecting to be at home and it is more than likely that he and his friends hatched a plot that night to convince Apel of his dire need and that it resulted in the draft letter that Minna was to copy. The evidence therefore seems to suggest that the 'imprisonment' was not a fact but a desperate ruse, and a successful one because Apel was parted from yet more of his money.

Other than *Rienzi* and *Der fliegende Holländer* the Paris years did not bear a great deal of creative fruit. A number of songs were written on French texts in an attempt to trade on the celebrity of popular and influential singers (see p. 285) and one of his first efforts in Paris was the composition of an aria, 'Norma il predisse', which he unsuccessfully offered the bass Lablache as an interpolation for Bellini's *Norma*. At the end of 1841 Wagner made a prose sketch for an opera in five acts called *Die Sarazenin* (The Saracen Woman); a draft of this subject was elaborated in 1843 but the versification barely begun. Another abortive project was *Die Bergwerke zu Falun* (The Mines of Falun) after E.T.A. Hoffmann, whose fantastic tales had caught his imagination as a boy. A Bohemian composer by the name of Josef Dessauer, who was temporarily resident in Paris, requested a libretto from Wagner and he worked out a prose draft on Hoffmann's story set among a mining community in the Swedish

[6] *Sämtliche Briefe*, i, p. 416.

town of Falun. Wagner never proceeded beyond this scenario because the idea was turned down by the Opéra.

Among the many acquaintances he made in Paris were Heinrich Heine and Berlioz, whose works he regarded with qualified admiration. But his most intimate friends, forming a quartet of comrades in hardship, were Gottfried Anders, Ernst Kietz and Samuel Lehrs. Anders ('Otherwise') was a librarian with musical interests who had abandoned his original surname. Kietz, who was Wagner's first portraitist, was said to take so long cleaning his brushes that he never completed a commission. Lehrs, a philologist, was responsible for providing him with valuable background material on the *Tannhäuser* and *Lohengrin* legends as well as introducing him to some philosophical concepts that were to play a significant part in his future works. Proudhon's *De la propriété* was published in Paris in 1840 and Ludwig Feuerbach's *Das Wesen des Christentums* (The Essence of Christianity) in Germany the following year. There is no evidence that Wagner read either work but it may well have been in his philosophical conversations with Lehrs that he became acquainted with the ideas promulgated in them. The fundamental tenet of Proudhon (who was also a virulent anti-semite, incidentally) – that the ownership of property is theft – was to be given dramatic expression in the *Ring*, especially *Das Rheingold* with its theme of the corrupting power of money. Of the ideas of Feuerbach expounded in *Das Wesen des Christentums* and other writings Wagner seems to have been most impressed by the assertions that God is but a projection of humanity who has made him in its own image, and that religion is justified only as a force of active humanity in the present life.

In spite of Meyerbeer's freely given support and help – and his influence undoubtedly smoothed the path for the premiere of *Rienzi* in Dresden and the later Berlin production of *Der fliegende Holländer* – Wagner was not enjoying the fame and prosperity he thought he deserved. That Meyerbeer was still the rage of both France and Germany galled him. In 1841, while still in Paris, his resentment began to show itself in articles written under the pseudonym 'W. Freudenfeuer'. The following year in a 'Letter from Paris' that Schumann printed in his *Neue Zeitschrift für Musik*, Wagner went further: he said that Halévy was 'not a deliberately cunning swindler like Meyerbeer' (Schumann moderated the description to '*filou* [rogue] like M.') When, in 1843, Schumann perused

Wagner's *Holländer* score, he touched a raw nerve by commenting on 'echoes of Meyerbeer'. By this time, the last thing Wagner wanted was to be regarded as a protégé or follower of Meyerbeer. In reply to Schumann he explicitly and strenuously distanced himself from the insipidities of Meyerbeer the musician.[7] Doubtless combined with this perceived threat to his artistic integrity were feelings of envy and frustration and probably also shame at his earlier self-abasement.

Deeply disillusioned with Paris Wagner and Minna began to make their way back, on 7 April 1842, to Dresden, where preparations for the premiere of *Rienzi* were under way. It was, as Wagner describes it in the *Autobiographical Sketch*, an emotional return: 'I saw the Rhine for the first time; with tears swelling in my eyes I, a poor artist, swore eternal loyalty to my German fatherland.' Shattered as he was by the misery of poverty and rejection in Paris, his spirits began to rise as they passed through the Rhineland, so rich in legendary associations. Another bright moment was afforded by a superb view of the Wartburg; the impression of the castle high in the mountains remained with him and eventually transformed itself into the stage picture for Act III of *Tannhäuser*.

Within a week of arriving back in Germany Wagner was making his way to Berlin where there was hope of staging *Der fliegende Holländer*. The work had been recommended to the Intendant, Count Redern, by Meyerbeer and accepted, but following the success of *Rienzi* in Dresden, Wagner requested the return of his *Holländer* score. In addition, Redern retired soon after and was succeeded by Theodor von Küstner; there was now less enthusiasm for the project and it fell through.

In June he took a holiday in Teplitz (Bohemia) with Minna and his mother, during which time *Tannhäuser* began to take shape. He returned to Dresden where rehearsals for *Rienzi* were to take place under the Kapellmeister, Karl Gottlieb Reissiger. A warm friendship sprang up between Wagner, Wilhelm Fischer, the stage manager and chorus master, and Ferdinand Heine, the costume designer. The first performance took place on 20 October in the Royal Saxon Court Theatre, its immense success undoubtedly due in part to the fact that

---

[7] For a discussion of ways in which Meyerbeer's music left its mark on Wagner, see Max Brod, 'Some Comments on the Relationship between Wagner and Meyerbeer', Leo Baeck Institute, Year Book ix (London 1964), 202–5.

it caught the spirit of the times. The German middle classes were calling for national unity, constitutional reform, press freedom and participation in political decision-making. Rienzi brings an end to the corrupt rule of the aristocracy and is made tribune of the people, but he too falls, the victim of conspiracy and of his own ambition. The part of Rienzi was taken by Joseph Tichatschek and that of Adriano by the singer who was reported to have so inspired the younger Wagner, Wilhelmine Schröder-Devrient.

She also took the leading female role at the premiere of *Der fliegende Holländer* which followed on 2 January 1843, at the same theatre. The brooding quality of this work did not appeal to the first audiences, but it was by no means a total failure. A close friendship developed with Schröder-Devrient and indeed she helped him out at this time with a loan of 1000 Talers. Some he sent to Kietz in Paris; his original intention in negotiating the loan had been to bring Kietz to Germany, but when the money eventually materialized it went to pay off some of his debts to Kietz and to other creditors from Paris and Magdeburg.

Wagner introduced himself to the German public with his *Autobiographical Sketch*, published by Laube in two parts on 1 and 8 February in his *Zeitung für die elegante Welt*. The King of Saxony's court at Dresden was looking for a new Kapellmeister and although Wagner had deep reservations about accepting such a post he was prevailed on and on 2 February the appointment was announced, with a salary of 1500 Talers. He had turned down the offer from Von Lüttichau, the Intendant, of a subordinate post – that of Musikdirektor, or assistant conductor – making it clear that he required full authority to bring about the administrative changes he deemed necessary. A nineteenth-century German Kapellmeister was responsible not just for the music of a church or royal chapel (as in Bach's time) but for all the musical activities of the court, including opera and orchestral concerts. At the Dresden court the chief responsibilities were those of conducting operatic, instrumental and choral performances and composing pieces for special court occasions. They were shared by two Kapellmeisters; the other was Reissiger.

Wagner scored an early success at Dresden with his conducting, in March, of Gluck's *Armide*. But he was less happy with the performance of *Das Liebesmahl der Apostel* (The Love-Feast of the Apostles), a work for men's voices that he wrote in May and June for a gala event planned for the combined male choral societies in Saxony. In the spring of 1843 he completed the versification of *Tannhäuser* and its famous march was foreshadowed in another work for male voices, *Gruss seiner Treuen an Friedrich August den Geliebten* (Salute to the Beloved Friedrich August from his Faithful Subjects); this choral greeting on the return of the king from England was just one of the occasional pieces that his appointment required him to produce.

When Breitkopf & Härtel expressed interest in full scores of *Rienzi* and the *Holländer* but failed to offer him a fee, Wagner decided to take the risk himself. He concluded an agreement in 1844 with the Court publisher C.F. Meser by which Wagner provided the capital (three friends including the faithful Anton Pusinelli, his doctor, put up the money) and Meser took 10 per cent commission. The works did not prove as popular as expected but even after *Tannhäuser* and *Lohengrin*, and in spite of Wagner's increasing reputation, Meser continued to be circumspect. As Wagner put it more bluntly to Uhlig (14 September 1851): 'Of all the music publishers in the world *he* is the most incompetent for such a business; and if you distilled the quintessence of the most shit-scared, the most unreliable and the most cowardly philistine, what emerges is precisely Meser.'

Wagner threw his weight behind a campaign to have Weber's remains transferred from London to his home town of Dresden. In spite of official obstruction, the ceremony eventually took place on 14 December with a torchlight procession and funeral music written by Wagner; many were moved by the solemnity of the occasion. On the following morning at the graveside Wagner paid tribute to the idol of his youth in a stirring oration couched in the nationalistic language that his audience instinctively understood and responded to. An ensemble of male voices then sang a setting by Wagner of a poem written by himself.

The library that he was building up in Dresden contained a vast range of literature, ancient and modern, emanating from both Germany and abroad; the catalogue, which was published in 1966, bears witness to the catholicity of his reading. Among the authors to be found there, mostly in German translation, are Aristophanes, Byron, Calderón, Chaucer, Dante, Gibbon, Goethe, Hegel, Homer, Horace, Lessing, Molière, Ossian, Plato, Schiller, Shakespeare, Sophocles, Tacitus, Thucydides, Virgil and Xenophon. The library also contained versions of Gottfried von Strassburg's *Tristan*, editions of the Parzival and Lohengrin epics, and a number of volumes on the life and times of the medieval cobbler-poet Hans Sachs. Thus the subjects of Lohengrin and all the great music dramas to follow the *Ring* were germinating in his mind during these years; a first prose draft was actually made for *Die Meistersinger* at Marienbad in 1845.

After completing the composition of *Tannhäuser* and seeing it on to the stage in 1845, Wagner took three months out of a busy schedule to prepare a report itemizing improvements that he considered essential if Dresden was to retain a respected place in the musical world. *Concerning the Royal Orchestra* was dated 1 March 1846 and dispatched to Lüttichau the following day. It recommended changes in the policy of hiring orchestral players, a rationalization of their work-load, raising of their salaries, and improvements in the layout of the orchestra so that players could hear each other and see the conductor clearly. He also suggested a series of winter orchestral concerts which could but enhance the stature of the Dresden court. Wagner's proposals were eminently practical and worked out in methodical detail. Had they been implemented Dresden might have assumed an even more dominant position in German opera, possibly under Wagner's direction, but too many people felt themselves criticized by such a report and threatened by such changes; after a year's wait, Wagner was informed that his proposals had been rejected.

A benefit concert for the Royal Orchestra's widows' and orphans' pension fund gave Wagner a chance to demonstrate both his powers as an orchestral conductor and his determination to get his own way. Once a year the old opera house (not that designed by Gottfried Semper) was turned over to a performance of an oratorio, the proceeds going to the fund; subsequently a symphony was traditionally added. Wagner's desire to use this Palm Sunday concert in 1846 for a performance of Beethoven's Ninth Symphony was greeted with horror by the trustees of the fund, who were convinced that this notoriously forbidding and incomprehensible work would spell disaster for their receipts. Wagner pressed ahead, countering the opposition from the orchestra's management and his own superiors with press announcements that so whetted the appetite of the public that the performance was an overwhelming financial success. Such was the enthusiasm and resolution he generated – the choir was apparently whipped into an ecstatic fervour and the cellos and basses had twelve special rehearsals to perfect the difficult recitative-like passage at the beginning of the finale – that the concert was also judged a resounding artistic success.

His financial position continued to be precarious. He could not be accused of habitual extravagance at this period; his salary was simply insufficient to cover essential outgoings. Schröder-Devrient suddenly, and rather unreasonably, turned against Wagner and through her lawyer demanded back the money she had loaned him in the early days of his Kapellmeistership. Wagner was forced to appeal to his employers and he was loaned, at interest, the sum he requested but was simultaneously required to take out at further cost a life insurance policy. Thus his meagre salary was depleted still more. It was during the difficult Dresden years that his marriage was at its most stable. But even these straitened circumstances compared favourably with the destitution of Paris; Minna managed the household, revelled in the status of Kapellmeister's wife and looked forward to more prosperous times. Wagner, however, bewailed their childlessness (this, though no fault of Minna, was to be a factor in their eventual separation) and joked wryly that they had to make do with pets – at this time another dog, Peps, and a parrot, Papo.

At the beginning of the new year (1847) Wagner was engaged in preparations for a production of Gluck's *Iphigénie en Aulide*. Drawn to Gluck's operas, especially the later ones, by their propensity to relinquish regular melodic periods in the interests of dramatic flow, he undertook a revision of the work which was performed with success in his own staging on 22 February. His arrangement was, according to the lights of his time, a sincere and sensitive attempt to present the opera in an acceptable form. Finding the arias and choruses 'disconnected', he linked them by means of preludes, postludes and transitions, taking care to make as much use as possible of Gluck's own melodic ideas. The orchestration was also revised but with restraint and always with the aim of highlighting features of Gluck's own score. His major alteration was to eliminate what he regarded as the predictable and sentimental marriage of Achilles and Iphigenia at the end; in order to effect this return to the spirit of Euripides it was necessary to introduce a new character (Artemis) as well as some recitatives.

During the year, while working on *Lohengrin*, he was studying Aeschylus (the *Oresteia* trilogy), Aristophanes and many other

Greek authors in German translations. It is of some significance that the *Oresteia* translation he read was the new one of Johann Gustav Droysen (1808–84). Droysen's translation and commentary interpreted Aeschylus' dramas as a Greek celebration of nationhood and freedom. Droysen's clear parallels between the Greek situation and the German were not lost on Wagner. The influence of Aeschylus on Wagner is discussed in the chapter on the *Ring* (p. 193). Also discussed there is the use he made of the Scandinavian sagas and epic poems of the twelfth and thirteenth centuries; it is sufficient to note here that Wagner had editions of many of these in his library at Dresden and was at this time deeply absorbed in study of them.

He succeeded in having *Rienzi*, his greatest popular success to date, put on at the Berlin Court Theatre, but it did not achieve the desired effect of securing a commission for *Lohengrin* from the King of Prussia. Nor was he paid for his two months of rehearsals, the Intendant, Küstner, claiming that the theatre had expressed a 'wish' and not issued an 'invitation'.

Early the next year, on 9 January 1848, Wagner's mother died in Leipzig. He was much moved by the serene expression on her face as she lay on her deathbed and realized that this was the breaking of his last link with his family, as his brothers and sisters were now all preoccupied with their own. His sense of loneliness was mitigated by work on *Lohengrin* and preparations for a series of three orchestral and choral concerts in Dresden. Among the works he conducted were symphonies by Haydn, Mozart and Beethoven, Bach's motet *Singet dem Herrn* and Palestrina's Stabat Mater. This last was given in an arrangement by Wagner himself. It is not true, as is sometimes stated, that Wagner destroyed the antiphonal character of the work in his version. In a very few places he does combine the two choirs but otherwise he preserves Palestrina's effects throughout. Dynamic, expression and tempo indications are added and these naturally conform to nineteenth-century rather than sixteenth-century taste.

With his remaining family ties cut, his indignation with conditions at the Dresden court rapidly rising to a peak, and his desire to create something new continually frustrated by stultifying forms and conventional taste, Wagner was ripe for the surge of revolutionary activity that was about to break in Germany.

4

The bourgeois revolutionary (1848–9)

The Germans were not natural revolutionaries: Napoleonic rule had taught them to equate the concepts of equality and emancipation with exploitation and the humiliation of conquest. But discontent rooted in the structures of the German Confederation was an undercurrent whose flow achieved increasing momentum in the years between 1815 and 1848, known as the *Vormärz* era ('pre-March', a reference to the outbreak of revolution in the March of 1848). The German Confederation set up in 1815 at the Congress of Vienna consisted of thirty-nine states under the presidency of the Austrian emperor. For all that it was carried out in a spirit of benevolent paternalism, many of these petty principalities were ruled in an archaic, even feudal manner; the princes were autocratic and insensitive to the needs of the populace.

But if the poverty, the squalor and the famine were not dealt with by the princely rulers, they were observed by middle-class liberals who were radicalized into protest against social deprivation. Many of the prominent liberals of 1848 were former firebrands, men who had suffered imprisonment for their earlier political activities. They were now academics (predominantly university professors) and lawyers, part of the establishment, albeit without political influence, and less favourably inclined towards the revolutionary solution. Their social position now, however, seemed to be threatened. Fear of revolution was outweighed by fear of their own proletarianization.

An uprising in Paris in February 1848 was followed by one in Vienna in March, an event which Wagner heralded with a signed poem of enthusiastic approbation, 'Greeting from Saxony to the Viennese', published in the *Allgemeine Österreichische Zeitung*. The people of Dresden took to the streets and pressed the king with their demand for electoral reform and social justice. Barricades were erected in some cities and the princes hastily capitulated to the extent that a pre-Parliament was allowed to assemble at Heidelberg and then, in May, a German National Assembly in Frankfurt.

Also in May, Wagner submitted to the relevant cabinet minister a *Plan for the Organization of a German National Theatre for the Kingdom of Saxony*. The chief proposals in this document were that the director of this institution be elected by its staff and by an association of dramatists and composers which was also to be inaugurated. A drama school was to be set up, chorus singers properly trained, the existing court orchestra expanded, salaries increased and its administration put under self-management. Naturally these democratic ideas were unacceptable to both the cabinet and the theatre management, but what rankled most with Reissiger was that Wagner was proposing to 'promote' him to the innocuous sphere of church music while the Intendant, Lüttichau, would be removed and all affairs placed under the direction of one Kapellmeister — Wagner himself, of course.

He put his career in even greater jeopardy when he wrote an article for the Vaterlandsverein, the leading republican political grouping. *How do Republican Endeavours stand in Relation to the Monarchy?* was published anonymously this time but since Wagner had the day before been prevailed upon to deliver it — to wild acclaim — as an address at a public meeting organized by the Vaterlandsverein, there was little secrecy about its authorship. The piece included a denunciation of communism but at the same time it portrayed money, and especially usury, as the root of all evil; humanity would only achieve its full potential for happiness when individual talents were realized. What caused the storm to break over his head, however, was his vision of the downfall of the aristocracy, particularly the end of its privileges at court, and his proposal of a people's militia dispensing with class distinctions, even if the whole was tempered by the compromise proposition that in Saxony the king was fit to remain at the head of the new republic, as 'the first and truest republican of all'. The last was by no means an idiosyncratic notion of Wagner's. The bourgeois liberal intelligentsia wanted constitutional and representative government, not revolutionary social change. They were not seeking the overthrow of kings and indeed in 1848 they remained in closer alliance with monarchies than with the working-class movement. There were demands for Wagner's dismissal, but the management decided for the time being to do nothing.

Wagner continued to carry out his duties at court and throughout the year he was engaged on several important creative projects. The scoring of *Lohengrin* was completed in April, while his conception of *Der Ring des Nibelungen* began to crystallize in *The Nibelungen Myth as Sketch for a Drama*.[1] The latter prose résumé of the drama was turned into the libretto *Siegfrieds Tod* (Siegfried's Death) that autumn and read to a group of friends in December. It has always been supposed that the essay *The Wibelungen: World History out of Saga* predates *The Nibelungen Myth as Sketch for a Drama* and *Siegfrieds Tod*, but it has now been established that it followed them.[2] Back in 1846 Wagner had made a sketch for a five-act work (probably an opera) on the subject of the twelfth-century emperor Frederick Barbarossa. In *A Communication to my Friends* and *Mein Leben* he tells us that he abandoned the idea as soon as he realized the greater potential of the Nibelungen myth for revealing the essence of 'utterly *true* humanity'. This cannot be correct because a sketch exists for the second act of *Friedrich I* which is written in Roman script. Wagner abandoned Gothic script and capital letters under the influence of the Grimm brothers in mid-December 1848 *after* completion of *Siegfrieds Tod*; the inadequacy of a historical subject was evidently not so immediately apparent.

In January of the new year, 1849, Wagner began to treat another subject, *Jesus von Nazareth*, probably also as an opera (a musical sketch exists); both projects were aborted. *Jesus von Nazareth* again has a five-act scenario, this time bringing together themes with which Wagner's mind had been occupied over the last decade and more. Jesus is portrayed as a social revolutionary of whom not the Romans but the Jewish priestly aristocracy have more reason to be afraid. When love is subjugated to money, misery is the result. The influence is apparent of such Young Hegelians as David Friedrich Strauss and Bruno Bauer, who had recently challenged the credibility of the Gospel stories. That of Feuerbach can be seen in the discourses on the self-sacrificial nature of true love, which is given of the free will, and in the assertion that humanity is essentially divine. Other passages reflect the revolutionary fervour of the time and in par-

---

[1] *Der Nibelungen-Mythus. Als Entwurf zu einem Drama* was the title Wagner gave it in his collected writings. The 1848 manuscript is actually headed *Die Nibelungensage (Mythus)*.

[2] John Deathridge, 'The Ending of the *Ring*', paper read at colloquium at Goldsmiths' College, London, 16 January 1984; publication forthcoming.

ticular the ideas of Proudhon. The protection of property is a crime against nature: without the evil of property there would be no crimes against property. The person who stores up treasures takes from his neighbour what his neighbour had need of and tempts the thief to steal. Who then is the thief: the one who took from his neighbour what his neighbour had need of, or the one who took from the rich man what he did not need? Modern scholarship suggests that Wagner's reading of Jesus may not be so far wide of the mark. The gospels had to explain away the awkward and dangerous fact that Jesus had been executed, for sedition, by the Romans. He was a revolutionary leader who posed a threat to the Jewish priestly aristocracy that policed the Jews while their country was under Roman occupation, and his followers included one of the Zealots – Peter was known as a 'terrorist' – a group who prepared armed resistance.[3]

As discontent continued to grow in the early part of 1849 Wagner found a kindred spirit in August Röckel, his assistant conductor and friend since 1843. Röckel, dismissed from his post for subversive activities, had begun in August 1848 to publish the *Volksblätter*, a weekly republican journal. They had many animated conversations on the subject of socialism and Wagner contributed articles anonymously to the *Volksblätter* (soon proscribed by the authorities). These were inflammatory tirades directed against the princes, against privilege and inequality.

Wagner's court duties became more and more intolerable to him and the theatre management for their part regarded him with increasing suspicion. One Sunday he was so immersed in *Tannhäuser* that he completely forgot that he should be conducting the music for Mass. He was accused of fostering disaffection among the orchestra members and of dereliction of duty. A performance of *Tannhäuser* in February at Weimar under Liszt set the seal on a magnificent friendship that was to last, admittedly with its vicissitudes, for the rest of Wagner's life.

In March the *Volksblätter* published his poem *Need* [*Die Not*], treating the Feuerbachian concept of necessity, the unstoppable compulsion that underlies human endeavour and existence. It was a concept that was to be central to his writings from *The Artwork of the Future* on. In the present poem the necessity was for the destruc-

---

[3] See S.G.F. Brandon, *The Trial of Jesus of Narazeth* (London 1968), for a full exposition of this interpretation, with citation of sources.

tion of capital and its concomitant evils greed and usury. (Feuerbach's philosophy was given a social and political dimension by others, notably Marx.) Interestingly it was exactly at this time that Wagner was introduced by Röckel to Mikhail Bakunin, the Russian anarchist. On their common interests of music and politics they held diverging views but Bakunin was personally acquainted with Marx, Engels and other leading socialists and there can be no doubt that their ideas became the topic of many an earnest discussion.

Meanwhile liberal politicians were coming to see Protestant Prussia as a suitable alternative to Catholic Austria as the dominant power in Germany and on 28 March 1849 the Frankfurt Parliament decided to offer the imperial crown to Friedrich Wilhelm IV, the King of Prussia. He rejected it five days later with the observation that he would not 'pick up a Crown from the gutter'. Five days later still, on 8 April, appeared a thundering torrent of rhetoric from Wagner's pen, entitled *The Revolution*:

> I [Revolution] will destroy every wrong which has power over men. I will destroy the domination of one over the other, of the dead over the living, of the material over the spiritual, I will shatter the power of the mighty, of the law and of property. Man's master shall be his *own* will, his *own* desire his only law, his *own* strength his only property, *for only the free man is holy and there is naught higher than he*. Let there be an end to the wrong that gives one man power over millions . . . *since all are equal I shall destroy all dominion of one over the other*.[4]

The 'anarchistic egoism' with its celebration of the freedom of the individual is reminiscent not so much of Bakunin as of Max Stirner (1806–65), another early socialist whose ideas must have been circulating in the smoke-filled rooms of Dresden. Both Wagner and the posthumous launderers of his reputation subsequently attempted to represent his role in the uprising as a peripheral one: that of a spectator rather than an activist. It is understandable that in later years he should have been at pains to minimize the extent of his involvement. In the 1850s he was seeking an amnesty to allow him to return to Germany from exile; in the 1860s, when dictating *Mein Leben*, he had the sensibilities of a royal benefactor to consider. While it may be true that a primary impulse of his revolutionary

---

[4] Translation by P.R.J. Ford from *Wagner: A Documentary Study*, ed. H. Barth, D. Mack and E. Voss, p. 172.

fervour was the desire for artistic reform – the demand for improved theatrical conditions such as would lend themselves to his new conception of drama – it is undeniable that the events of 1848–9 fanned the radical flame in him; his idealism reached its peak in these years and its inspiration was social as well as artistic. Nor, of course, did his personality allow him to occupy a back seat: he always had to be a leader, always at the hub of things. And there was to be action as well as stirring oratory. At least two political gatherings took place in his garden and the arming of the populace was discussed. It seems that Wagner, possibly with Röckel, and possibly on behalf of Bakunin, instructed a brass founder to manufacture hand-grenades and fill them with explosives.

In Saxony, as elsewhere, the king, Friedrich August II, refused to acknowledge the constitution agreed at Frankfurt and in fact flagrantly violated it by dissolving both chambers of Parliament and sacking the cabinet. Röckel fled to Prague to escape arrest and Wagner took over responsibility for the *Volksblätter* in his place. As it became clear that Saxony was about to be invaded by the Prussian army Wagner wrote to Röckel (2 May 1849) urging him to return to Dresden. 'A decisive conflict is expected, if not with the king, at least with Prussian troops. There's only one thing to be afraid of, namely that a revolution could break out *too soon*.' This letter, found on Röckel at his arrest, was cited by the Dresden police as evidence incriminating Wagner.

Despite the rhetoric Wagner could never bring himself to see the masses as his equals. He was one of the many bourgeois liberals who had no wish to see a victory for the proletariat then developing, and who feared the excessive spilling of blood. If the Saxon army were to side with the people against the invading Prussians, he reasoned, it might yet be possible to persuade the king to accept the constitution and usher in a new era of enlightened, democratic government. He had some small posters printed with the words 'Are you with us against foreign troops?' and pressed them, at considerable risk, on the Saxon soldiers himself.

Just before the struggle began in earnest he jotted down some ideas for a three-act drama on the subject of Achilles; as with *Friedrich I*, its themes – a free hero, the gods yielding to humanity – were superseded by the *Ring*. On 5 May he climbed the tower of the Kreuzkirche in order to report on the movements of the troops for those attempting to co-ordinate the strategy from the city hall. He spent the night in the tower, engaging in philosophical debate with a schoolmaster. This characteristic touch does not, however, indicate lack of involvement: the tower was under fire, his task was an important one and others reported on him being caught up in the excitement of events.

The amateurish organization of the provisional government was no match for the well-drilled Prussian troops and resistance began to collapse. By 9 May the insurrectionists were in retreat. In her diary Clara Schumann noted the terrible atrocities committed by the troops: an innkeeper was made to stand and watch while twenty-six students found there were shot one after the other; men were said to have been hurled into the street by the dozen from the third and fourth floors. Röckel was arrested, as were three of the leading rebels, Bakunin, Otto Heubner and his aide C.A. Martin. Wagner escaped arrest only by the most providential of misunderstandings. Heubner and his two comrades walked into a trap when they took up an invitation to set up headquarters at Chemnitz. Wagner would have travelled with them but having missed their coach he arrived in Chemnitz independently and fortunately took a room in a different inn from theirs: they were seized in their beds early the next morning.

Heubner, and Röckel too, received a death sentence; it was commuted to life imprisonment and Röckel was to spend the next thirteen years in gaol. Wagner would undoubtedly have been treated similarly, though at first he scarcely realized what trouble he was in, even contemplating a possible return to Dresden. To both his friend Eduard Devrient and to Minna he wrote, just a few days after the failure of the uprising, that the likes of them could never be true revolutionaries. They had not the necessary reckless determination. They wished to build a better future while the true revolutionary had first to destroy – this could only be carried out by 'the scum of the common people' (letter to Minna, 14 May 1849). Henceforth he abjured revolution, he announced.

Wagner had meanwhile made his way via his brother-in-law, Heinrich Wolfram, at Chemnitz to Weimar. There Liszt sheltered him but on 19 May the *Dresdner Anzeiger* published a warrant for his arrest and Wagner realized that he would have to leave the country without delay.[5] Liszt was of the opinion that he would stand

---

[5] Martin Gregor-Dellin has reconstructed in fascinating detail the chronology of Wagner's activities during the uprising; see pp. 168–80 of *Richard Wagner: His Life, His Work, His Century*.

the best chance in Paris; reluctant as he was to return to the scene of his misery and degradation, Wagner was obliged to pretend to accede since Liszt was providing the money for him to leave Germany. He made his way on a false passport to Switzerland and from there to Paris on a passport of his own, which provides us, if it is accurate, with the only authoritative evidence of his height: 5 ft 6½ in. (1m. 69.16cm.).[6] Revisiting Paris briefly in 1849 and 1850 made his gorge rise. Nothing had changed: 'Spare me from expatiating in more detail on the shocking baseness of artistic activity in Paris, especially as regards opera', he wrote to Ferdinand Heine (19 November 1849). And the following year he indulged in orgiastic fantasies of vindictive destruction: 'I no longer believe in any other revolution than that which begins with the burning down of Paris', he wrote to his former Dresden friend Theodor Uhlig (22 October 1850), describing this necessary treatment as a 'fire-cure' (*feuerkur*). Inflammatory words for one who had abjured revolution.

[6] The passport actually reads '5 Fuss, 5½ Zoll' (i.e. 5ft 5½in.), but the Swiss foot was divided into 10 rather than 12 inches. Gregor-Dellin's calculation (op.cit., pp. 536–7), concluding that Wagner's height was nevertheless 5ft 5½in. in modern terms, is incorrect in that he takes the modern foot as equivalent to 30 rather than 30.48cm.

5

Exile (1849–55)

Settling down in Zurich Wagner was adopted by a circle of literary intellectuals who befriended him and provided pecuniary support; one of the two cantonal secretaries, Jakob Sulzer, was a particularly valued friend. In July 1849 he launched the series of 'Zurich essays' which addressed themselves, in a maelstrom of words and ideas, to a vast range of artistic and political matters. The first three, *Art and Revolution*, *The Artwork of the Future* and *Opera and Drama*, are nothing less than a fundamental reappraisal of the function of art, providing a theoretical basis for what emerges as the only legitimate medium of the future: the Wagnerian music drama.

Art and Revolution, the most intensive and polemical of the three, deplores the debasement, during the Christian era, of the glorious Greek drama which combined all the arts. Modern corrupt society was reflected in its mercenary, vacuous theatre. The artwork of the future, uniting all the media within the framework of a drama, would embrace the spirit of a newly liberated humanity: nationality would therefore be no more than an ornament and art would be taken out of the realm of capitalist speculation and profit-making. All this could be achieved only by the great revolution of mankind.

In *The Artwork of the Future*, written later the same year – it was completed on 4 November 1849 – Wagner elaborated his theories in the repetitive, tortuous prose that has made them notorious. In essence he was saying this. The three basic elements of the original Greek drama were dance, music and poetry. In isolation their potential remains unfulfilled; working in conjunction in a united artwork each can attain its full maturity. Similarly, the arts of architecture, sculpture and painting will regain their classical and authentic stature only as constituents in the artwork of the future. Traditional theatres are unable to serve art adequately because of the requirements of speculation for gain on the one hand, and luxurious ostentation on the other; auditoria are at present stratified in order to fence off the various classes of society. The architect of the theatre of the future, however, will be guided solely by the law of beauty and will aim to bring the dramatic action to the eye and ear of the spectator in an intelligible fashion. Sets will be executed by landscape painters, and the stage is thus prepared for the actor of the future, in whom the three sister arts are united: he is dancer, musician and poet.

Interestingly, *The Artwork of the Future* allows for occasional use of the spoken word, though this possibility was not explored either in *Opera and Drama* or in the music dramas themselves. Finally, the new work of art will be brought into being not by a single creative artist but by a fellowship of artists. It is a communal work and can be created only in response to a communal demand. The artist of the future is, in a word, *das Volk* (the People).

The reunification of the arts into a *Gesamtkunstwerk*, or 'total work of art', was not a new notion: among those who had previously advocated some sort of unification, either in theory or in practice, were Lessing, Novalis, Tieck, Schelling and Hoffmann, while the idea of the regeneration of art in accordance with Classical ideals can be identified with such writers as Winckelmann, Wieland, Lessing and of course Goethe and Schiller. Of Wagner's more individual ideas it may be noted that the 'stratification' of the audience was indeed virtually abolished by the amphitheatrical auditorium of the Bayreuth Festspielhaus when it was eventually built. Every member of the audience was brought into close contact with the drama on stage, and there was no 'luxurious ostentation' (the wooden seats remain numbingly bare to this day). As for the designing of the stage sets by academic artists, those for the *Ring* in 1876 were indeed done by such a man, Joseph Hoffmann, though they were executed by professional scene-painters.

There is an element of fantasy in Wagner's outline of the future music drama: it was perhaps a utopian vision that he did not expect to see carried out in every detail. In any case its philosophical basis is evident. He describes the artistic creation of the *Volk* as the product of sheer necessity: in other words, the process is one of historical inevitability. This is a concept that was in general circulation around the time of the 1848–9 risings and both the ideas and the language of the essay are redolent of such revolutionary thinkers as Marx (whom Wagner may or may not have read) and Ludwig Feuerbach (the original dedication to the latter was removed when the piece was reprinted in Wagner's collected writings).

Wagner's idealization of the *Volk* is not to be identified with Marx's proletariat; the working class, referred to by Wagner as 'the rabble' (*der Pöbel*), he considered the abnormal product of a corrupt society, offering no brighter hopes for the future than the autocrats and capitalists who currently held power. The *Volk* was rather the cultivation of an idea long familiar in German thought. For those bourgeois intellectuals like Wagner who wished for social change but who were also keeping an anxious eye on their hard-won privileges, the concept of the *Volk* provided a convenient rallying-cry. The *völkisch* ideology had evolved with the rise of national consciousness in the eighteenth century and acquired impetus as a reaction against the new technological world and the 'insidious' forces of liberalism and modernism which were associated with the invading foreigners of the Napoleonic wars. German nationalism was thus intrinsically reactionary even in its early days. The characteristically German solution of a *tabula rasa* was embodied in the *völkisch* outlook, which urged a return to a remote primordial world where peasants of pure Germanic blood lived as a true community. This nostalgic yearning for a lost national identity was to underpin the whole course of German nationalism up to and including its tragic consequences in the present century. Wagner's fellowship of artists, in which the individual genius figure has given way to the *Volk*, was thus not a new notion, but a formulation of ideas in general circulation.

At the beginning of 1850, before finally despairing of Paris, Wagner made a prose draft for a three-act opera that he envisaged being performed there. The story of *Wieland der Schmied* concerns a smith who is forced to work for the enemies who have lamed him but who finally makes his own wings to soar above the world and join his beloved, Schwanhilde, the swan bride. There are many pre-echoes of the *Ring* and other works, for example in the giving of a ring as a pledge and the forging of a sword, but it is the central character who is of most interest. Wieland is at the same time a smith and an artist. Languishing in bondage, he is compelled to create according to the instructions of his master. Inspired by a faithful bride he finds the means to escape his miserable fate. Wagner soon decided that the Germanic hero Wieland could never be translated into a French context and abandoned the plan.

Suddenly his luck seemed to have turned when he heard that two of his (female) admirers were proposing to provide him with an annual allowance of 3000 francs, a sum substantial enough to free him from the tiresome worries of everyday expenditure. It would probably be true to say that Wagner was as delighted at the discerning recognition of his potential shown by these benefactresses as he was by the prospect of being able to devote his life to the kind of works that he now believed it was his destiny to accomplish. Frau Julie Ritter, a widow from Dresden, was already known to him as the mother of Karl Ritter, a musician and poet who was to become a member of his circle. Karl Ritter had visited him in Dresden in the company of Jessie Laussot (née Taylor), an Englishwoman by birth who gradually allowed a passion for Wagner's music to fill the vacuum in her life left by her unfulfilling marriage to a Bordeaux wine merchant, Eugène Laussot. She (with the help of her family) was the second benefactress and with her good looks and cultural sophistication appealed strongly to Wagner. She spoke fluent German and had the intellectual capacity to comprehend Wagner's artistic intentions; at the keyboard she displayed considerable skills though her singing left something to be desired. At Bordeaux Wagner found the warmth and receptivity that he so longed for; from his own wife he could expect nothing but recriminations – Minna regularly and stridently reminded him that he had thrown up the security of a Kapellmeistership for the sake of political extremism and Wagner responded in kind.

But the inevitable affair with Jessie Laussot swiftly took a remarkable turn. Wagner conceived the impulsive idea of leaving behind all the squalor of his existence and seeking oblivion in Greece or Asia Minor. Jessie thrilled him by hinting that she would be prepared to abandon her unhappy marriage and cast in her lot with him. He wrote an emotional but trenchant letter of farewell to Minna, salvaging his conscience, perhaps, by pressing her to accept half of his expected allowance. But Jessie miscalculated by confiding the plan to her mother who promptly informed Eugène. Trusting in his powers of persuasion Wagner hastened to Bordeaux only to be warned away from the town by the police, who had been alerted. And so the idyllic vision faded, though Julie Ritter did make him an annual allowance of 800 Talers which continued from 1851 to 1859. Wagner wrote a self-justificatory letter to Minna, on which the latter commented with cynical remarks in the margin: 'obvious lie', 'shameful!' and so on. They came together again in Zurich to torment each other once more.

A debate in the *Neue Zeitschrift für Musik* on the use of the term 'artistic taste of the Hebrews' prompted Wagner to contribute pseudonymously an article which soon created an unforeseen stir. *Jewishness in Music* (as *Das Judentum in der Musik* is best translated in this context) included an attack on his erstwhile benefactor Meyerbeer (without actually naming him), but beyond that there was nothing new: all the points made in Wagner's closely argued anti-semitic diatribe echoed the prejudices and obsessions of an ever-increasing number of nineteenth-century Germans. His argument may be summarized as follows. The emptiness of a society that hankers only after money and material things is epitomized by Jewish musicians. Jews have no culture of their own and therefore no true artistic feeling; as aliens in the society in which they live, and as a race wedded to commerce, they will never be able to create anything of real artistic value, but are condemned to imitate. A famous Jewish composer [Meyerbeer] has prospered by entertaining his bored audience with triviality dressed up as glittering novelty. The Jews' artistic insensitivity should be evident from their displeasing physical appearance, the shrill, sibilant buzzing of the Semitic voice, the superficial blabbering of their conversation, and the grotesque gurgling one hears in the synagogue. Only by renouncing Jewishness can Jews be redeemed.

Contemporary caricature of Meyerbeer conforming to the anti-semitic stereotype.

The less penetrating, more racially abusive part of Wagner's tract belongs to an identifiable tradition of anti-semitism. What was regarded as the characteristic Jewish physiognomy was caricatured as early as the fifteenth century; along with the emancipating reforms of the late eighteenth century the long nose and short build entered polemical literature and by the mid-eighteenth century the stereotype was fixed. The Jew's supposed physical ugliness, insensitivity to the German language, and general rapacity and untrustworthiness had been depicted by 1850 in countless novels, often written by people with otherwise impeccably humanitarian credentials. Among the novels embodying this stereotype were two of the most popular of the century – both written by liberals: Gustav Freytag's *Soll und Haben* (Debit and Credit) of 1855 and Wilhelm Raabe's *Hungerpastor* (Poor Pastor) of 1862. The stereotypical image of the Jew was, as George Mosse put it, 'the focal point for the feeling of aggression inherent in the [*völkisch*] ideology'.[1] But this ideology is what also underlies Wagner's more discerning analysis of Jews in relation to culture, in particular the German culture of his time. His argument is that because Jewish artists are rootless and working in an alien tradition they are incapable of reflecting the inner feelings and emotions of the German people. The preoccupation with 'feeling' – seen both here and throughout the other Zurich and subsequent essays – is entirely characteristic of the trend in nineteenth-century German thought. More specifically it is connected with the *völkisch* ideology: the inspiration of the native soil, the instinctive affinity with one's countrymen and women.

In the *völkisch* outlook the Jew, as outsider, was necessarily lacking in true feelings and spirituality. However, if Jewishness was intrinsically un-German, it was thought to be possible for individual Jews to be assimilated. Again it was the more liberal view which called on the Jews to reject their 'superstitions', their habits and trade and undertake a programme of re-education. The history of German literature from the Enlightenment to the fall of the Third Reich is a despicable catalogue of anti-Jewish sentiment; sympathizers were rare. In varying degrees both major and minor figures expressed hostility to or contempt for the Jews: Clemens Brentano and Achim

---

[1] *Germans and Jews*, 18. See chap. 1 (pp. 3–33) for the origins and development of the *völkisch* ideology, and chaps 2 and 3 (pp. 34–76) for much perceptive material on anti-semitism in the nineteenth century.

von Arnim (the compilers of the folksong collection *Des Knaben Wunderhorn*), the Grimm brothers, Ludwig Tieck, Hegel (in early life), Schopenhauer, Karl Marx, the liberal Hoffmann von Fallersleben. The list could be infinitely extended; indeed, it could be taken back to Luther who inveighed against the Jews and proposed the burning of their synagogues, and to the even earlier anti-semitic obsessions of the medieval age.[2] The ending of Marx's *On the Jewish Question* (1843) is remarkably similar to that of Wagner's essay: 'The social emancipation of the Jews is the emancipation of society from Judaism.'

In the reactionary aftermath of 1848–9 the Jews, already a popular target of abuse, played the role of a scapegoat. They were blamed by some for fermenting the revolt and by others (such is the logic of racism) for provoking it, by their unscrupulous exploitation as bankers and traders. Wagner, the frustrated egoist, needed a scapegoat more than most. Large head and exaggerated features contrasting with a short body almost to the point of deformity, uncertain of paternity (possibly even Jewish, he thought), unsuccessful in love, thwarted in career, now uprooted and denied contact with his native public: all the classic ingredients for an inferiority complex, and one that could take refuge in an absurdly irrational and repulsive racist mentality. But the wound goes deeper. He cast himself, in an exquisitely masochistic identification, in the role of Ahasuerus, the Wandering Jew, the rootless suffering artist.[3] He longed to be important to his countrymen and women, to belong. The Jews, by reputation rich and successful, inspired his envy. With more passion than logic he claimed that they had no conception of community: in fact, for all that many of them experienced difficulty in reconciling their Jewishness with their German nationalism, they had both a strong sense of ethnic identity (albeit with no fatherland)

---

[2] See Alfred D. Low, *Jews in the Eyes of the Germans*, for a detailed study of the phenomenon from the Enlightenment to Imperial Germany, and Léon Poliakov, *The History of Anti-Semitism*, esp. vol. III (From Voltaire to Wagner) for an exhaustive treatment of the subject.

[3] On Wagner's 'Ahasuerus Consciousness' see H. Zelinsky, 'Die "feuerkur" des Richard Wagner oder die "neue religion" der "Erlösung" durch "Vernichtung" ', 94–5. The intention of the article, to prove that Wagner's whole life was orientated around the destruction of the Jews, is highly questionable, but many interesting points are raised.

and, in the Old Testament, a national myth. But they served admirably as a scapegoat, and whether or not we accept that Mime and Beckmesser were intended as Jewish caricatures, there are good reasons for supposing that Wagner's villains – just like his antisemitism – are to a large extent projections of his frustration, guilt and self-hatred.[4]

On 28 August 1850 *Lohengrin* received its world premiere at Weimar under the direction of Liszt; Wagner himself was to be denied the satisfaction of hearing his latest score for another eleven years. Having attempted and abandoned the composition of *Siegfrieds Tod* (later to become *Götterdämmerung*), he set about his major theoretical work, the longest of his essays: *Opera and Drama*. This immense discourse – it runs to some 100,000 words – on musical aesthetics is written in Wagner's most high-flown rhetorical style. For pages at a time his rhapsodic prose hovers on the perimeter of comprehensibility; often it roves beyond. But the third and final part of the essay is of considerable interest as it contains the fundamentals, outlined in comprehensive detail, of the proposed artwork of the future: i.e. the music drama.

After a lengthy discussion of word accentuation in speech and music, Wagner concludes that diverse emotions can be expressed all the more forcefully by a mode of verse-setting that pays strict attention to both the sound and the meaning of words. The device of *Stabreim* (an old German verse form using alliteration) opens up a vast range of possibilities for the composer. Moreover, in the new kind of melodic verse (*Versmelodie*) poetry and music are uniquely united because the melody will grow out of the verse. A system of presentiments and reminiscences, functioning as 'melodic impulses' (*melodische Momente*), will develop into, as it were, 'signposts for the emotions' (*Gefühlswegweiser*). Once an emotion has been expressed in the melodic verse in such a manner (i.e. with a leitmotif, though Wagner does not use the word) it can become the property of pure music; a subsequent rendering of the idea by the orchestra alone will then be enough to realize that emotion for the listener.

A duplication of such a vocal melody in the orchestra would be utterly superfluous; the orchestra is the medium in which the har-

---

[4] The portrayal of aspects of Wagner's character in his heroes and villains is too large a subject to be treated here; for a stimulating psychological analysis see Peter Wapnewski, *Der traurige Gott*.

mony is created. Nor will one voice serve as harmonic support for another, except in rare cases where it is justified for a deeper understanding of the situation. Choruses and other ensembles will thus disappear, and only when the characters are engaged in a communal expression of feeling, at the peak of lyrical effusion, is there an opportunity for vocal polyphony; but even here the composer must ensure that the individuality of each participant is guaranteed by a definite melodic utterance. Also of great importance in ensuring individuality is gesture: the new drama will prescribe in detail each character's bearing and movements as well as their appearance and costume. The way in which these principles were put into practice by Wagner is discussed later, in the chapter on the *Ring*.[5]

Six months after completing the labour of *Opera and Drama* he embarked (July 1851) on an extensive preface to accompany the projected publication of the librettos of *Der fliegende Holländer*, *Tannhäuser* and *Lohengrin*. This preface, which he called *A Communication to my Friends*, was intended to explain to all those 'who feel a need and inclination to understand me' the reasons for his change of direction from history and legend to a new concept of drama based on the Nibelung myth and related sagas. Although it provides an interesting retrospect of an artist's life and work some of its facts and judgments require to be treated with caution.

In the hope of alleviating his dual complaints of erysipelas and severe constipation he took the waters at the hydropathic establishment at Albisbrunn, near Zurich. The regimen was brutally severe and although he sustained it for nine weeks his brief description in the Annals[6] sums it up: 'Water torture'. Minna was more sceptical

---

[5] See also chapter 10, pp. 125–28 and the chapters on *Tristan, Die Meistersinger* and *Parsifal*. For more detailed expositions of *Opera and Drama* see Frank Glass, *The Fertilizing Seed*, Bryan Magee, *Aspects of Wagner*, and Jack M. Stein, *Richard Wagner & the Synthesis of the Arts*.

[6] From August 1835 Wagner kept notes for his future autobiography in the Red Pocketbook. Using these notes he began, in July 1865, to dictate *Mein Leben* to Cosima (at the request of his new patron, Ludwig II). When the story had reached the year 1846 Wagner decided to transfer his notes from the Red Pocketbook into the leatherbound Brown Book Cosima had given him. These new notes, called the 'Annals', deal with the years of his revolutionary activities and his affairs with Jessie Laussot and Mathilde Wesendonck – all matters of a sensitive nature as regards Cosima and Ludwig. This possibly accounts for the transfer and for the fact that all but

about its efficacy; even success wouldn't convince her, he told Kietz, because she would attribute that to something entirely different. But Wagner himself counted it a failure and his condition on arriving back in Zurich – 'Dreadful nervous state: very thin and pale. Total insomnia.' (Annals) – was relieved only by the more congenial home in the Zeltweg that Minna had moved them into. It must have been with some satisfaction that he told Kietz (28 May 1852): 'You need no other address for me than *Richard Wagner* in *Zurich*. That is enough.'

In this last month of 1851 he still had high hopes of the following year which he confidently expected to bring the revolution, starting in France. Even the coup d'état of Louis-Napoleon on 2 December 1851, which resulted in a dictatorial suppression of the opposition and dissolution of the Assembly – and a year later in the proclamation of the Second Empire – did not at first seem to him more than a minor setback. In expectation of what the new year would bring he continued to count its days as 32, 33 December etc. A letter to Theodor Uhlig of 22 January 1852 is dated '53(!) December 1851'. Wagner's letters to Uhlig, who as well as being a composer and a member of Wagner's orchestra in Dresden sympathized with his political views, are the most revealing as to his outlook in the years immediately following the 1849 uprising. Indeed, he expressed himself so forcefully there that when the correspondence was prepared for publication in 1888 Cosima (possibly with Wagner's approval before his death) found it necessary to strike out passages in seventy of the ninety-three letters. The deleted matter became available to Wagner scholars only in 1951, on the publication of the Burrell Collection.

Early in 1852 Wagner was introduced to a couple who were destined to play leading roles in the events of the Zurich years: Otto and Mathilde Wesendonck. (They spelt their name thus, incident-ally; it was not until after 1900 that their son adopted the form

the first four pages of the Red Pocketbook were destroyed, though it is doubtful whether the survival of these original notes would have revealed a great deal: even those of the early years are compressed to such an extent that they were clearly intended to serve as no more than a mnemonic aid. A transcription of the four remaining pages of the Red Pocketbook can be found in vol. 1 of the Sämtliche Briefe (not yet translated); the Annals (1846–1868) appear in the English translation of the Brown Book (see Bibliography for full details of both).

'Wesendonk'.) Otto had made his fortune as a partner in a New York silk company; Mathilde, who was thirteen years younger – she was only twenty-three when she made the acquaintance of Wagner – had some talent, falling rather short of genius, as a writer of poetry and prose. But this was not a vein she tapped until much later. With the exception of the five poems which Wagner set to music in 1857–8 her role was mutually accepted to be that of muse. Wagner did not want, did not need the stimulus of a corresponding creative talent in order to generate the sparks of his own imagination. On the contrary, Mathilde's receptive young mind provided endorsement, encouragement and inspiration.

Otto's role, considered by Wagner to be no less important to the creative artist, was to care for his material needs. From the start he displayed generosity through loans and other financial support; eventually, in 1857, he fulfilled Wagner's dream of a sanctuary from the buffetings of the world by putting a small house at his disposal.

A few months after meeting the Wesendoncks, Wagner was introduced by his friend Georg Herwegh (another 1849 activist in exile) to François and Eliza Wille, a couple whose pleasantly appointed house at Mariafeld, overlooking Lake Zurich, was frequently visited by Wagner; Eliza was to become a supportive friend and trusted confidante. In April and May 1852 Wagner conducted four performances of *Der fliegende Holländer* but his steadily increasing reputation as a conductor and composer were not enough to dispel moods of gloom and depression. Several letters from later in the year speak of a loveless, cheerless existence; more than once he contemplated suicide. These moods continued until 1857, the time of his occupation of his new home, the Asyl; they returned to him in Venice after the conclusion of the affair with Mathilde Wesendonck.

Meanwhile the text of the *Ring* had been taking shape and on four successive evenings beginning on 16 February 1853 he recited it to an invited audience at the Hotel Baur au Lac in Zurich. By all accounts readings such as these were far from the tedious business one might suppose. Wagner's tremendous histrionic abilities are well attested: he was able to transform himself into the various characters and bring the drama to vibrant life simply with gestures of his hands and nuances of intonation. At about the same time he had fifty copies of the poem printed at his own expense; they were sent to various friends including Liszt and Röckel.

In May, Otto Wesendonck's patronage allowed him to present

and conduct three concerts of excerpts from his earlier works. Throughout his career he accepted the necessity of performing what have since become known as 'bleeding chunks' – necessary both to raise funds and to keep in the public eye. But it was not a practice he relished and towards the end of his life Cosima reported that 'presenting fragments from his works is particularly repulsive to him' (Diaries, 12 May 1872).

Wagner and Minna had now moved into a larger apartment on the second floor of 13 Zeltweg and furnished it in a more luxurious manner that they mistakenly thought would be justified by increasing prosperity. It was to there that Liszt came in July for a keenly awaited visit. The two composers gave each other enormous pleasure with their company and each was impressed and stimulated by the other's works. Wagner later gave generous praise to the symphonic poems and *Faust* Symphony, which Liszt played him on this occasion, though he was more reticent about the undeniable influence on him of their bold harmonic style.

With Otto Wesendonck's help he was able to make a trip to Italy, which according to *Mein Leben* was cut short by the sudden onrush of inspiration for *Das Rheingold* – coming to him as he lay in a half-sleep in a hotel room in La Spezia. Even if our suspicions were not aroused by the fact that he communicated this momentous event to no one – not even Liszt, to whom he mentioned La Spezia just a week later – and that by his own account he nearly changed his mind about returning when he reached Genoa, even so it would be necessary on strictly musicological grounds (see p. 198) to regard the story as probably yet another example of Wagner's incorrigible tendency to romanticize his life. But however mythical his account, it is evident that he now realized himself to be on the threshold of a new phase in his career, and it was in the succeeding months that the music of the *Ring* at last began to take shape.

In October Wagner saw Liszt again, this time in Basle along with Hans von Bülow, Joseph Joachim and Peter Cornelius – pianist, violinist and composer respectively. The company was joined by Liszt's companion the Princess Carolyne von Sayn-Wittgenstein and her daughter Marie, an attractive, pensive fifteen-year-old who unwittingly captured Wagner's heart. A few days later, Wagner and Liszt came together again in Paris. Now Liszt was accompanied by the three children of his liaison with Marie d'Agoult, and thus it was that Wagner met Cosima. He did not later present it as a destiny-filled moment; he records simply that he was struck by the shyness of the sixteen-year-old Cosima and her sister Blandine. It is generally when his life impinges upon his art that Wagner finds it necessary to embroider.

By the middle of the following year, 1854, the heart condition from which Minna was suffering had become serious enough for her to take a 'whey cure' at Seelisberg on Lake Lucerne. The disease was taking its toll on her looks and she had also resorted to laudanum for her insomnia. Her increasing nervous excitability exacerbated their marital problems. Minna flew into rages more frequently and Wagner infuriated her further by remaining totally calm: 'she once told me that nothing had ever so enraged her as my calmness during a scene in Zurich', Wagner later said to Cosima (Diaries, 30 November 1881). Minna's inability to bear a child distressed them both and they considered adoption. Malvida von Meysenbug, who knew the couple well, assessed the situation thus: 'A man so dominated by his elemental spirit should from the beginning have had a high-minded and understanding woman at his side – a woman who understood how to mediate between the genius and the world by realizing that the two were bound to be eternally poles apart. Frau Wagner never realized this. She tried to mediate by demanding concessions towards the world from the genius, which the latter could not and must not make.'[7]

His old friend Kietz, still in Paris, had been importuning him for a loan but Wagner had to explain that he too was still in difficulties: his works were not yet bringing in the expected receipts and in addition he was having to support not only Minna and Natalie but Minna's parents as well. By September 1854 he reckoned his debts at 10,000 francs; Wesendonck agreed to settle these and provide a regular allowance in exchange for the receipts from future performances of Wagner's works. Wesendonck's patience (though not his money, it seems) was fast running out; this was to be the last time, he said. Wagner's portrayal of Wesendonck in *Mein Leben* is certainly not abounding in gratitude; but neither is it quite the shabby, mean-spirited treatment that is sometimes represented (even in the original, uncut version). Wagner tested his friendship to the limit with his requests and Wesendonck certainly reacted magnanimously,

---

[7] Translation by P.R.J. Ford from *Wagner: A Documentary Study*, ed. H. Barth, D. Mack and E. Voss, p. 188.

though he never pretended that the coffers were bottomless or that returns were not expected: the loans were always regarded by both parties as repayable and a rent was charged on the house that was to be provided for Wagner next to Wesendonck's villa. But above all Wagner simply had no respect for accumulated capital. As a child of the revolution and as an impoverished man he believed vaguely in the redistribution of wealth; as a creative artist he believed sincerely that it was the duty of others to make sacrifices in return for the torments he underwent and the pleasure he delivered. It is perhaps easier to sympathize with that proposition in so far as it relates to material things; less so when it is extended to benefactors' wives. But as regards the comparative esteem in which wealth and art are held, there is little doubt that if Wagner had been able to look more than a century into the future he would have been appalled to see that priorities have not changed.

Minna returned to Saxony in September, for the first time since the 1849 uprising, to visit her parents and various acquaintances. Another of her missions was to address a petition to the new Saxon king, Johann. Wagner was very sensitive about these appeals for clemency, several of which had to be made before his full amnesty was eventually granted in 1862; he was not at this stage prepared to accept that he had done anything wrong. The warrant for his arrest had been reissued the previous year and he was still evidently under surveillance. According to an official communication of the Vienna police (1 July 1853), 'He was highly flattered on hearing that the warrant for his arrest had been printed in the *Polizei-Anzeiger*, and is said to take no little pride in the fact that he is described as a prominent supporter of the revolutionary party.' They knew too that he was about to make a trip to St Moritz in the Engadine, which borders on Austria: '. . . we shall send the necessary notice to the Tyrol police to have him kept under observation during his stay in the neighbourhood of the Imperial frontiers.'[8] Agents employed abroad by the Dresden police reported back on the suspicious company Wagner kept; some of his friends were regarded as nothing short of terrorists. These acquaintances included Gottfried Semper, Wilhelm Heine (the son of the costume designer Ferdinand), Marschall von Bieberstein – all active in the uprising – and Georg Herwegh, whose differences with the authorities went back still

[8] Quoted in W. Lippert, *Wagner in Exile*, 46. Trans. by Paul England.

further; his correspondence with Röckel in Waldheim gaol would of course have been no secret. Then there were Ede Reményi, the Hungarian violinist, himself under close surveillance, and Malvida von Meysenbug, likewise constantly watched as a dreaded socialist and a confidante of the Italian subversive Giuseppe Mazzini. The Vienna police concluded that Wagner 'is still trying by his speeches and his writings [*Art and Revolution*, presumably, or had some pitiable junior officer been assigned *Opera and Drama* to comb for subversive utterances?] to bring about a revolutionary movement by means of his art, and to this end is in communication with all the literary and artistic forces of revolutionary propaganda.' The surveillance was indeed far-reaching because the police report ends, astonishingly, with this musicological judgment: 'Belief in his "music of the future" is notably on the wane, as it becomes more and more evident that his works, in spite of their brilliant orchestration, possess neither soul nor melody – what melodies are to be found in them he has stolen from others.'[9] The appeal for clemency was rejected.

Ironically, it was one of these 'dangerous' political refugees, Georg Herwegh, who by introducing him, in September or October of 1854, to the philosophy of Arthur Schopenhauer ensured that Wagner would never again look seriously to revolution for a solution of the world's evils. The impact on Wagner of *Die Welt als Wille und Vorstellung* (The World as Will and Representation) – Schopenhauer's chief work, published in December 1818[10] and universally ignored for over three decades – was overwhelming. He read it four times in all between then and the following summer, continued to read it throughout his life, especially at the periods of his greatest creative fecundity, and never ceased discussing it and recommending it (Schopenhauer is referred to no fewer than 284 times in the Diaries that Cosima kept between 1869 and Wagner's death in 1883). The importance of Schopenhauer for Wagner was twofold: his aesthetics and his pessimistic philosophy of life.

Kant had shown that the world was divisible into noumenon and phenomenon, but Schopenhauer believed that he, rather than Kant, could show what these really consisted of. All phenomena in

[9] Quoted *ibid.*, 50–1.

[10] But with the date 1819 misleadingly printed on the title-page.

time and space (i.e. what we regard as the material world) are, he taught, merely the objectification of an energy to which he confusingly gave the name 'will'. Schopenhauer is not here using the term 'will' in the sense we understand it – one of conscious volition – but in almost the reverse sense: the 'will' or noumenon is an undifferentiated force (like gravity, for example), it is impersonal and it is all-encompassing. He also refers to the 'will' as 'the inner nature of everything', 'the thing-in-itself'. Direct knowledge of the noumenon is only possible through its manifestation in individual objects, including ourselves. These objectifications of the noumenon are the phenomena of the everyday world which, therefore, all consist of both noumenon and phenomenon. Now the arts, with the exception of music, are representations of the natural world (sculpture is a tangible example), but they also allow us glimpses of the noumenal; they therefore inhabit an intermediate region between the noumenon and phenomena. Music, however, has no point of contact with phenomena; it is a direct articulation of the noumenon. Thus it is able to speak of the inner essence of things and express the seemingly inexpressible in a way beyond the power of the other arts.

Schopenhauer's elevation of music above the other media cut across Wagner's own theories, so comprehensively expounded in *The Artwork of the Future* and *Opera and Drama*, where he had proposed the reunification of the arts on the basis of equality. But Schopenhauer's formulation now seemed the only right one and curiously enough it required less a betrayal of his principles than a shift of emphasis to bring his work into line (the changing balance, or synthesis, of poetry and music is traced in the second half of this book, in the *Ring* and subsequent chapters).

So much for Schopenhauer's aesthetics. What Wagner also responded to was his philosophy of life. According to this deeply pessimistic outlook, existence is a meaningless round of striving, suffering is inescapable, and pleasure is merely release from pain. The will to live is reprehensible and the only escape from the burden of life lies in denial of the will (in our sense of the word), in extinction or nirvana – the Buddhist state of cessation of individual existence. The extent to which Wagner's philosophical outlook, as expressed in his later music dramas, was affected by Schopenhauer can scarcely be overstated; Schopenhauer's impact on the outcome of the *Ring*, the utterly Schopenhauerian ideas and language of *Tristan*, the final reconciliation in *Parsifal* – all these are discussed in the relevant chapters of the present book.[11] But it must not be forgotten that Wagner was already something of a Schopenhauerian *avant la lettre*: *Der fliegende Holländer*, *Tannhäuser* and *Lohengrin* all deal with the concept of redemption, i.e. release from the phenomenal world, and with the necessity of compassionate concern for others. And, of course, the text of the *Ring* was already written when he discovered Schopenhauer. That the text and music of the *Ring* seem at times to be almost a vehicle for the philosophy of Schopenhauer merely bears witness to the extraordinary affinity that Wagner felt for the older man. They were never to meet. Wagner had the opportunity to visit him once but he seems to have been daunted; the admiration he had for Schopenhauer was unique – no other living person evoked such reverence from him. For his part, Schopenhauer regarded Wagner as talented rather than a genius – he died before any of the works after *Lohengrin* were performed. It was for a long time thought that Schopenhauer did not know that Wagner had tried to establish a chair of Schopenhauerian philosophy at Zurich, but a letter of Schopenhauer to Julius Frauenstädt (28 March 1856) makes it clear that he did.

It is difficult to say exactly when Wagner's affectionate feelings for Mathilde Wesendonck blossomed into love and at precisely what point he began to identify their relationship with that of Tristan and Isolde, but it was probably shortly after his first reading of *Die Welt als Wille und Vorstellung*, in the autumn of 1854, that he sketched the first outline of his story. The idea was thus already committed to paper some time before he felt compelled to break off the composition of the *Ring* in June 1857 and turn his attention to the subject that was by then increasingly preying on his mind.

In the last week of 1854 Wagner was approached by the Philharmonic Society with a view to his conducting a series of eight concerts in London the following year. Ferdinand Praeger, the author of the notorious fabrication *Wagner as I Knew Him* (London 1892), claimed to have been responsible for the invitation to

---

[11] See also Bryan Magee's *The Philosophy of Schopenhauer* (to which this book is indebted) for an eminently intelligible exposition of Schopenhauer. Magee devotes an extended appendix (pp. 326–78) to the influence on Wagner and his work. A less detailed but equally lucid introduction to Schopenhauer is provided by R.J. Hollingdale in his edition for Penguin Classics of *Parerga und Paralipomena*, entitled *Schopenhauer: Essays and Aphorisms* (Harmondsworth 1970).

Wagner. Ernest Newman thought that he had put the record straight in attributing the initiative to Prosper Sainton (leader of the Philharmonic Orchestra and on the board of directors) and his friend Charles Lüders, on the basis of Wagner's account in *Mein Leben*. But the publication in 1982 of the minutes of the Philharmonic Society's board meetings and related correspondence[12] shows that this version too is an imaginative reconstruction of events by Sainton, which Wagner had no reason to disbelieve. According to Sainton, the Philharmonic was faced with the refusal of the regular conductor, Sir Michael Costa – following a quarrel – to direct the coming season. The treasurer, George Frederick Anderson, had asked Sainton for advice and Sainton had recommended Wagner, largely on the strength of Lüders' enthusiasm on reading *Opera and Drama*.

As the minutes of the relevant board meeting reveal, the truth was somewhat different. The directors had attempted unsuccessfully to make Costa change his mind. They then approached Spohr, the violinist and composer, who was Kapellmeister in Cassel. When he declined they decided to ask Berlioz on condition that he did not take up an invitation to conduct the series of the rival New Philharmonic Society. At the same meeting it was agreed also to write simultaneously to Wagner, asking whether he would accept the engagement if it were to be offered. Sainton was present at all of these meetings but the minutes do not record that he so much as uttered the name of Wagner; nor was he either the proposer or seconder of the motion concerning the invitation to him. Berlioz declined, on the grounds that he could not renege on his agreement with the New Philharmonic. Wagner expressed interest but wished to be satisfied on two conditions: first, that a second conductor would take charge of the smaller concert pieces for instrumentalists and singers; second, that he would be allowed what he considered to be the adequate number of rehearsals. The board of directors decided that Anderson, the treasurer, should go to Zurich to negotiate with Wagner and it was resolved 'that he be instructed not to concede either of the points specified in Herr Wagner's letter'.[13] Anderson duly visited Wagner and was able to secure his services 'for the sum of 5000 francs [£200 Sterling] and on the conditions specified in the Minutes of [the] last

[12] See 'Wagner in London (1)', *Wagner*, iii (1982), 98–123.

[13] *ibid.*, p. 102 (minutes of 7 January 1855).

Meeting'; he was congratulated by his fellow-directors for 'the zeal, activity, and judgment'[14] with which he carried out this diplomatic coup, and indeed Wagner was obliged to do most of the conducting himself, while one rehearsal per concert was all he was allowed (with two for the concert including Beethoven's Choral Symphony).

His four-month stay in England was far from happy: in a letter to Liszt (16 May 1855) he described his existence as like that of 'a damned soul in hell' (he had been reading Dante). He was apprehensive about the extended potpourris that stood for programme planning at the Philharmonic's subscription concerts. The second of the series was typical in its juxtaposition of a Weber overture and the Mendelssohn Violin Concerto with an aria by Cherubini; there was also an instrumental selection from *Lohengrin* and the concert was rounded off by Beethoven's Ninth. With no English at his command he found the language an insuperable barrier, the foggy London weather uncongenial, the customs of the inhabitants alien, and their tastes philistine. To Otto Wesendonck he characterized the English as sitting stoically through hours of oratorio fugues in order to reap the heavenly reward of their favourite Italian opera arias. Certainly they found the unconventional timbres and harmonies (even of the pre-*Ring* works) a challenge for which they were not equipped. And Victorian morality was outraged as much by the 'licentiousness' and 'degeneracy' of the music itself as by that of his *Tannhäuser* subject.

In spite of the chasm between Wagner and his audience, they were willing to give him a fair hearing and many liked what they heard. But he had to contend with a ferocious press campaign conducted by men who had neither the intelligence to understand what he was about, nor the tolerance that might have persuaded them to look for the answer beyond their own limited musical horizons. To his credit, but also to his severe disadvantage, Wagner refused from the first to pay court to the critics in the customary fashion. The all-powerful J.W. Davison of *The Times* (and editor of the *Musical World*) was particularly affronted by the failure of the foreign visitor to offer the expected fulsome courtesies and tributes – even bribes – and he took his revenge in colourful prose.

It was also with the English – critics, audiences and players alike – that Wagner's interpretative style as a conductor led him into the deepest mires of hostile incomprehension. London audiences were

[14] *ibid.*, p. 103 (minutes of 21 January 1855).

used to the conducting of Mendelssohn and Sir Michael Costa, which tended towards a uniform *mezzo forte* and a standard, inflexible tempo (Mendelssohn himself told Wagner that he liked to adopt a brisk tempo for everything as the best means of concealing orchestral flaws). Wagner, on the other hand, whose aim was always to reveal the drama inherent in a symphonic conception, liked to point up contrasts of *forte* and *piano*. In his opinion it was vital to establish a tempo appropriate to the movement in question, according to whether it was characterized by cantabile phrasing or rhythmic figuration. Moreover, a Beethoven allegro comprised more than one mode of expression – an assertive first subject giving way to a more lyrical second subject – and these different modes required to be accommodated by modifications of the main tempo. Wagner, for example, would slow down for cantabile passages, and to introduce an important idea or a recapitulated theme he would use a notable ritardando. These principles, which heralded the passing of mere time-keeping and the birth of modern conducting, were spelt out by Wagner some years later in his essay *On Conducting* (1869).

The penultimate concert of the series was attended by Queen Victoria and Prince Albert, who led the applause for the performance of the *Tannhäuser* Overture (which was substituted, at Wagner's insistence, for the March). They delighted him even more by receiving him in a manner both respectful and friendly during the interval. He valued their support and did not fail to point out to Liszt the irony of the royalty of England consorting with one considered guilty of high treason in his own country.

The other highlight of his London visit was the opportunity to make the closer acquaintance of Berlioz. Wagner detected a deep sense of world-weariness in the older composer and his heart went out to him. They passed some companionable hours together discussing artistic and other matters, but Wagner continued to react unpredictably to Berlioz's music and was unimpressed by his conducting of the classics. Less happy was a brief encounter with Meyerbeer: the pair amazed the company present by staring at each other and walking away without exchanging a word.

6

Blighted hopes (1856–63)

Wagner arrived back thankfully in Zurich. His work on the scoring of *Die Walküre* had been severely disrupted and the expense of living in London had left him with a mere 1000 francs (£40) out of his fee of 5000 francs. But Zurich was not enough. He wanted to be able to hear *Lohengrin* and his other works played in German theatres. By spring of the next year, 1856, he was ready to compromise a fraction if it had the desired effect: on 16 May he addressed a plea to King Johann of Saxony for the first time acknowledging 'my grievous fault in deserting my proper sphere of art for the field of politics' and pledging that he would never again indulge in such 'reckless action'. It was once again rejected. Between finishing the score of *Die Walküre* and taking up work on *Siegfried*, and on the same day that he drafted his appeal, he also made a short prose sketch for an opera on a Buddhist subject: *Die Sieger* (The Victors). Dealing with the themes of passion and chastity, renunciation and redemption, the idea clearly stemmed from his immersion in Schopenhauer, whose philosophy had many points of contact with oriental religion. Wagner thought he saw special scope in the treatment of reincarnated souls for his newly-developed technique of motivic reminiscence. In the event, nothing came of *Die Sieger*, largely because its preoccupations were subsumed into *Parsifal*. But as Cosima's Diaries show, he continued to toy with the idea until the end of his life.

Relations with Minna were unimproved, though it was her daughter Natalie (still thought to be Minna's sister by the world at large, as well as by Natalie herself) who was upsetting Minna now. In June Wagner insisted that Natalie leave their house; they ensured that she was looked after by relations back home and Wagner later assumed financial responsibility for her. But these ructions, together with the worries over his work and financial situation, were playing havoc with his health. He had suffered more than a dozen attacks of erysipelas since the beginning of the previous winter; they were painful and debilitating and it was a considerable relief to him when a doctor by the name of Vaillant diagnosed his complaint as a nervous allergy and set him on a successful course of treatment. The musical environment of the Zeltweg – his neighbours included five pianists and a flautist – was not conducive to the composition of *Siegfried*, which he started in September. In particular, it was necessary to come to a working arrangement with a tinsmith who lived opposite. He agreed to confine his hammering to certain times and was rewarded by having his industry immortalized in *Siegfried*: Wagner went to his piano and pounded out the angry G minor passage in which Siegfried impatiently criticizes Mime's forging.

Otto Wesendonck came to the rescue of the *Ring* and its creator by offering him the tenancy of a small house adjacent to the villa he was having built in a suburb of Zurich called Enge. The house, for which Wagner and Minna were to pay an annual rent of 800 francs – the same as that for the lodging in the Zeltweg – seemed to be the answer to his prayers: a quiet, secluded home where he could work unmolested by the troublesome world. He called it his 'Asyl' (Refuge). The move had an immediately beneficial effect, generating an inspiration on the subject of Wolfram von Eschenbach's *Parzivâl* that resulted in a first prose sketch. The incident is described in *Mein Leben* as follows. After living in temporary rented accommodation and then a hotel, both in Zurich, he and Minna were able at the end of April to move into the Asyl. It was cold and damp; they were both ill. One morning he woke up to find the sunshine flooding in – the first time he had experienced that in this house. Buds were opening in the little garden, the birds were singing and he went to sit 'on the verandah of the little house' to enjoy the tranquillity. He suddenly recalled that it was Good Friday and remembered how the significance of that holy day had struck him when reading Wolfram's *Parzivâl* in Marienbad. (It was to have a central significance too in his own composition.) He immediately made a hasty sketch for a drama. The story has a charming sense of poetry and one hesitates to dispel the illusion. However, it was not Good Friday on which all this happened. Good Friday fell that year on 10 April, at which time the Wagners were still living in the Zeltweg. If the *Mein Leben* account of events is broadly accurate (and the dates of Wagner's movements are supported by letters written at the time), then Good Friday is ruled out. The suggestion has been made[1] that Wagner walked out to the

---

[1] Curt von Westernhagen, *Wagner: A Biography*, I, p. 226.

Asyl on Good Friday while it was still in the builders' hands. But this theory is contradicted by Wagner's mention of waking up in the Asyl.[2] The matter is clinched by Cosima's Diaries in which Wagner admits that he was 'mistaken' about the date. The entry for 22 April 1879 reads 'R. today recalled the impression which inspired his "Good Friday Music"; he laughs, saying he had thought to himself, "In fact it is all as far-fetched as my love affairs, for it was not a Good Friday at all – just a pleasant mood in Nature which made me think, 'This is how a Good Friday ought to be.' " ' (See also 13 January 1878.)

The transferral of date may have started on Good Friday 1865, when in a letter to King Ludwig, Wagner spun a yarn about the significance for him of Good Friday, and how *Parsifal* had been conceived on that day in the Asyl. (The *Mein Leben* account is supplemented by a mention of bells ringing in the distance.) But the entry in Cosima's Diaries suggests that the mythmaking was initiated straightaway in 1857 when Wagner first noted down the experience, and the Annals for the relevant part of April 1857 read: 'Good omens: Good Friday. Fantasy on the verandah: conceive *Parzival*.'[3] Already this shorthand note fuses two separate occasions and paves the way for an embroidered re-creation of the work's conception – one, indeed, with bells on. It is entirely in character. For Wagner, everything had to be sacrificed to his art: friends, money, social status and, if need be, factual accuracy as well. Good Friday disobligingly occurred at the wrong time in 1857, but that was swiftly put right with a leap of the imagination and a few strokes of the pen.

The Wesendoncks moved into their villa in August and the ensuing propinquity of the two couples caused the long-suppressed affection of Wagner and Mathilde for each other to burst into full flower. But before this could reach a critical conclusion the Wesendonck home provided the setting for a dramatic tableau fraught with marital tension. The pianist Hans von Bülow and his young bride

---

[2] For relevant documents and a discussion see Sämtliche Werke, xxx, p. 13.

[3] 'Gute Anzeichen: Charfreitag. Phantasie auf der Zinne: *Parzival* conzipirt.' (*Das braune Buch*, ed. J. Bergfeld, Zurich and Freiburg im Breisgau 1975, p.127) The translation in the English edition is an inspired misreading: 'Good signs: Good Friday. Imagination at peak: conceive "Parzival".'

Cosima were visiting Switzerland on their honeymoon and Wagner invited them to stay for a few weeks at the Asyl. Bülow's musicality and mastery of his instrument deeply impressed Wagner; he was able to make a convincing job of reading from Wagner's drafts for Acts I and II of *Siegfried*, with the composer taking all the vocal parts. But Wagner had already laid the *Ring* aside in favour of a new subject, *Tristan und Isolde*, which had been making increasingly insistent claims on his attention. Wagner and Mathilde could scarcely disguise the fact that they had thrown themselves into the roles of Tristan and Isolde. On completing the poem on 18 September he had taken her the last act and she had then, it seems, given the first real indication that his passion was reciprocated. She had led him to a chair in front of the sofa, put her arm around him and declared that she was ready for death since she had nothing more to wish for. If that protestation indeed opened the floodgates, the true state of affairs must have been abundantly clear to anyone in the vicinity. One can scarcely imagine the atmosphere on the occasion when Wagner read his completed *Tristan* poem to the assembled company: his wife, his lover and his future wife, and both their husbands. The reaction of Wesendonck and Bülow is not recorded but the audience generally was much moved and Mathilde had to be consoled.

As the composition of *Tristan* got under way, Mathilde's visits to Wagner's first-floor workroom became more frequent. She wrote a cycle of five poems steeped in the aroma of *Tristan* and he set them to music. Minna and Otto were understandably becoming more edgy and there may even have been rows; the Annals refer coyly to 'neighbourly confusion'. In any case, Wagner took himself off to Paris where Berlioz read him his libretto for *Les Troyens*; with a growing sense of despair Wagner realized that they were not on the same wavelength at all. On his return to Zurich it was only a matter of time before the storm broke. The catalyst was a handsome but harmless Neapolitan, Francesco de Sanctis, who was coaching Mathilde in Italian. Consumed with jealousy at de Sanctis' close contact with his pupil, Wagner one evening, in his absence, railed at his interpretation of Goethe's *Faust*. The next morning, to make amends to Mathilde he sent her a 'Morning Confession' rolled in a pencil sketch of the *Tristan* Prelude. Most of the long letter deals with *Faust* and the aspects of its interpretation that had been under discussion, but Minna, when she intercepted the messenger bearing the letter and read its contents, noticed only the sentences of extravagantly phrased devotion: 'In the morning I was reasonable again, and from the depth of my heart could pray to my angel; and this prayer is love! Love! My soul's deepest joy lies in this love, the source of my salvation!' And later: 'Look at me, then everything becomes indisputably true to me, then I am so sure of myself when this wonderful, holy glance rests on me and I submerge myself within it!'

According to Wagner, in a letter to his sister Klara Wolfram (20 August 1858), the 'Morning Confession' was not about love but about 'resignation'. Certainly it was an innocuous enough letter and it could indeed be that the whole relationship was actually one of resignation, of unfulfilled longing. Wagner always insisted, to Minna, Klara and others, on the 'purity' of the relationship; Mathilde had been frank with her husband about it long before the 'Morning Confession' crisis and Otto appears to have accepted it on that basis. Nothing can be proved either way but perhaps *Tristan und Isolde* is the best evidence. Could that monumental expression of yearning have been composed while its creator was in the throes of ecstasy? Wagner's love for Mathilde indeed wrung from him some of the most passionate music ever to be composed, but it is surely the effusion of one who is *denied* the ultimate satisfaction. It is not so much a question of Mathilde inspiring *Tristan* as of Wagner's artistic creation causing him to idealize the woman in the real world who most closely corresponded to that vision.

Minna did not, of course, stop to consider all this. She angrily confronted Wagner with the letter and listened disbelievingly to his innocent explanation. Her next step was to brandish it in front of Mathilde with the words 'If I were any ordinary woman I should go to your husband with this letter'. Mathilde, affronted by the imputation that she had secrets from Otto, immediately told him what had happened. Wagner was reproached by the Wesendoncks for being less frank with Minna than they had been with each other. Minna was persuaded to take a cure at Brestenberg, from which she finally returned three months later. Wagner was clearly concerned for her welfare and tried to effect a reconciliation. It is true that continued tenancy of the Asyl depended on a healing of the breach, but he had also been warned by the doctor that Minna's weak heart might any day prove fatal. Partly to pacify her he broke off relations with the Wesendoncks, though at some point he also suggested to

Mathilde (not seriously, he later said: Diaries, 14 March 1873) that they both leave their spouses and marry.

During these months of grasswidowerhood, as he described them, he enjoyed consolation in the shape of a youthful prodigy sent to him by Liszt. Carl Tausig, though still only sixteen, was an enormously gifted pianist; Wagner said that his furious playing made him tremble but he was equally impressed by his sensitivity and receptivity. Wagner was particularly fascinated by the blend of boyish exuberance and mature intellect. He found himself acting like the father he had always longed to be.

Minna returned from Brestenberg in July to find that the gardener had erected over the door a kind of triumphal arch bedecked with flowers. Knowing that it could be seen from the Wesendoncks' villa, Minna insisted that it be left up for several days, as though to claim victory. Since Mathilde had previously declared that Minna must not be allowed to enter the Asyl again, she was understandably galled by this gesture of defiance. The atmosphere on the Green Hill darkened. There was a constant stream of visitors but it could not be concealed from them that the rift was growing ever wider. Wagner gradually came to terms with the inevitable: he would have to leave the Asyl.

It was on 16 August that he bade farewell to Mathilde and the following day he left Zurich, his destination as yet undecided. At Karl Ritter's instigation, and in his company, he travelled to Venice and rented an apartment in one of the deserted Giustiniani palaces on the Grand Canal. The grand piano which Madame Erard had recently given him as a gift followed him there and his secluded quarters provided an environment conducive to the completion of the second act of *Tristan*. Ritter, too, proved an amiable and stimulating companion. During these months in Italy Wagner was discouraged from communicating with Mathilde Wesendonck and she returned letters unopened. He confided his feelings towards her in the so-called Venetian Diary; the journal, which was not read until later by Mathilde, records his experiences (mostly in Venice) between 21 August 1858 and 4 April 1859. It has been variously described as containing 'intimate personal revelations' (Westernhagen) and as 'exhibitionistic' (Gregor-Dellin). Both, curiously, are right. The personal note seems to be exemplified in Wagner's new identification of himself and Mathilde as the characters Ananda and Savitri in his earlier projected Buddhist drama *Die Sieger* – joyfully fulfilled and redeemed in their renunciation of passion. But how genuine is this? Is it not a further example of Wagner imposing an artistic fantasy onto the circumstances of his real life? A revealing clue is contained in the fact that he maintains the intimate 'du' form right up to the end of the Diary in April 1859, whereas in his actual letters to Mathilde, resumed just before the end of the previous year, he reverts first to the more formal 'Sie' and then to 'Freundin', the gracious lady friend of happier days.

His stay in Venice was marred by two things: bad health, including dysentery and a painful ulcer on the leg; and police harassment. Venice was still part of the Austrian Empire and as soon as the Viennese chief of police, Baron Kempen von Fichtenstamm, heard that he was there he began to make enquiries of the local police. His next step was to notify the Austrian Minister of Foreign Affairs that a former revolutionary was residing in the Imperial dominions, though no one except Kempen appeared to be unduly agitated by this discovery. In particular, the local police official responsible, Angelo Crespi, sent regular reports from Venice in which he made an admirable job of fending off Kempen's persistent onslaughts. But by the spring of 1859 it was clearly dangerous for him to delay any longer in Venice when a clash between Italian nationalists and the Austrian military became imminent. He left Venice on 24 March and arrived in Lucerne four days later; it was in that town, at the Hotel Schweizerhof, that he completed *Tristan* in August. In September he revisited the Wesendoncks in Zurich and although he was initially reluctant to accept an unsolicited offer of financial help from Otto to finish the *Ring*, he did devise a business deal: Wesendonck would buy the copyright in the four scores for 6000 francs each and enjoy the proceeds, Wagner receiving the revenues from public performances. Wagner insisted on a legal deed of sale, which was duly signed.

He planned another assault on Paris, proposing to conquer the French this time with *Tannhäuser*, *Lohengrin* and *Tristan*. By arrangement, Minna rejoined him there, but their doctor, Pusinelli, had been asked to advise Minna against engaging in sexual intercourse, on the grounds of her 'state of health'. Another musical doctor, Auguste de Gaspérini, helped him over the hurdle that had so disastrously impeded his French venture of two decades earlier, by introducing him into influential Parisian musical circles. When, at the beginning of 1860, he conducted three concerts of excerpts from his works there was a buzz of anticipation in the Théâtre Italien audience, which included such distinguished figures as Berlioz, Meyerbeer, Auber, Gounod, the novelist Champfleury and the poet Baudelaire. With the exception of the Prelude from *Tristan*, which neither audience nor orchestra could understand, his music was gratifyingly well received; that did not, however, prevent an overall deficit of 11,000 francs.

The music publisher Franz Schott of Mainz had expressed interest in Wagner's operas and was offered *Das Rheingold* for 10,000 francs. Wagner fully intended to return to Wesendonck the 6000 francs he had already received from *him* for this piece, but the new deficit on the concerts necessitated a reappraisal. Instead, he shrewdly asked Wesendonck to regard the 6000 francs he had paid for *Rheingold* as an advance payment for the fourth work in the tetralogy, not yet written. Wesendonck generously agreed.

The powerful friends Wagner had made in Paris now made the production of *Tannhäuser* at the Opéra a reality. The decree for its performance was that of the emperor, Napoleon III, but the woman largely responsible was Princess Pauline Metternich. Partly through her personality and partly because, as wife of the Austrian ambassador in Paris, her role was seen as that of mediator between the French and the Austrians – who were still regarded with suspicion – the Princess was disliked in certain court circles. This was the seed of rancour that was to be given such devastating expression at the performances of *Tannhäuser* the following year.

Now that he was being hailed in major cities as one of the leading composers of the day, the Saxon authorities could no longer ignore the pleas for an amnesty made by and on behalf of Wagner. But when the King of Saxony finally steeled himself to permit the former revolutionary to re-enter German territory, he made his concession as ungracious as possible. The king refused to deal with Wagner himself, so whenever he proposed to enter a state within the German Confederation he would be obliged to seek Saxony's permission through that other state. Most important of all, he was still prevented from returning to Saxony itself. When on 12 August 1860 he set foot again on German soil, for the first time in eleven years, Wagner, who doubtless thought he deserved something more like a hero's welcome, found that this time he shed no tears for the fatherland. Germany had yet to honour him as her own.

Rehearsals for *Tannhäuser* at the Opéra began on 24 September. From the start his artistic integrity seemed to court disaster. He refused outright the management's request for a second-act ballet, in accordance with Opéra custom: their aristocratic patrons habitually arrived late at the theatre after dining well, and wished only to see the performance of the ballet dancers, with whom they were intimately acquainted. The new music he wrote for the Act I Venusberg bacchanal was, in its demonic, orgiastic frenzy, not intended to pacify the young aristocrats of the Jockey Club, nor did it. And rehearsals were dogged by other problems. Unable to flout another Opéra tradition – that all performances had to be directed by the resident conductor – Wagner was obliged to accept the incompetent Pierre-Louis Dietsch, the very man who twenty years earlier had set to music a rival version of the Flying Dutchman legend. His Tannhäuser, too, Albert Niemann, wishing to save his voice for the last act, insisted on the cutting of some crucial lines in the second-act finale; Wagner had no option but to comply.

After no fewer than 164 rehearsals the curtain rose on 13 March 1861 on one of the great scandals in the annals of opera history. The bacchanal survived unscathed but as the following shepherd's pipe sounded there was a co-ordinated and prolonged outburst of laughter and catcalls from the white-gloved humorists of the Jockey Club. It was hoped that the louts might be content with ruining the premiere but, displaying a not unfamiliar blend of puerility and ruthlessness, they came back for the second performance armed with dog whistles. In spite of the presence of the emperor and empress the evening was little more than a contest of abusive whistling and counter-cheering accompanied by snatches of *Tannhäuser*. After an equally disrupted third performance, Wagner was allowed to withdraw the production. The cause of the demonstration had been not so much the lack of a second-act ballet as political: Wagner was paying for the support of the despised Austrian princess. Casting round for scapegoats Wagner seized on the hostile reviews in the press which he regarded (not without some justification) as being under the influence of Meyerbeer. A legend even grew up that Meyerbeer had been present at the *Tannhäuser* fiasco and delighted in it. The truth is that Meyerbeer was not in Paris at the time, but in Berlin. It was there that he heard what had happened and recorded his reaction in his diary. Notwithstanding Wagner's ill-concealed hostility towards him, the entry betrays no malice. In fact, untypically for his diary, he comments on the artistic value of *Tannhäuser*:

it is, he says, 'in any case a very remarkable and talented work' and its reception seems to be 'the result of intrigues and not of real judgment'.[4]

Wagner now switched his attention to *Tristan und Isolde* and pinned his hopes on its first performance being given in Vienna rather than Karlsruhe, as originally planned. He was travelling extensively at this time but Vienna provided a particularly congenial base when Dr Josef Standhartner, the Empress's physician, offered him the use of his house while away on holiday. Since both house and Wagner were to be looked after by the doctor's niece, the adorable young Seraphine Mauro, this was an offer he could not refuse. His friend Peter Cornelius, who was Seraphine's lover, probably had good reason to be jealous.

The inability of the tenor for *Tristan*, Alois Ander, to memorize his part, and his sudden loss of voice all contributed to the myth, rapidly acquiring accretions, that the work was unperformable. Accepting an invitation to visit the Wesendoncks in Venice at the beginning of November, he found them flourishing and Mathilde pregnant for the fifth time (two of her children had died in infancy). Their demeanour, though friendly, convinced him immediately that his secretly cherished desire to return to the Asyl was an impossible dream. Together the three went to see Titian's *Assumption of the Virgin* and Wagner tells us in *Mein Leben* that he was so overawed by the masterpiece that he determined forthwith to embark on the composition of *Die Meistersinger*, characteristically omitting to mention that he had already expressed precisely that intention to Schott in a letter dated 30 October.

By 5 February the following year, 1862, the poem of *Die Meistersinger* was ready for a public reading at Schott's house in Mainz. Everyone present was moved and impressed by his brilliant rhetorical performance. The occasion also provided an example of the personal devotion Wagner could inspire. Peter Cornelius, as well as being expected to share Seraphine, was concerned about his own independence as a composer. The guests assembled and Cornelius had not arrived, although Wagner had expressly urged him to come and even sent him his fare from Vienna. As the clock struck seven, Cornelius appeared at the door: he had been caught up in floods as

[4] *Giacomo Meyerbeer: Briefwechsel und Tagebücher*, ed. H. Becker (Berlin 1960–).

the Rhine burst its banks, and he had lost his overcoat on the way, but he was there, come hell or high water.

Wagner took up lodgings in Biebrich, across the Rhine from Mainz, and there set to work on the composition of *Die Meistersinger*. Minna joined him but it was only a short time before they were at loggerheads over a Christmas present that arrived belatedly from Mathilde Wesendonck. Minna was jealous and suspicious and the couple had few points of contact – intellectual or emotional. 'Ten days in hell' was how Wagner described it to Cornelius (4 March 1862), acknowledging that his wife also found *her* hell in his company. He could not bring himself to divorce Minna, believing that such a declaration would be unforgivably cruel to a woman as sick as she now was. Instead he suggested setting her up in Dresden with a room put aside for him to make occasional visits (his full amnesty was announced that month, allowing him to visit Saxony). He did also charge Pusinelli with the delicate task of suggesting a divorce to Minna, but retreated in the face of her furious response. Unwilling to hurt her, he assured her (falsely) that Pusinelli had exceeded his brief. The hapless Pusinelli accepted the blame.

Divorce no doubt seemed an alluring proposition all the more in view of the abundance of female admirers flitting around him. In addition to Seraphine Mauro, there was Liszt's elder daughter, Blandine, married briefly, before her early death in September 1862, to the French lawyer and politician Emile Ollivier (there is no evidence to give substance to the rumour that Wagner's intimate friendship with Blandine amounted to anything more than that). To Mathilde Maier, the twenty-eight-year-old daughter of a notary he had met at Schott's, he felt a great attraction, but she was reluctant to get involved with him on account of her incipient deafness. There was also Friederike Meyer, the sister of the soprano once intended for the role of Isolde in Vienna: Luise Dustmann. Friederike was an actress who was having an affair with her theatre director, one Herr von Guaita. She soon disappeared from Wagner's circle. And then there was Cosima, at first hovering silently and mysteriously on the sidelines, but soon to cast her long shadow over the proceedings.

Hans and Cosima von Bülow visited Wagner in Biebrich in the July of 1862. Ludwig Schnorr von Carolsfeld, who had recently impressed him in a performance of *Lohengrin*, and his wife Malvina were there at the same time and Wagner coached them in the roles of Tristan and Isolde, with Bülow at the piano. (He had not yet given up on Ander and Dustmann, but it was to be the Schnorrs who ultimately brought the work before the public three years later.) During a visit to Frankfurt, Cosima gave spectacular evidence that she was unwinding from the introspective aloofness that Wagner had noted in her. In a sudden burst of high spirits he suggested that he convey her across the square to their hotel in a wheelbarrow standing empty near by. Equally impetuously she consented, but Wagner's nerve failed him and they covered the distance by more conventional means. In November he visited Minna, now in Dresden, leaving after a few days. It was to be their last meeting.

At the end of the year, for publication in 1863 – ten years after the private printing of the *Ring* poems – Wagner prepared a new edition with a foreword. In it he set out his plan for the public performance of the tetralogy, under festival conditions, with performers and audience alike able to devote themselves wholly to the matter in hand. A temporary theatre would be built, perhaps just of wood; the auditorium would be structured like an amphitheatre and the orchestra would be concealed. A German prince, Wagner concluded, could easily supply the funds for such a venture by diverting the resources allocated to his own opera house. 'Is such a prince to be found?'

Meanwhile, in May 1863 Wagner rented the upper floor of a house in Penzing, near Vienna. With breathtaking disregard for the consequences, he had it furnished in luxurious style: violet drapes with gold borders in one room, scarlet damask curtains in another, velvet everywhere.[5] Naturally for one in his precarious financial position, criticism was expressed. He justified himself in a famous outburst to Eliza Wille: 'I am a different kind of organism, my nerves are hypersensitive, I must have beauty, splendour and light! The world owes me what I need! I cannot live the miserable life of a town organist, like your Master Bach!'[6] Not that he was at all selfish in indulging his extravagant tastes. The Christmas of that year was celebrated with friends round the tree in Wagner's house, each receiving what he called 'an appropriate trifle'. 'A wonderful heavy

[5] Wagner's own plan of the apartments, with details of the furnishings, is reproduced in *Wagner: A Documentary Study*, ed. H. Barth, D. Mack and E. Voss, 203.

[6] Translation by Mary Whittall from *Wagner: A Documentary Study*, ed. H. Barth D. Mack and E. Voss, 204.

overcoat – an elegant grey dressing gown – a red scarf, a blue cigar-case and tinder box – beautiful silk handkerchiefs, splendid gold shirt studs – the *Struwwelpeter* [a popular book written by Heinrich Hoffmann] – elegant pen-wipers with gold mottoes – fine cravats – a meerschaum cigar-holder with his initials': and that was only for Peter Cornelius.[7] His friends at the time were no less shocked than future commentators were to be. Again it is Wagner's heretical disrespect for the value of money that has given offence. In addition we can see the same tendency towards gigantism that characterizes so many of Wagner's conceptions: just as *Rienzi* had to outdo every existing grand opera in the immensity of its scale, so the Wagnerian Christmas tree had to be a display of unsurpassable generosity.

Inevitably, debts began to overwhelm him. Under threat of imminent arrest he left Vienna and took refuge with Eliza Wille at Mariafeld. On 10 March 1864 a new monarch ascended the throne of Bavaria: Ludwig II. Seeing a portrait of the eighteen-year-old king in a shop window, Wagner was struck by his youth and beauty. The story of his miraculous intervention in the affairs of Wagner's life is well known. In one sense, it was an entirely unexpected occurrence. And yet Wagner, with his limitless confidence that destiny would one day be fulfilled, seems almost to have predicted it. From the depths of his despair about his financial position, he wrote to Cornelius on 8 April 1864, less than a month before Ludwig's advent: 'My situation is very uneasy; I am living on a knife-edge . . . A light must show itself, someone must arise to give me vigorous help now'. Cornelius himself wondered whether the new king might not take a special interest in music, and particularly Wagner. The same thought must surely, at the very least, have passed through the composer's mind.

---

[7] Letter from Cornelius to his sister Susanne, 11 January 1864. *Peter Cornelius: Literarische Werke*, Bd I: *Ausgewählte Briefe*, Bd I, ed. Carl Maria Cornelius (Leipzig 1904), 748.

7

Royal patronage and fulfilment of a dream (1864–76)

Ludwig II's cabinet secretary, Franz von Pfistermeister, had been on Wagner's trail for two whole weeks before tracking him down in Stuttgart. Wagner at first tried to avoid him, assuming that he was a creditor, but when Pfistermeister was eventually able to introduce himself he announced that King Ludwig was an ardent admirer of Wagner's work and wished to respond to his published cry for help; a ring and portrait of the king were handed over as tokens of his good will. Wagner had his first audience the next afternoon; so overcome were the pair by mutual esteem and affection that it lasted an hour and a half. Ludwig offered Wagner the opportunity to continue his work untroubled by financial constraints: within days he had received 4000 Gulden to pay off creditors.

As a boy, Ludwig had already shown some of the traits that were to characterize his colourful years on the throne. He was shy, haughty, highly strung, generous, a dreamer. From an early age he had a passion for building grand edifices: when he was six it was with toy bricks – later he was to lavish millions on fantastic castles set high in the Bavarian mountains. An arch-Romantic from his youth, he was drawn to the ancient German legends, to swans, to the solitude of the forests and hills. When at the age of fourteen he began to have hallucinations, it was feared that inbreeding in the family was giving rise to mental instability.

Having occupied the royal castle Schloss Berg, overlooking Lake Starnberg (south-west of Munich), Ludwig installed Wagner at the Villa Pellet, just across the lake. Almost every day they met, sometimes contemplating each other in complete silence – a love relationship without the physical element. Wagner, as ever, was looking for female companionship. He wrote to Mathilde Maier begging her to come to Villa Pellet as 'housekeeper'. In a letter addressed to her mother (who never received it) Wagner gave assurances that his intentions were strictly honourable. Nothing came of the suggestion, chiefly because Wagner was already entangled in another direction. The previous November he and Cosima von Bülow had found themselves alone, taking a carriage ride through Berlin. Cosima had never been really happy with Hans. He suffered from neurotic disorders, including a severe inferiority complex, and Cosima had married him more out of pity than affection. Now she and Wagner instinctively recognized in each other the profound sorrow of unsatisfied love. In a passage suppressed from the official edition of *Mein Leben* and not published until the complete text was made available in 1963, Wagner described how they sealed, with sobs and tears, the avowal that they belonged only to each other.

And so when, at Wagner's invitation, Cosima, her two young daughters and a nurserymaid arrived at Starnberg (Bülow had been delayed in Berlin), Wagner had hurriedly to break off his overtures to Mathilde Maier. That Wagner was pressing Mathilde at the very time he was expecting a visit from Cosima can presumably only be explained by the assumption that Wagner was not prepared for Cosima's total acquiescence. All we know is that some time during the week before Hans arrived on 7 July the couple consummated their union; their first child, Isolde, was born on 10 April 1865.

In October 1864 Wagner moved into the spacious house at 21 Briennerstrasse in Munich, made available to him by the king. In addition to the initial payment already made, Ludwig had authorized an annual stipend of 4000 Gulden (comparable to that of a ministerial councillor), another gift of 16,000 Gulden in June and a further 4000 Gulden for removal expenses. Now on 18 October Ludwig became the third owner of the *Ring* copyright for a sum of 30,000 Gulden. Martin Gregor-Dellin points out that the 131,173 Gulden paid out by the royal exchequer represented one third of the annual sum that the king had at his disposal, or one tenth of his entire civil list.

The Munich house was decked out in a similarly luxurious fashion to the one in Penzing and with the help of the same Viennese milliner and seamstress, Bertha Goldwag, that had supplied his furnishings before. She sent him the special coloured satins he could not obtain in Munich and in addition to his velvet drapes and portières he requested for himself a wardrobe of dressing gowns and suits in silk lined with fur (in various colours with matching slippers and neckties), shirts and underclothes in silk and satin, and delicate scents with which to perfume the atmosphere. Bertha made two visits to Munich, travelling incognito according to Wagner's wishes. To allay the curiosity of customs officials she told them that her cargo of silks and perfumes was for a countess in Berlin. In spite of her discretion, Wagner's style of living could not long remain a secret and his enemies were to make much capital out of it. Wagner's letters to his *Putzmacherin*, setting out his requirements in exotic detail, fell into the hands of an unscrupulous journalist who published them in 1877, still in the composer's lifetime. His voluptuous tastes have earned him much snide criticism, on grounds of both extravagance and of a decadence which has been seen to smack of 'effeminacy' and 'degeneracy'. Wagner, for his part, claimed that he needed sumptuous surroundings and sensual perfumes as a stimulus for creative inspiration. Given his psychological make-up and the predominant role of eroticism, there is probably much truth in that. Nor can he be blamed for the necessity to minister to his sensitive skin. These hedonistic years, however, must have been a testing time for his devotion to Schopenhauerian philosophy with its welcoming acceptance of suffering and renunciation. In his works Wagner continued to express that philosophy, but in his manner of living we are bound to conclude that he was something of an armchair Schopenhauerian.

Ludwig decided that Munich was the place for a festival theatre to produce the *Ring*, and he summoned Wagner's old Dresden friend Gottfried Semper to design one. This proposal marked the beginning of the official opposition to Wagner in Munich, since it was welcome neither to the vested interests of the musical establishment nor to the cabinet ministers who controlled the exchequer. In particular, the recently appointed prime minister of Bavaria, Ludwig von der Pfordten, had already come up against Wagner in Saxony in the late 1840s and was now no less opposed to him on ideological grounds. Nor did Bülow, for whom Wagner had secured an appointment as performer to the king, enjoy the favour of Munich. To the fact that he was an alien Prussian in Bavaria, he added a natural abrasiveness.

The correspondence between Wagner and Ludwig, which runs to several volumes, is couched in the kind of high-flown Romantic language calculated to raise eyebrows: 'O my King! You are divine!', 'Unique one', 'Beloved and only friend!' 'My love for you . . . will endure for ever!' Given Ludwig's homosexual inclinations it was inevitable that sooner or later aspersions would be cast on the nature of the relationship between the two men. But sexuality was not at the root of it. On Ludwig's side it was attraction to the man who could conjure up those Romantic, legendary scenes about which he loved to daydream. For Wagner the relationship was perhaps less passionate: 'my bewildering, marvellous, relationship to this young king', he once described it to Bülow (8 April 1866). But to suggest that Wagner to some extent played up to Ludwig is not necessarily to impute cynical motives. There were times when he was able to abuse the king's somewhat naive trust, but the charge that he merely used Ludwig to further his ambitions is not borne out by his letters to intimate friends, by his own self-communings, or by Cosima's Diaries.

Contemporary caricature on the subject of Wagner's projected music school.

At the beginning of 1865 Wagner suffered his first real ill-treatment at the hands of the king's officials and the Munich press. In conversation with Pfistermeister, Wagner had shocked the courtier by referring to Ludwig as '*Mein Junge*' (My boy). Pfistermeister not only rebuked him but also apparently deliberately misled the king over a payment for a portrait supposedly being demanded by Wagner. The upshot of it was that when Wagner arrived at the

Residenz at 1 o'clock on 6 February for an audience, the king refused to see him. His displeasure lasted only a few days but in the meantime the press, seizing their opportunity, had leapt into action. Wagner was branded as an ex-revolutionary turned sybarite; Ludwig was criticized for indulging the composer's extravagant tastes.

A further target for their attacks was Wagner's proposal for a German music school to be established in Munich. In a report submitted to Ludwig and published in 1865, Wagner argued that the traditional institutions were incapable of teaching students a performance style appropriate to the nature of German music and drama. His new school would concentrate on the art of singing and inculcate a true understanding of the requirements of both classical and modern works.

Rehearsals for *Tristan* at the Court and National Theatre were meanwhile progressing. The conductor was to be Bülow and the lead roles were to be played by Wagner's latest discovery Ludwig Schnorr von Carolsfeld and his wife Malvina. Schnorr grasped the composer's intentions so rapidly that Wagner was soon able to leave him to his own devices. After many rehearsals the day fixed for the performance, 15 May, arrived. It was a day of double catastrophe. First creditors sent in the bailiffs and Wagner had to apply to the king for immediate financial help. And then in the afternoon Malvina Schnorr lost her voice. Another Isolde was out of the question and the performance had to be postponed, to the delight of those busily putting around the story that the work was unperformable. Eventually it was given on 10 June, with three subsequent performances. There was some hostility from those who found the work licentious or its music incomprehensible, but there were many who realized that they were witnessing the inauguration of a landmark in the history of music. Only three weeks after the final performance came the appalling and tragic news that Schnorr had died in Dresden. The cause of death is uncertain but Wagner recalled that he had complained of the icy draught blowing across the stage as he lay sweating profusely after his exertions. Wagner was numbed by the event: in part he was grieving at the loss of a fine friend and his favourite singer; in part also he was torturing himself with the idea that he and his work were responsible for Schnorr's death. It was three years before he could bring himself to pay his final tribute to the singer in his *Recollections of Ludwig Schnorr von Carolsfeld*.

At the request of the king, Wagner began, on 17 July 1865, to dictate his autobiography to Cosima, using notes from his Red Pocketbook (see note 6 on pp. 49–50). The following month, when they were temporarily separated (by the Bülows' visit to Liszt in Hungary), Wagner made his first entry in the Brown Book. This was a leather-bound notebook given him by Cosima for the purpose of jotting down thoughts and communications which she could then subsequently read. It was used chiefly in this way up until 1868, when they began their permanent cohabitation at Tribschen, but it was also the repository of all sorts of fascinating ideas and fragments, from the original prose sketch for *Parsifal* to some discarded bars of music headed 'Romeo and Juliet'.

By the October of that year neither the plans for Wagner's music school nor those for Ludwig's festival theatre had come to anything. Indeed, hostility, both in court circles and from the people of Munich at large, was steadily mounting. Wagner successfully negotiated an annual stipend of 8000 Gulden and an additional payment of 40,000 Gulden needed to discharge more pressing commitments. But treasury officials took the opportunity to publicize the matter and cause maximum embarrassment by confronting Cosima, when she arrived to receive the money, with sacks of coin instead of banknotes. Nothing daunted, Cosima called for two cabs and herself helped to load the sacks into them.

When Wagner began increasingly to offer Ludwig advice on matters of state and went as far as to urge that his now chief enemies Pfistermeister and Pfordten ('Pfi' and 'Pfo', as he had dubbed them) be dismissed, the king's ministers led a campaign to have Wagner banished from Bavaria. Under enormous pressure from all sides, and with heartfelt reluctance, Ludwig finally gave the order at the beginning of December.

To the misery of Wagner's enforced absence from Cosima was added the blow of Minna's death the following month. He was on the move when he received the news but did not travel to Dresden for the funeral. Instead, on hearing a few days later that his beloved dog Pohl had also died, he disinterred the animal and gave it a sorrowful reburial. The bizarre ceremony apparently allowed him to come to terms with his profound grief.

While Bülow was away on tour, Cosima joined Wagner in Geneva and from there they travelled to Lake Lucerne, where they spotted the house called Tribschen on a promontory overlooking the lake. They decided to make it their home. (Wagner invented the spelling 'Triebschen' for it in order to associate the name with the promontory supposedly formed by silt (*angetrieben*) on which it stood – he could never resist the temptation to find an etymological explanation for something.) Cosima visited him at Tribschen on 12 May with her three daughters Daniela, Blandine and Isolde (that the latter, now thirteen months old, was also Wagner's child must have been suspected by Bülow as well as by others).

Ludwig, weighed down by affairs of state, was talking of relinquishing the monarchy, a proposal that dismayed Wagner who relied so completely on his royal benefactor. On 22 May, Wagner's birthday, he received a surprise visit at Tribschen from the king, who had left Munich in secrecy and who now arrived at the door calling himself Walther von Stolzing. Ludwig was accompanied by his aide and friend Prince Paul von Thurn und Taxis just as Wagner was accompanied by Cosima, yet his innocence about sexual matters was such that he accepted the explanation that Cosima was there as the composer's amanuensis.

Further and worse deception of the king became necessary when a reference in the Munich *Volksbote* to ' "Madame Hans de Bülow" . . . with her "friend" (or what?) in Lucerne' brought discussion of the scandalous liaison out into the open. Bülow's response was to challenge the editor of the paper to a duel, but he was contemptuously brushed aside. He then tendered his resignation to the king. Wagner's letter to Ludwig of 6 June 1866 deplored the shabby public treatment of Bülow forcing him to leave Munich and that meted out to 'his noble wife'. He urged the king to write a letter to Bülow, which he might then publish, expressing his satisfaction with the conductor and his indignation at the disgraceful way he had been treated. The following day Cosima sent her own plea to Ludwig, taking the deception a stage further: she begged him to write the letter for the sake of her three children 'to whom I owe the duty of transmitting the honourable name of their father free of stain'. That one of these children, Isolde, was Wagner's is almost beyond doubt, and certainly the one with which she was now pregnant was his. With his own letter to the king, Wagner had enclosed a draft of his suggested letter for Ludwig to send to Bülow. After speaking of the honour of his valued conductor and his respected wife, it went on to promise an investigation into 'these criminal public libels', with the intention of ensuring 'that the culprits are brought to justice with merciless severity'. Ludwig wrote the letter almost as drafted, and

Bülow published it. It is a measure of their desperate situation that Wagner and Cosima found it necessary to stoop to such a level of deceit. They knew that if Ludwig were to be made aware of the truth of the rumours about their liaison, the consequences could be grave: even if his anger at their lack of honesty with him did not alienate him for ever, it was clear that the public outrage at the impropriety of a monarch encouraging such nefarious activities would pose a real threat. They stood to lose either the royal allowance or each other – or even both. The charade could hardly have been sustained indefinitely and their base act was born of blind panic rather than calculation. In psychological terms it must have cost them dearly: Wagner himself had once said that lying was the worst sin. In practical terms it achieved the desired effect for the time being. Nobody could publicly contradict the king's statement and the *Volksbote* editor was fined by the courts.

At the height of the whole affair Bavaria found herself caught up in a war between Prussia and Austria. The ostensible cause of the war was the disputed administration of the Schleswig-Holstein duchies, but there was a much more fundamental principle at stake: who should be the leader of the emerging national state of Germany: Prussia or Austria? The former leadership of Austria had recently been challenged by the economic and military superiority of Prussia, now under the prime ministership of Otto von Bismarck. In 1866 Prussia took on not only Austria but also the Confederation itself in an attempt to determine – successfully as it turned out – the issue of Austrian/Prussian rivalry once and for all. Bavaria had to decide which to support. Wagner's advice to Ludwig, strongly influenced by the views of the conservative federalist Constantin Frantz, had been that Bavaria should steer her own independent course between the two powers. In a letter of 29 April 1866 he suggested that Bismarck, whom he described as 'an ambitious Junker', 'is deceiving his weak-minded king in the most insolent manner' (an ironic comment this, in the circumstances). And on another occasion he gave his opinion that 'The German will enjoy what is advantageous to him only when Bismarck and similar poor imitations of the most un-Germanic spirit are completely finished.'

When war broke out, Bavaria was forced to take sides. She supported Austria, as did other states in the Confederation including Hanover, Saxony and Württemberg. But it was only a short time before Prussia emerged victorious. As a result of the war, the German

Confederation collapsed and Prussian hegemony was incontrovertibly established. Even before the decisive Battle of Königgrätz on 3 July, Wagner's attitude to Bismarck had undergone a transformation. On 23 June he advised Röckel: 'My Friend! If you want to and must pursue politics, then adhere to Bismarck and Prussia. God help me, I know no other way.' This change of heart is not especially remarkable and certainly not one experienced by Wagner alone. Bismarck's liberal opponents in Prussia were also impressed by his success and believed that it would pave the way for national unification, a liberal administration and increased democratic participation. Indeed, the victory was even depicted in some quarters as one of Prussian liberalism over the obscurantism of Catholic Austria. 'North Germany is about to be saved from the Jesuits and from economic ruin' was how a speaker at an election rally in Berlin put it in July. Wagner's obsession with Jesuits, like that with the Jews, was shared by many.

At the end of October (1866), Hans Richter, the future conductor of the *Ring*, entered his circle as secretary and copyist, joining the household at Tribschen. Bülow was staying at Basle; in addition to Cosima and her three daughters there was a governess and a nurse for the children, a housekeeper (soon to be joined by her husband), two manservants, a parlourmaid and a cook. Only a few months after the *Volksbote* scandal had died down, the whole affair came to the surface again in an extraordinary manner. Malvina Schnorr, the creator of the role of Isolde, arrived in Tribschen on 10 November. The death of her husband had left her with a grief that for the rest of her days she tried to assuage by communicating with the spirit world. Contrary to allegations soon to be flung at her, she was not deranged, though the pupil accompanying her, Isidore von Reutter, does appear to have been suffering from neurosis and delusions. Isidore claimed that she was in touch with Schnorr's spirit who had announced that she, Isidore, was destined to marry King Ludwig, while Malvina's mission was to help Wagner to create a culminating masterpiece. Wagner jumped to the conclusion that Malvina was angling for him and that in any case Isidore was a charlatan. Malvina became incensed with Cosima not, probably, out of jealousy but out of anger that she was obstructing the destined course of events. When Wagner lost his patience with the pair, Malvina denounced the liaison with Cosima to the king. This sudden new threat caused Wagner and Cosima to react in a particularly vicious way. They both wrote to Ludwig trying to convince him that Malvina was insane and cunningly suggesting that her real victim was the king himself. Malvina persisted in enlightening Ludwig as to the truth of the matter, even divulging the facts about Wagner's deceitful conduct in the *Volksbote* affair. In return, Wagner relentlessly pursued Malvina but failed in his attempts to have her banished from Munich or her royal pension stopped. Not until the autumn of 1868 did Malvina finally leave Bavaria, by which time irreparable damage was done. Wagner and Cosima had, in their desperation, acted with a savage bestiality which must have seared their consciences for life; and Ludwig was at last forced to accept the truth: 'if it should really be a case of adultery – then alas!' (Letter to Dufflipp, 13 December 1867).

At the end of 1866 Wagner's two arch-enemies, Pfistermeister and Pfordten, were both removed from office. Early the next year, on 17 February 1867, Cosima gave birth to Wagner's second child, Eva. The announced engagement of Ludwig to his cousin Sophie Charlotte was to prove less fruitful and was broken off later in the year. The surge of popularity caused by Ludwig's engagement boded well for the proposed music school and Wagner was able to secure appointments for Bülow as its director and as Court Kapellmeister. Wagner's influence in Munich was increased still further by the appointment, in December, of Hans Richter as repetiteur at the Court Theatre.

The gossip about Cosima, Bülow, Wagner and their circle, combined with Ludwig's own observations, caused relations between the king and his beloved idol to plummet. Disagreement, too, between Semper and the court came to a head in March 1868 when Semper finally threatened to institute legal proceedings to enforce payment for the work he had already done on designs for the proposed festival theatre. Since Wagner himself was only lukewarm about the project – it became increasingly clear to him over these and the following years that Munich was not the place for the *Ring* – the concept was never realized.

Wagner's greatest artistic triumph since the Dresden years came on 21 June 1868, when *Die Meistersinger* received its premiere under Bülow in the Court Theatre. The performance was given to rapturous acclaim though for some Wagner blotted his copybook by taking a bow from the royal box – a shocking breach of etiquette. During 1868 Cosima spent much time at Tribschen but had not yet formally broken with her husband. The manner in which this should be done even led to some friction between Wagner and Cosima. Wagner was in favour of an immediate divorce, whereas Cosima was more cautious. She knew that Bülow did not regard divorce as inevitable and in any case would have been unwilling to condemn her publicly as would have been required (their marriage, solemnized under Prussian law, could not be dissolved by mutual consent). In addition, Cosima was a Catholic and Wagner wished her to change her faith in order that their children might be brought up as Protestants. But Cosima's father, Liszt, had by now taken minor orders in the Catholic Church and Cosima was reluctant to hurt both her father and her husband unnecessarily. These conflicts found artistic expression in a prose sketch of August 1868 called *Luthers Hochzeit* (Luther's Marriage). For Wagner, as for his countrypeople generally in these years of culminating German nationalism, Luther was a national hero. The year 1868 was celebrated as the 350th anniversary of the Reformation and marked by the erection of a Luther memorial at Worms. In the same year Sachs' ode to the 'Wittenberg Nightingale' was taken up by the *Volk* at the end of *Die Meistersinger*, and now in *Luthers Hochzeit* Wagner celebrates one of the decisive acts of the Reformation: Luther's rejection of his priestly celibacy and his marriage to Catharina von Bora. It would seem that Wagner did not find the subject suitable for musical treatment – no composition sketches are known – and ten years later he was expressing a desire to write a play on the subject in prose (Diaries, 5 July 1878).

After a trip to Italy with Wagner, Cosima finally took the fateful step and moved into Tribschen with Isolde and Eva. For the time being, their cohabitation was not announced, though Ludwig had already been officially informed – albeit in somewhat oblique terms – of their relationship. On 1 January 1869 Cosima made the first entry in the diary that she was to keep until the end of Wagner's life. The devotion of Cosima and Wagner to each other is so remarkable, and their relationship so important to the last fifteen years of his life, that they merit some discussion. One of three illegitimate children of Franz Liszt and the Countess Marie d'Agoult, Cosima suffered in her childhood from the itinerant life of her virtuoso father and from the separation of her parents. The education she received in Paris was a strict one, concerned as much with deportment and breeding as with modern languages. She emerged from it accomplished and self-confident, her knowledge extensive but shallow, her outlook cultivated but narrow-minded. In spite of a somewhat haughty and forbidding exterior, she was burdened with doubts and psychological insecurities so potent that at different times she was persuaded it was her mission to help and succour two men clearly in need: first Bülow, then Wagner. While not physically attractive in the conventional sense, like the succession of women to whom Wagner had previously been drawn, Cosima had beautiful long light-brown hair over which he never ceased to marvel. More importantly she possessed a whole series of qualities that provided the foundation for the only enduring sexual relationship of his life. She had the intelligence to follow Wagner's impromptu theorizing, the erudition to enable her to converse with him on any subject from Voltaire to vegetarianism, and the servility necessary to accommodate his dictatorial, egoistic manner. One thing she never had doubts about – like Wagner himself – was that he was a genius, who occupied a central position in the history of Western culture.

Reading the Diaries, one gets the impression that for all Wagner's sonorous declarations that she was vital to his artistic creativity, it was not a relationship based on true intellectual reciprocity. The number of occasions on which she influenced the actual course of a composition – as in the case of Sachs' final monologue in *Die Meistersinger* – is few. Her opinions seem to be subsumed into his, so that frequently it is impossible to tell whose are being expressed. 'In the evening R. sings a theme from a Mozart quartet which he finds uniquely graceful and beautiful, but unfortunately it soon gives way to banality' (31 March 1878). Clearly the criticism is Wagner's, but did Cosima also take that view? Probably she was not given the opportunity to venture an opinion. From the start she willingly accepted the role of servitude. When she first arrived at Tribschen – as Wagner later recollected and Cosima duly recorded – she had had, like Kundry, 'only one wish, to serve, to serve!' (16 November 1878). Joyfully pandering to every bodily need of her husband, she even accepted his ill-tempered barbs as a gift from God. As one writer has put it: she is 'the embodiment of anti-emancipation'.[1] Idolatry reaches its limits in the entry for 27 July 1878: 'In the morning, he gives me the single hairs from his eyebrows which had grown too long above his left eye, and I am carrying them around with me.'

---

[1] Hilde Spiel, 'Living with a Genius. On the Marriage of Cosima and Richard Wagner'.

However, as has been well said by Geoffrey Skelton, the English translator of the Diaries: 'In the ordinary affairs of life, as in his art, he had to dominate, and to him love and loyalty meant a complete subjugation to his will. Those who were willing to submit to him did not, unless they wished to, become mere slaves. They were repaid with kindness and sympathy, and this was Wagner's way of expressing his gratitude, for behind the urge to dominate lay a constant desire for reassurance.'[2]

Furthermore, for all Cosima's passivity, and for all her apparent lack of influence on artistic matters, she did have a decisive, if concealed, impact on many issues. Her secret was that she was able to persuade Wagner that it was his view that was prevailing even when it was in fact hers. By such subtle engineering, she had her own way over the divorce, for example. She also opened his letters, including those from Minna, and suggested replies. Time and again we can see her hand in the direction of events. Firm but tactful, she had a certain ruthlessness that bordered on cruelty, but at the same time her education and upbringing had endowed her with the grace and diplomacy that Wagner so disastrously lacked. He loved her poise and the aristocratic pretensions that went with it; they gave his dealings with royalty and high society a legitimacy that he could not supply himself. It was their mutual recognition of these complementary qualities that provided the solid basis for their blissful union.

In a letter of 10 February 1869 Ludwig showed that he had forgiven Wagner. But his olive branch gave cause for concern. The reason was that it also expressed Ludwig's desire to see *Das Rheingold* premiered in Munich. Wagner had not even completed the third work of the cycle yet and he knew that the *Ring* could not be performed to his satisfaction under conventional conditions. It was with foreboding that he agreed to the start of rehearsals. Wagner did nothing to help his cause by deciding to reprint *Jewishness in Music*, and with a new preface protesting about Jewish persecution – of himself, that is. Most of his friends, even Cosima, thought that this was a mistake and there was indeed a storm. It is not without significance that the pamphlet was published only a few months

---

[2] Geoffrey Skelton, *Richard and Cosima Wagner*, 105. This book is a well-documented history of the Wagners' marriage. See also George Marek's *Cosima Wagner*.

7 Wagner photographed in Paris by Pierre Petit & Trinquart,
February/March 1860.

8 King Ludwig II of Bavaria in the year of his accession.

9 Second complete draft of Siegfried's Funeral March, substantially as it appears in *Götterdämmerung*. Note the instrumentation sketched in the margins, and the stage directions, already an integral part of the conception.

Richard Wagner im Himmel.

10 'Richard Wagner in Heaven'; Viennese caricature dating from the year of Wagner's death. Top (left): angels blow Wagnerian brass instruments; (right) Wagner gives instruction to Mozart and Beethoven. Centre: Wagner gives Offenbach another roasting. Bottom: St Peter heralds a celestial performance of Wagner's 'trilogy', given daily.

prior to the full emancipation of the Jews. In July 1869 this was enshrined in a law passed, with Bismarck's blessing, in the North German Confederation. The reprinting of *Jewishness in Music* gave notice that in spite of the formal abolition of discrimination, prejudice was still rampant.

On 17 May a young philosopher came to Tribschen as guest. Wagner had met Friedrich Nietzsche briefly the previous November and invited him to come and stay. Nietzsche had been overwhelmed by the power of Wagner's music, especially the 'dangerous fascination', the 'horrible, sweet infinitude' of *Tristan und Isolde*. This attitude towards Wagner's art was ultimately uncontainable and was to explode violently. In 1869, when still only twenty-four, he was appointed Professor of Classical Philology at Basle University; thus he came to take up Wagner's invitation and he was present at Tribschen when Wagner and Cosima's third child, Siegfried, was born on 6 June. For Wagner the birth of his son and heir was an event of cosmic proportions. Cosima now asked her husband for a divorce and requested the custody of Daniela and Blandine; Bülow immediately agreed.

Three equally congenial visitors arrived in July: Judith Mendès-Gautier (daughter of the poet Théophile Gautier), her husband Catulle Mendès, and their friend the poet Philippe Auguste Villiers de l'Isle-Adam. They were all unashamed admirers and several convivial evenings were passed with discussions and readings. Wagner was particularly struck by the beauty and discerning intelligence of Judith; he showed his exuberance by scuttling up trees at the side of the house.

Wagner's forebodings about the world premiere of *Das Rheingold* shortly to take place in Munich in no way diminished as reports reached him of the grotesquely inadequate staging. When he and Cosima first saw the costume designs, they dismissed them as 'very silly and unimaginative' and although that particular aspect was improved, the opinion of those who observed the production on their behalf and reported back was that the work was mutilated. Ludwig was determined to see *Rheingold* staged and although Wagner tried every ploy to prevent it – he even considered breaking with him – the king was victorious. Shortly before the premiere Hans Richter, with Wagner's encouragement, submitted his resignation as conductor. Wagner and he hoped that this would force the king to abandon the project, but he battled on, vowing to do without either man. A succession of conductors refrained from taking up the baton out of deference to Wagner. Eventually Franz Wüllner, a local and relatively inexperienced conductor, agreed and was not even deterred by Wagner's admonitory outburst: 'Hands off my score! That's my advice to you, sir; or the devil take you.' When the premiere took place, on 22 September 1869, Wagner was pointedly absent. It was not the unmitigated disaster predicted, but no one present imagined that real justice had been done to the work.

Reinforced in his determination to establish a festival exclusively for the production of the *Ring*, Wagner continued to ponder on the most suitable venue. The Upper Franconian town of Bayreuth was mooted and Cosima urged him to look it up in the encyclopedia. To their delight the town boasted a theatre – the Markgräfliches Opernhaus, dating from 1748 – which might prove suitable. In the meantime, nothing could be done to prevent *Die Walküre* being given publicly in Munich alongside *Das Rheingold*. It was premiered on 26 June 1870, once again under Wüllner. That the performance was received well did nothing to reconcile Wagner to the fact that it had taken place at all.

Ludwig was by now preoccupied with affairs of state. Bismarck's policy of Prussian expansion had led many observers to conclude that a war between France and Prussia was only a matter of time. But such were his political skills that when the war broke out in July 1870 he was able to represent it, successfully, as a battle to preserve German liberties in the face of French aggression. Against a background of increasing prosperity and self-confidence, a mood of national pride had established itself which, at the onset of war, transformed itself into rabid jingoism. The south German states, including Ludwig's Bavaria, had no hesitation in allying with Prussia; France, finding herself confronted by a vastly greater and better disciplined army, was soon forced to capitulate. Germany proclaimed the Second Empire, Wilhelm I of Prussia became the Kaiser on 18 January 1871 and ten days later the armistice was signed between France and Prussia.

Nowhere did anti-French feeling run higher than at Tribschen. The bitter humiliations Wagner had suffered in that country were never to be forgotten and they most certainly coloured his already prejudiced opinion of French culture. Neither did Cosima betray any sentimental attachment to the past, to her Parisian upbringing: 'arrogant and wicked' was how she characterized the French and their behaviour during the crisis of July 1870. Their French friends Catulle and Judith Mendès visited them in the company of Villiers de l'Isle-Adam, the composers Saint-Saëns and Duparc, and others, arriving on the very day war was declared. Almost inevitably there was trouble. On the last day of their visit Villiers gave a reading which offended Wagner by what he felt was bombast and theatricality. He responded by criticizing the French and 'the objectionable nature of their rhetorical poetry' (Diaries, 30 July 1870). This insult was but a foretaste of a play he wrote later in the year (November) for musical setting, describing it as 'a comedy in the antique manner'. Entitled *Eine Kapitulation* (A Capitulation), this heavy-handed farce has generally been seen as a tasteless and humourless jibe at the expense of the Parisians suffering during the siege of their city. Wagner may have had just a moment's doubt about its taste – though not, apparently, about its humour – for when he published it three years later he explicitly declared in his foreword that the piece was certainly not intended to ridicule the Parisians for their misfortunes; on the contrary, the French, for all their foolish fripperies, always managed to be original, whereas the Germans were capable only of a disgusting imitation of the French. Although the expected capitulation of Paris is clearly alluded to in the play, the central irony is that in cultural terms it is Germany which has surrendered to France. In a final speech, Victor Hugo invites the Germans into Paris, not as invaders, but as friends, in order to enjoy their cafés and restaurants, their theatres and concerts. 'Who would find your *Faust* appetizing?', he asks. 'Gounod first made it delightful.' Similarly, he continues, Don Carlos, William Tell and Mignon have all been popularized by the French. In other words, this is yet another variation on Wagner's theme that German culture, and especially opera, has been swamped by the crowd-pulling frivolity of French or French-inspired works.

A more serious contribution written in the same year, and published to coincide with the centenary celebrations of his idol, was Wagner's essay *Beethoven*. Once again he addressed himself to the fundamental question of the relationship of poetry to music in the music drama. And now, since *Opera and Drama* had been written before Schopenhauer's philosophy had revealed to him the true path, he felt it necessary to attempt a rapprochement. Wagner by this time takes it for granted that words and music cannot operate on the basis of total equality; in company with Schopenhauer he now holds that music is the ultimate vehicle of expression and that the words must occupy a subordinate position. However, the union of the two provides a range of emotional expression far beyond the limitations imposed by the different media in isolation. Not any poetry would serve the purpose and only a poet-musician such as himself, claimed Wagner, was able to provide the kind of libretto suitable for musical treatment.[3]

It was while working on *Beethoven* that Wagner and Cosima were at last able to sanctify their relationship. On 18 July came the news that Cosima's marriage to Bülow was legally dissolved and their wedding took place in the Protestant church in Lucerne on 25 August. Their happiness was sealed by Wagner's gift of the intimate *Siegfried Idyll* (see chapter 20).

In April of the following year, 1871, they visited Bayreuth and established that the Markgräfliches Opernhaus was too small to accommodate the *Ring*. Considering the idea of a purpose-built theatre, they turned their attention to the raising of capital. The cost of building and equipping a theatre, together with all the necessary administrative expenses, was estimated at 300,000 Talers, which could be raised, it was thought, by issuing 1000 'patrons' certificates' at 300 Talers each.[4] Carl Tausig was put in charge of the scheme but that July the brilliant young virtuoso succumbed to typhus and died at the age of twenty-nine. Happily there was no lack of energetic helpers: Countess Marie von Schleinitz co-ordinated the prospective patrons in Berlin, while Emil Heckel, a music dealer from Mannheim, proposed and initiated a network of Wagner Societies which would enable less affluent enthusiasts to contribute jointly to the cause.

Another solid supporter was to be Friedrich Feustel, a banker and chair of the town council of Bayreuth. When in November 1871 Wagner wrote to inform him of his choice of Bayreuth for his enterprise, Feustel immediately secured the authority of his council

---

[3] In contrast to Jack Stein and most other writers, Frank W. Glass in *The Fertilizing Seed* argues, convincingly, that the theories of the later essays, including *Beethoven*, together with the mature music dramas themselves, do not contradict *Opera and Drama* in its basic premise: that the 'poetic intent' inspires a musical response and brings it to life as drama.

[4] The Taler in the 1870s had the value of approximately 3 Marks. Cf Wagner's annual salary of 1500 Talers in Dresden.

to offer him any site he chose for the construction of a festival theatre. This was fortunate indeed, for Wagner had already announced his intention of holding the first festival in Bayreuth in 1873.

Ludwig was not pleased that the *Ring* was to be given outside Munich, but he accepted it with good grace. This too was important because the task of inaugurating the Bayreuth Festival turned out to be more arduous and more perilous than anyone had envisaged; Ludwig was again to be the saviour when it seemed certain to founder. In February 1872 Wagner acquired a site adjoining the palace gardens for his future home, Wahnfried. As for the theatre itself, two proposed sites had fallen through but eventually an ideal one was found: the 'Green Hill' of Bürgerreuth, the commanding position which the Festspielhaus occupies to this day.

The ceremony for the laying of the foundation stone was fixed for 22 May, Wagner's birthday. Liszt's friendship with him had cooled since Cosima's separation from Bülow and remarriage in a Protestant church (she was then converted officially to Protestantism on 31 October 1872), but Wagner wanted to heal the rift. He invited him, in warm tones, to attend the ceremony, acknowledging the debt he owed him; Liszt did not come but he sent his good wishes. The 22nd was a rainy day and those attending the stone-laying had to negotiate ankle-deep mud on the Green Hill. After the ceremony, speeches were delivered in the old opera house, on account of the rain, and Beethoven's Ninth Symphony was performed.

At the end of September the Wagner family moved into a temporary home in Bayreuth at Dammallee 7, but in November Wagner and Cosima set off on a tour that took them to most of Germany's important opera houses to look for singers. By the end of the following August, 1873, it was apparent that there were still unresolved problems: Wagner was obliged to announce to his patrons that the festival would not take place until 1875. He had been able to secure the services of Karl Brandt and Joseph Hoffmann, the former to design and construct the stage machinery, the latter (a painter of historical subjects, as Wagner wished, in preference to a mere scene-painter) to make the stage designs. But he was having less success with King Ludwig, whose generous subsidies were no longer forthcoming. In January 1874 he was met with a flat refusal for funds to complete the festival theatre. As a desperate measure – and contrary to all the utopian ideals he had entertained for a popular celebration of art – he turned to the Reich, but his appeal was rejected before it reached the Kaiser. Just as he was yielding to despair, Wagner received a passionate letter from Ludwig, indicating a change of heart: 'No, no and again no! It must not end like this; help must be given! Our plans must not founder!' (25 January 1874). His financial help took the form of a loan of 100,000 Talers. As with the scheme of 'patrons' certificates' the loan, which necessitated the selling of admission tickets, ensured that entry to Bayreuth was to be just another pastime for the privileged rather than the communal theatrical experience for the ordinary people originally intended. But this was not a time for ingratitude and Ludwig made a further sum available for the completion of the villa next to the palace gardens. The Wagners moved in on 28 April 1874 and christened their new home 'Wahnfried', roughly translatable as 'peace from illusion'.

Wagner had been proceeding with the composition of *Götterdämmerung* and it was on 21 November 1874 that the score was finally completed. What should have been a joyous day was marred by a misunderstanding. Cosima came to Wagner's workroom and deliberately averted her eyes from the score lying completed on his desk, thinking he had been too tired to finish it. Instead she showed him a letter from her father. But Wagner's temper was particularly unpredictable where Liszt was concerned; he resented, possibly out of a bad conscience, any affection being diverted to Cosima's father and away from him. He reproached her bitterly for caring more about her father's letter than about his own completed masterpiece. Cosima was so upset that she discontinued her diary for over a week. She took comfort only in the fact that her suffering was atonement for a nameless guilt.

Even 1875 had turned out to be too optimistic a forecast for the opening of the festival: it was not until the following year that the final preparations could at last be made. A major problem was the lack of a suitable Siegfried. Albert Niemann, his Paris Tannhäuser, coveted the part but Wagner was determined not to give it to him – in any case he was to be Siegmund. A tenor from the Mannheim Opera, Georg Unger, was physically among the most prepossessing candidates but he clearly required close supervision in learning his role. Wagner went to the lengths of engaging a singing teacher from Munich, Julius Hey, to instruct Unger in the part. He sang in all three cycles of the first festival but his creation of the role of Siegfried was not counted among the successes. The Brünnhilde, Amalie Materna from Vienna, also had to be groomed for the part; an advantage was that these singers responded the more readily to Wagner's direction. Franz Betz, who had sung Hans Sachs at the premiere of *Die Meistersinger*, was a known quantity: Wagner was obliged to put up with his temperament in order to secure a first-class Wotan.

Wagner was assisted in his coaching of the singers – who all agreed to be paid expenses but no fee – by the members of what he called the 'Nibelungen Chancellery', a small group of disciples earlier employed in copying parts. They now included Hermann Zumpe, Anton Seidl, Joseph Rubinstein and a Greek, Demetrius Lalas; the group was occasionally augmented by Franz Fischer and Felix Mottl. Mottl, a fine musician in his own right, and soon to become one of the leading Wagner conductors of his age, was, along with Seidl and Fischer, involved in a vital part of the proceedings for *Das Rheingold*. It was their task to co-ordinate the movements of the swimming machines into which the three Rhinemaidens were strapped (and which were each operated by two other men) with the music.

The man responsible for movement and gesture on the stage was Richard Fricke, though Wagner retained overall control of the direction. Much was improvised according to the needs of the instant: with each singer Wagner sought to work out stage actions that came naturally to them. When Cosima took over the direction after his death, she attempted to impose an authoritative style – the one supposedly ordained by Wagner himself – on her performers. But Wagner required only that his central conception of the work be accepted; within that conception he gave singers the freedom to find their own most convincing portrayal of the character.[5] Another of Wagner's protégés, Heinrich Porges, at his request documented and preserved for posterity everything that was said by him at rehearsals. Porges' record is of much interest, particularly as regards Wagner's approach to performance style. Porges sums this up as the combination of 'the realistic style of Shakespeare with the idealistic style of antique tragedy': the union of 'an art rooted in fidelity to nature' with a more stylized form 'striving for a direct embodiment of the ideal'.[6] Wagner's observations and instructions, so faithfully

[5] Geoffrey Skelton's *Wagner at Bayreuth* is essential reading for the history of stage direction at Bayreuth.

[6] *Wagner Rehearsing the 'Ring'* (Eng. trans. by Robert Jacobs), 4–5.

recorded by Porges, provide a valuable insight into the composer's intentions on that occasion. They should not, however, be regarded as a formula for effecting some sort of 'definitive' production: all the evidence is that Wagner thrived on the inspiration of the moment, on improvisation,[7] on the discovery of new and alternative possibilities. And in any case he was far from satisfied about the staging of those first performances: Fricke wrote in his diary that Wagner told him afterwards 'Next year we'll do it all differently'.

Nor was Wagner happy about the conducting of Hans Richter, though the latter was by this time an experienced and highly competent conductor. Wagner told him bluntly that his tempos were not to his liking and Richter may have attempted to accommodate Wagner's objections within his own interpretation, because the result seems to have been confusion. In a post mortem on the performances held by Wagner and Cosima, Richter's contribution was summarily dismissed: 'Richter not sure of a single tempo – dismal experiences indeed!' (Diaries, 9 September 1876). After Wagner's death, however, he returned to conduct at Bayreuth on many occasions.

There were three cycles, beginning on 13 August 1876. Musicians, critics, admirers and notables had gathered from all over Europe. The composing fraternity was represented by Bruckner, Tchaikovsky, Saint-Saëns and Grieg, among others, while the monarchs present included Kaiser Wilhelm I of Germany, Dom Pedro II of Brazil (who two decades earlier had invited Wagner to conduct his works in Rio de Janeiro) and, of course, Ludwig II of Bavaria. Ludwig attended the dress rehearsals and then the third cycle, avoiding the public, as was his habit, as far as possible.

Another observer at the rehearsals was Nietzsche. He had been a regular visitor at Tribschen and Wahnfried until 1874, but his health had now deteriorated drastically. Suffering from blinding headaches, bouts of nausea and frequent fainting fits, he had had to leave his post at Basle University temporarily in February 1876 (he was eventually obliged to resign the professorship in 1879). It would seem – though it has never been conclusively proved – that he was afflicted by a syphilitic infection contracted during a sexual encounter in his youth. The weakening of his eyesight and his later sad

[7] On Wagner and the art of improvisation see Dieter Borchmeyer, *Das Theater Richard Wagners*, 57–63, 206–30.

Hans Richter

drift into insanity certainly support such a diagnosis. Shortly before the *Ring* premiere in 1876 the fourth of Nietzsche's *Unzeitgemässe Betrachtungen* (Thoughts out of Season) appeared. Entitled *Richard Wagner in Bayreuth*, it was, on the surface, a celebration of Wagner and his achievement and was welcomed accordingly: 'Friend! Your book is tremendous! Wherever did you learn so much about me?', wrote Wagner on 12 July. But the essay is profoundly ambiguous, reflecting in Nietzsche's characteristically cryptic style the deep-seated uncertainties he entertained about Wagner and his art. On many occasions right up to the end of his life, Nietzsche spoke movingly of how Wagner's music pierced him to the core; yet it was precisely that seductive quality, to which he so readily succumbed, that troubled him. He was coming to see the renunciatory, quietistic impulse that had informed Wagner's art since his 'surrender' to Schopenhauer as a betrayal of the challenging, affirmative spirit that he had formerly greeted as being so in accordance with his own iconoclastic outlook on life. Wagner, it seemed, was no longer pricking the artistic and social conscience of his era; instead he was

95

becoming something of a figurehead for the German Reich. And now, with his essentially theatrical approach to art, Wagner was offering the public, sensed Nietzsche, exactly that self-indulgent artificiality it hankered after: in Wagner's theatre of illusion, audiences were invited to surrender their intellectual and critical faculties and wallow, transported, in emotion. Nietzsche railed against Wagner's Schopenhauerian espousal of the 'philosophy of pessimism' and of pity as the source of morality. But it was above all the pathological content of Wagner's work that he now complained of: Wagner was a neurotic, he claimed, who relished characters suffering from convulsive passions and hysteria.

What provoked the violence of Nietzsche's reaction against this 'degeneracy' and 'decadence'? Wagner, it is true, was rapidly becoming an emblem of bourgeois culture; but Nietzsche had also moved. Back in 1868 (8 October) he had identified for his friend Rohde the aesthetic pessimism, tinged with decadence, that drew him to Wagner: 'What pleases me in Wagner is that which pleases me in Schopenhauer: the ethical breeze, the whiff of Faust, the Cross, death, the grave etc.'[8] In what is sometimes referred to as his 'second period' (1876–82) Nietzsche turned against art as romantic illusion and condemned those, like Schopenhauer and Wagner, who refused to say 'yes' to life. The bitterness in his writings of these and later years is undoubtedly due to the fact that he had once embraced the tendencies that he now recognized as so dangerous, and indeed continued to be susceptible to their allure.[9]

Nietzsche attended rehearsals for the premiere but found himself more and more alienated from the enterprise and irritated by

---

[8] *Nietzsche Briefwechsel: Kritische Gesamtausgabe*, ed. G. Colli and M. Montinari, Abt. 1, Bd 2 (Berlin and New York 1975), 322.

[9] For a fuller account of the Wagner/Nietzsche relationship see Roger Hollinrake, *Nietzsche, Wagner and the philosophy of pessimism*; R.J. Hollingdale, *Nietzsche, the Man and his Philosophy*; Ronald Gray's chapter 'The German Intellectual Background' in *The Wagner Companion*, ed. P. Burbidge and R. Sutton; and Dietrich Fischer-Dieskau, *Wagner and Nietzsche*.

For the fascinating correspondence between Wagner and Nietzsche's doctor – Wagner considered that Nietzsche's troubles were the result of habitual masturbation – see Martin Gregor-Dellin, *Richard Wagner: His Life, His Work, His Century*, 451–8.

the behaviour of the public and press.[10] It was chiefly, however, ill health – in particular incessant and violent headaches – that drove him from Bayreuth, as he disclosed to his sister Elisabeth. He returned for the start of the festival and attended the first cycle in the company of Elisabeth; they disposed of their tickets for the second cycle. The dishonesty of Elisabeth Förster-Nietzsche's testimony as to the breach between Wagner and Nietzsche was methodically exposed long ago by Ernest Newman.[11] Her purpose was to support Nietzsche's own claim that he had tolerated and encouraged Wagner's talent as a reflection of his own genius, but that with the *Ring* and *Parsifal* Wagner's betrayal compelled him to break the ties forthwith. As an example of Elisabeth's technique might be mentioned the fact that in the biography of her brother she deleted all references from his letters as to his ill health during the weeks in Bayreuth; she represented his sudden departure as solely for reasons of aesthetics.

Similarly, her account of the last meeting of Nietzsche and Wagner provided the basis for a tenacious myth. They came together in Italy, at Sorrento, a few months after the festival. While walking on the cliffs Wagner is supposed to have described the subject of his next music drama, *Parsifal*. Nietzsche, disgusted with Wagner for yielding to Christianity, strode off and never saw him again. Now it is true that Nietzsche was becoming deeply disillusioned about Wagner, whom he regarded as becoming a representative of the bourgeois Christian culture he so loathed; in a new preface, written in 1886, to *Menschliches, Allzumenschliches* (Human, All Too Human) he was to write that Wagner 'suddenly sank down, helpless and broken, before the Christian cross'. And it is also true that the Sorrento holiday was to prove their last meeting. But on the other hand both Nietzsche's correspondence and Cosima Wagner's Diaries disprove the notion that there was any abrupt break that autumn. Indeed, Nietzsche was to write to Cosima a year later (10 October 1877), in a letter not published until 1964: 'The glorious promise of *Parcival* may console us whenever we are in need of

---

10 Newman considered that Nietzsche probably had not attended the rehearsal of *Siegfried*. But Roger Hollinrake, *op.cit.*, believes that he did (p. 244).

11 See chapters 25–27 of vol. iv of his *Life*.

consolation.' In any case, Wagner's treatment of the *Parsifal* story could not have come as any surprise to Nietzsche in 1876 because at Tribschen on Christmas Day 1869 Wagner had read him his prose draft of 1865 – a detailed working-out of the subject in which the Christian symbolism is fully elaborated.

Another visitor to the festival had been Judith Gautier, now divorced from her husband but enjoying the attentions of an amateur composer called Ludwig Benedictus. Wagner had a seat reserved for himself in the theatre between Judith and Benedictus and occupying it as the lights went down he whispered to her that he would like to listen to all his works in her arms. When they were alone, they embraced and kissed, though Judith was understandably anxious that their intimacy should not develop into a fully-fledged affair and urged him to forget her. They continued to correspond for some eighteen months, until February 1878, and Judith supplied him with silks, satins and exotic perfumes from Paris. Substituting these for her bodily presence, he was able to conjure the atmosphere and mood he allegedly needed to compose *Parsifal*. A local barber acting as a factotum ensured that their intimate correspondence remained a secret from Cosima. Even when, in December 1877, she was informed about the fact that they were in communication, she was not told all. Cosima's Diaries reveal very little about the affair or her attitude to it, but it does appear that the following month, January 1878, she caught Wagner burning some correspondence, and that then, or soon after, the whole story came out.[12] Displaying the calm determination that has already been noted, she dropped hints to Judith that the game was up, and effectively warned her off, though managing to do it in such a way that her own reasonably cordial relationship with her was not impaired. On 15 February the 'affair' came to an end, with a last letter from Wagner to Judith. What little evidence there is for the whole incident suggests not that the tolerant, understanding Cosima turned a blind eye – the traditional view – but that in her skilful, resolute manner she was once again successful in getting her own way.[13]

[12] See Diaries, 12 February 1878 and 29 October 1879.

[13] This is the conclusion of Geoffrey Skelton, with which I agree. In his *Richard and Cosima Wagner*, Mr Skelton considers all the available evidence, including that of Judith Gautier's goddaughter Suzanne Meyer-Zundel; see pp. 226, 230–31, 244–8.

In the immediate aftermath of the festival Wagner's chief concern was in respect of the deficit, which amounted to 148,000 Marks. The German people had disappointed him: they had not had the vision to embrace the new concept of art he offered, rooted in the German spirit. The reason is perhaps easier for us to see. The *Ring* had initially been inspired by contempt for a materialistic society; it looked forward to a transformed world. But its ultimate audience was not an idealized *Volk*: it was a prosperous bourgeoisie and one which, in the early years of the Reich, derived little pleasure from the contemplation of a radically reconstructed society. The irony is that Wagner himself was now an accredited member of that social class and shared many of its convictions and prejudices. Yet he was still enough of an idealist to feel betrayed. He considered handing over the festival to the Munich Court or even to the Reich, suggesting that Ludwig order the matter to be raised in the Reichstag. But when he had recovered from his depressive phase – induced in part by utter exhaustion – he began to consider new schemes for making the festival viable.

8

A new creed (1877–83)

Several different ideas were put forward by Wagner and his supporters for saving the festival. He had hoped that for future years, now the major expenditure in connection with the establishment of the theatre was out of the way, it would be possible to meet annual expenses out of receipts, to attract larger audiences by reducing seat prices and to offer the singers a suitable fee. The renewed approach to the Reich had come to nothing and it soon became evident that another festival could not be launched until at least 1878. A firm of concert agents in London, Hodge & Essex, invited Wagner to give a series of twenty instrumental and vocal concerts in the recently opened Royal Albert Hall. The capacity of the hall being 10,000, good receipts seemed to be assured and he accepted. Unfortunately the inexperience of the agents had caused them wildly to over-estimate the potential audience for a series of concerts. Furthermore, they had overlooked the fact that a sizeable proportion of the 10,000 seats belonged to subscribers towards the cost of building and maintaining the hall: these seat-holders paid an annual rate but they were at liberty either to occupy the seats at no extra charge or to leave them vacant – they were not for general sale. As a result, the series had to be reduced – eight concerts were eventually given – and although the performers' fees, already agreed, were adjusted, they remained artificially high. In contrast to his earlier visit to London in 1855, Wagner was now an international celebrity and he was well received. Excerpts from the *Ring* and other works were conducted by Wagner and Richter; many must have been hearing this music for the first time. In spite of the interesting personalities to whom they were introduced – the poet Robert Browning, the painter Edward Burne-Jones, William Morris, George Eliot and her companion George Henry Lewes (Wagner was once again presented to Queen Victoria, this time at Windsor) – it was not a happy tour for him. Nor did the financial proceeds do much to sweeten the pill. In the circumstances a profit of £700 was not as bad as might have been expected, but it was considerably less than the sum originally envisaged.

Over the summer Wagner had been toying with the idea of emigrating and leaving his problems behind. An impresario had offered him a tour of the United States and he was seriously considering the possibility of selling Wahnfried and crossing the ocean to start a new life with his family in America, never to return. The hope of finding 'a fresh and vital soil' in which to cultivate his art, untainted by 'the decay of European culture' was, he later told Friedrich Feustel (4 March 1880), what attracted him. Instead, he threw himself with renewed vigour into two projects designed to regenerate the society he condemned as corrupt. The first was *Parsifal*, of which he had made the libretto in March and April 1877, then setting it to music between September 1877 and April 1879. The second was the *Bayreuther Blätter*, which was to provide the vehicle for *Parsifal's* literary and ideological counterpart. The idea of a monthly journal devoted to Wagner and his work was the brainchild of Hans von Wolzogen, who took up residence in Bayreuth in October 1877 and produced the first issue the following January. Over the remaining five years of his life Wagner contributed a series of articles to the *Bayreuther Blätter*, establishing it as a flagship of a line of intellectual enquiry that led from the nationalistic aggrandizement of the Second Reich to the inhuman excesses of the Third.

Before tracing this path it is necessary to record the ultimate settlement of the question of the Bayreuth deficit, which also had important consequences for the future. The discharging of the debt of 98,634 Marks to the Bavarian Court was resolved on the basis of a plan evolved by Feustel and approved by Perfall, the Intendant of the Munich Court Theatre. By the terms of this agreement of 31 March 1878 Wagner confirmed Ludwig's right to produce all his works in the Court Theatre without payment; the King, however, voluntarily offered to set aside 10 per cent of all such receipts until the deficit was cleared. In essence, this amounted to a 10 per cent royalty on all works mounted in Munich; it has often been pointed out that if such a favourable arrangement had applied throughout his life Wagner would probably not have been in a permanent state of insolvency. Not until 1906 was the Bayreuth debt discharged by Wagner's heirs, but a more immediate consequence of the agreement stemmed from a different clause. Wagner agreed that the first performance of *Parsifal* (either in Bayreuth or Munich) should be given with the orchestra, singers and artistic personnel of the Munich Court Theatre, after which Munich was to have unrestricted rights over the work. It was this clause that was to compel Wagner to accept the Jewish Hermann Levi as the conductor of *Parsifal* in 1882.

The series of essays written in Wagner's last years for the *Bayreuth Blätter* have often been dismissed as senile and irrelevant ramblings. The charge is both unfair and dangerously misconceived. In the first place these writings are not, judged by Wagner's own standards, especially incoherent; indeed, they are often a great deal easier to comprehend than is *Opera and Drama*, written in his prime. In the second place, they expound and codify a strain of Wagner's thought which has jostled with contrasting, even contradictory ideas throughout his life, which now in his final years becomes established as a system of moral values, and which was to have untold consequences for the history of Bayreuth. The ideology behind these essays is one to which many German intellectuals were able to respond with enthusiasm both in Wagner's time and in the decades following his death. It strikes us today as a disturbingly reactionary ideology and deplorably, if not risibly, racist. But in view of its import and crucial impact it is one that must be confronted, not ignored.

The first essay, *Modern* (1878), asserts that present-day culture is dominated by Jews. But whereas the Jews presume that 'modern' trends were brought about by them, in fact it is the Jews themselves who are the novelty. They have appropriated the national heritage of the Germans, especially their language, which they mangle. The concept of 'modern' itself they purloined from the Young Germans of the 1830s, who were opposed to orthodoxy. All this will result in people speaking without meaning, and composing without inspiration. *Public and Popularity*, dating from the same year, addresses itself initially to the relationship between artist and audience. In the final part of the essay Wagner turns to science and religion: conventional religion has come to be seen as anti-scientific as well as unintelligible. 'That the God of our Saviour should have been interpreted as the tribal god of Israel is one of the most terrible confusions in world history.' Might not theology take the step of relinquishing Jehovah, thus granting to science its indisputable truth and to the Christian world its pure God revealed in Jesus? Perhaps the People will one day, through science, produce an answer to this unacceptable situation.

Work on the composition of *Parsifal* was meanwhile proceeding and in his next essay, *Shall we hope?* (1879), Wagner made explicit reference to the link between his ideological and artistic trains of thought. The essay is a call for the renewal of the German spirit and a strengthening of the German intellectual fibre. Wagner's answer to the challenging question of his title is affirmative: 'That I myself have not yet abandoned hope is attested by the fact that I have been able to complete the music of my *Parsifal* in the last few days.'

At the end of July an appeal was made to him to lend his voice to a crusade against vivisection. After reading Ernst von Weber's book *Die Folterkammern der Wissenschaft* (The Torture Chambers of Science) he told Cosima with anger and indignation that 'if he were a younger man he would not rest until he had brought about a demonstration against such barbarism' (Diaries, 31 July 1879). The new religion they preached ought to, he said, begin with compassion for animals. This compassion – which Wagner had displayed since his boyhood days – was treated at length in an Open Letter to Herr Ernst von Weber, one of his more humane contributions to the *Bayreuther Blätter*.

Suffering from depression and ill-health, Wagner was advised to seek a milder climate. On 31 December he left Bayreuth with his family for an extended stay in Italy; they remained there for most of 1880, not returning until the end of October. As in Tribschen and Wahnfried, where the Wagners always kept an open house, the company that assembled in the Villa d'Angri, overlooking the Bay of Naples, was large. They had taken with them all five children, their servants and a governess. Siegfried's new tutor, Heinrich von Stein, a young philosophy student, joined them, and soon after they were visited by the twenty-five-year-old composer Engelbert Humperdinck and the Russian painter Paul von Joukovsky. The latter, who was invited to be the designer for *Parsifal*, became part of the household with his young servant and companion Pepino; in regard to homosexuality, at least, Wagner was a true liberal.

In Italy he stumbled on two settings that struck him as perfect models for stage pictures in *Parsifal*. The Palazzo Rufolo at Ravello was a Moorish-style castle with an exotic garden that echoed his conception of the second act. In the visitors' book he wrote 'Klingsor's magic garden is found!' On another occasion they visited Siena, whose cathedral interior, with its lofty marble columns, greatly moved Wagner; its bizarre, almost fantastic grandeur evoked for him the Hall of the Grail. Joukovsky was asked to make sketches of both stage pictures and they were indeed used as the basis for the sets of the first production.

In *Religion and Art* (1880) Wagner picks up some of the ideas from his previous essays and develops them with a prodigal seasoning of home-spun biology and anthropology pathetically destitute of scientific merit. The earliest people on the earth were graziers and tillers of the soil; only later did they begin to kill animals for food and, acquiring a blood-lust, turn to murdering each other. Christ exhorted his followers to adopt vegetarianism, offering his own flesh and blood as expiation for all slaughtered flesh and spilt blood. The primary cause of the early decay of Christianity was the failure of his followers to abstain from animal food. Christ himself, Wagner continues, has been mistakenly identified with the Jewish creator of heaven and earth, and it is more than doubtful anyway that Jesus was of Jewish extraction. Invoking Jehovah, the Lord of War, nations today stand armed to the teeth preparing for mutual extermination; manifestly it is not Christ the Redeemer they serve. A return to natural food is the only basis of a possible regeneration of mankind. Vegetarians and animal-lovers should join forces with the temperance societies and socialists to help bring this about. Above all, such a regeneration must be rooted in the soil of a true religion. But the most effective way of communicating these ideas is through art, in particular the art of the tone-poet (i.e. music drama). Conventional religion has become artificial and dependent on dogma, whereas true art can express the essence of religion through its mythic symbols.

In a series of three supplements to *Religion and Art* Wagner repeated and expanded these ideas. *What use is this Knowledge?* (1880) adds little that is new, but in the latter part of *Know Thyself* (1881) he focuses his attention on what he had come to regard as the burning issue of race. The Romanic nations and the English, says Wagner, are often considered superior on account of their hybrid stock; however, in terms of producing a great and noble character, the pure-bred races such as the Germans have been much more successful. This character has steadily deteriorated and although in recent times there has been a renewal of the concept 'German', this has not yet amounted to a real rebirth of racial consciousness. The Jew, on the other hand, is 'the most astonishing example of racial consistency that world history has ever offered': Jewish characteristics seem capable of surviving any alien contact. The German race would therefore appear to stand at an enormous disadvantage and yet there has been recently a reawakening of the German instinct — perhaps it should be more properly termed 'the spirit of pure humanity'. Wagner finds the position of all the current political parties inadequate on the Jewish question. His penultimate paragraph looks forward to an absence of Jews, though he makes no proposals as to how this may be brought about.

Heroism and Christianity (1881) brings this racist demagoguery to its pernicious conclusion. Here, in particular, are found overtones of the French writer Count Joseph-Arthur de Gobineau; the Wagners had made the acquaintance of the French aristocrat in Rome in 1876, had met him again in Venice in 1880, and now, prior to writing *Heroism and Christianity*, Wagner had read several of his works including the one for which he is chiefly remembered, the *Essai sur l'inégalité des races humaines* (Essay on the Inequality of the Human Races). *Heroism and Christianity* begins by citing Gobineau on the degeneration of the species through corruption of blood. As Wagner points out, Gobineau attributes this corruption not to a change of diet (as Wagner himself had done) but to miscegenation, i.e. interbreeding between races. Gobineau became a regular and favoured visitor at Wahnfried, yet the better acquainted he and Wagner became, the more they realized that their views diverged. One of the leading exponents of the racist Aryan ideology, Gobineau postulated a hierarchy of three basic stocks: whites, yellows and blacks, with a super élite of Aryans within the highest category, the whites. His outlook was a pessimistic one in that he believed some degree of miscegenation was essential for the continuation of civilization; at the same time he was convinced that it was responsible for the corruption and decay of the species. In contrast to Gobineau's stoic acceptance of this conclusion, Wagner's more optimistic view was that redemption was possible through the agency of Christ. This is the line of argument pursued in *Heroism and Christianity*. The Saviour's blood was pure – the highest possible development of the human species. The Redeemer's blood perhaps flowed, suggests Wagner, in a supreme endeavour of redoubled power to save humanity from final decay. By partaking of that blood, as symbolized in the sacrament of the Eucharist, even the lowest races might be raised to the most godly purity.

Nauseating as many of these ideas may be to the present-day reader, they cannot simply be discounted as the quirky idiocies of a senile mind; nor can it convincingly be argued that they have no connection with Wagner's music dramas (this latter aspect is discussed in the chapter on *Parsifal*). In order to understand Wagner's role in the cultural history of Germany it is necessary, once again, to evaluate his contribution in the context of the prevailing spirit of the times. Many Germans, including prominent writers and scholars, had seen the military victory of 1871 as a victory of German culture. (It was Nietzsche, incidentally, who had pointed out that technical and administrative proficiency had nothing to do with cultural or moral superiority.) But the unification finally achieved in 1871 had an adverse effect for many of the intellectuals who, as liberal nationalists, had struggled for it. An industrial bourgeoisie had emerged and seized power from the intellectuals who previously had commanded considerable respect and influence in society. The political allegiance of many of the latter shifted from liberalism to a form of romantic conservatism, Wagner's case being a prominent and well-known example. Resenting their demotion and shamed by it, they began to rationalize the situation by constructing comprehensive philosophies of history. Possibly the most influential of these was *Die Grundlagen des 19. Jahrhunderts* (The Foundations of the Nineteenth Century) by Houston Stewart Chamberlain, Wagner's son-in-law (he married Eva in 1908). More often than not, such histories reserved a special place in their demonology for the Jews. Wilhelm Marr, Eugen Dühring, Theodor Fritsch, Bernhard Förster, Adolf Stöcker and many like them pandered to a new wave of anti-semitic sentiment in Germany. Since the 1820s anti-semitism had been quiescent, but the economic crash of 1873 helped to revive it; the Jews, who were identified with the stock market and unearned capital, played the classic role of the scapegoat in times of insecurity and low morale. The removal of outstanding civic and legal disabilities from Jews in the aftermath of the unification of Germany increased rather than reduced hostility towards them.

Wagner, of course, had always been inclined to take a global view of his affairs and as a long-standing anti-semite he fell in easily with the idea of his contemporaries that the 'Jewish problem' was a historical one that had to be confronted in a radical way. What is idiosyncratic about Wagner's anti-semitism, as manifested in the so-called 'regeneration writings' described above, is the way he lifted it into the realm of theology. Wagner (unlike the Nazis) had no programme of action for dealing with the Jews and he was unspecific about how regeneration, or redemption, was to be achieved, but it was apparently some sort of mystic experience to be made accessible by art rekindling the inspiration of religion.

Thus, in spite of Wagner's obsession with Jews – and Cosima's Diaries reveal that any imperfection within his field of vision was liable to be attributed to their influence – it would seem that in the later years it is Judaism the religion rather than Jews, individually and collectively, that has become his prime target. This goes some way to explain the paradox, frequently commented upon, that so many of the musicians with whom Wagner surrounded himself were Jews: Tausig, Porges, Rubinstein, Levi, to name but a few. As individuals he could neither fault their behaviour nor deny their talent; it was only as representatives of 'Jewishness' that they ranked as second-class citizens. In an earlier chapter (see p. 46) it was mentioned that according to the *völkisch* view individual Jews could be assimilated; this possibility is stated more clearly in Wagner's 1850 essay *Jewishness in Music* than in the 'regeneration writings', where the 'decay' is held to have set in terminally. But an even darker aspect of the psyche appears to be at work in Wagner's relationship to his Jewish acquaintances: he exploited them (as indeed he did all his friends), he vilified them, he dominated them and he revelled in flaunting his generosity before them. One is obliged to ask why the victims of such sadistic treatment so meekly accepted it and even returned for more. It may be supposed that part of the reason is the phenomenon of Jewish self-hatred – one result of the psychological conflict experienced by many Jews in the decades following Emancipation.[1] In some cases this had the effect of Jews accepting the current anti-semitic analyses and even joining in the abuse. As the anti-semite Dühring put it, they were receiving indulgence for the cardinal sin of their Jewishness. Other Jews, conscious of the lack of an old folk culture of the kind Romanticism advocated – and the sense of security, of belonging, it afforded – coveted such a *Gemeinschaft* when they observed it elsewhere.[2] Wagner's *Gemeinschaft*, based on the *Volk*, on mythology and on a revival of the German spirit, acted as a magnet to those bereft of a *Gemeinschaft* of their own.

[1] See Léon Poliakov, *The History of Anti-Semitism*, iii, pp. 259–60.

[2] See Ernest Gellner, 'Accounting for the horror', *TLS*, 6 August 1982, pp. 843–5.

Wagner's refusal to sign Bernhard Förster's 'Mass Petition against the Rampancy of Judaism' is sometimes cited as evidence in his favour, as are such remarks as that to the Jewish impresario Angelo Neumann: 'I have absolutely no connection with the present "anti-semitic" movement. An article by me shortly to appear in the *Bayreuther Blätter* [*Know Thyself*] will demonstrate that in such a manner that it should be impossible for intelligent people to associate me with that movement' (23 February 1881). However, the reason he gave for not signing the petition was that it was unlikely to be effective (Diaries, 16 June and 6 July 1880) and such declarations as that to Neumann betoken not a lack of sympathy with the aims of the anti-semitic movement but a preference for addressing the question in a less personalized, more theoretical manner – one in accord with a Wagnerian view of world history and religion.

Neither can Wagner be given credit for his engagement of Hermann Levi for the premiere of *Parsifal*. By the terms of his agreement of 31 March 1878 Wagner was obliged to accept the company of the Munich Court Theatre and its conductors Hermann Levi and Franz Fischer for *Parsifal*. The thought of his final masterpiece, with its re-enactment of the most sacred Christian ritual, being conducted by a Jew caused Wagner considerable disquiet. In fact, he even rejected Levi but Ludwig, who was impatient with Wagner's anti-semitic bigotry, presented him with an ultimatum: *Parsifal* with the Munich forces and Levi, or not at all.[3] Wagner gave in but continued to embarrass and torment Levi about his Jewishness, even making an unsuccessful attempt to persuade this son of a rabbi to submit to baptism before undertaking *Parsifal*.

Levi was perhaps the supreme practitioner of self-abasement in the face of Wagner's relentless and aggressive anti-semitism. But even before he met Wagner he had been determined to prove that he was a 'good German'; Jewish self-hatred was deeply rooted in his character and expressed itself in the form of chauvinism and anti-semitism. His friend Wilhelm Busch, the poet and illustrator, though a less strident anti-semite than Wagner, behaved in a similar manner to him – one so common as to be regarded as an acceptable mode of behaviour: while enjoying many genuine friendships with Jews, Busch was wont to lace his poems and drawings with belligerently anti-semitic caricatures based on the grotesque stereotypes. Levi not

[3] See Egon Voss, *Die Dirigenten der Bayreuther Festspiele*, 15–17.

only permitted such jests but himself indulged in activities of the same kind – a psychological mechanism known as 'identification with the aggressor'.[4] It remains only to mention Levi's attitude when confronted with the prospect of conducting *Parsifal* – the greatest challenge, to both conscience and musicianship, of his career. Although he later thought better of it, his immediate reaction, long before Wagner began to be exercised about the matter, was that he had 'no alternative' but to have himself baptized.[5]

Daily life in Wahnfried was conducted appropriately in a spirit combining the ceremony of the Church with the theatricality of the stage. The diary of Susanne Weinert, a governess to the Wagners' children in 1875–6, affords fascinating insights into everyday affairs.[6] Wagner always treated Cosima with 'the most delicate courtesy'; the servants (of whom there were six or seven) were expected to be very submissive towards members of the family, even the children; the children themselves had to stand and kiss their mother on the hand whenever she entered the room. Cosima's own diary furnishes the most comprehensive detail on life at Tribschen and Wahnfried. For Wagner's birthdays she would organize dramatic representations, elaborate pantomimes and recitations given by the children; sometimes they would dress up as characters from his operas; Joukovsky even portrayed them as the Holy Family. We have seen that throughout his career Wagner, inspired by a need to make myths, was constantly stage-managing events, in order to bring life and art closer together. As the Romantic artist *par excellence* he was engaged in a continual process – operating on both conscious and subconscious levels – of blurring the edges between the two. The theatricality of Wahnfried brings to mind Blake and his

---

[4] Discussed by Peter Gay in his illuminating and scrupulously documented article 'Hermann Levi: a Study in Service and Self-Hatred', in his collection *Freud, Jews and Other Germans*, 189–230.

[5] Letter to Paul Heyse of 1 January 1878, quoted on p.223 of Gay's collection cited in previous note. This letter, incidentally, precedes even the fateful agreement of 31 March 1878 (see p. 108), but Levi, as Ludwig's Kapellmeister in Munich, doubtless realized, even as he read the partially set libretto, that he was in line to conduct *Parsifal* one day.

[6] See John N. Burk, ed., *Letters of Richard Wagner*, 430–38.

wife sitting naked in the garden of their Lambeth home and reading *Paradise Lost*, to the consternation of the neighbours.

Wagner's health continued to cause Cosima anxiety. In addition to rheumatism and his other familiar complaints – including bowel disorders and a recurrence of erysipelas – he suffered chest pains in 1881 that his doctor failed to diagnose as a heart condition. It is possibly his tiredness and ill-health that account for the severity of the portrait of him sketched in oils by Renoir on 15 January 1882 in Palermo. The cardiac spasms continued in 1882 and at the end of March he had his first major heart attack.

Shortly before rehearsals began for *Parsifal*, the system of financing the festival was altered. The Society of Patrons was discontinued so that admission was open to anybody who paid for tickets in the usual way (though his undertaking to existing patrons was to be honoured by the giving of two special private performances). At the same time the *Bayreuther Blätter* took on a new role: instead of acting as a journal merely for members of the Society it was to spread the word to the nation as a whole. The idea of a music school was finally abandoned, but in order that students and other deserving people who could not afford to buy tickets might be enabled to attend the festival, he proposed the launching of a stipendiary foundation to provide a certain number of free places together with expenses. The principle of the scholarship fund that was set up in response to this proposal has been maintained to the present day.

Sixteen performances of *Parsifal* were given in July and August 1882 under Levi and Fischer. At the last one Wagner descended from the wings into the orchestra pit during the third act, took the baton from Levi and brought the work to its conclusion. In contrast to 1876 Wagner felt that broadly speaking justice had been done to the piece in terms of both singing and staging; the 1882 festival also produced a profit large enough to permit festivals in future years. To Wagner's regret and annoyance King Ludwig did not attend. In fact, they were not to see each other again: Ludwig spent the remaining years of his life increasingly isolated from the world and seeking consolation in music, mythology and fantastic castles. In 1886, three years after Wagner's death, he was officially declared insane and five days later he was found drowned in Lake Starnberg with his doctor.

Wagner took much pleasure in his flowermaidens at these performances, especially, it seems, one of the six solo singers, a young English soprano called Carrie Pringle. It has sometimes been suggested that Wagner and she had a sexual relationship, but although the possibility certainly cannot be ruled out, there is no positive evidence of such an affair.[7]

Still troubled by the insalubrious climate of Bayreuth Wagner moved with his family and entourage to Venice, where they occupied the mezzanine floor of the Palazzo Vendramin. His heart spasms continued but did not prevent him from rehearsing and performing his youthful C major Symphony on Christmas Eve in celebration of Cosima's birthday. In the last month of his life, February 1883, he began an essay entitled *On the Feminine in the Human*, which connected with some of the themes from a jotting in the Brown Book of nearly a year previous. He inveighs against the loveless marriages encouraged by society, advocates true love as the 'moulder of all noble races', and in the interests of culture and art recommends the elimination of the rigid, unequal division of the sexes. Although he had long since abandoned any political solution to the problems of social progress – indeed, in many respects he was now opposed to it – Wagner had continued to concern himself with such matters during his final years. Reflecting to Cosima on the shuttered, unoccupied Venetian palaces, he brought together his earlier social views and his later racial ones: ' "That is property! The root of all evil. Proudhon took a far too material view of it, for property brings about marriages for its sake, and in consequence causes the degeneration of the race" ' (Diaries, 5 February 1883).

On the day of his death, Tuesday 13 February 1883, Wagner rose late. According to the testimony of their daughter Isolde, he and Cosima had a furious row during the morning, apparently provoked by the announcement of a visit from Carrie Pringle. In any event, Wagner retired to his study to continue with *On the Feminine in the Human*, while Cosima went to the piano – a rare occurrence – and played Schubert's *Lob der Tränen* (In Praise of Tears), weeping as she played. Joukovsky arrived for lunch and at two o'clock Wagner sent word that they should not wait for him. The maid, Betty Bürkel, was the only one within earshot when Wagner suffered his final, fatal heart attack. She hurried in when he cried out and found him at his desk, the essay lying unfinished in front of him. Cosima was called

---

[7] See Herbert Conrad, 'Absturz aus Klingsors Zaubergarten' and Curt von Westernhagen, 'Wagner's Last Day'.

and the doctor summoned. Siegfried later recalled that his mother had left the room in such a frenzy that when she collided with the half-open door it almost splintered. Some time after three o'clock Wagner died. Cosima remained clasping his knees right through the night and could not be separated from him for twenty-five hours. She had always wanted to die with him and for some time it was feared that her neglect of her health would indeed bring this about.

The report of Wagner's Venetian physician, Dr Friedrich Keppler, described the primary disorders as being located in the stomach and intestines. He noted that the consequent strain on the heart was exacerbated by Wagner's vigorous participation in a wide range of social and artistic matters, and concluded: 'The actual attack which precipitated the abrupt end of the Master's life *must* have had a similar cause, but I cannot engage in speculation on the subject.' It would appear that Keppler knew or suspected what had agitated Wagner on that last day but was prevailed upon to keep silence. Whether or not Wagner had had, or was intending to have, an affair with Carrie Pringle, it may well have been the English flowermaiden who, with the announcement of her visit, was the unwitting cause of his death.[8]

Wagner's body was taken in a draped gondola to the station, from where it was conveyed by rail, with due ceremony, to Bayreuth. The town was in mourning: black flags fluttered from almost every building and the bells of all the churches tolled as the funeral pro-·cession wound its way from the station to the gates of Wahnfried. The burial took place in private, in the grounds of Wahnfried, attended by a restricted number of mourners. But the countless obituaries and memorials, as well as the tributes that flowed in from monarchs, statesmen, friends and fellow-artists, bore witness to the extraordinary and unique hold that Wagner had over the imagination of his time. Of all the epitaphs composed, perhaps the most honest contemporary appraisal was contained in that of Debussy some years later: '. . . Wagner's art will never perish utterly. It will be the victim of inevitable decay, time's brutal distraint upon all that is beautiful; all that remains will be beautiful ruins in whose shadows

---

[8] For more on the subject see the two articles cited in the previous note, and Martin Gregor-Dellin, *Richard Wagner: His Life, His Work, His Century*, 508, 518, 521.

our grandchildren will dream of the former greatness of this man who was underendowed only in humanity to be truly great.'[9]

[9] From 'Parsifal et la Société des Grandes Auditions de France', first published in *Gil Blas* on 6 April 1903. The article appears in an English translation in *Wagner*, iii (1982), 45–7.

9

'Bayreuth Idealism': the catastrophe

No attempt is made in this final chapter of the 'Life' to provide a complete history of Bayreuth or its stage productions,[1] nor to deal with the vast and complicated subject of Wagner's influence on later composers. Similarly, to treat adequately the impact of Wagnerian thought in non-musical spheres throughout the twentieth century is beyond the scope of this book.[2] Instead the present chapter picks up some of the important threads in the preceding story in order to follow through one aspect – but a crucially significant one – of the legacy of Wagner. By once again setting Wagner against a cultural and historical background it is possible to see what became of the institutions established by him and perhaps thereby to understand a little more clearly the nature of his idealism.

Already in Wagner's lifetime his tendency to behave as a monarch surrounded by a court was a subject for acerbic comment. One has only to recall Wagner's habit of gathering admirers round and dominating them, the autocratic manner in which he and Cosima dealt with most of their contemporaries, the expectation of utter subjugation to their wishes, the hierarchical way in which they ran Wahnfried, to realize that the commitment to democracy was merely skin-deep. Combining that with the sense of divine mission exuding from the later writings and the kind of self-aggrandizement expressed, for example, in the early days of King Ludwig's patronage – 'we three are immortal'[3] – it is not difficult to see why Wagner was

---

[1] See Geoffrey Skelton, *Wagner at Bayreuth*, for an informative treatment of the subject.

[2] The following studies may be of interest: John L. DiGaetani, *Richard Wagner and the Modern British Novel*; Anne Dzamba Sessa, *Richard Wagner and the English*; Raymond Furness, *Wagner and Literature*; Stoddard Martin, *Wagner to 'The Waste Land'*.

[3] *Brown Book*, 82.

often lampooned as enthroned or deified. His conviction that he was the ultimate expression of the German spirit – 'I am the most German being, I am the German spirit'[4] – caused him to be publicly reminded once that he did not have the monopoly of the German spirit.

As for the Bayreuth Festival, it was conceived as what appeared to be a 'democratic' and 'progressive' institution. Its purpose was to offer the new concept of music drama – the 'artwork of the future' – and the harmonies and orchestration of the latter were just two features that put Wagner among the avant garde of his day. After all, the enterprise was to ensure a complete break with the commercial theatre and its meretricious entertainment. But for all the progressive features of the festival idea, it contained within it the seeds of reaction. Wagner's insistence on an emotional rather than an intellectual response from his audience was an aspect of the strain of irrationalism in the nineteenth-century Germany psyche that was to be grotesquely cultivated in the Third Reich; the way in which all things un-Wagnerian were rejected as mediocrity had more than a whiff of élitism about it; and élitism and exclusivity were combined in the determination to ward off competition (particularly in the case of *Parsifal*). The exaltation of genius and inequality is, as Hans Mayer has pointed out,[5] central to all Wagner's major undertakings: the writing of an autobiography, the publication of the collected writings, the founding of the *Bayreuther Blätter*, the patronage of the Richard Wagner Societies.

The national component, élitism and reaction against social progress were synthesized by Wagner at the symbolic inauguration of the Festspielhaus, that is in the speech he made at the laying of the foundation stone (1872): on the one hand the venture could only succeed through the rebirth of the German spirit; on the other there was, he said, a danger that true genius was being smothered by what was generally regarded as 'social progress'. An article containing the text of this speech was sent to Bismarck with a letter angling for

---

[4] *Brown Book*, 73.

[5] *Richard Wagner in Bayreuth*, 35. I have found both Professor Mayer's book and the documentation on which it draws (Michael Karbaum, *Studien zur Geschichte der Bayreuther Festspiele (1876–1976)* invaluable in the writing of this chapter.

unspecified support: evidently the fear of becoming a state musician was less than that of the festival foundering altogether. Nonchalantly playing off Prussia against Bavaria, Wagner also approached Ludwig with renewed appeals, the success of which made Bayreuth possible but also had incalculable consequences for the future. It had always been Wagner's intention that Bayreuth should be independent both of the state and of the theatre establishment: the agreement with Munich ensured that it was neither. The settlement made to deal with the enormous deficit of the 1876 festival meant that Bayreuth was beholden to Munich until 1906, when the debt was repaid, and even beyond that.[6] And two separate attempts to launch a music school (first in Munich, then in Bayreuth) which could produce a new breed of singer had to be abandoned: artists therefore came from the traditional theatre circuit and Bayreuth was no more autonomous than any other major European opera house.

Another problem was never solved; how to make the festival accessible to the ordinary people. The institution of Richard Wagner Societies whose members could club together to subsidize a number of places was an improvement on the basic scheme of patrons' certificates, which restricted admission to a wealthy, privileged élite. Later schemes also enabled a few students to be present on scholarships, but none of this altered, or has ever altered, the essential class composition of the audience. The 1876 festival was attended by four crowned sovereigns and a host of aristocrats and representatives of the higher echelons of the bourgeois establishment. One hundred years later little had changed.

It was with considerable reluctance that Wagner accepted many of the necessary compromises: in order to inaugurate a festival at all he was forced to watch his Zurich ideal transform itself into the pragmatic reality of Bayreuth. Unfortunately, the measures improvised to deal with a series of crises became permanent and fossilized.

Nobody regarded Cosima as the natural successor in 1883, but she took over the direction with an assurance born of utter devotion to the wishes of her husband. Indeed, her production style was marked by so rigid a concept of fidelity to 'the Master's' ideas that it sacrificed the essential spark of inspiration and improvisation. Cosima herself was a natural actress and many of her stylistic principles were well motivated; however, in her determination to impress

---

[6] Michael Karbaum, *op. cit.*, 26, 53–6.

them on her performers she succeeded only in cramping their style and thus stifling any innovatory impulse on the Green Hill. To her credit, Cosima did succeed in founding a short-lived music school in Bayreuth in 1892, which produced a couple of singing actors who appeared in a succession of festivals, and she was often able to choose relatively inexperienced singers from the smaller German opera houses and groom them according to the 'Bayreuth style'. Of the early conductors, Richter, Levi, Mottl, Seidl and Fischer had all worked under Wagner and knew exactly what was required of them.

Ironically, Cosima came to be criticized by an influential faction of conservative Wagnerites at Bayreuth for *lack* of sympathy with Wagner's ideological principles. Her French background and connections were regarded as insidiously cosmopolitan. In a letter to the anti-semitic nationalist Ludwig Schemann, Martin Plüddemann, formerly a trusted friend of Wagner, wrote: 'Cosima's spirit, I fear, will finally be the grave of the *true* Bayreuth spirit. . . . Wagner's works can only be fully understood and reproduced from the depths of the German soul and of German music . . . More dangerous is the Bayreuth internationalism which through the essentially French – or in any case from top to toe un-German – nature of Cosima will bring about the ruin of Bayreuth!'[7]

Proposals for the succession on Wagner's death had included Liszt and Bülow. The latter's refusal was understandable but unfortunate because an administration by performers such as these might have encouraged innovation and creative experiment. Instead a dynasty was established that was based around Wahnfried and that, according to Cosima's will of 1913, ensured a male succession by specifically disendowing Siegfried's sisters.[8] Just as Cosima had stopped her diary on the day of Wagner's death, so she orientated the administration of the festival to the embalming of Wagner and his works. But even this preservation ritual did not satisfy the old guard. There were attempts to use the Richard Wagner Societies against her, and Cosima felt obliged to dissociate herself from the Gobineau Association set up in 1894 by Schemann and other members of the 'Bayreuth Circle'.

Cosima retired from the administration, through ill health and

[7] Letter of 25 February 1896; M. Karbaum, *op. cit.*, 50.

[8] Cosima's will dated 13 August 1913; M. Karbaum *op. cit.*, 59.

failing eyesight, after the 1906 festival, but she lived until 1 April 1930, dying at the age of ninety-two just a few months before Siegfried himself. The latter always maintained that his management of the festival was independent from his mother's influence, but her presence was certainly one to be reckoned with and in the years before the war (1908–14) there was little perceptible progress. In his five festivals following the reopening of the theatre in 1924 Siegfried made some cautious innovations: three-dimensional stage sets replaced the old flat painted scenery; the lighting was modernized; the composer's stage directions were even deliberately flouted. But Siegfried did not stray far from the path of hallowed tradition and rarely offended the old guard. The innovations of Adolphe Appia continued to be rejected; the Expressionist *Der fliegende Holländer* of Klemperer and Fehling at the Kroll Opera in Berlin inspired horror at Wahnfried; and Siegfried set his face against both the avant-garde composers of whom he was a contemporary (for example the Second Viennese School) and the experimentalists in the field of music theatre. His last new production, *Tannhäuser* in 1930, heralded a certain degree of emancipation, not least in the engagement of Arturo Toscanini – the first conductor in the history of Bayreuth to be summoned from outside Germany, a man progressive in outlook (as well as an outspoken anti-fascist), and an established 'star' as opposed to one groomed in the Bayreuth stable. There was also, in 1930, some evidence of a rapprochement with the new techniques and ideas of contemporary music theatre, but Siegfried's death makes the likely outcome of this a matter for pure speculation.

Siegfried Wagner was a man of liberal views who would not countenance racial discrimination. In 1921 he refused to exclude Jewish artists from Bayreuth, commenting: 'If the Jews are willing to help us that is doubly meritorious because my father attacked and insulted them in his writings ... whether a person is Chinese, a Negro, an American, an Indian or a Jew is to us a matter of complete indifference.'[9] Siegfried's retreat, in his own compositions, into a world of fairytale naivety may perhaps be regarded as a symptom of the same irrationalism that was then building to such a devastating climax in Germany, but regarding himself as an apolitical man, he attempted to distance himself from current trends. He had little

[9] Letter to August Püringer, reproduced in H. Zelinsky, *Richard Wagner: ein deutsches Thema*, 165.

sympathy with the 'Bayreuth Circle' which by now had harnessed an array of anti-progressive, anti-democratic forces in its self-appointed mission to preserve the works and perpetuate the ideas of Wagner. It was this militant nationalist group that was responsible for the outbreak of 'Deutschland, Deutschland, über Alles' after the performance of *Die Meistersinger* in 1924. Siegfried was furious, but partly because he believed in the separation of politics and art, and partly because he was concerned for Bayreuth's image among the festival's international clientèle. At this stage he was by no means unsympathetic to the rising Nazi movement, as is demonstrated by a little-known letter to him from Hitler while the latter was in detention after the failed Munich putsch[10] and Siegfried's appallingly naive comment about 'the power of love one finds in Hitler and Ludendorff'.[11]

A few words are necessary on the man who in 1923 actually brought Hitler to Wahnfried. It was Houston Stewart Chamberlain, the English aristocrat who, regarding his place of birth as a misfortune, took German nationality, married Wagner's daughter Eva and became one of the most influential ideologues of the pre-Nazi era. His *Grundlagen des 19. Jahrhunderts* (Foundations of the 19th Century) was an epic pseudo-history of the kind so in favour and its marked proclivity towards anti-modernism and racial prejudice confirmed its success. The book went through three editions in the year of publication, 1899, and by 1938 had sold a quarter of a million copies. Anti-semitism was fundamental to Chamberlain's analysis and he called for Teutonic blood to be purged of poisonous elements, of which the Jews were the foremost. He became a Nazi party member but should properly be regarded as a Wilhelminian, whose contribution was to popularize the proto-fascist doctrines that were circulating in Bayreuth and elsewhere.

Tracts were appearing in their hundreds celebrating the resurgence of the German spirit, advocating policies of militant aggression towards 'aliens', and addressing themselves to the 'Jewish question' in terms that varied between those of philosophical enquiry and rampant racial bigotry. So many took *Parsifal* and Wagner's later writings as their starting-point that the conclusion is

[10] Letter of 5 May 1924; M. Karbaum, *op. cit.*, 65.

[11] See Hans Mayer, *op cit.*, 104–7.

inescapable that these intellectuals saw themselves as carrying on his 'mission'.[12] An early example of this appeared in the year of Wagner's death, 1883: *Parsifal-Nachklänge. Allerhand Gedanken über Deutsche Cultur, Wissenschaft, Kunst, Gesellschaft* (Echoes of *Parsifal.* Sundry thoughts on German Culture, Learning, Art, Society),[13] gathered by Bernhard Förster. The work, which bears the Parsifalian epitaph 'Weisst Du, was Du sahst' (Do you know what you have seen), is dedicated to 'all true followers [*Anhänger*] of Richard Wagner, especially his dear friend and comrade-in-arms [*Mitstreiter*] Baron Hans Paul von Wolzogen in Bayreuth'. Förster, the brother-in-law of Nietzsche and the originator of the mass petition of 1881 against the Jews, refers in his introduction to *Parsifal* as 'God's son' and 'the son of a supreme genius truly begotten in the plenitude of his powers'. Alluding to the composer as the 'prophet of his People', he asks, 'What position does Richard Wagner occupy in the development of the German, Aryan culture?'

In the *Bayreuther Festblätter* of the following year the atmosphere and language of Wagner's late writings are reflected in an otherwise harmless poem called *Regeneration* by Heinrich von Stein,[14] the tutor of Siegfried Wagner. In 1894 the court chaplain Adolf Stöcker, an anti-semite admired by Cosima Wagner, contributed an article to the *Musikalisches Wochenblatt*[15] interpreting *Parsifal* in a narrowly Christian manner and comparing Bayreuth and *Parsifal* with Oberammergau and the Passion Play.

But the chief forum for the exposition of the doctrines that became known as 'Bayreuth Idealism' was the *Bayreuther Blätter*, the periodical established by Wagner and Wolzogen under the latter's editorship in 1878. A couple of examples must suffice here. In an issue of 1890[16] Alexander Ritter begins a piece with Liszt,

---

[12] An overwhelming, and sobering, selection of these documents is reproduced in H. Zelinsky, *op. cit.*

[13] H. Zelinsky, *op. cit.*

[14] H. Zelinsky, *op. cit.*

[15] *Musikalisches Wochenblatt*, xxv (1894), 454–5. Reproduced in H. Zelinsky, *op. cit.*, 84–5.

[16] Vol. xii, p. 380. Reproduced in part in H. Zelinsky, *op. cit.*, 75.

moving on to Wagner's essay *The Public in Time and Space*, only to develop an argument contrasting an 'Aryan philosophy of art' with a 'Semitic' one. Wolzogen himself responded to the mood of 1914 with an article elevating the spiritual art of which he and other right-thinking people were the guardians over the tawdry profanities of the world.[17] In mystical terms he urges his fellow-strivers after truth to 'watch over the treasure of art which may one day with God's grace transform itself again into a Holy Grail'. Wagner's Festspielhaus is, of course, the shrine as well as something more: 'Bayreuth is not only a sanctuary, a refuge, but also a power station of the spirit of that inner world which we might in a word term idealism. And so we who gladly call ourselves idealists should be as it were the conduits through which the spiritual power of idealism flows forth to other distant souls, as many as are responsive to it, in the world outside, which cannot satisfy truly living souls.' Nothing illustrates better the perniciously hermetic and narcissistic place Bayreuth had become by 1914 than this sanctimonious gibberish.

Wolzogen edited the *Bayreuther Blätter* for all six decades of its existence, 1878–1938. During that time it became the organ of more and more societies and leagues, all with similar names and all devoted to the promotion of 'unsere Sache' ('our affair' or 'mission'). One of them, the Richard Wagner-Gesellschaft, founded in 1926, adopted the so-called 'Aryan paragraph' in its constitution.

Nor, with Hitler's rise to power, can all Wagner conductors and scholars be exculpated: some went no further than allowing themselves to be carried away on the wave of nationalist hysteria; others were NSDAP sympathizers or even members. The cases of Strauss and Furtwängler are well known; those of Karajan and Böhm have also been documented elsewhere.[18] Of the scholars, Karl Grunsky wrote an anti-semitic pamphlet entitled *Richard Wagner und die Juden* as early as 1920,[19] the distinguished Wahnfried archivist Otto Strobel paid fulsome tribute in 1933 to 'our great Chancellor *Adolf Hitler*', than whom no previous leading statesman has done

[17] 'Nach 1913', vol. i/iii (1914), 3. Reproduced in H. Zelinsky, *op. cit.*, 128.

[18] See Fred K. Prieberg, *Musik im NS-Staat*, for an admirably documented study of music and musicians in the Third Reich.

[19] See H. Zelinsky, *op. cit.*, 164.

more to promote and protect German art;[20] Curt von Westernhagen, in his 1935 publication *Richard Wagners Kampf gegen seelische Fremdherrschaft* (Richard Wagner's Struggle against Spiritual Foreign Rule), celebrated Wagner as 'a German of the Nordic stamp' (*Deutscher nordischer Prägung*), protagonist in the struggle against alien racial elements – 'for the German revolution is a *revolution of the blood*';[21] the work and impact of the influential musicologist Alfred Lorenz are discussed in the next chapter.

During the Third Reich the Bayreuth Festival, now administered by Siegfried's wife Winifred, with Heinz Tietjen as artistic director, came under the personal protection of Hitler. As a devotee of Wagner and a close friend of Winifred, Hitler was a regular visitor to Bayreuth. Images of the Festspielhaus patronized by the Nazis and of Wagner used as propaganda have burned themselves into twentieth-century consciousness. Interestingly, many leading Nazis did not share Hitler's predisposition towards Wagner's music, but that did not prevent him favouring Bayreuth with privileges and money. Wagner's wishes were fulfilled in bizarre circumstances when the Reich took over 11,310 tickets in the price range 15–30 Marks, in order to make them available to people in low-income brackets.[22] In the years 1936–9 the Reich Chancellery provided an annual subsidy of about 100,000 Marks and there was also strong support from the organization Kraft Durch Freude (Strength Through Joy), who put up 1,600,000 Marks in 1942 alone.[23] Subsidies such as these may best be regarded as a continuation of the tradition of financial support given to Bayreuth by state and business interests from the time of its foundation.

The purpose of this chapter is not to argue that Wagner was a proto-Nazi or that if he had been born a few decades later he would have abandoned his purple silk shirt for brown cloth drill. Rather it is an attempt to trace part of the course of idealism in Germany and point up the continuity of a cultural and ideological tradition.

---

[20] 'Zum Geleit' in the *Bayreuther Festspielführer* for 1933; see H. Zelinsky, *op. cit.*, 215. See also F. Prieberg, *op. cit.*, 40f.

[21] See H. Zelinsky, *op. cit.*, 234.

[22] See Hans Mayer, *op. cit.*, 137.

[23] *loc. cit.*

Wagner's unparalleled mastery as a composer and his extraordinarily charismatic personality encouraged many people in his own time and later to regard him as an exceptional cultural phenomenon. The reality is that in countless ways he was an entirely characteristic symptom of his age, reflecting its outlook, its prejudices and its neuroses. But the power and individuality of his utterance were such that he seemed to speak for his era. He acted as a focus for German idealism and reflected and magnified its values, appearing to give them definitive expression. Thus it was that as idealism ran its course and approached its catastrophic culmination Wagner, like Nietzsche, could be seen as a patriarchal figure and to later generations, in retrospect, as a progenitor of Hitlerism instead of just a highly influential artist who was working in a particular tradition.

It must be repeated that this chapter has attempted to describe only part of the history of Bayreuth in the decades since Wagner's death: the part that connects most directly with the cultural and ideological outlook dealt with in the preceding chapters. There is a more favourable aspect, another story which could also have been told: that of the artistic innovations made in and after 1951; the reappraisal of Wagner's aesthetics by Mann, Adorno, Bloch and others; the determination shown by historians to confront and illumine the terrible facts of the past; the efforts of musicologists to find new, more appropriate ways of analysing and evaluating Wagner's music. Without that aspect the story is admittedly incomplete but until we are able to accept the full implications of Wagner and all he stood for, we are not properly equipped to face the future.

10
The music

The logical place to begin an examination of any composer's music is with the sketches, which often provide revealing clues as to the method of composition. In Wagner's case they help us to establish some of the facts of the initial stages of conception and elaboration, as opposed to the composer's autobiographical fantasies, which have for too long been promulgated as gospel truth (see, for example, the chapter on the *Ring*, especially pp. 196–200).

The first thing to observe about Wagner's manuscripts is the handwriting. His preliminary sketching, done in pencil very rapidly, has often proved difficult for scholars to decipher accurately. However, when he came to write out his scores in ink, the hand is neat and stylish: Wagner's are some of the most beautiful composer's autographs in existence. The sketching of *Rheingold, Walküre, Siegfried* Acts I and II and most of *Tristan* coincides with Wagner's relationship with Mathilde Wesendonck, who no doubt took some pleasure in inking over his initial drafts in pencil. Her task was lightened by cryptic little love messages that Wagner wrote to her. The sketch for Act I of *Walküre* includes the following: 'L.d.m.M.?' ('Liebst du mich Mathilde?'/Do you love me, Mathilde?) and 'D.b.m.a.!!' ('Du bist mir alles'/You are everything to me).

A general word is also necessary here on the nomenclature of the sketches. The nomenclature devised by the Bayreuth archivist Otto Strobel when, between the wars, he undertook the enormous task of cataloguing the sketches, is still used by many writers today. But other scholars find the terminology inadequate: 'composition sketch' for the first continuous draft, for example, suggests that the compositional process was limited to this stage, while 'orchestral sketch' gives the impression that the work was immediately elaborated into something like an orchestral score. Neither is true, but the terms are further misleading in that they take no account of the fact that Wagner's method changed as he progressed from his early works to the later ones. To apply the term composition sketch both to the sketches for individual numbers in *Der fliegende Holländer* and to the continuous advanced draft of *Walküre* is to imply that they were conceived in a similar way, words and music pouring out in a simultaneous stream of inspiration. For those who have wished to present the early works as music dramas rather than operas, Strobel's nomenclature has been a useful smokescreen; indeed, Strobel himself is not guiltless.

More about the various stages in Wagner's composition can be found in Robert Bailey's informative article 'The Method of Composition'.[1] But Bailey's nomenclature, though a vast improvement on Strobel's, is not beyond reproach[2] and I have preferred in this book to use the terms adopted by the *Wagner-Werkverzeichnis*[3] which are likely to become the most widely accepted and authoritative. A table showing the stages in each of the works is given in Appendix E.

Wagner's major contribution to the history of music was, of course, the music drama. To a greater or lesser extent, opera composers before him had subjected dramatic considerations to musical; for Wagner the 'absolute melody' of Rossini seemed to bear no relation to the words or to the dramatic action. Wagner's aim was for a musical declamation that carried all the nuances of the text and through which the dramatic action could be articulated, while maintaining interest in purely melodic terms. Such a process is foreshadowed in the operas *Der fliegende Holländer*, *Tannhäuser* and *Lohengrin*, but it is only in the music dramas, from *Das Rheingold* on, that it can be seen to have come to fruition.

Wagner's concept of the ideal musico-poetic line, a synthesis of the melodic and dramatic functions, was formulated in *Opera and Drama*, the chief of the series of theoretical essays dating from his first years of exile in Zurich. The chapters following chart his progress towards the prescriptions put forward in those essays, and the extent to which he adhered to or departed from them is discussed. The central idea of the Zurich essays is the *Gesamtkunstwerk*, or 'total work of art', by which Wagner meant a union of all the

[1] In *The Wagner Companion*, ed. P. Burbidge and R. Sutton, 269–338.

[2] See John Deathridge, 'The Nomenclature of Wagner's Sketches'.

[3] J. Deathridge, M. Geck and E. Voss, *Verzeichnis der musikalischen Werke Richard Wagners und ihrer Quellen*.

disciplines: music, poetry, dance, architecture, sculpture and painting. The term is used in *The Artwork of the Future* alongside similar terms such as 'the complete work of art of the future' and 'the universal drama':[4] all refer to the same idea, and underlying it is the assumption that it is the dramatic representation of the subject matter to which all the elements contribute.

Wagner's ideas on the comparative importance of music and poetry underwent several changes during his career. In his essays, stories and letters of the 1830s and early 1840s there are many references to music as an inimitable mode of expression; however, from his tendency to vacillate one may best conclude that at this time he was seeking the ideal terms on which to base a marriage of music and poetry. The emphasis on drama, or rather the 'poetic intent', in the Zurich essays contrasts with this earlier outlook, but not long after, with his conversion in 1854 to the philosophy and aesthetics of Schopenhauer – according to which music was the medium uniquely capable of expressing the inner meaning of existence – came a shift in priorities from drama to music. The new ascendancy of music can be seen in *Tristan* and *Die Meistersinger* and is also evident in the description of his works that can be found in an 1872 essay: 'deeds of music that have become visible'.[5] In the same essay, Wagner repudiated his earlier designation of them as 'music dramas', but this is the term by which all the works from *Das Rheingold* on are now known, and the term seems unexceptionable.

Another much-discussed term found in Wagner's writings is 'unending melody'.[6] The product of this concept was a continuous melodic line that evades cadence and avoids periodicity. The line is not always literally unbroken in the vocal part – if only on account of the necessity for the singer to breathe – but any gaps are likely to be filled in by the orchestra. The latter also serves to bridge changes of rhythm or tempo, so that a smooth, continuous flow is achieved. The end of a phrase in the vocal line may be elided with the beginning of a

---

[4] 'Gesamtkunstwerk': Sämtliche Schriften, iii, 156; 'das vollendete Kunstwerk der Zukunft': *ibid.*, 96; 'das *allgemeinsame* Drama': *ibid.*, 96.

[5] *Über die Benennung 'Musikdrama'*, Sämtliche Schriften, ix, 306 ('*ersichtlich gewordene Taten der Musik*').

[6] 'Unendliche Melodie'; '*Zukunftsmusik*', Sämtliche Schriften, vii, 130.

new motif in the orchestra, or the voice may come to the end of a phrase with no orchestral accompaniment, at which the orchestra enters and leads off with a new motif or a new tonality, or both. The importance of this concept for Wagner, however, lay not so much in its technical manifestation as in its aesthetic principle. For Wagner, and nineteenth-century composers generally, every musical idea had to contribute something original to justify itself; formulas, such as merely cadential figures, were not admissible. Wagner rejected the traditional idea of a melody – exemplified in extreme form for him by Rossini – because its symmetrical, periodic structure was bound to result in 'filling-in' with non-essential matter. Instead he advocated the Beethovenian kind of melody in which nothing was superfluous; this unbroken, 'unending' melody formed the basis of his musico-poetic synthesis.

It is in the major essay *Opera and Drama* that Wagner expatiates on the system of motifs that subsequently became known as leitmotifs. The leitmotif, an anglicization of the German *Leitmotiv* (leading motif), is a short musical idea associated with a particular character, object, emotion or concept. The principle of such a recurring motif had been used by earlier composers[7] but it was Wagner's self-liberation from closed forms like the aria (in *Der fliegende Holländer* onwards) that opened the way for a new, revolutionary application of the idea. For Wagner it was an ideal structural device because it was able to bind together ideas that were linked in musico-poetic terms: unlike, say, sonata form it was not a purely musical procedure. Referring to leitmotifs as 'melodic impulses' (*melodische Momente*), Wagner said in *Opera and Drama* that these impulses, consisting of presentiments and reminiscences, would be strictly connected with the dramatic situation and he saw them being developed by the orchestra, in the course of the construction of the drama, into something like 'signposts for the emotions' (*Gefühlswegweiser*). Wagner did not himself use the word 'Leitmotiv' – at least not in his writings;[8] other terms used in his essays include 'thematisches Motiv', 'Hauptmotiv' and 'Grundthema'.

[7] For a good summary see the article 'Leitmotif' in the *New Grove*. See also Robert T. Laudon, *Sources of the Wagnerian Synthesis*, esp. 22–86.

[8] I know of only one reference: *Über die Anwendung der Musik auf das Drama*, Sämtliche Schriften, x, 185. Wagner there refers noncommittally to Wolzogen's use of the term.

If one takes leitmotif in the strict sense of motif of reminiscence as prescribed in *Opera and Drama* (that is, the motif originates in the musico-poetic line but subsequent appearances are in the orchestra), it is only in the *Ring* that Wagner comes at all close to meeting all his own demands. The principle is faintly discernible in *Die Feen, Das Liebesverbot* and *Rienzi*; in the *Holländer* the Redemption motif is the main motif of reminiscence; *Tannhäuser* has almost none; in *Lohengrin* there is an approximately equal proportion of motifs of reminiscence (or something similar) and ordinary motifs. By *Das Rheingold* the larger part of the motifs are now motifs of reminiscence; the subsequent fate of the leitmotif is dealt with fully in the chapters on the *Ring, Tristan, Die Meistersinger* and *Parsifal*. Although structure in Wagner's works is not simply a matter of motivic integration – rather a combination of this with underlying tonal processes – it may be pointed out that it is only in the mature music dramas that the leitmotif acquires a role of real significance in terms of the large-scale structural organization.

In Wagner's day his music was advocated and deprecated equally as 'music of the future'. The description refers primarily to the new conception of music drama, but to many nineteenth-century ears Wagner's harmonic style was also bewilderingly avant garde. It was not, however, the harmonic vocabulary that was unfamiliar so much as the way it was used. Wagner seized on a wide range of devices that had become increasingly prominent in the first half of the century: he adapted them, expanded them, and thereby enriched the musical language of his day.

The chord of the $\frac{6}{4}$, or second inversion, for example, is a tonic chord sounded over a dominant bass, which thus contains a fundamental ambiguity that threatens the tonic/dominant polarity of the tonal system, a possibility already realized by Beethoven and Schubert and much exploited by the later Romantics. use of the $\frac{6}{4}$ in the Classical and Romantic eras was governed by universally accepted rules, but Wagner felt free to employ the chord at the beginning or end of a period, or indeed anywhere if it provided the required effect – generally one of instability. The instability, however, is frequently short-lived; it may colour, but does not ultimately undermine the primacy of, the root-position major and minor triads.

Serving a similar function of enhancement is the chord of the diminished 7th, ubiquitous in Romantic music and used to excess by some composers (though its association with the melodramatic and the supernatural did not, in pre-Hollywood times, have quite the hackneyed ring that it came to acquire later). In Mozart's music the diminished 7th actually reinforces the status of the tonic, because it usually resolves onto either the dominant or the tonic itself. In Wagner's later works the chord is used as a means of suspending the sense of tonality. Even when it is used for pictorial effect (as in the Dutchman's music in the *Holländer*) there are always wider implications for the tonality.

The chord of the dominant 7th, which held a commanding position in the hierarchy of the Classical tonal system, is given a new dimension by Wagner. His constant refusal to resolve his dominant 7ths onto their expected tonics is another aspect of his enrichment of tonality. Without the usual cadential resolution there is much less certainty as to which is the predominant key at a particular time. Higher-powered chords of the dominant – the 9th, 11th and 13th – also appear frequently. Often these will resolve conventionally onto a dominant 7th (which may or may not then itself resolve); in such a context, the experience of the dominant 7th becomes one of relative relaxation. Thus it is that perceptions of dissonance have shifted.

The whole range of secondary 7ths form another part of Wagner's harmonic vocabulary. They are used in all inversions and with all the accidentals arising from the various major and minor forms. These variants thus frequently take on the appearance of chromatically altered chords and because of their unconventional usage it is sometimes difficult to distinguish the two. A particularly favourite chord is the secondary 7th on the second or seventh degree of the scale, which results in a distinctive configuration of two minor 3rds and a major 3rd. It is often resolved onto a diminished 7th (Ex. 1a) or a dominant 7th (Ex. 1b):

Ex. 1

This chord is also sometimes known, rather confusingly, as the 'half-diminished' 7th.

A characteristic feature of Wagner's harmonic style is his use of augmented chords, especially those of the 5th and 6th. The former crops up regularly as a method of giving spice to the ordinary major triad. The following, from *Siegfried*, is the beginning of a long series of augmented 5ths:

Ex. 2

The chord is particularly common in *Die Meistersinger* and can be heard prominently in the scene in Act II in which Sachs teases Beckmesser by hammering an accompaniment to his serenade.

The augmented 6th is a familiar chord in Romantic harmony. Wagner uses it in all three of its common manifestations: the 'Italian 6th' (with major 3rd), the 'French 6th' (with major 3rd and augmented 4th, as in Ex. 3a below) and the 'German 6th' (with major 3rd and perfect 5th or doubly augmented 4th). In his mature harmonic style Wagner more often than not dresses up the approach and resolution of the chord with chromatic passing notes. The conventional resolution of the augmented 6th is onto the dominant or onto the dominant preceded by the $\frac{6}{4}$ of the tonic, but Wagner's resolutions are unpredictable: if it is the dominant it is almost certain to be embellished or protracted in some way, but it is equally likely to be a 7th or even a 9th in a remote key. Ex. 3, from *Götterdämmerung*, Act I, scene 3, shows a typical Wagnerian resolution:

Ex. 3 (a)

(a) shows the conventional resolution onto the dominant; (b) shows how Wagner draws it out. The A flat and F sharp, which form the

Ex. 3 (b)

Brünnhilde

Dass sein Zorn sich ver - zo - gen, weiss ich auch.

augmented 6th itself, resolve onto a unison G, but the resolution of
the C is suspended. Meanwhile, the upper G continues on a chromatic
path through G sharp, which is treated as an appoggiatura intensifying a dominant 7th. The dominant 7th is repeated (as dictated by
the vocal line) and the resolution onto G is eventually achieved.
Ultimate resolution is never in doubt: the delays and embellishments
are merely for expressive effect.

There is a deeper significance in the use of augmented chords
than that they add a chromatic spice: they also serve to divide the
octave symmetrically, whereas the tonic/dominant polarity of the
Classical tonal system depends on an asymmetrical division. The
whole-tone scale is a symmetrical division of the octave, and both the
tritone and the augmented 5th can be extracted from the whole-tone
scale. So can the augmented 6th, and the 'French' form, with augmented 4th (see Ex. 3), has a special whole-tone flavour. Minor 3rds
also divide the octave symmetrically, and it is for that reason that the
diminished 7th (which is made up of minor 3rds) is an effective
means of suspending tonality over short periods. Symmetrical
division of the octave in the music of Wagner – and of certain
contemporaries, notably Liszt – represented a challenge to the tonal
system. But even while testing and stretching its limits, Wagner never
abandoned that system.

The same is true in respect of his predilection for the mediant
and submediant relationship, in place of the Classical dominant.
Whereas Haydn and Mozart had firmly established the dominant as
the main subsidiary key in their sonata structures, the key in which

the second subject would appear and one of the possible tonalities for the slow movement (occasionally the submediant or flattened submediant was employed for exotic effect), Beethoven and Schubert began consciously to explore the possibilities of third-related keys. Composers of the Romantic period eagerly seized the opportunities for sensuous indulgence offered, in the process enhancing the expressive potentiality of the Classical tonal system. Wagner constantly deployed keys a 3rd apart: the central polarity of Act I of *Götterdämmerung* is E flat/B, an association signalled in a characteristic way by the opening two chords of the act – B being spelt here as C flat; the F sharp minor of the pivotal *Todesverkündigung* (Annunciation of Death) scene in Act II of *Die Walküre* is a 3rd away from the A minor which opens the act and a 3rd away from the D minor which closes it; third-relationships in *Tristan* are discussed in chapter 17. But the fact remains that the dominant is still in Wagner's style the chord of most importance after the tonic: asymmetry and third-relations achieve their effect primarily as deviations from the norm.

It will have been noticed that none of the elements of Wagner's harmonic style is new: his innovations lay in his revolutionary application of them. His unprepared and unresolved 7ths and 9ths, his elliptical treatment of traditional progressions, and his anticipation, embellishment and suspension of them, all contributed towards the emancipation of the dissonance. Ex. 4, from *Götterdämmerung*, Act I, scene 3, shows a typical Wagnerian ellipsis:

Ex. 4

The dominant 13th at (a) might have been resolved with a dominant 7th under the C sharp at (b), but instead there is another dissonance – the C sharp being treated as an appoggiatura. This in turn might have resolved onto a G major chord, but Wagner gives the screw another twist by harmonizing the B with a chord of the 7th (c).

It is often hard to distinguish harmonic from non-harmonic notes, because the contexts of which they are a part are so rapidly changing. Ex. 5, also from *Götterdämmerung* (Act II, scene 4), shows the devices of anticipation and suspension working to an even greater effect of intensification:

Ex. 5

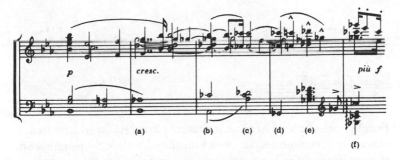

The dominant 13th at (a) fails to resolve in the usual way, the G instead beginning a chromatic descent which is only completed at (f). Meanwhile, at (b) the chord of A flat minor is anticipated in the lower register; it follows two beats later in the upper register, by which time a dominant 7th on D flat has sounded (c). The resolution of the G flat is, however, suspended for a beat and this F is in turn suspended at (d). At (d) the resolution of the D flat 7th is anticipated but it is finally achieved only at (e) and then onto another 7th which requires resolution onto (f). No new harmonies as such, then, but a radical way of treating the old ones, by compression and elision. Looked at in the broader context of the underlying tonal progression (E flat to C flat) one might describe the passage rather differently: as an example of Wagner's enrichment of tonality by means of prolongation.

Another traditional device that Wagner took over and adapted for his own ends is the sequence. Whereas Baroque and Classical composers tended to proceed sequentially by steps of a tone up or down (often with intermediate dominants or dominant 7ths), Wagner gave himself complete freedom to move in cycles a semitone, a tone, a minor 3rd, major 3rd or a 4th apart. The 3rd especially was

favoured as this gave an extra expressive thrust, both on account of
the leap of a 3rd and because the sensation of modulating from, say,
C to E or A was an appealing one in itself. Wagner's sequential moves
are quite unpredictable, but the apparent anarchy is deliberate and
controlled. Another common procedure of his is to detach smaller
units from a larger sequential phrase; the sequential treatment of
the smaller, foreshortened units gives the music an added sense of
urgency, as in these bars from *Tristan*, Act II:

Ex. 6

Usually melodic and harmonic elements are developed simultaneously, but sometimes sequences are disguised, so that the progression
is completed in the harmony while the melodic line moves on to a
new idea. The sequence is a central feature of Wagner's style; a large
part of its attraction for him must have lain in its potential for
offering unity in diversity. Repetition is a standard means of achiev-
ing unity (cf. the recapitulation in sonata form), but the Wagnerian
style is essentially mobile and evolutionary; sequential repetition
satisfied both demands. In addition it allowed him to move through
keys that were adjacent but tonally remote (e.g. C, D and E major),
because sequential progression integrates potentially alien harmonies.[9]

   Wagner's tonal procedures naturally changed during the course
of his career; increasing subtlety and complexity mark his shaping of
a technique that has been called an 'associative' use of tonality.[10]

[9] See Ernst Kurth, *Romantische Harmonik*, 333ff (unfortunately not
available in an Eng. trans.) for a classic analysis of the Wagnerian
sequence.

[10] See Robert Bailey, 'The Structure of the *Ring* and its Evolution', 51ff,
where he also discusses an 'expressive' use of tonality, and Patrick
McCreless, *Wagner's Siegfried: Its Drama, History, and Music*, for an
exhaustive analysis of the musical structure of *Siegfried*.

This can take one of two forms. In the first, a motif or melody is associated with notes of a particular pitch. An example is the horn call in *Der fliegende Holländer*, which is usually based on a B minor triad. Its appearances are mostly made in contexts of B minor and only very occasionally is the horn call used to swing the music round to that key. However, in the mature music dramas this is precisely what such calls are often made to do. The nightwatchman's horn in *Die Meistersinger* sounds a single note: F sharp. Each of its appearances in Act II initiates a switch to the Romantic midsummer night's key of B major. It thus plays an important part in determining tonal direction. Siegfried's horn call in *Siegfried* and *Götterdämmerung*, on the other hand, tends to have a more short-term effect. It is always heard in F major when played on the stage – rather than by an instrument in the orchestra pit – but it does not necessarily affect the overall tonal orientation of the scene. The other form of 'associative' use of tonality is the identification of particular tonalities with particular characters or ideas. In the following chapters (see pp. 176–7, 189 and 217–18) it is demonstrated how a simple association between a single character and a tonality (e.g. Lohengrin and A major, Elsa and A flat major) gives way in the later works to a considerably less clear-cut procedure.

Whenever the question of Wagnerian formal analysis comes up, the name of Alfred Lorenz is inescapable. Lorenz was a German musicologist active in the 1920s and 30s who aimed to show that Wagner's works could be broken down into units of different formal types, chiefly the *Bogen* (arch: ABA) and *Bar*, the medieval verse form – borrowed for *Die Meistersinger* (two identical strophes and an after-song: AAB).[11] Lorenz propounded his theory with devastating thoroughness, and the obedient manner in which period after period – over enormous canvases – allowed themselves to fall into place in his scheme gave the analyses an air of conviction and authority that went virtually unchallenged for a generation.

Lorenz's approach to Wagner has to be seen as an aspect of his ideological outlook. In the *Zeitschrift für Musik* he wrote in April 1939 a eulogy of Hitler entitled 'Music greets the Führer'. It ends as

---

[11] Three of Lorenz's articles have been translated and published in *Wagner*, ii (1981), nos 1, 2 and 3. Gerald Abraham devoted several pages to Lorenz, including an analysis of Act I of *Die Walküre*, in *A Hundred Years of Music*, 121–9.

follows: 'The true, secret, strong music of our time still lives on outside musical composition. This rings out in the march step of the regiments, in the rhythm of work, in the throbbing of engines and propellers; it rings out in the final *harmony of German hearts*, in the will to elevate the German people, in the will to power! *Hail to our saviour and leader!*' (Lorenz's italics).[12] The obsessive desire to press every constituent unit into the service of a higher, all-encompassing master-plan is characteristic of the fascist mentality: the individual is submerged into the collective, and single bars achieve validity only as elements ordered in a larger structure. Lorenz's methodology was so perfectly attuned to the prevailing ethos of the Third Reich that it became impregnable: criticism of his approach would have been all but impossible during the Nazi years.

In the 1960s and 70s Lorenz's findings began to be challenged in an academically rigorous manner, and Carl Dahlhaus and a new generation of scholars (predominantly German) brought Wagnerian formal analysis to maturity. By 1981 it was possible to say: 'The seemingly indigestible lump of Lorenz has finally been broken down, its nutritious portions digested, its harmful ones expelled.'[13] One of the lessons learned is that it is dangerous and misleading to regiment Wagner's music into preordained schemes.[14] The acts of his operas – as, indeed, is the case with operas of other composers – do not behave according to the dictates of symphonic form: the demands of the text, the dramatic motivation and the sheer time-scale of an opera render that particular mode of tonal cohesion inappropriate. Instead, the unity of Wagner's works depends on large-scale tonal processes, still with the Classical tonal system at the root, but enlarged to suit the needs of the drama. In such a macrocosm a

---

[12] The piece is reproduced in H. Zelinsky, *Richard Wagner: ein deutsches Thema*, 236.

[13] Anthony Newcomb, 'The Birth of Music out of the Spirit of Drama: an Essay in Wagnerian Formal Analysis'.

[14] A critique of Lorenz accessible for a non-specialist audience is Egon Voss's essay 'Noch einmal: das Geheimnis der Form bei Richard Wagner', in *Theaterarbeit an Wagners Ring*, ed. D. Mack. An Eng. trans. of this can be found in *Wagner*, iv (1983), 66–79. The more rigorous critiques are listed on p. 218 of David R. Murray's useful 'Major Analytical Approaches to Wagner's Musical Style'.

modulation may be undertaken simply to allow the curse on the ring to sound in B minor, or the sword in C major, but the tonal framework of the act is not necessarily affected. Moreover, many of Wagner's larger units are governed by 'directional tonality', that is to say a tonal system in which the centre of gravity shifts from one key to another.[15]

Lorenz claimed that his system was based on Wagner's own exposition of the 'poetic-musical period'.[16] But Wagner was describing passages in which the *Stabreim* (alliteration) of the text was complemented by the modulations of the musical setting, and this is an aspect ignored by Lorenz. The greatest error is to try to divide Wagner's music into anything like regular units. While he did not altogether abandon four- and eight-bar phrases after *Lohengrin* (they can still be found in *Götterdämmerung*, for example), periodicity has unquestionably given way in the music dramas to less regular groupings. The characteristic style of the post-*Rheingold* works is a kind of musical prose, consisting of regular and irregular units juxtaposed; indeed, irregular patterns are no longer experienced as deviations from a norm.

Vestiges of traditional forms like the strophic song (repeated stanzas with or without refrain) are still to be found even in the music dramas, but always modified in some way so that expectation is thwarted. The result is that Wagner's works are assemblages of disparate and hybrid structures. A conventional song form, ABA, may be initiated and turn into something quite different. Wagner's structures are constantly evolving; their dynamic nature is determined from the inside. Consequently any attempt to impose from the outside an architectonic structure – such as would be appropriate for a Mozart symphony – is doomed. A convincing analysis is much more likely to reveal spontaneous generation and ambiguity than neat sectionalized patterns.

The tonal structure of these works is correspondingly complex. One of the most characteristic media in the music dramas is that which Schoenberg called 'wandering' or 'floating tonality'. In passages of this kind, the music passes through a succession of keys

---

15 On 'directional' tonality, and also 'associative' tonality, see Patrick McCreless, *Wagner's Siegfried*.

16 See *Oper und Drama*, Sämtliche Schriften, iv, 152–5.

for each of which the primary relationship is with that preceding and following it: the tonalities are links in a chain, and there is no necessary connection for any except the adjacent tonality. In passages of 'expanded tonality', on the other hand, a particular key is felt as the central force shaping the structure; either subsidiary keys or passages of chromatic flux may intervene but the ultimate effect is that of reinforcing the tonality that has been established as the tonic.[17] (As an example of this, the end of *Siegfried* might be given, where C major is firmly established as the tonic from the moment of Brünnhilde's awakening; several keys are traversed in the following duet but the final return to C is experienced as inevitable.) Against these two forms of tonality, pure diatonicism is comparatively uncommon in the music dramas, but the beginnings and ends of *Rheingold* and *Parsifal* may be cited as examples. In passages where chromatic flux is in evidence, shape may well be provided by less traditional means: tonally stable and unstable passages may be contrasted, or a referential sonority such as a diminished 7th or the '*Tristan* chord' may be used.

The following chapters trace the development of Wagner's style from the gradual loosening of the 'number' structure in the early works, through the division of *Der fliegende Holländer* into scenes, through the nearly continuous *Tannhäuser* and *Lohengrin*, to the varied and intricate structures of the music dramas. Did Wagner achieve his aim of creating the artwork of the future? Or was he, in Debussy's famous phrase, a 'beautiful sunset that was mistaken for a dawn'? In terms of opera as a medium, things were never the same again: Wagner's innovations may not have gone entirely according to plan, but they were a necessary stage in the evolution of the genre. In terms of harmonic language there is a sense in which Debussy was absolutely correct: Wagner's expansion and enrichment of the Classical tonal system may also be seen – and this is perhaps the more traditional view – as the dissolution of tonality. From this perspective it marked the end of an era (an end that was protracted by others for a considerable time) and it fell to Schoenberg to undertake the task of constructing a new system. Wagner's emancipation of the dissonance, his discovery that music could actually convey the en-

---

[17] The various writings of Arnold Whittall (see Bibliography) have done much to establish the notion of Wagner's 'enrichment' rather than 'dissolution' of tonality.

joyment of pain,[18] and that ambiguity was a valid mode of expression: all this changed the language of music for ever, but it was left to others to build anew on the foundations of the old.

[18] In Adorno's estimation Wagner was the first to stretch the expressive values of harmony beyond their traditional function. Consonance and dissonance no longer necessarily stood for affirmation and fulfilment on the one hand, negation and suffering on the other. Instead, a single chord could tell 'both of the poignant pain of non-fulfilment and of the pleasure that lies in the tension'. See *In Search of Wagner*, 67.

11

Die Feen and Das Liebesverbot

Wagner's first three operas – discounting *Die Hochzeit*, of which only an introduction, chorus and septet were set to music – are the product of a talented young composer, one who is confident that he has something to communicate to the world, but who has not yet cultivated a personal voice with which to articulate it. As we shall see, *Das Liebesverbot* turned to the buoyant, effervescent French-Italian style for a solution, while *Rienzi* was an attempt to find favour with the popular genre of grand opera.

For *Die Feen* (The Fairies), however, Wagner chose the style which came most naturally to him: German Romantic opera was in his blood. As a boy he had regarded Weber as something of an idol and he had been especially attracted by *Der Freischütz*. Later he became familiar with the music of Heinrich Marschner: during Wagner's first season as chorus master at Würzburg he had the task of rehearsing *Der Vampyr* (though it was not, as is sometimes stated, put on until the new season, which it opened on 29 September 1833), and that was closely followed by *Hans Heiling*, the work with which Marschner had recently scored a brilliant success in Berlin. A performance of *Fidelio* (though probably without Schröder-Devrient) had provided him with a memorable theatrical experience, and he was also acquainted with many lesser repertory works – not all, to be sure, German or Romantic.

Wagner's later sensitivity about musical influences does not seem to extend to the earlier works. He readily admitted that Weber and Marschner had been his models in *Die Feen*, and, indeed, Weber's *Freischütz* and *Oberon* were also among the operas it was his duty to rehearse at Würzburg in the first few months of 1833. The conscientiousness with which he took his job at the theatre did not leave him much time to set to music the libretto he had written that winter, but staying in Würzburg during the summer break to work on it, he was able to complete the first act by 6 August. With the composition of the overture, the score was finished on 6 January 1834.

The plot of *Die Feen* was taken by Wagner from a tale by the eighteenth-century Venetian dramatist Carlo Gozzi, *La donna serpente* (The Snake Woman); in his adaptation he took over the names of characters from his earlier unfinished work *Die Hochzeit*, which in turn were taken from poems by 'Ossian' and others. Arindal, Prince of Tramond, out with his huntsman one day, is spirited away into the magic realm of Ada, who is half fairy, half mortal. She agrees to marry Arindal on condition that he refrains for eight years from asking who she is. Curiosity eventually overpowers him and when he asks the forbidden question the magic realm disappears. Morald and Gernot, from the court of Tramond, find Arindal in a rocky wilderness and persuade him to return home where on the death of his father he has become king and is needed to repulse the enemy. Ada sends Arindal back to his court; she longs to join him as his wife on earth, but a 'fateful decree' ordains that she is to be punished for marrying a mortal. She makes him promise that whatever happens he will never curse her. He swears, but is ignorant of the fact that their reunion is conditional on his successfully undergoing a series of tribulations to be inflicted by Ada herself. He fails, and goaded beyond endurance curses her. Ada now reveals all and tells Arindal that she is condemned to be turned to stone for a hundred years (in Gozzi's story she becomes a snake). Arindal's despair drives him insane, but following Ada into the underworld he finally restores her to life by singing and playing the lyre. His courage is rewarded with immortality and, renouncing his earthly kingdom, he departs to reign with Ada in fairyland.

In both story and music, there are pre-echoes here of themes and gestures familiar from Wagner's later work. Redemption and the forbidden question are the two most prominent examples, though in *Die Feen* it is the man rather than the woman who is the agent of redemption and whose human weakness causes him to ask the question. Arindal's Act III lyre song, with which he regains his bride, bears little more resemblance to Walther's Prize Song in *Die Meistersinger* than an identity of key, but the former gives an interesting foretaste of a musical set-piece being projected to the focal point of the work. That Wagner had the confidence at the height of his career to set himself the task of composing a song that would outshine all competition and form a fitting pinnacle to the whole music drama is remarkable enough: here in *Die Feen* we find him setting himself a similar task if on a more modest scale. A brief glimpse forward to another mature music drama occurs in Arindal's mad scene (Act III): he imagines that he is out hunting and the baying of the dogs is depicted in the same manner (repeated diminished 7ths with acciaccaturas) as that Sieglinde fancies she hears in Act II, scene 3 of *Die Walküre*.

If we did not know about the early musical training that Wagner plays down so much in his autobiography, it would be difficult to account for the sudden blossoming of talent in *Die Feen*. The young chorus master of Würzburg seems to have been seized by the desire to show what he could do, and proves himself resoundingly. Taking up the challenge of all the conventional forms – aria, recitative, romanza, cavatina, various ensembles (trio, quartet, septet) – he demonstrates a capacity for creative imitation far in advance of the piano pieces of a year or two earlier.

Particularly worthy of note in Act I are Ada's cavatina, in which her sadness at losing Arindal is expressed in throbbing appoggiatura dissonances, and the final ensemble, which is a masterly deployment of multiple voices (a septet joined by full chorus) in vigorous acknowledgment of Arindal's oath and acclamation of Queen Ada.

Acts II and III each have a fine scene and aria: that in Act II concerns the making of Ada's decision to accept a mortal's fate on earth rather than live eternally without Arindal ('Weh' mir, so nah' die fürchterliche Stunde'); that in Act III represents the distracted imaginings of the tormented Arindal. Whereas most of *Die Feen* was written by a young composer content to exercise his abilities within the conventional number form, the scene and aria was an opportunity for Wagner to stretch himself a little. The latter is a complex in which recitative, arioso and aria are juxtaposed; it was not the invention of Wagner, of course, but it is a fair indication of the direction of his thoughts that he should find it of value. A few years later he was, in *Der fliegende Holländer*, to extend the principle over a larger canvas, so that in a sense the whole opera is a succession of miniature scenes. The final stage of the process was to be the through-composed music drama.

One of the most delightful things in *Die Feen* is not actually typical of the work: the comic duet for Drolla and Gernot (Act II). As in *opera buffa*, the differentiation of social classes is reflected in the music: here, the detached pattering of Drolla and Gernot marks them off as the representatives of the 'lower orders'. Suspecting each other of infidelity, they end in each other's arms, but on the way the music sparkles with wit and invention: their lines overlap as they quarrel, there are unexpected twists of harmony as their tiff enters new phases, felicities of scoring abound. The duet is untypical because *Die Feen* is otherwise notable for its solemnity. Derivative the opera may be, but there is no suggestion of parody: Wagner was taking his musical development too seriously for that. In his next work he allowed himself to relax a little; the duet is much closer to the spirit of *Das Liebesverbot*.

The summer holiday in Bohemia with Apel that was responsible for the genesis of *Das Liebesverbot* (The Ban on Love) was embarked on by the two young men in an access of high spirits. 'I was then twenty one years old, inclined towards enjoyment of life and a happy view of the world; *Ardinghello* and *Das junge Europa* filled every fibre of my being', wrote Wagner in his *Autobiographical Sketch*. Heinrich Laube's *Das junge Europa* (Young Europe), of which the first part appeared in 1833, propounds free sensual pleasure, religious, political and national emancipation, women's liberation and equal rights for Jews. The author of *Ardinghello und die glückseeligen Inseln* (Ardinghello and the Blessed Isles), Wilhelm Heinse (? 1749–1803), was of an earlier generation. His poetry is identified with the *Sturm und Drang*, and *Ardinghello* appeared in 1787. Its eponymous hero is a 'universal man', the ideal of the Italian Renaissance. He is an advocate of free love, and eventually after many adventures settles with his followers on the Greek islands of Naxos and Paros; there they proscribe ownership and make possible the development of latent human talents. Heinse's vision is not, incidentally, without its regressive aspects: the concept of a nobleman enjoying his privileges beyond the bounds of property and family in an individualist élite society based on slavery is at once a progressive and a reactionary one. But as an alternative to bourgeois morality it was eagerly seized on by the Young Germans and by Wagner.

The heady ideas in these two novels – in particular the self-indulgent enjoyment of sensuality – set his pulse racing on his Bohemian holiday, and his creative springs gushing. The story he chose as the basis for *Das Liebesverbot* was Shakespeare's *Measure for Measure*. In the spirit of his newly found hedonism he transferred the action to sun-soaked Sicily and made the butt of his onslaught not simply hypocritical puritanism but bourgeois morality *per se*.

The Regent Friedrich has outlawed all licentious behaviour –

even love itself, it seems, certainly that expressed outside the sancti-
fying bond of wedlock – on pain of death. The first victim is Claudio,
whose sister Isabella is persuaded by Luzio to appeal to the Regent.
It transpires that Friedrich was once married to Isabella's friend
Mariana but for the sake of ambition repudiated her; he now falls for
Isabella and proposes to set Claudio free in exchange for her favours.
Isabella pretends to agree, but in fact sends Mariana – Friedrich's
own wife – to the rendezvous, which is the fancy-dress carnival
forbidden by the Regent himself. Thus, Friedrich, to satisfy his lust, is
forced to break his own decree. He is exposed and is willing to accept
the penalty imposed by his law, but the people will have none of it.
They set him free and a new era of unfettered pleasure is heralded by
the return of their own king.

This celebration of free love was seen by Alfred Einstein as both
foreshadowing values in the *Ring* and as an expression of the
'revolutionary' strain in Wagner's character that was to make itself
more forcibly felt over the next few decades: 'From its immorality
there was one day to develop the grandiose immorality of the *Ring*;
from the tumultuous apotheosis of sensual enjoyment the idea of
transfiguration through love; the revolutionary tendentiousness of
the Vormärz [the period between 1815 and the March uprising of
1848] would be transformed into something which was in the highest
sense revolutionary . . . '[1]

In August 1834 Wagner set to work versifying the prose scenario he had made two months earlier in Bohemia. The following
January he began the music and it was completed early in 1836.
While elaborating the poem of *Das Liebesverbot*, he was not only
busy with his theatrical duties (his ensemble was on tour in Rudolstadt, Thuringia), but his mind, and heart, were also full of Minna
(and one or two other women), whom he had met that summer. In
spite of this, Wagner felt (he tells us in *Mein Leben*) a greater
assurance in working out *Das Liebesverbot* than he had in *Die Feen*.
Laube might criticize his 'presumption' in writing his own libretto
but his verdict was encouraging.

While the influence of his Italian and French models is clear –
particularly Bellini in the former case (though Verdi is brought to

---

[1] 'Richard Wagners "Liebesverbot" ', *Zeitschrift für Musikwissenschaft*, v
(1923), 382–6. Translated and annotated by Gert R. Dämmerung in
Wagner, old series, 50 (1976), 3–6.

mind in the amusing 'trial' of Dorella by Brighella, Friedrich's police chief) and Auber in the latter – this is not tasteless imitation. There is, for one thing, genuine characterization. The Act II trio for Isabella, Dorella and Luzio admirably catches Luzio's casual gallantry – he is faithless to Dorella and quite unmoved by her demurring. As in *Die Feen* the finales to both acts are well contrived, though that to Act I is overlong, introducing by its prolixity an unintentional note of self-parody. Other numbers worthy of mention are the duet for Isabella and Claudio, with its slow middle section depicting the hero's fall from his lofty plane of martyrdom as he realizes that in glorious death he will not enjoy the pleasures of love, and Friedrich's scene and aria (also Act II), in which the puritanical tyrant with a human heart tunefully battles with his conscience.

An important step forward in *Das Liebesverbot* is marked by the handling of motifs. Whereas in *Die Feen* a few characteristic ideas return but with scarcely sufficient persistence to merit the term 'leitmotif', *Das Liebesverbot* boasts a handful of recurring motifs, sometimes appearing in true leitmotif fashion. Foremost of these is the motif associated with Friedrich's ban on love. It is first heard in the overture in the following form:

Ex. 7

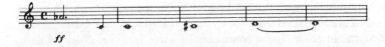

but on subsequent appearances the downward leap ranges between anything from a perfect 4th or 5th to a diminished 7th. It does not arise, as Wagner later stipulated it should, out of a musico-poetic line (unsurprisingly, for he was not yet preoccupied with such a synthesis), but it does occasionally act as a comment on the proceedings. A couple of such comments which rise above the level of routine may be noted. In the Act I finale, as Isabella begs Friedrich to show mercy to her brother, the Regent's stony heart is moved: 'Wie warm ihr Atem, wie beredt ihr Ton; bin ich ein Mann?' (How warm her breath, how eloquent her tongue; am I a man?) and a compressed form of Ex. 7 sounds ironically on oboes and clarinets. Earlier, in the more lighthearted 'trial' of Dorella, the motif is ubiquitous in different guises throughout Brighella's absurdly pompous assumption of power. He threatens Dorella with punishment for infringing the new law, but led on by her finds himself overcome by her charms. In a richly farcical exchange, Dorella asks him to speak as she is hanging on his every word; the orchestra answers with a jaunty, trilling version of Ex. 7, intimating that it is not the *banning* of love that is in Brighella's mind.

Two other motifs (though they are substantial enough to be called themes) may be mentioned. Claudio's plea to Luzio to seek Isabella's help returns at the beginning of Act II just before Claudio enters with 'Wo Isabella bleibt'. More importantly, a melody first heard (like the 'ban on love' motif) in the Overture reappears several times throughout the work as an expression, rather than repression, of love:

Ex. 8

When Isabella pleads for her brother's life, it sounds in the orchestra as Friedrich is stirred by love for her. Later, at the carnival, it is heard as Friedrich looks round lustfully for Isabella. None of these examples should be claimed as an 'advanced' use of leitmotif: in each case its appearance is immediately followed by a clarification put into the mouth of the character concerned. No irony is intended, no hidden meanings are being signalled. The principle of leitmotif, then, is only dimly foreshadowed in *Das Liebesverbot*, and primarily by Ex. 7.

What is often overlooked is the fact that, in spite of the predominating Italian/French influence, the work also exhibits a number of German traits. In the essay cited above, Alfred Einstein singles out 'the Marschner-influenced melody of the motif which symbolises Friedrich's subjection to love [Ex. 8], the strange reminiscence of Beethoven in the first finale, and above all the almost word-for-word imitation of Leonore's "Töt' erst sein Weib!" at the climax of the trial scene ("Erst hört noch mich")'. To these examples may be added first, the use in the nuns' Salve Regina (Act I) of the 'Dresden Amen' (this simple but evocative chordal progression was to reappear in a religious context in both *Tannhäuser* and *Parsifal*), and second, the vigorous, thrusting E major melody, heavy with appoggiaturas, that is heard in Isabella's Act II scene 'So sei's!' – this could easily be taken for something out of *Tannhäuser*.

Das Liebesverbot was produced in Magdeburg on 29 March 1836. The one and only performance was a fiasco: none of the singers had mastered their roles, and one of them was obliged to fill in the gaps in his memory with chunks of *Fra Diavolo* and *Zampa*. A projected second performance failed even to get off the ground on account of a violent back-stage marital dispute just before curtain-up. On meeting further resistance to the staging of the opera a few years later, Wagner lost interest in it and turned his attention to other matters. He presented the score to King Ludwig II at Christmas 1866 with the now famous dismissive lines: 'Once I erred and now should gladly atone for it; and how might I absolve myself from that youthful transgression? I humbly lay its work at *your* feet, that your clemency might be its redeemer.' *Das Liebesverbot* was not given in Germany until 1923 (in Munich) and in England until 1965.

12

Rienzi

To the less objective of Wagner's admirers *Rienzi* has always been an embarrassment. How could the future composer of the *Ring* and *Tristan* have turned so blatantly to grand opera and have produced a piece with so much unmemorable music? Glasenapp (the first 'official' biographer) and others connected with Wahnfried minimized the operatic aspects of the work and attempted to place it in the tradition of the Wagnerian music drama, seeing the whole oeuvre as a continuous, logical process culminating in *Parsifal*. In order to justify that distorted view – and it is one that is still current in certain quarters even today – much had to be ignored or glossed over. Selective quotation from 'the Master' was one method; another was the implementation of severe cuts in the score. A full score published by Fürstner in 1898–9, purporting to be 'based on the original score', omits choruses, word repetitions and other 'operatic' tendencies; it was in fact based on a version by Cosima Wagner and Julius Kniese (a member of the Bayreuth entourage) attempting to transform the work into a music drama.

There can be no doubt, however, that Wagner himself envisaged *Rienzi*, and subsequently regarded it, as a grand opera. In his 1860 essay '*Music of the Future*' he pointedly separated it from the maturer works composed since:

> I lay on this work, which owed its conception and formal execu-
> tion to the earliest impressions of Spontini's heroic opera
> [*Fernand Cortez*, which Wagner had heard in Berlin in 1836],
> together with the brilliant Parisian genre of the grand operas of
> Auber, Meyerbeer and Halévy, all of which demanded emulating,
> – I lay, as I say, on this work . . . no special emphasis, for in it there
> is not yet evident any important instance of the view of art which I
> later came to assert . . .

Wagner's primary source for *Rienzi, der letzte der Tribunen* was the novel *Rienzi, the Last of the Tribunes*[1] by Sir Edward Bulwer-Lytton, the English writer and politician. Wagner had read the novel in Blasewitz, near Dresden, in the summer of 1837 and was immediately inspired to sketch an outline for an opera. (The idea of using Rienzi for a subject may, as John Deathridge plausibly speculates, have been suggested to him a few years earlier by Apel.)[2] This brief sketch (merely a few lines written in pencil on a small – octavo – double sheet) was elaborated into the prose draft which Wagner began probably soon after taking up his post in Riga in August the same year.[3] The prose draft is written largely in the form of dialogue, most of which was taken over intact into the final libretto. The verse draft, which came next, has fragments of music in the margin, a fact which has led to the claim that verse and music in *Rienzi* were conceived simultaneously. This claim, intended to demonstrate that Wagner was 'a musical poet', even at this early stage, is not borne out by the evidence; it would be more accurate to describe the poetic and musical conceptions as inter-relating.[4]

After making a number of fragmentary composition sketches, Wagner used these to write out in ink a continuous composition draft in a form rather like a vocal score. The composition draft of the first two acts were completed by 9 April 1839. A short gap followed, during which time the journey to Paris occurred and work was started on *Der fliegende Holländer*. Work on *Rienzi* was recommenced with Act III in February 1840 and concluded with the Overture (dated 23 October 1840 in the composition draft); all that remained for Wagner was to write out part of the score.

Rienzi is the story of a man who is swept to power on the strength of his promise to make Rome a great city once again; the streets will be made safe, as all, noble or plebeian, shall be subject to

---

[1] First published London 1835. Later editions were entitled *Rienzi: the Last of the Roman Tribunes*.

[2] *Wagner's 'Rienzi': A reappraisal based on a study of the sketches and drafts*, 24.

[3] For the dating of the prose draft see Deathridge, *op. cit.*, 159–60. Deathridge's book is invaluable as a critique of *Rienzi* by way of a detailed analysis of the manuscript sources, and also for the light it throws on Wagner's method of working.

[4] Deathridge, *op. cit.*, 42–50.

the law. His fortunes then suffer a reverse: there are murmurings against the pomp and splendour of Rienzi's life-style, against the taxes levied to pay for the protection of the citizenry, and there are allegations that the man of the people is making secret deals with the nobles to further his ambitions. Rienzi's demand that Rome choose her own emperor makes an enemy of the Emperor, and the Church also turns against him: his excommunication causes many to desert him. Adriano, a nobleman of the Colonna family, veers between loyalty to his clan (swearing to avenge their deaths at the hand of Rienzi) and to Rienzi, whose sister Irene he loves. The People finally set fire to the Capitol and the building collapses burying Rienzi, Adriano and Irene.

The idealized portrait of Rienzi, not endorsed by his twentieth-century biographer Konrad Burdach (whose transcriptions of Rienzi's letters show him to be an ambitious, if enlightened, politician rather than a philanthropist selflessly concerned for the state of his native city),[5] was taken over by Wagner from Bulwer. (In 1835, when his Rienzi novel was published, he was still Edward Lytton Bulwer. When he inherited Knebworth in 1843 he took the additional name -Lytton, although he was still known as Bulwer.) Bulwer alludes to Rienzi's pomp, his levying of taxes, and the rest; however, he concludes that Rienzi fell not through any vice of his own but through the fault of the People. They deserted him at the crucial moment; above all, they put too much faith in one man:

> If I judge not erringly, it [the moral of Rienzi's life and of the novel] proclaims that, to be great and free, a People must trust not to individuals but to themselves – that there is no sudden leap from servitude to liberty – that it is to institutions, not to men, that they must look for reforms that last beyond the hour – that their own passions are the real despots they should subdue, their own reason the true regenerator of abuses.[6]

Rienzi throws some interesting light on Wagner's social and political beliefs in the 1830s. The uprisings in Paris and other places – including Leipzig, where he was studying – at the beginning of the decade had imbued him with revolutionary fervour. Bulwer's novel,

---

[5] Konrad Burdach, *Briefwechsel des Cola di Rienzo*, 5 vols (Berlin 1913–29), i, 499.

[6] 1840 edn (London), appx I, p. 538.

11 The Festspielhaus at Bayreuth as it looked in 1876.

12 The bells used in the Grail ceremony scenes in the original Bayreuth performances of *Parsifal*.

13 Portrait of Wagner by Lenbach.

14 The Palazzo Vendramin in Venice, in which Wagner spent the last five months of his life with his family and servants; they occupied the mezzanine floor.

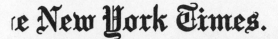

THE WEATHER.

Rain; brisk southwest to west winds.

NEW YORK: FRIDAY, DECEMBER 25, 1903.—TWELVE PAGES.   ONE CENT

"PARSIFAL" AN ARTISTIC TRIUMPH

Production Unrivaled in History of Opera in New York—Immense Audience, Deeply Impressed with Wagner's Festival-Play, Listens Breathlessly Throughout the Performance.

15 Enthusiastic acclaim for the Metropolitan Opera's 1903 production of *Parsifal*. Thus the thirty-year embargo on stagings outside Bayreuth was broken – to the fury of Cosima and Wahnfried.

BAYREUTHER
BÜHNEN
FESTSPIELE
1933
★
21. JULI BIS 19. AUGUST
PARSIFAL
MEISTERSINGER
RING
★
MUSIKALISCHE LEITUNG
TOSCANINI R. STRAUSS
ELMENDORFF
GESAMTINSZENIERUNG
TIETJEN
★

16 Hitler's assumption of power brought a principled refusal from Toscanini to conduct at Bayreuth. Richard Strauss, however, felt able to accept an invitation to conduct *Parsifal* in his place.

17 Cosima Wagner, the 'Mistress of Bayreuth', in dignified old age.

describing the irresistible force of a populace goaded beyond endurance by oppression and injustice, and swayed by the rhetoric of a charismatic leader (himself of plebeian origin), who overturns the old, corrupt order and puts in its stead a 'buono stato', a Good Estate: all this made a direct appeal to Wagner's heart. However, neither Wagner's nor Bulwer's revolution was to establish an egalitarian society. In Wagner's prose draft, as in the finished score, Rienzi wins over Adriano by reminding him of the debt owed by Adriano as a Colonna – a Colonna had killed Rienzi's brother. But in the prose draft (though not in the score) an important objection of Adriano's is answered by Rienzi: the Tribune declares that he has no intention of abolishing the nobility – a matter in which Adriano naturally takes some interest. He simply wants to institute the rule of law and bring the nobles within it.

This change was surely made for dramatic rather than political reasons (Adriano's love for Irene and consequent divided loyalties were made by Wagner into a central feature of the plot). Nevertheless, it should be seen alongside the Vaterlandsverein speech of 1848 (see p. 34), in which Wagner pragmatically proposed a new social order without a ruling class, but consisting of a republic headed by a monarch. (This aim was entirely in accordance with the aspirations of German bourgeois liberals in the 1840s.) Wagner's Rienzi actually refuses kingship but he accepts office as Tribune, the People's magistrate and protector. It should also be noted briefly that the doctrine of the Saint-Simonians (reflected in some of Wagner's early writings as well as in *Rienzi*) favours a 'genius leader' who mediates between the governing élite and the governed by his natural, inspiring authority. Wagner's Rienzi follows Bulwer's here. Bulwer's evident revolutionary enthusiasm is perhaps surprising in a Member of Parliament (he entered the Commons in 1831), even more so in a member of the landed gentry. But his Tribune makes it clear that he harbours no 'mad scheme to level the ranks which society renders a necessary evil'[7] – a useful loophole for Bulwer, who was to crown his political career with a seat in the Lords.

Wagner's attitude towards the character of Rienzi is of critical importance in view of the work's alleged proto-fascistic tendencies, which we have still to examine. Did he present him as an unblemished leader whose sacred mission would brush aside all scruples? If so, the

[7] 1840 edn, p. 220.

school of thought that regards *Rienzi* as foreshadowing the Nazi horror would have powerful ammunition. To begin with, it must be said that Wagner does not make of his hero quite the idol that Bulwer makes of his. It is true that the omission from the score of another important detail in the prose draft makes Rienzi appear less like an opportunist: in the draft of the Act I trio, Rienzi sharply observes the attachment of Adriano to Irene ('*Rienzi* hat beide scharf beobachtet'), which clearly suggests that in that instant he sees the possible desirability of an alliance with the nobles. However, in Act IV, Baroncelli, a citizen, alleges that Rienzi sought such an alliance, and although the charge is not proved, neither is it dismissed by Wagner as similar charges against Rienzi are by Bulwer. (Not that Bulwer had moral objections to political opportunism: he entered Parliament as a Whig but refused to allow narrow Party principles to stand between him and the Colonial Secretaryship in a Tory Government.) So although Wagner's Rienzi is brought down largely by political manoeuvring – in which his excommunication plays an important part – there is an area of uncertainty. Baroncelli's allegations, and the treatment of the character of Adriano, leave the question slightly open; in this, Wagner shows a political awareness that is lacking in Bulwer, and that argues against a total identification with the character of Rienzi in the irrational manner of a proto-Nazi.

And yet there remains the uncomfortable fact that a performance of *Rienzi* in 1906 or 1907 made an unusually strong impact on the young Adolf Hitler: indeed, he later stated, with reference to the Nazi movement, that 'In jener Stunde begann es' (In that hour it began).[8] Doubtless Rienzi the eloquent orator, inspiring the masses with his rhetoric, appealed to Hitler. He also responded to Rienzi as redeemer, whose mission it was to restore Rome to its former greatness. The extravagant pomp and ceremony which were seen by Rienzi's anonymous contemporary biographer[9] as a major contributory factor to his downfall – though dismissed by Bulwer – are reflected in musical terms by Wagner. Indeed, the abundance of choruses, festive dances, processions and marches was dictated by the very choice of the genre of grand opera.

Adorno, who neatly described Rienzi as 'the last Roman tribune

[8] August Kubizek, *Young Hitler: the Story of our Friendship* (trans. E.V. Anderson), London 1954, pp. 64–6.

[9] *La Vita di Cola di Rienzo*, ed. Zefirino Rè Cesenate (Fiorli 1828).

and the first bourgeois terrorist' – a reference to the incomplete nature of the revolution noted earlier – drew attention, with special reference to *Rienzi*, to 'Self-praise and pomp – features of Wagner's entire output and the emblems of fascism'.[10] Pomp, and of an undeniably self-regarding kind, is certainly present throughout the opera. There is also a tendency to cudgel listeners, to overwhelm them with accumulating banks of sound – a tendency, it is true, that characterizes all Wagner's music, but intensified in *Rienzi* to an unparalleled degree. The sense of oppression would be considerably less were it not that this extravagant treatment is lavished on such vacuous ideas. The rhetoric is powerful but empty.

Sometimes, as Deathridge is able to show by his analysis of the sketches and drafts,[11] the mass effects were added during the composition of the music. But the fact that they were not in some cases part of the initial conception – often they were grafted on so as to disguise technical inadequacy – does not affect the validity of the fascistic charge: they are an intrinsic part of the work as Wagner gave it to the world. That he seemed to be partly conscious of these tendencies in *Rienzi* is to his credit, but the charge cannot, if Wagner's work is to be understood in all its aspects, be dismissed out of hand.

As was mentioned at the beginning of this chapter, Wagner clearly regarded *Rienzi*, both at the time of composition and subsequently, as an opera – more specifically as a grand opera – which is not to deny that there are traces of music drama, simply to assert the work's true paternity. But mere imitation was unlikely to satisfy Wagner:

> 'Grand opera', with all its scenic and musical splendour, its effect-ridden, musically massive strength of passion, stood before me; my artistic ambition demanded not merely that I should imitate it but that I should outdo all previous examples with sumptuous extravagance. (*A Communication to my Friends*)

From Paris (January 1842), Wagner wrote to Ferdinand Heine, the costume designer at the Dresden Court Theatre where *Rienzi* was to be performed:

[10] *In Search of Wagner* (trans. by Rodney Livingstone of *Versuch über Wagner*), London 1981, pp. 12 and 14.

[11] Deathridge, *op. cit.*, 89–90, 141–2.

> I shall not give up a single detail of the musical pomp on the stage;
> ... See to it that the trumpeters and trombonists accompanying
> the warlike procession of Colonna and Orsini in the first act are
> chosen from the cavalry and appear on horseback: this (as I
> imagine it) will look splendid and appropriate and it can certainly
> be done on the Dresden stage.
>
> The director must spare no expense and no pains, for in
> operas like mine it's all or nothing – you understand me!

In his *Autobiographical Sketch* Wagner admits that from the
outset he planned the work on such a scale that it could not be given
in a small theatre: he was determined to avoid a repetition of the
disaster that had befallen *Das Liebesverbot*. The result is a generous
endowment of marches, processions and ballets. March rhythms
obtrude even into vocal numbers: the Act I trio for Irene, Adriano
and Rienzi, referred to earlier, culminates in a vigorous B flat march.
So much of the choral work is in quadruple-time march rhythms that
it comes as a relief to find some breaking the mould, such as the
atmospheric conspirators' exchanges opening Act IV.

Occasionally too there is a broad sweep of melody that carries
no martial or other sinister connotations: the effulgent orchestral
introduction to the Chorus of the Messengers of Peace that begins
Act II is as splendid as anything in the work, and the main melody of
the Overture (and of Rienzi's Act V prayer), dignified and majestic-
ally eloquent, is surely one of Wagner's finest inspirations:

Ex. 9

Ernest Newman had some harsh things to say about *Rienzi*. He
found it the least satisfying of all Wagner's works – 'far less enjoy-
able than *Die Feen* or *Das Liebesverbot*'. Inveighing against its
wooden characters, the 'pretentious poverty' of its musical invention
and its 'intolerable prolixity',[12] his observations, though intemper-
ately expressed, are accurate. Finales in *Rienzi* – such as that to Act II
– are not as skilfully constructed as those in the earlier works.

[12] *Wagner as Man and Artist*, 310–12.

Adriano's Act III scene and aria 'Gerechter Gott!' also makes an interesting comparison. In the aria the melodic line becomes increasingly tortured as Adriano agonizes over his conflicting loyalties. Admittedly, the number was written with Wagner's idol Schröder-Devrient in mind, and it is true to the grand operatic style in which the whole work is conceived; yet it is difficult not to feel that Wagner achieved more in comparable situations in *Die Feen* with considerably less outward show.

While acknowledging that *Rienzi* is grand opera, it is necessary to point to a small but significant change in style during the course of the work. As mentioned earlier, Wagner's composition of the music was interrupted for some ten months by his move from Riga to Paris. Acts I and II, written before the break, are unequivocally in the Italian and French style of grand opera that he admitted taking as his model. By the time he came to write Acts III to V, Wagner had not only begun to question the validity of that style: he had also set in train a process that was ultimately to lead to the *Gesamtkunstwerk* and its musico-poetic synthesis.

His writings of the period bear witness to this change of heart. Several of the Paris essays and novellas show Wagner wrestling with the inadequacies of operatic form and in one in particular, *A Pilgrimage to Beethoven* (1840), he clearly foresees the arias, duets and trios of conventional opera being superseded by a form unifying poetry and music, the voice and the orchestra. In the latter part of *Rienzi* this new approach is heralded by a more expressive, more poetically aware use of recitative that has begun to break down the barrier between recitative and aria, and by a slightly more mature use of the orchestra that comments on the action in an independent manner.

The division of *Rienzi* into two stylistic parts should not be exaggerated. One of the most forward-looking uses of motif, for example, the Vengeance motif, whose pointed recurrence allows us to consider it a forerunner of the motif of reminiscence, occurs in the first part. Interestingly, the two phases of style do not seem to have been detected by the composer.

According to *Mein Leben*, the premiere on 20 October 1842 lasted more than six hours (including intervals): from 6 o'clock to after midnight. But in spite of its inordinate length the work was an unmitigated success: Schröder-Devrient, in the opinion of Ferdinand Heine, was stunning. Wagner immediately turned his attention to cuts[13] and encountered benevolent opposition from the singers, especially Tichatschek (Rienzi). A truncated version was performed and it was also tried as before but over two evenings, the first part being called *Rienzi's Greatness* and the second *Rienzi's Fall.* Wagner's truncated version was reverted to and the work has been dogged by the problem of cuts ever since, a problem exacerbated by the absence of an original uncut score. No printed score was ever made from the autograph without cuts being made, and the autograph itself disappeared with Hitler, in whose possession it was.

Rienzi is perhaps the most extraordinary work of Wagner's career. Hugely, uniquely successful in his lifetime, it catapulted him to fame – if not to fortune – overnight, but it has been savaged by his critics, distorted by his admirers and never given at Bayreuth.

[13] Cuts had already been suggested by Wagner (in letters from Paris to Heine and Wilhelm Fischer, the chorus master at Dresden), though it is not certain precisely which were made at the first performance. For more information on cuts and corrupt versions, see Deathridge, *op cit.*, esp. 147–54. See also vols iii (1–4) and xxiii of the Sämtliche Werke, ed. Carl Dahlhaus; and Reinhard Strohm, ' "Rienzi" and Authenticity'.

13

Der fliegende Holländer

As mentioned in the last chapter, Wagner had already been giving some attention to his next work even while *Rienzi* was in progress. His main source for *Der fliegende Holländer* was Heinrich Heine's telling of the legend[1] in *Aus den Memoiren des Herren von Schnabelewopski*, published in 1834. But, according to Wagner, it was a real-life episode that ignited his imagination. The flight from Riga and the hazardous voyage from London aboard the *Thetis* were described in chapter 3; Wagner recounts the events in inimitable style in *Mein Leben*, and it was on this voyage, as the storm raged, the wind whistled through the rigging, and the crew's shouts echoed round the Norwegian fjords, that the *Holländer* was supposed to have taken shape in his mind. There are good reasons to doubt this account, as will shortly be seen.

Heine's story relates the legend of the man doomed by the Devil to sail the seas until the Day of Judgment unless he can be redeemed by a woman's fidelity. It is an ironic, detached retelling, ostensibly of a play seen by the author in a theatre in Amsterdam; he deliberately interrupts the narrative (in order to debunk it) with a recital of his adventures with an admirer at the theatre. Wagner, true to his nature, took the story much more seriously, particularly the theme of redemption by a woman. His Dutchman is driven by storms to a Norwegian harbour and is eventually rescued from his plight by Senta who, not only in pity but also in the belief that she is fulfilling destiny, forsakes her own lover Erik.

Wagner identified himself closely with all this: he too was persecuted, uprooted, harassed from all sides, and unfulfilled in love. Years later, in a letter to Liszt (11 February 1853), he pictured

---

[1] The figure of the Flying Dutchman had already acquired a legendary status by the time of his first appearance in literature, which occurred as late as the beginning of the nineteenth century. See Eduard Reeser, 'Die literarischen Grundlagen des "Fliegenden Holländer"'.

himself, in a fit of depression induced by his social isolation, as the melancholy Dutchman; but for himself, he said, there was no salvation – only death. The story also had a deep mythic resonance for him. 'The figure of the "Flying Dutchman" is the mythical poem of the People: a primeval trait of man's essential nature expresses itself here with heart-enthralling power' (*A Communication to my Friends*). The Greek world had embodied the myth, he said, in Ulysses and his longing after home, house, hearth and wife; the Christian world epitomized it in the figure of the Wandering Jew (Ahasuerus, with whom Wagner also identified himself). The redeeming woman, however, was

> no longer the Penelope of the *Odyssey* wooed in ancient times, caring for the home, but woman in general, though a woman who does not yet exist, one who is longed for and dreamed of, the infinitely womanly woman – let me express it in one phrase: *the woman of the future*.

But Wagner's close identification with his subject should not allow us to accept uncritically his *Mein Leben* account of the inspiration of the work. Describing the stormy *Thetis* voyage and their taking refuge in the small Norwegian harbour of Sandwiken on 29 July 1839, Wagner writes:

> The sharp rhythm of this call clung to me like a consoling augury and soon shaped itself into the theme of the [Norwegian] sailors' song in my *Fliegender Holländer*. Already at that time I was carrying around with me the idea of this opera and now, under the impressions I had just experienced, it acquired a distinct poetic and musical colour.

What he does not mention is that his story was originally set not in Norway at all, but in Scotland. Erik and Daland were called 'Georg' and 'Donald' (or 'the Scotsman') and in the prose sketch Senta was 'Anna' (but never 'Minna' as asserted by both Kapp and Westernhagen[2]). The Scottish setting obtained until just a few weeks before the work's premiere; the change to Norway was presumably motivated, at least in part, by the desire to bring life and art more

---

[2] See Julius Kapp, *Richard Wagner und die Frauen* (Berlin 1929), 305; Curt von Westernhagen, *Wagner: A Biography*, I, 65.

closely together.[3] Undoubtedly *Der fliegende Holländer* reflects aspects of Wagner's personality and experiences; it was a characteristic touch that the genesis of the work should be presented in such a vividly autobiographical way. Wagner would have been delighted to know that he had so successfully pulled the wool over the eyes of generations of commentators.

Wagner wrote his poem for the *Holländer* in Meudon, just outside Paris, in May 1841. The first numbers to be composed were Senta's Ballad, the chorus of the Norwegian sailors and the chorus of the Dutchman's crew. 'So possessed was he by the subject and so easily did his ideas flow that the whole work was completed in seven weeks, the overture being written last', writes Newman,[4] and the 'seven weeks' (first mentioned by Wagner in his *Autobiographical Sketch*) has become as durable a legend as that of the Dutchman himself. But this is not quite accurate. Parts of the work were sketched, or even completed, before those weeks in the summer of 1841. To begin with, we can presume that the three numbers mentioned above were written some time between 3 May and 26 July 1840, that is between the date on which Wagner informed Meyerbeer that he was about to send Scribe his prose sketch for the work and that on which he announced that the three pieces were ready for audition. Even allowing for the element of fantasy in the *Mein Leben* account quoted above, it is quite possible that some music was indeed jotted down in the months following the *Thetis* voyage, though no musical sketches survive to support such a conjecture.

In the second place there are two documents providing specific evidence that the conceptions of *Holländer* and *Rienzi* overlapped. A composition sketch (fragment) transcribed and discussed by John Deathridge,[5] that was formerly part of the Burrell Collection, and a

---

3 There are other factors. Dietsch's *Le Vaisseau fantôme*, based on the Flying Dutchman legend – though not, as Wagner claimed, on his scenario – came to the Paris Opéra stage in the same month (November 1842) as rehearsals for *Der fliegende Holländer* began in Dresden; such an unfortunate coincidence must surely have rankled with Wagner. He may well have wished to distance himself at the same time from the Scottish setting of Heine.

4 *Wagner Nights*, 27.

5 *Wagner's 'Rienzi': A reappraisal based on a study of the sketches and drafts*, 127–33.

manuscript in the Princeton University Library[6] both juxtapose ideas for the two works, the Burrell fragment (concerning the two overtures) so closely that they would seem to have been written down at the same time. The common source of inspiration is almost certainly Beethoven's Ninth Symphony, a work which Wagner says he learnt to appreciate only under Habeneck in Paris. The pulsating, openfifth beginning of the *Holländer* Overture has an elemental quality very similar to that of the beginning of Beethoven's Ninth.

Wagner's own recollection of the genesis of the *Holländer*, recorded a decade later in the *Communication to my Friends*, has to be treated with caution:

> I remember that before I proceeded to write *Der fliegende Holländer* at all, I first sketched Senta's second-act Ballad, composing both the text and the melody; in this piece I unwittingly planted the thematic seed of all the music in the opera: it was the poetically condensed image of the whole drama, as it was in my mind's eye; and when I had to find a title for the finished work I was strongly tempted to call it a 'dramatic ballad'. When I came eventually to the composition, the thematic image I had already conceived quite involuntarily spread out over the entire drama in a complete, unbroken web; all that was left for me to do was to allow the various thematic germs contained in the Ballad to develop to the full, each in its own direction, and all the principal features of the text were arrayed before me in specific thematic shapes of their own making.[7]

Senta's Ballad may well have been the core of the work for Wagner – its conceptual nucleus – but the idea that the remainder of the music developed from the 'thematic seed' of the Ballad is a retrospective interpretation of events. It is a formulation that suits Wagner's theorizing about music drama in the early 1850s, but as regards illuminating his compositional process in the *Holländer* it is of little help except to those determined to find at all costs the consistency of the later works throughout the composer's oeuvre.

It is true that the elements of Senta's Ballad appear elsewhere, and it is true that these occurrences include some of the central

---

6 See Paul S. Machlin, 'A Sketch for the "Dutchman" '.

7 Trans. by Mary Whittall from C. Dahlhaus, *Richard Wagner's Music Dramas*, 18.

numbers of the work, for example the Dutchman's Monologue, Erik's dream, the duet for Senta and the Dutchman, the finale. Senta also sings (to a form of what we might call the Redemption motif) two lines from the Ballad, 'Ach! möchtest du, bleicher Seemann, sie finden!', after hearing Erik's prophetic dream, a reminiscence interrupted by the dramatic appearance of the Dutchman himself. But while the Redemption motif comes closer than anything else in the *Holländer* – or in *Tannhäuser* for that matter – to the authentic post-*Opera and Drama* motif of reminiscence, it is misleading to regard these quotations and allusions as comparable in any way to the method of structural organization in the *Ring*. In the latter, large numbers of motifs are developed and integrated in complex arrangements so that they do indeed 'spread out over the entire drama in a complete, unbroken web'. In the *Holländer*, on the other hand, they tend rather to stand outside the structure, as with Senta's repetition of 'Ach! möchtest du', or to adorn it, with or without a commentating function.

Wagner's original intention for *Der fliegende Holländer* was a work consisting of one act. The reasons for this, he tells us in *Mein Leben*, were that it might have a better chance of acceptance: one-act dramas were often given as a curtain-raiser before a ballet at the Paris Opéra. But he also hoped thereby to concentrate on the dramatic interaction of the principal characters and exclude 'the tiresome operatic accessories'. (He was eventually obliged, on practical grounds, to conform to the traditional three-act scheme, though following Cosima's example when she introduced it at Bayreuth in 1901 it is often now given as one act – with its taut transitions an improvement on the three-act version.)

Despite his good intentions, Wagner was not able at a stroke to rid himself of the accessories of conventional opera. Recitatives, arias, duets, trios, choruses: all are present. There is a mode of declamation that can be identified with recitative in all the works up to and including *Das Rheingold*. In the *Holländer*, such passages (which are always, of course, accompanied by the orchestra, or else unaccompanied altogether – the age of the harpsichord continuo is past) are still, in places, referred to in the score as 'recitative'. In *Tannhäuser* and *Lohengrin*, more effort is made to conceal them, and in *Rheingold* we are hardly aware of recitative as such, not so much because the nature of the recitative has changed but because the distinction between recitative and aria has been eroded: the characteristic line at this point combines the declamation of recitative with the lyricism of the aria.

As for arias and duets, it was described in Chapter 11 how Wagner used the 'scene and aria' in *Die Feen* and how the principle was to be extended in the *Holländer* so that the work was no longer a 'number opera' nor yet a through-composed music drama, but what might be called a 'scene opera'. The number opera was on the way out even before Wagner. Weber's *Euryanthe*, for example, written in 1822–3, is virtually through-composed: there is no *secco* recitative and breaks are minimal, though the set number is still in evidence.[8] The *Holländer* score is also divided explicitly: no. 4, for instance, is a 'scene, duet and chorus'.[9] Such divisions were soon to be abjured entirely by Wagner, but meanwhile there are also some revealing clues as to the drift of his thoughts at this time.

No. 8 is ostensibly a duet for Erik and Senta (after Senta's Ballad, Erik has come in to announce that his prospective father-in-law is on the way, only to find Senta in ecstasies over a portrait of the Dutchman). But it is not a duet in the conventional sense, with one singer beginning alone, being joined by the other, each commenting on the situation. Here, after a brief exchange, Erik launches into a passionate protestation of loyalty that sounds very much like an aria (Ex. 12). There is another longer exchange; Erik repeats his protestation; another heated dialogue; then Erik recounts his dream. Only then do the voices come together right at the end, at moments of high intensity, for a few brief bars. What has happened is that Wagner has found the poem too important to submerge in a welter of harmony. He has become increasingly concerned that all the words should be heard, and although there is no consistency in the word-setting – sometimes there are brief snatches of phrase, sometimes regular four-bar periods – we can see that this is the road leading to his ideal synthesis of poetry and music.

---

[8] For a detailed account of the development of opera up to and beyond Wagner, see Opera, § IV: Germany and Austria in the *New Grove*.

[9] Wagner adopted a pragmatic attitude to the individual numbers, emphasizing their saleability as an extra reason for the publication of the score. See previously unpublished letter to Härtel, 24 January 1844, Egerton MS 2159, ff.102^r–102^v; reproduced and trans. in *Wagner*, iv (1983), 107–10.

For ensembles, as for duets and trios (Wagner was to write in *Opera and Drama*) there was to be no place in the music drama of the future: no individual was merely to provide harmonic or melodic support for another character. He did not adhere rigidly to that rule; nevertheless there is not in the mature works a single chorus that is not dramatically justified and that is not woven seamlessly into the musical fabric. In the *Holländer*, however, there are choruses treated in the old-fashioned manner: the Sailors' Chorus that brings down the curtain on Act I, and the Spinning Chorus opening Act II, neither propel the action forward nor are they well integrated. In their defence one might point out that the Spinning Chorus, with its pretty but not very profound music, accurately characterizes the colourless, soulless spinning girls and their humdrum but happy existence; the two choruses are also cleverly linked (in both the single-act and three-act versions) by the orchestra's development of a dotted figure common to both.

On the other hand there is some extended chorus work in Act III that is much easier to justify. The two ships are lying side by side in the harbour, the Norwegian brightly lit with much merrymaking and revelry on board, the Dutch dark and silent: 'the stillness of death reigns over it', the stage directions read. The Norwegian sailors and womenfolk shout out to the others, offering food and drink. For a long time there is nothing but a ghostly silence. Eventually the Dutch crew strike up a diabolical and terrifying chorus. Daland's men desperately try to impose their own merry chorus, while tossing waves and a howling wind are portrayed vividly in the orchestra. Then follows a marvellously effective superimposition of the two choruses, fighting each other, as it were, for supremacy. The Dutchmen finally triumph and the Norwegians retire in horror. All this is depicted in powerful and exciting choral writing – with pictorial help from the orchestra, of course.

Two worlds are strikingly contrasted in the *Holländer*, the 'interior' world of the imagination inhabited by Senta and the Dutchman, and the 'exterior' world of reality to which belong Daland, Erik, the spinning girls and the sailors. An awareness of the dramatic possibilities of psychological penetration begins to dawn, complementing Wagner's developing technique: one might almost say that the two worlds are differentiated by the capacity of the various characters to depart from traditional operatic habits. Erik's third-act cavatina, for example, despite some intensifying modulations into distant keys, falls tunefully into two-bar phrases that pose little threat to the established order of things: Senta needs no further proof of her incompatibility with the earth-bound huntsman. Daland's introduction of the Dutchman to Senta, 'Mögst du, mein Kind' – in the middle of which he breaks into a little cadenza of ecstasy at Senta's beauty and the Dutchman's approval of it – is melodic and harmonic invention of a banality almost embarrassing, until we realize how perfectly it captures the bluff, hearty sea-captain, and how well it counterbalances Senta's own spellbound recognition of the Dutchman.

Neither of the two central expositions of the 'interior' world, Senta's Ballad and the Dutchman's Act I Monologue, entirely manages to break free from the constraints of regular periodic structure, but the latter comes closer to doing so. It begins with a recitative, 'Die Frist ist um', followed by a strong C minor section in which the Dutchman bewails his curse and endless voyaging. The turbulence of the sea and of the Dutchman's mind is portrayed in a rocking motif prefigured in the Overture and also heard in Senta's Ballad, her duet with the Dutchman, and elsewhere:

Ex. 10

Then the Dutchman pleads for some angel to show him the way to deliverance in a passage, 'Dich frage ich', of the kind Berlioz justly criticized for excessive use of tremolo.[10] The Monologue ends with a splendid piece of Verdian blood-and-thunder, 'Nur eine Hoffnung', whose long, sweeping, rising phrases and double dots add up to a telling characterization of this formidable figure.

Significantly, the Dutchman's edited account of his voyaging to Daland shortly after (naturally he does not wish to mention the curse or his punishment) falls into standard four-bar phrases. The Dutchman's style is modified by the presence of Daland and his crew, and

10 'Concerts de Richard Wagner: La Musique de l'Avenir', in *A Travers Chants* (Paris 1862), 293–302. Trans. in *Wagner: A Documentary Study*, ed. H. Barth, D. Mack and E. Voss, 189–192.

in the following duet, 'Wie? Hör' ich recht?', his rugged individuality is completely submerged by Daland's blandness. The trite duet expresses both the superficial, meretricious character of the father and his joy at receiving so much wealth in exchange for such a trifle as his daughter.

A greater duet – indeed, the highpoint of the work – is that for Senta and the Dutchman at the end of Act II. But the most advanced passage, in the context of the development of music drama, comes from an unexpected source. Erik's recital of his dream, 'Auf hohem Felsen', achieves its dreamlike quality by its irregular, broken phrases:

Ex. 11

Notice how accented syllables are set with long notes and unaccented ones dismissed with short. The setting may have little melodic charm but it matches precisely the poetic line. Compare a few bars of Erik earlier in more conventional vein:

Ex. 12

Here the two syllables of 'Treue' and that of 'bis' are all stretched out in order to fit the four-bar tune. The unmelodiousness of Ex. 11 shows that Wagner had some way to go to attain the perfect musico-poetic synthesis, but in principle the passage might be regarded as a precursor of the narrations of Tannhäuser (see p. 176) and Lohengrin (p. 184–5).

To sum up, Wagner's attempt to purge his writing of operatic 'accessories' in the *Holländer* is partially successful, especially where he is concerned with the interior world inhabited by Senta and the Dutchman. The numbers, which are predominantly organized in structures of two (or multiples of two) bars, are assembled to form through-composed scenes. The work cannot claim to be any more than an inchoate music drama, but the unprecedented attention given to dramatic considerations, the consistency of its background colour and the strength of its characterization justify Wagner's assertion (in *A Communication to my Friends*) that with the *Holländer* began his career as a poet, and ended that as a mere manufacturer of librettos.

Aspects of *Der fliegende Holländer* continued to worry Wagner for the rest of his life and small modifications began to be made already for the first performances. The most important subsequent changes were as follows: first in 1846 some revisions were made to the orchestration for a projected performance in Leipzig (which did not take place) – these had the effect of toning down the brassiness which Wagner had reluctantly inherited from the French grand opera. Then in 1852 when performances were planned for Zurich and Weimar (the work was given four times in Zurich in April and May 1852, and a number of times under Liszt in Weimar, beginning in February 1853), he took the whole work in hand with a view to revisions. In the event he contented himself with changes to the scoring and an improved ending to the Overture, declaring that for the rest the 1846 Leipzig version should be considered the authentic one. In 1860, when the *Holländer* Overture formed part of the programme given in a series of three concerts in Paris, the coda of the Overture was remodelled and the ending of the whole opera adapted in accordance; this remodelling does not, as sometimes stated, date from 1852. The 1860 revision produces textures that are more intricate and subtle than before, so that the orchestra is used less like a battering-ram with inexorable block changes of harmony at the half-bar. These post-*Tristan* changes are a revealing indication of just how far Wagner had come since the composition of the *Holländer* in 1841.[11]

---

[11] For more information on the revisions see Paul S. Machlin, 'Wagner, Durand and "The Flying Dutchman": the 1852 Revisions of the Overture', and Gerald Abraham, 'Wagner's Second Thoughts', chapter in his *Slavonic and Romantic Music*. The most detailed and reliable work on the subject is by Isolde Vetter: 'The "Ahasverus of the Oceans" – Musically Unredeemed? The Flying Dutchman and its Revisions', and her dissertation '*Der fliegende Holländer' von Richard Wagner. Entstehung, Bearbeitung, Überlieferung*; see also Sämtliche Werke, iv, for her critical edition.

14
Tannhäuser

The question of 'versions' is a much more pressing one in *Tannhäuser*, since between the time he put the finishing touches to his autograph on 13 April 1845 and the end of his life Wagner made at least thirty changes to the score: some small, some radical. Until the very end he was talking of revisions to *Tannhäuser*. We will be looking more closely at the alterations later in this chapter: suffice it to recall here (as mentioned in chapters 3 and 6) that the work was first given in Dresden in 1845 and that it was revised by Wagner for an ill-fated run in Paris in 1861.

The stories of Tannhäuser and the song contest on the Wartburg were familiar in the nineteenth century in several different versions. Among these were first *Der getreue Eckart und der Tannenhäuser* (The Faithful Eckart and Tannenhäuser), from Ludwig Tieck's collection of fairytales *Phantasus*, in which is told the story of Tannenhäuser and his dallying in the Venusberg, his pilgrimage to Rome and his repulsion by the pope. Second, E.T.A. Hoffmann's story *Der Krieg der Sänger* (The Singer's Contest), from his *Serapions-Brüder*, which tells of a competition on the Wartburg in which the participants include Wolfframb von Eschinbach and Heinrich von Ofterdingen. Third, a typically ironic poem, *Der Tannhäuser*, by Heine.[1]

Tieck and Hoffmann are acknowledged in *Mein Leben*, where Wagner also tells us about a crucial occurrence: a chap-book ('Volksbuch') chanced to fall into his hands, in which the stories of Tannhäuser and the song contest, hitherto quite separate, were linked. For a long time the existence of such a chap-book was doubted: Wagner's memory, Newman supposed, was at fault.[2] But it is now almost certain that the chap-book can be identified with

---

[1] A full discussion of these sources and their usefulness to Wagner may be found in Newman's *Wagner Nights*, 58–74.

[2] *ibid.*, 66.

Ludwig Bechstein's collection of Thuringian legends, *Der Sagen-schatz und die Sagenkreise des Thüringerlandes* (1835–8), which erroneously and anachronistically associates the two stories.[3] The link was no more than hinted at but it was reinforced when Wagner's friend Samuel Lehrs appeared one day with a volume including a paper on the Wartburg contest, submitted by C.T.L. Lucas to the Royal German Society of Königsberg. In that paper, Lucas argued – his theory has not subsequently been accepted – that Heinrich von Ofterdingen, one of the competitors on the Wartburg, was the same man as Tannhäuser, the minnesinger.

In the same volume Wagner found for the first time the full text of the medieval poem. With that and especially with the discovery of Jacob Grimm's *Deutsche Mythologie* – a comprehensive study of German mythology – a completely new world was opened up to him. In recreating that world of a bygone age, Wagner was more faithful to its values in many ways than were his contemporaries, with their pseudo-mystical, nationalistic Catholic outlook. That faithfulness may not be evident from the unhistorical linking of separate traditions – though we may surely grant poetic licence for that – but for his firm and instinctive grasp of medieval literature, a knowledge which he was steadily increasing, he commands our respect.

At Aussig (now Ústí nad Labem) in the Bohemian mountains, a detailed prose draft was worked out in the summer of 1842 in a little notebook that is now in the Wahnfried Archive.[4] It consists of ten sheets, part in pencil, part in ink; characters and scenes are indicated, and the dialogue sketched in brief. Preparations for the first performance of *Rienzi* (October 1842) and *Der fliegende Holländer* (January 1843), both in Dresden, prevented Wagner from versifying *Tannhäuser* until the spring of 1843. A feverish excitability in turn impeded work on the composition of the music (except for some sketching of music associated with the Venusberg and the pilgrims).

[3] See Stewart Spencer, '*Tannhäuser: mediävistische Handlung in drei Aufzügen*' (article in English), in *Wagner 1976*, ed. S. Spencer, 40–53.

[4] This first draft (a second followed immediately after) is dated in Wagner's hand: '28 June 1842', incorrectly interpreted by some authorities as 2–8 June 1842. Wagner did not arrive in Teplitz (from where he started his mountain ramble) until 9 June.

It may be inferred from Wagner's account in *Mein Leben* that a single, continuous draft of each act was the first stage in the compositional procedure. This is also the impression given by writers for whom it is an article of faith that all Wagner's works, both early and late, were conceived semi-miraculously, in an unbroken stream of inspiration. Curt von Westernhagen, for example, tells us, with reference to the (fragmentary) complete draft: 'Like all the composition sketches of the later works, this first continuous draft on two or three staves was written down in sequence and with hardly any alterations. Here and there details of characteristic instrumentation are given.'[5] The misleading analogy made between the compositional processes of an early work like *Tannhäuser* and the later works can be traced back to Otto Strobel, who applied the term 'composition sketch' indiscriminately to the first stage of composition, whether of *Tannhäuser* or the *Ring*, whereas the fragmentary initial sketches of the former bear little resemblance to the continuous drafts for the latter. Likewise, in his use of the single term 'orchestral sketch' for both early and late works, Strobel created a false parallelism between them. This stage of the pre-*Ring* works, the (continuous) complete draft, is an elaboration on two staves (with additional staves for extra vocal or choral parts) of the accompaniment from which Wagner could later make a full score; it has relatively few references to orchestration and represents a less advanced stage of composition than its counterpart in the later works (see Appendix E).

The important point about the genesis of *Tannhäuser* is that the first complete draft (surviving only in fragmentary form), which is the one referred to in *Mein Leben*, was preceded by a number of sketches for individual sections. The continuous complete draft then followed act by act, the first being completed in January 1844, the second not till October of that year, and the third in December. The overture was written next and the full score completed on 13 April 1845.[6]

Those who seek to perceive compositional processes in the earlier works similar to those in the mature music dramas, cite a

---

[5] *Wagner: A Biography*, I, 75.

[6] Newman and Burk give 15 April, but the final page of the score is dated clearly, in Wagner's hand: 'Dresden, 13 April 1845'.

letter from Wagner to the Berlin music critic Karl Gaillard, of 30 January 1844:

> Before starting to write a verse, or even to outline a scene, I am already intoxicated by the musical aroma [*Duft*] of my subject. I have all the notes, all the characteristic motives in my head, so that when the verses are ready and the scenes ordered, the opera proper is also finished for me and the detailed musical treatment is rather a calm and considered afterwork which the moment of real creation has preceded.

This is indeed interesting and must be taken into account, the more so because it was written by Wagner at the time and is not therefore one of the fanciful retrospective reinterpretations of events in which he was later to indulge. And yet, how reliable is the artist's own testimony? We have just seen how Wagner's *Mein Leben* account effectively puts us off the scent of the early *Tannhäuser* sketches. How far was that intentional? In any case, the letter to Gaillard scarcely seems to argue for *simultaneity* of composition of words and music; once again 'inter-relation' would be more accurate. Only a close analysis of the early sketches might reveal something more of the order and method of composition.

Wagner's treatment of the Tannhäuser story was, he tells us, influenced by the disgust he was feeling for the trivial sensuousness and hedonism of modern life. He was longing

> to find satisfaction in some more elevated and noble element which, unlike the immediately recognizable sensuality in life and art which was all around me in the present, I conceived as being something pure, chaste, virginal and inaccessibly and unfathomably loving. And what else could this loving desire be, this noblest of sentiments which it was in my nature to feel, but the longing to vanish from the present, to perish in that element of infinite love which was unknown on earth, in a way that only death seemed able to achieve?[7]

So *Tannhäuser* is not the celebration of sensuality that *Das Liebesverbot* was. Wagner's perspective had changed. Paris had convinced him of the emptiness of operatic entertainment as it existed, and his

---

[7] *Eine Mitteilung an meine Freunde*, Sämtliche Schriften, iv, 279. Trans. by Stewart Spencer.

sense of disillusion took on a global significance. Freedom, in *Tannhäuser*, becomes associated not with the unbridled expression of love but with asceticism. Tannhäuser desires to escape from the suffocating joys of the Venusberg. As Adorno has observed: 'His wish is to take the image of pleasure away from the *Venusberg* and return with it to earth: his parting from Venus is one of the authentic political moments in Wagner's works.'[8]

But more destructive forces are also at work. 'The socially determined experience of pleasure as unfreedom transforms libido into sickness';[9] like Tristan and Amfortas, Tannhäuser is 'sick' because he yields to his desires. Wagner may still be attacking puritanical hypocrisy – the pope's failure to forgive is clearly criticized, and Wagner spoke elsewhere of 'the distortion of God's mercy at the hands of a callous priesthood'[10] – but his bourgeois sensibilities impose their own limit. Sex, sexual 'excess', and sexual disease become confused. If some of his attitudes underwent revision during the course of his life, a puritan streak in him remained consistent: in his youth he had participated in a riotous attack on a Leipzig brothel; at the other end of his life he put forward as an objection to vivisection that such experimentation was being carried out to assist in the treatment of venereal disease. Wagner was persuaded to change the title of *Tannhäuser* from his original *Der Venusberg* (The Mount of Venus) because, as was pointed out to him, obscene jokes were likely to be made. The change was prudent, but prudish too: Wagner said he was disgusted.

His social and political perspective had broadened since the 1830s. In Paris he had suffered cruelly from the inequitable concentration of wealth and power in the hands of a bourgeois élite; returning to Germany he found economic conditions no better and social consciousness rising as a result. In spite of his royal appointment he sympathized with the liberal and republican movement. The court at the Wartburg, which banishes Tannhäuser for his outrageous conduct at the song contest, epitomized the reactionary feudal structures of art and life which had to be overthrown.

In terms of Wagner's compositional development, *Tannhäuser*

---

[8] *In Search of Wagner*, 92.

[9] *ibid.*, 93.

[10] Letter to Karl Gaillard, 5 June 1845.

marks an advance, though not a great one, over the *Holländer*. As in all the pre-*Ring* works, thematic ideas tend to be substantial, often complete melodic lines. Certainly the leitmotif is still a thing of the future: in *Tannhäuser* there is only one motif at all comparable in function to the Redemption motif in the *Holländer*, which we saw to be a forerunner of the motif of reminiscence as later used by Wagner. The key-changing perfect 5ths associated with Venus' sneer that Tannhäuser will never find the happiness he seeks if he leaves the Venusberg (towards the end of Act I, scene 2) resurface dramatically in the Act II Prelude, and in a gentler recollection of foolish longing in Elisabeth's Act III Prayer.

Ex. 13

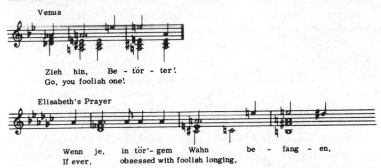

Even this idea makes far fewer appearances than the Redemption motif in the *Holländer*, and not always in the orchestra. There are other effective – though no more thoroughgoing – examples of thematic recall. A felicitous one is that of Elisabeth's 'Ich fleh' für ihn' (I supplicate for him) – an expressive thematic idea based on two rising consecutive perfect 4ths; it appears first during Elisabeth's intercession for Tannhäuser after the minstrels and nobles have drawn their swords on him, and reappears on winds in the orchestral introduction to Act III.

Wagner was never fully satisifed with *Tannhäuser*, and the work's lack of motivic integration must have been one factor in that dissatisfaction; another was his failure yet to master the art of transition. When his complete draft was all but finished he wrote to Kietz (18 December 1844) 'I feel that in it I have approached my ideal with giant steps', a comment which reveals at once his awareness of the significance of *Tannhäuser* and a consciousness of its shortcomings. The absence of a leitmotivic technique and of the smooth transitions both vital to music drama betokens *Tannhäuser*'s allegiance still to opera. As Dahlhaus points out, music in opera 'does not explain or connect but asserts and establishes'; abrupt contrasts and a certain dramatic incoherence are therefore in order. With music drama, on the other hand, everything is linked and motivated; ungainly joins must be obliterated.[11]

In the famous letter to Mathilde Wesendonck of 29 October 1859, in which he expounds the art of transition with special reference to *Tristan und Isolde*, Wagner notes that it was in *Tannhäuser* that he 'first worked with a growing sense of the beautiful, convincing necessity of transition'. As an example of its possibilities he quotes the transition at the end of the Song Contest (Act II, scene 4), in which the outburst of horror at Tannhäuser's confession gradually subsides into a respectful silence for Elisabeth making her intercession. This is indeed a skilfully effected transition, but less happy examples occur elsewhere. The gap, for instance, between the ecstatic Tannhäuser/Elisabeth duet (Act II, scene 2) and the Song Contest (Act II, scene 4) is bridged not by a mature piece of Wagnerian connecting tissue, but by a short scene for Elisabeth and the Landgrave (Act II, scene 3). Its beginning brings us back to earth with a bump of C major and Wagner makes only a token attempt to graft this scene on to its neighbours – almost none to integrate it into the larger work, for example by use of characteristic motifs.

Wagner may not yet be the master of transition, but he is aware of its potential; he is aware, too, of the major importance of drama in his opera, though he has not yet perfected a musico-poetic synthesis. He was concerned that people would respond to the Song Contest as primarily a display of contrasting numbers, as on the concert platform, whereas his preoccupation was with the dramatic conception, the 'poetic intent'. Several letters written at the time of the earliest productions of *Tannhäuser* attest to Wagner's anxiety that the work's dramatic impact would be sacrificed to its musical attractions. Again referring to the Song Contest, Wagner told Baron von Biedenfeld (17 January 1849) that a musical contest alone, with grace notes and cadenzas, would not have served the purpose: the drama must predominate, helped by musical expression, and the catastrophe must be precipitated by the dramatist's or poet's art.

[11] *Richard Wagner's Music Dramas*, 26–7.

Wagner's uneasiness about *Tannhäuser* plagued him for the rest of his life. As Cosima's Diaries record, the subject cropped up several times, right up to the last weeks of his life. On 19 October 1881 she writes: 'As far as *Lohengrin* is concerned, R. says he is completely satisfied with it, but in *Tannhäuser* he would criticize some still-remaining traces of operatic tradition (which mean that in the duet between Elisabeth and T., for example, the singers have almost to change places).' On 6 October 1882 he says 'he would like to stage *Tannhäuser*, which he regards as a consummate drama, but then again not, since he feels that musically some things are insufficiently expressed.' More intriguing are two references the meaning of which is not entirely clear: 'He asks himself whether he will retain enough strength and desire to stage his other works, besides *Parsifal*, there [Bayreuth]; he says he ought to take them all up again, with close attention to detail – *Tannhäuser*, for instance.' Is it a staging or a further musical revision that is in his mind? The two possibilities are also contained in Cosima's recording of an elliptical and oft-quoted remark (23 January 1883): 'He says he still owes the world *Tannhäuser*'. In Reinhard Strohm's opinion, the latter remark 'did not refer only to the planned production in Bayreuth, but demonstrably also to a revision of the score which in the end he never managed to carry out.'[12]

Wagner was right to be self-critical about the musical setting of *Tannhäuser*, and yet it does represent an advance over that of the earlier works. The verse, rhymed or unrhymed, is in a variety of metres, but already showing a strong tendency towards free verse. It is set, in many instances, with regard for the true accentuation of words – that is, regular musical periods are not allowed to dictate matters entirely. Even the most egregious example of old-fashioned aria-writing in the work, Wolfram's 'O du mein holder Abendstern' (O Star of Eve), shows consideration for the natural emphasis of the verse, and there are not many passages where it is disregarded as blatantly as in the Act II duet for Tannhäuser and Elisabeth:

Ex. 14

Von Won - ne-glanz um - ge - ben lacht mir den Son-ne Schein

12 'On the History of the Opera "Tannhäuser" ', 22.

The proportion of music written in declamatory recitative to that in formal numbers (aria, duet, chorus) is vastly increased in *Tannhäuser*, especially in Acts II and III. For the first time in a Wagner opera the former outstrips the latter, even if the melodic content of this declamation leaves something to be desired. One passage in *Tannhäuser* is actually the longest and most advanced dramatic recitative (one might equally call it 'arioso') in any of the works before *Opera and Drama*, that is including even *Lohengrin*. It is Tannhäuser's Rome Narration, in Act III, scene 3. Here the narrative is the main concern and the setting of the words to music is completely geared to that narrative; awkward accentuations are avoided and the nature of the melodic line actually changes as the verse in turn describes Tannhäuser's fervent state of mind on beginning his journey, his memory of Elisabeth, the heavily oppressed pilgrims, and so on.[13] It is a powerful piece of writing, and in the melodic interest of its vocal line and the harmonic elucidation provided by the orchestra it surpasses the comparable narration of the hero in *Lohengrin*: 'In fernem Land' (Act III). (We may note in passing how skilful Wagner was in transforming the awkward but necessary back-narrative into interesting music: the narrations of Tannhäuser and Lohengrin and the Dutchman's 'Die Frist is um' are among the most memorable moments in those works.)

The role assumed by the orchestra in Tannhäuser's Rome Narration is already hinting at things to come in later works. An increase in richness of texture (as opposed to sheer density) was achieved in the *Holländer*, contrasted with *Rienzi*, though there was still virtually no harmonic integration, i.e. use of the orchestral texture in making dramatic points from the text. However, in the Rome Narration, and indeed in *Tannhäuser* generally, we can appreciate a growing awareness on the composer's part of the potentiality of the orchestra for expressive, illustrative purposes; it is becoming more emphatically the medium responsible for generating tension, for effecting modulations, and for bearing the burden of the dramatic argument.

The 'associative' use of tonality described in chapter 10 is heard

[13] This point is made more fully and with music examples by Jack Stein in *Richard Wagner & the Synthesis of the Arts*, 45–7. Stein's study is strongly recommended as an easily comprehensible analysis of the changing relationship of text to music in Wagner's works.

to fine dramatic effect in *Tannhäuser*. The opposing spheres of the sensual and the divine are represented respectively by E and E flat major, the former being the key associated with the Venusberg, and the latter not with Elisabeth (who is represented by no single tonality) but with the pilgrims, and the ideas of salvation and asceticism. Wolfram ends his Act II address to holy love, as he began it, in E flat; Tannhäuser bursts in, in profane defiance, with E major. The two spheres, and their representative tonalities, are again effectively juxtaposed in the final act: Tannhäuser's Rome Narration attains a resonant E flat tonality as the expectant appearance before the pope is reached; after a series of modulations, the Venusberg temptations return with their identifying key of E. Tannhäuser's ultimate salvation restores E flat. As has been pointed out elsewhere,[14] the composition of the Overture presented Wagner with a problem: if he were to present the two spheres together he would not only have to negotiate a skilful deployment of two tonalities a semitone apart (a capacity he did not yet entirely possess), but he would also have to end the Overture in a different key from its beginning (an unsatisfactory prospect, since the Overture was bound to be played on its own). His solution was to give the pilgrims' music for once in E major, instead of E flat.

Associated tonalities are one way in which the two spheres are characterized; another is the incidence of diatonicism and chromaticism. Broadly speaking, the music identified with holiness and holy love is diatonic, while the sinful joys of the Venusberg are portrayed in 'dissolute' chromaticism. Thus the Pilgrims' March, the songs of Wolfram and Walther, and Elisabeth's 'Hall of Song' aria are predominantly diatonic, although sometimes they are affected by chromatic twists, as in a prominent winding passage in the Pilgrims' March which seems to speak poignantly of Tannhäuser's suffering.

Tannhäuser is often referred to as existing in two versions: Dresden and Paris. But as Reinhard Strohm points out in the preface to his edition for the Collected Works (vol. 5), of which the first part appeared in 1980, there are, in fact, at least four major 'versions':

1. the autograph, which was used for the Dresden premiere
2. an 1860 edition, with altered ending, published by Meser Verlag

---

[14] Robert Bailey, 'The Structure of the *Ring* and its Evolution', 52.

3. an 1861 version (not published), as performed in Paris
4. an 1875 edition, as performed in Vienna, published by Fürstner.

Of these, no. 2 is usually, but misleadingly, known as the 'Dresden version', and no. 4 as the 'Paris version'. Wagner himself did not refer to 'versions' but preferred the terms 'new scenes' (*neue Szenen*) or 'alterations' (*Abänderungen*).

A full discussion of the *Tannhäuser* variants cannot be attempted here; instead a few other studies may be indicated, and some general remarks offered. Ernest Newman's chapter on *Tannhäuser* in *Wagner Nights* is useful, as is Carl Dahlhaus's in *Richard Wagner's Music Dramas*, while 'Wagner's Second Thoughts' by Gerald Abraham, in his collection of essays *Slavonic and Romantic Music*, includes an excellent examination of the way a work of 1844 was recast sixteen years later by the recent composer of *Tristan und Isolde* (causing stylistic inconsistencies far greater than those in *Der fliegende Holländer* and which were commented on adversely, even by Wagner's admirers, right from the start). Reinhard Strohm's essay 'On the History of the Opera "Tannhäuser" ' in the Bayreuth Festival programme for *Tannhäuser* of 1978 (in German, English and French) includes a detailed account of all the alterations made by Wagner, and his new edition (referred to above) presents two complete performing scores showing all the variants, an enterprise which will greatly facilitate future studies.

As with the *Holländer*, Wagner began to tamper with the score even before the first performance and more adjustments were made before the second. The chief changes made for Paris concerned the Venusberg scene (Act I) and the Singers' Contest (Act II). The former was expanded, the bacchanal being made more orgiastic and the part of Venus being elaborated to improve the delineation of the character. Walther's solo in the Contest was deleted, because of the inadequacy of the singer who was to take the part. The once-prevalent misconception that Wagner shortened the Overture for Paris and ran it straight into the new Venusberg music seems at last to have been laid to rest. He did indeed intend to do so but was forced to forgo his plan.[15] The ending of the opera, where in the original version Venus does not appear (the Venusberg being suggested by a red glow in the

---

[15] See Reinhard Strohm, 'On the History of the Opera "Tannhäuser" ', 26.

distance) and Elisabeth's death is announced only by bells tolling
from the Wartburg, was changed by Wagner at an early stage; in
spring 1847 he reworked the ending, allowing Venus to reappear
and Elisabeth's death to be signalled by the entrance of knights with
her bier. This was one of the many changes that were incorporated in
the Meser score of 1860.

The foregoing concern the major revisions Wagner made to his
score. Gerald Abraham's essay, mentioned above, deals with the
fascinating subject of the differing treatment of the same passage by
the less and more mature composer, pre- and post-*Tristan*. Abraham
draws attention to the greater mastery of orchestration in the later
music and the more skilful use of transition; summarizing the broad
principles of Wagner's touching-up of the vocal line – as distinct
from its complete rewriting – he mentions 'lengthening of note-
values, imparting a freer, bolder sweep to the line, avoidance of
repeated "reciting" notes and elimination of vocal cliché, with a
(doubtless unconscious) moulding of outlines into more "personal"
melodic shapes.' Much more besides could be gleaned from
Wagner's reworking of his own material, and we still await a complete analysis of the different 'versions' of *Tannhäuser*. It is to be
hoped that the new edition will encourage such investigations.

15
Lohengrin

It was while he was researching the *Tannhäuser* legend in Paris during the winter of 1841–2 that Wagner first became acquainted with the *Lohengrin* subject.[1] Then in the summer of 1845, while taking the waters at Marienbad, he had the opportunity to delve further. He had taken with him editions by Simrock and San-Marte of *Parzival* and *Titurel* by the poet Wolfram von Eschenbach (*c.* 1170 – shortly after 1220),[2] and an edition by Johann Joseph von Görres[3] of the anonymous epic *Lohengrin*. These he absorbed and he soon found an overwhelming desire welling up to give his own poetic expression to Wolfram's subject. *Lohengrin* 'stood suddenly revealed before me, complete in every detail of its dramatic construction', he later wrote in *Mein Leben*. And indeed the prose scenario, which he completed on 3 August, is remarkably close to the final version of the poem which he subsequently worked out in Dresden.

The changes made at this stage, however, reveal much about Wagner's compositional processes: here a detail was expanded or deleted in order to highlight a dramatic point; there the composer provided himself with an opportunity for emotional elaboration or intensification.[4] One example must suffice here. The second act

[1] C.T.L. Lucas's *Ueber den Krieg von Wartburg* (Königsberg 1838) contained a commentary on both legends.

[2] Wolfram von Eschenbach, *Parzival und Titurel, Rittergedichte*, trans. and commentary by Karl Simrock (Stuttgart/Tübingen 1842), 2 vols; *Lieder, Wilhelm von Orange und Titurel von Wolfram von Eschenbach und der jüngere Titurel von Albrecht*, an abridged trans. with essays on the life and works of Wolfram von Eschenbach and the legend of the Holy Grail, ed. San-Marte (Magdeburg 1841).

[3] *Lohengrin, ein altteutsches Gedicht, nach der Abschrift des Vaticanischen Manuscriptes von Ferdinand Gloekle*, ed. J. Görres (Heidelberg 1813).

[4] A full account of these changes is given in the relevant chapter of Ernest Newman's *Wagner Nights*.

concludes with Lohengrin and Elsa leading the procession towards the minister. In the prose scenario all doubts are temporarily dissipated and the crowd enthusiastically cheers them on; but in his libretto Wagner introduces the dramatic stroke that makes such a thrilling effect in the theatre. As she reaches the top step of the minster, Elsa's gaze falls on Ortrud below, who stretches out her arm threateningly. Elsa is horrified and, turning away, presses herself anxiously to Lohengrin.[5] The motif of the forbidden question rings out on trumpets and trombones, the F minor colouring casting a menacing shadow over the radiance of the predominating C major.

Ex. 15

Wagner's *Lohengrin* poem is a masterly development of a number of medieval sources. Having thoroughly familiarized himself with all the interconnecting legends and their variants, he took from each exactly what he required and fashioned all the elements into a libretto which had dramatic conviction while retaining a legendary and historical flavour. The historical background was important to Wagner. The German king who at the beginning of the opera urges the Brabantines to take up arms with him against the Hungarians was Henry I, Duke of Saxony (Henry the Fowler), who reigned from 919 to 936. For Wagner it was essential that Saxons and Brabantines should be clearly distinguished, just as there should be a clear antithesis between the old world of Germanic paganism (personified by Ortrud) and the new one of enlightened Christianity. As *A Communication to my Friends* makes clear, there are also overtones of the philosophies of Feuerbach and Young Germany. The 'necessity of love', the essence of this love as the 'longing for complete material reality', satisfaction of all the senses, pride in human rather than

---

[5] The stage direction in the score is slightly different: there Elsa and Lohengrin embrace *before* Ortrud is observed making her gesture. There are countless such discrepancies between the directions in the librettos (later taken over by Wagner without correction into his collected writings) and the scores. Each source has a legitimate claim to be authoritative, a fact often overlooked by those for whom the sanctity of Wagner's 'stage directions' is an article of faith.

divine achievement: it is the language as much as the ideas that acknowledges the debt.

When the poem was all but complete, Wagner read it to a group of friends. The general opinion was favourable, though Schumann, who was there, was initially perplexed by the absence of musical numbers. Wagner, tongue in cheek, proceeded to read parts of it to him in the form of arias and cavatinas, whereupon Schumann laughed and declared himself satisfied.

Shortly afterwards, Wagner's confidence in his own artistic judgment was shaken by the opinion of a respected friend, Hermann Franck, concerning the tragic ending. Franck considered that Elsa's punishment by the departure of Lohengrin, while in keeping with the nature of the legend, was not in the best interests of dramatic realism in the theatre. At first he suggested that Lohengrin die immediately on stage, then that he be prevented by some supernatural power from leaving Elsa. Wagner could not agree to these suggestions, but he was sufficiently perturbed by Franck's opinion to seek a way for Elsa to leave the world with Lohengrin as a form of penance. His mind was put at rest, however, by the discerning Frau von Lüttichau, the wife of the Intendant at Dresden, who assured him that his original dénouement was the only possible one. A few years later, he was completely thrown by an opinion similar to Franck's being expressed by the writer Adolf Stahr. Reacting over-hastily, Wagner dashed off a letter to Stahr telling him he was right. After suffering agonies of indecision for a few days, Wagner announced emphatically to Liszt that Stahr had been wrong.

But to return to the composition of *Lohengrin*. Preparing the following May (1846) to set his poem to music, he approached the task with a different method from that used in *Der fliegende Holländer* and *Tannhäuser*. In the former, making use of his preliminary musical sketches (simply jottings) he had worked out fuller sketches of individual numbers or whole scenes; these were then assembled, with some transpositions of sequence. In *Tannhäuser*, the sketches made from his jottings almost formed a complete draft, but for *Lohengrin* Wagner did actually make a through-composed draft for the whole work, if only on two staves (one for the voice, one indicating harmonies – often just by a bass) and amounting to little more than 'a very hasty outline' (*Mein Leben*).

Having thus made his first complete draft, Wagner's next step was the all-important second complete draft, in which the accom-

Elsa's Dream

paniment was elaborated on two staves, with more staves being used for extra vocal and choral parts (see Appendix E). In the case of *Lohengrin*, Wagner made various changes to the poem at this stage, especially in Act III;[6] uniquely for him, he decided to make his second complete draft for Act III before those for Acts I and II. The full score was written out between 1 January and 28 April 1848.

If *Lohengrin* has a special fascination it is surely because this opera, more than any other in Wagner's oeuvre, stands tremulously balanced on the brink of music drama. Wagner was too steeped in the heritage of German Romantic opera to throw off all its trappings – even if he wished to – at once; the first true music drama, *Das Rheingold*, was to follow only after an infertile gap of five years – infertile, that is, apart from a couple of pieces for piano, the *Ring* poems and the very considerable group of theoretical writings.[7]

Lohengrin is still decked out in the spectacular garb of traditional opera. There are conspirators, a colourful bridal procession,

6 For an analysis of one such change and an extensive quotation from the first complete draft of this act, see Robert Bailey, 'The Method of Composition', in *The Wagner Companion*, ed. P. Burbidge and R. Sutton, 269–338.

7 Wagner also sketched some music for *Siegfrieds Tod* and *Der junge Siegfried* in 1850 and 1851, as will be seen in the next chapter.

183

and a knight in shining armour. The musical counterpart of all this is to be found in the vestiges of the old number form (recitative, aria, duet, chorus), in the squareness of phrase structure, and in the relative stability of tonality. To take the first of these: two of the best-known numbers from *Lohengrin* are Elsa's Dream, 'Einsam in trüben Tagen' (Act I), and Lohengrin's Narration, 'In fernem Land' (Act III). Each of them has the feel of a set piece and, indeed, each has acquired a special popularity by being performed in isolation from its context; and yet such performances do scant justice to the efforts Wagner was making to integrate numbers into a continuous musico-dramatic structure. For example, Elsa's second stanza, in which she describes the knight in her vision, is introduced by the Grail motif, first heard in the Prelude:

Ex. 16

and this motif is later to provide the substance of Lohengrin's Narration. The link between the two numbers is reinforced by the similar melodic contours of the opening of Elsa's second stanza and of Lohengrin's Narration:

Ex. 17

Ex. 18

Even the few bars' pause before Elsa opens her mouth contain more than just the conventional pizzicato string chords that are apparent in the score: the timing of those chords suggests the 'expectant silence' of the stage direction. Not, to be sure, a transition of the masterly kind later to be found in *Tristan*; nevertheless a step in the right direction.

As for phrase structure, the entire work is permeated by periods consisting of multiples of two- and four-bar phrases. There are exceptions; for example, both Elsa's Dream and Lohengrin's Narration begin with conventionally balanced phrases but develop into a freer structure more appropriate to narrative as the unfolding of the tale seizes the imagination of teller and listener. The ponderous quality of *Lohengrin* is due largely to these quadratic phrase patterns, together with the virtual absence of triple time. On the other hand, the verse, which is more regular than that of *Tannhäuser* and has many more rhymed lines, moves along faster than that of the earlier opera. The poem of *Lohengrin* also shows a tendency towards the archaisms and alliteration that were to be such a feature of the *Ring*.

But if certain traits of the old-fashioned operatic style are still present, we can see Wagner struggling with all his might to loose himself from these shackles. When Liszt wrote: 'The music of this opera is characterized by such a predominant unity of conception and style that there is not a single melodic phrase, and even less a complete passage or ensemble, whose true sense and inner meaning are at all comprehensible if separated from the whole',[8] he could not have known how much truer a description this would be of Wagner's later works. A rigorous modern analysis would hardly come to the same conclusion as Liszt. Nevertheless, one can see his point: even the Bridal Chorus gains from being heard in its musical and dramatic context. It is possible, as Wagner did for Schumann, to divide the work up into numbers, but the divisions are far less apparent than in the *Holländer*. Recitative and aria give way to a new, continuous, arioso-like texture; not yet as fluid as it was to become, but such that Wagner could tell Liszt (8 September 1850) that the singers ought not to know that there were any recitatives in it. The chorus has

---

[8] *Lohengrin et Tannhäuser de Richard Wagner* (Leipzig 1851). An Eng. trans. of part of this essay appears on pp. 178–9 of *Wagner: A Documentary Study*, ed. H. Barth, D. Mack and E.Voss.

plenty of opportunity to make its presence felt, but crowd scenes do not occur unless they arise out of the dramatic action, and the chorus is more skilfully integrated into the musical texture than in Wagner's earlier operas. Note, for example, how at the beginning of Act I, scene 2 the men of the chorus describe the rapt appearance of Elsa as she enters, and how, in whispers, they comment on her enigmatic words.

These stylistic advances are fittingly anticipated, indeed epitomized, by Wagner, in an exceptionally beautiful Prelude marking considerable progress from the traditional opera overture. The convention for the overture that had crystallized during the second half of the eighteenth century was a slow introduction, to be followed by a fast movement, in common time, with little in the way of thematic development. An attempt was sometimes made, in the *opera seria*, to match the mood of the succeeding drama; Mozart's *Idomeneo* expertly exemplifies this, and in his famous preface to *Alceste* (1769) – a reform manifesto – Gluck expresses his conviction that 'the overture ought to apprise the spectators of the nature of the action that is to be represented'. Composers sometimes, as often with Weber, gave out notable tunes from the opera; sometimes they preferred to develop a smaller number of themes within a sonata or sonata-related structure. Wagner's achievement in *Lohengrin* is that finding himself dissatisfied with the 'scissors-and-paste' construction (to use Hans Gal's term) of the *Holländer* and *Tannhäuser* overtures, he was able to fashion a Prelude of perfect proportions, that was at once an exposition of some thematic ideas from the work and that depicted in music a visionary experience: the descent from heaven of a host of angels bearing the Grail, and their final return to heaven, having left the Grail in the care of holy men.

One scene towers above the rest in *Lohengrin*: Act II, scene 1. It is the magnificent dark-hued scene in which Ortrud exerts her malignant influence over her husband Telramund, telling him how Elsa's asking of the forbidden question ('Who is Lohengrin and where has he come from?') would ensure the downfall of both. While picking up the thread of the musico-poetic synthesis that had already been essayed in Tannhäuser's Rome Narration, this scene represents Wagner's most confident stride towards music drama to date. In order that the vocal lines could convey, by their shape and their inflections, the characters of Ortrud and Telramund, it was necessary first to liberate them from four-square phrase structures. Then, by interweaving motifs associated with a particular character or idea, Wagner was able to paint a canvas in which all the parts contributed to the effect of the whole, rather than standing as self-contained numbers within a scene. The new liberated line is neither recitative nor aria but a musical analogue of the forceful passions articulated by the text.

A prominent motif here is the one associated with Ortrud and her sorcery; it is first heard in the twelfth bar, menacingly given out by cellos and two bassoons:

Ex. 19

This motif, built on the diminished 7th chord – traditional in German Romantic opera for the depiction of the supernatural – sounds and resounds throughout Ortrud's music in this act, its baleful tones spreading like tentacles. We hear it first on the cor anglais, then taken up by other woodwind instruments on their own or in combination, as Ortrud reveals to Telramund the deadly secrets learned by her prophetic powers. Two other motifs repeatedly appear, the first originally uncoiling on cellos at the beginning of the act:

Ex. 20

and the second similarly expressive of sinister forces:

Ex. 21

All of these combine to give Ortrud a depth of character such as is found in none of Wagner's earlier works. He cannot yet resist the grand operatic revenge duet with which the scene ends (an ensemble of the kind that was shortly to be prohibited by Wagner), but there is no denying the power of the theatrical effect created by the two vocal lines in unison supported by tremolando strings and occasional woodwind and brass choruses. If the scenes of festivity and passages of narrative elsewhere in *Lohengrin* are the most obvious indication that Wagner was still short of complete maturity, Act II, scene 1 is a most impressive achievement and paves the way for the style of the · *Ring*.

A striking anticipation of the leitmotif technique – as it was shortly to be advocated by Wagner in *Opera and Drama* – is the motif of the forbidden question (Ex. 15). This conforms perfectly to Wagner's prescription in that it originates in the musico-poetic line – it is first heard to the words 'Nie sollst du mich befragen' (Never shall you question me) – and in that its reappearances always serve to remind the listener of Lohengrin's stern warning to Elsa not to ask his name or origin. Sometimes this will be in response to a specific reference in the text, sometimes it will form its own independent comment on events. One notable example has already been given: the closing bars of Act II, when Elsa, reaching the top step of the minster, is thrown into terror and confusion by the sight of Ortrud with outstretched arm (Ortrud, as already mentioned, is planning the couple's ruination by means of the question). Other examples occur earlier in the same act, during the Ortrud-Telramund scene, for instance, when Ortrud tells her husband of Lohengrin's vulnerability to the forbidden question. Even more telling is the appearance of the motif in the orchestra in the following scene (Act II, scene 2) as Ortrud sows the seed of doubt in Elsa's mind: 'Könntest du erfassen' (Could you only comprehend how strange his ways; may he never desert you as he by magic came to you!). Ortrud hypocritically shows concern, but the motif sounding quietly on cor anglais and bass clarinet makes it clear to the audience that Ortrud is trying to provoke Elsa to satisfy her curiosity about Lohengrin.

In spite of the advanced use of the forbidden question motif, this, like the motifs of *Lohengrin* generally, is of a different kind from many leitmotifs in the *Ring* and serves a different structural function. The motifs of *Lohengrin* are often fully rounded themes with matching phrases; some motifs in the *Ring* are of a similar sort but many are short, pregnant ideas capable of infinite transformation. (Compare, for instance, Ex. 15 and 19 with Ex. 29.) And whereas the former appear dutifully in connection with a character or concept but without making any impact on the design of the work, motifs in the *Ring* actually help to shape the structure: by being combined and divided, assembled and fragmented, they create the intricate motivic network which makes the *Ring* the unique work it is.

The 'associative' use of tonality is again present in *Lohengrin*. Lohengrin himself and the sphere of the Grail are represented by A major, the key in which the work begins and ends, and, naturally, the key of his Act III Narration, 'In fernem Land'. Elsa is associated with A flat major (and minor), while Ortrud and her evil attributes are depicted in F sharp minor (the relative minor of Lohengrin's tonality). There is a further notable conjunction between the king's trumpeters on stage and C major. The second and third scenes of Act I are a powerful demonstration of the expressive use to which such tonalities could be put. Scene 2 opens in A flat with Elsa's appearance. Her dream 'Einsam in trüben Tagen' is centred around that key but Lohengrin's swan-drawn skiff also brings A major with it in a glorious seven-bar modulation. When Lohengrin offers himself as Elsa's champion, the music switches back, in an even more economical key-change, to A flat. Shortly after, as the spotlight turns on Lohengrin again, there is another step-up to his tonality of A. Wagner's ability to play with two tonalities so close together (a far more difficult operation than with two more widely spaced keys) is yet another indication of his rapidly maturing talent.

The orchestration of *Lohengrin* was praised by both Liszt and Richard Strauss in extravagant terms. Liszt, as the first conductor of the work, had the opportunity to study the orchestration in detail, and in his long essay on *Lohengrin* and *Tannhäuser* (quoted from above) he described with overflowing enthusiasm how each of the elements in *Lohengrin* has its own distinctive colouring – strings for the Holy Grail, wind for Elsa, brass for the king – and how 'magnificent contrasts' were achieved when one followed another: for example, the soft, pure woodwinds are 'like a refreshing dew' as Elsa appears on the balcony after the 'blazing passion' of the duet for Telramund and Ortrud (Act II, scene 1).

Strauss, in his revised edition of Berlioz's treatise on orchestration,[9] gives a number of examples from Wagner's works; indeed, he boldly (and modestly) states that Wagner's scores represent 'the only

[9] *Instrumentationslehre von Hector Berlioz*, supplemented and revised by Richard Strauss (Leipzig, 1905), foreword.

progress worth mentioning in the art of instrumentation since Berlioz'. In his foreword he singles out *Lohengrin* for its masterly variety of tonal combinations, achieved largely by Wagner's handling of the wind, in particular his application of the 'third wind' (*dritte Bläser*) – by which he means the addition of the cor anglais to the two oboes, and the bass clarinet to the two clarinets, to form homogeneous and potentially independent choruses alongside the three flutes and three bassoons.

Important as these tonal groupings are, it should be stressed that the score of *Lohengrin* does not depend on the kind of 'rank' effects found in the works of the organist composers César Franck and Bruckner. Wagner uses his expanded resources to increase the range of combinations available, and it is in the blending of contrasting timbres that his mastery is evident. Restless innovator as he was, triple wind was not going to satisfy Wagner for long; in his next work he was to augment his forces to an extent hitherto undreamed of in the history of the modern symphony orchestra.

16

Der Ring des Nibelungen

'In this work I no longer gave a thought to the Dresden or any other court theatre in the world; my sole preoccupation was to produce something that should free me, once and for all, from this irrational subservience.' Thus wrote Wagner in *Mein Leben* about the *Ring*, and indeed he did produce something that was deliberately beyond the reach of provincial court theatres; better to risk remaining unperformed and be gloriously independent, he reasoned. But of course he soon had ideas about mounting a festival exclusively for the performance of his tetralogy of music dramas, and the staging of the *Ring* at the Festspielhaus in Bayreuth in August 1876 was the victorious culmination of Wagner's quarter-of-a-century-long struggle to realize his aims. The composition of the *Ring*, with a period of several years' intermission, took a staggering twenty-six years – from the writing of the first words in 1848 to the final touches on the score in 1874. The sustaining of the creative imagination over such a vast period of time and the single-minded determination that enabled Wagner to bring both music dramas and festival to fruition are one of the supreme achievements in the history of music.

Sources

Contrary to popular supposition the characters and events portrayed in the *Ring* are not all mythical. Certainly the deeds of gods and heroes described there are the stuff of myth, but human beings who later came to be given names like Siegfried, Gunther and Gutrune actually existed in the first millennium of the Christian era, even if it is not always clear with which individuals the characters are to be identified. Such real historical people and events were interpreted and reinterpreted by chroniclers and poets until eventually they were 'fixed' in the form of sagas and epic poems in the twelfth and thirteenth centuries. These were the sources plundered by Wagner.

Myth and history were intertwined from the beginning. Wagner claimed to have abandoned his drama *Friedrich I* (probably intended as an opera) on discovering the potentiality of myth, but he is contradicted by the chronology.[1] Moreover, it was the very over-lapping of his historical theme — centring around Frederick Barba-rossa, the Hohenstaufen emperor — with the Nibelungen story that induced him later to write an essay which he called *The Wibelungen: World History out of Saga*, a piece that indulged in some speculative etymology to prove certain connections.[2]

Wagner's main sources for the material of the *Ring* were as follows. First, the Poetic (or Elder) Edda, written in unrhymed verse with *Stabreim*. Second, the *Völsunga Saga*, a prose narrative that was perhaps his richest source, containing as it did a detailed account of the whole of Siegfried's life (Sigurd was his Norse name), together with the story of his parents, the Völsungs, which provided the essence of Acts I and II of *Die Walküre*. Third, the Prose Edda by Snorri Sturluson, a leading literary and political personality born in Iceland *c.* 1178. This was the source that offered the clearest outline of the story of Wotan (Odin) for *Das Rheingold*, as well as of the other gods, Valhalla, the Norns, the Valkyries, the giants, the dwarfs and Ragnarök (the fated end of the gods). These three sources were all compiled in Iceland, probably in the first sixty or so years of the thirteenth century.

Fourth, *Das Nibelungenlied*, an epic poem written in Middle High German around 1200, which furnished material for the story of Siegfried (but only from his arrival at the Hall of the Gibichungs). The poem recreates Siegfried's heroic deeds in the context of the time in which it was written: that is to say Siegfried is portrayed as a chivalrous medieval knight.

Fifth, *Thidreks Saga af Bern*, a prose narrative written *c.* 1260–70 in Old Norse but telling the story and featuring characters from Low German sources. This filled in the tale of the earlier life of Siegfried, describing how he was brought up in the forest by Mime, how he killed the dragon and understood the woodbird. It also provided a more authentic 'primitive' Teutonic atmosphere, treating the story in pagan, fairy-tale terms rather than those of Christian

---

[1] See p. 35.

[2] For the dating of *Die Wibelungen* see p. 35.

chivalry. It is not, however, on a par with the *Nibelungenlied* as a work of art.

All five sources, with the exception of Snorri Sturluson's Prose Edda, are anonymous. In addition to these five chief ones, a number of lesser sources were drawn on by Wagner, as well as various scholarly writings of his day in the form of essays and critical editions. In particular he was indebted to the formidable scholarship of the Grimm brothers – immortalized for a popular audience by their collections of fairy-tales, but also making an inestimable contribution to the nineteenth-century resurgence of interest in the early Teutonic peoples with their thorough research. Wilhelm Grimm's *Die deutsche Heldensage* (The German Heroic Saga) assisted Wagner in finding his way through this enormously complex mass of material, while Jacob Grimm's *Deutsche Mythologie*, a comprehensive study of German mythology, was invaluable to him.

Wagner's wholesale identification of the German gods with the Scandinavian ones occasionally drew on Wilhelm Grimm's authority but often far exceeded it. He also felt free to adjust the names orthographically on poetic grounds, turning, for example, Frikka into Fricka, Donar into Donner, and Wodan into Wotan (the last was a change made at a later stage of the composition).

Finally, the extent to which Greek drama influenced Wagner in the conception and working-out of the *Ring* has often been overlooked. In the summer of 1847 he read and was immediately gripped by the Greek tragedians, especially Aeschylus, whose *Oresteia* was available to him in a new translation by Johann Gustav Droysen. By the time he was writing *Art and Revolution* Wagner was regarding Greek drama as the perfect artwork whose principles should be copied as the solution to the sterility of present-day operatic entertainment: performers and audience united in a reinterpretation of mythology common to their understanding and given as a religious festival. But the influence went further than that. The *Oresteia* suggested to Wagner not only the framework of a trilogy (*Rheingold* was merely a 'preliminary evening') but also the possibility of linking successive episodes with the themes of guilt and a curse. It is even possible to see the leitmotif principle foreshadowed by Aeschylus' use of recurrent imagery; yet another Aeschylean technique adopted by Wagner is the confrontation of pairs of characters. It was such aspects of dramatic procedure, as well as the philosophical inspiration of hellenism – in particular its life-affirming idealism free of the dampening constraints of Christianity, the religion of consolation and the hereafter – that caused Wagner to say of his reading of the *Oresteia*: 'My ideas about the significance of drama and particularly of the theatre were decisively moulded by these impressions' (*Mein Leben*).

But it was the *Prometheus* trilogy that provided him with many ideas for the plot of the *Ring*. The authorship of *Prometheus* is now questioned by some scholars, but neither Droysen (who reconstructed the trilogy from its surviving fragments) nor Wagner had any reason to doubt that it was part of the Aeschylean canon. As examples of the many parallels between the *Ring* and *Prometheus* one might mention the following: Brünnhilde and Prometheus are both the offspring of an earth goddess who has the gift of prophecy; both defy the ruler of the gods and are punished by being bound on a rock by a fire-god; both foretell to a woman that her descendants will perform heroic deeds; both are freed by a hero.[3]

One cannot but marvel at Wagner's ability to absorb such a tremendous range of literature and scholarship. His capacity then to compress a number of divergent sources into a single, relatively unified poem, that carried a dramatic conviction all its own, has irritated some specialists but continues to dazzle those more sympathetic to the Romantic aesthetic by its sheer brilliance.[4]

Construction of the libretto

Not the least unusual feature of the *Ring* is the fact that the four music dramas were written in reverse order. Wagner began in autumn 1848 with *Siegfrieds Tod*[5] (Siegfried's Death) but finding

[3] The interaction of Wagner and Aeschylus is examined in greater depth by Hugh Lloyd-Jones in his article 'Wagner and the Greeks', and by Arthur Drews in 'Richard Wagner and the Greeks', *Wagner*, i (1980), 17–21 (trans. of an article first published in the *Bayreuther Festspielführer* for 1933). Michael Ewans' tendentious *Wagner and Aeschylus* deals with the purported parallelism of the *Ring* and the *Oresteia*.

[4] For more information on Wagner's sources and an enthralling account of his manipulation of them, see Deryck Cooke, *I Saw the World End*.

[5] Both in his sketches and the first printed copy Wagner spelt this *Siegfried's Tod*, but the apostrophe was later dropped and that is how it is now generally referred to.

that this involved an unacceptable amount of narration of earlier events he then in 1851 wrote *Der junge Siegfried*[6] (Young Siegfried). Working back, the poem of *Die Walküre* completed a cycle of works to be given over three evenings, which was then prefaced with a prelude, *Das Rheingold*.

However, it is often forgotten that Wagner's original conception of the story was in the 'correct' order. Shortly before embarking on the text of *Siegfrieds Tod* he mapped out in prose a résumé of the whole drama dated 4 October 1848 and called *The Nibelungen Myth as Sketch for a Drama*.[7] Incomplete as this sketch is, the story has been assembled substantially in the order which it was to follow in the completed work. At this point Wagner was intending to centre his drama around Siegfried's death: like a Greek tragedy, the final catastrophe was the point of focus, there were very few other main dramatic events, and preceding contributory incidents would be narrated. At this juncture the end was quite different. Brünnhilde purges the guilt of the gods by an act of self-immolation and the gods reign in glory instead of perishing.

When *Siegfrieds Tod* was then written, Eduard Devrient, Wagner's friend and former colleague at Dresden, felt that too much background knowledge to the story was presupposed: in particular he suggested that Siegfried and Brünnhilde should be shown 'in their true and calmer relationship' before they appear hostile to each other. Wagner saw the point and added the prelude: a scene for the three Norns provided more background, the scene of Siegfried and Brünnhilde's leavetaking on the mountain their 'true and calmer relationship'.

Wagner then put aside *Siegfrieds Tod*, perhaps unsure how to reconcile the diverging strands of the drama – divine myth and heroic tragedy – and in any case preoccupied in fleeing for his life after the abortive revolution. In summer 1850 Liszt came close to negotiating a commission for Wagner (now in exile in Zurich) to complete work on *Siegfrieds Tod*. Such a commission never materialized but in fact Wagner, as previously mentioned, was reluctant to be tied down to the requirements of any court theatre in the world; he also realized that a preliminary drama was necessary and began in May 1851 to

[6] Originally *Jung-Siegfried*.

[7] See chapter 4, note 1.

sketch *Der junge Siegfried*. The poem was written between 3 and 24 June. In 1856 Wagner was contemplating new titles, but not until 1863 was *Der Junge Siegfried* definitively renamed *Siegfried*; *Siegfrieds Tod* became *Götterdämmerung*.

Die Walküre and *Das Rheingold* followed, beginning with the earliest prose sketches in October/November 1851, proceeding through the stage of a prose scenario and reaching versification, or libretto form, in 1852 (*Walküre* 1 June–1 July; *Rheingold* 15 September–3 November). Next Wagner found himself in the position of having to revise *Der junge Siegfried* and *Siegfrieds Tod* in the light of *Walküre* and *Rheingold*. The alterations made at this point are of some significance: Siegfried was replaced as the central character by Wotan; the ending was changed so that the gods were no longer purged and allowed to reign in glory but instead doomed and due to go up in smoke with their home, Valhalla; the Norns scene in the added prelude was completely rewritten; a confrontation between Brünnhilde and the rest of the Valkyries became the telling scene we now know in which Waltraute comes to plead with Brünnhilde to give up the ring; several passages of narrative now rendered superfluous by *Walküre* and *Rheingold* were removed (though not enough for the taste of some listeners).

Composition sketches

Wagner's preliminary composition sketches are a fruitful field of study because so often they highlight discrepancies between his actual method and the one he described. In the case of the *Ring* the surviving sketches include a continuous draft for each music drama (first complete draft), a detailed continuous draft of *Siegfried* and *Götterdämmerung* (second complete draft), a first draft of the full score for *Rheingold*, *Walküre* and *Siegfried* Acts I and II and an autograph score for *Siegfried* and *Götterdämmerung* (those for *Rheingold* and *Walküre* are lost, having entered the possession of Adolf Hitler). There are also fragmentary sketches for both text and music, and Wagner's own copy of a libretto of the *Ring* privately printed in 1853 has many jottings and much correcting of the text made during the composition of the music.

The first complete draft for *Rheingold*, as for all Wagner's subsequent works, was in pencil, continuous and exhaustive (with rare exceptions), the text of the poem being set from beginning to end.[8] It is true that this complete draft drew on earlier sketches (as had the first continuous drafts of *Tannhäuser* and *Lohengrin*) but in those operas the preceding sketches had usually been of sections of text-setting; now they were only fragmentary sketches and jottings of musical ideas which were to be linked to a text in the complete draft. The vast challenge of writing for the first time for a hugely expanded orchestra such as was used in the *Ring* caused Wagner to make a draft for his full score, specifically to elaborate the orchestration; this he did only for *Rheingold*.

Wagner did not make a second draft for *Walküre* since he was by now familiar enough with his expanded orchestral forces to go straight into score. In spite of the greater degree of elaboration in the first complete draft of *Walküre* (often one vocal stave plus two instrumental, instead of one vocal plus one instrumental as for much of *Rheingold*) he experienced much agonizing when he tried to recall his inspiration in order to write out a score from that draft, on account of many delays and interruptions, not to mention the great length of the work.

These difficulties were forestalled in *Siegfried* by the making of a second complete draft in ink on three staves or more, in which ideas could be developed and the orchestral texture to some extent worked out.[9] *Siegfried*, moreover, was composed one act at a time; that is to say each act reached its score form before the next was started. For *Götterdämmerung* in particular Wagner made many sketches of individual motifs, working out possible combinations for them; this was necessary on account of the complexity of the texture of that work.

The composition sketches are transcribed and analysed in detail by Curt von Westernhagen in *The Forging of the 'Ring'*. Much can be learnt from this book about Wagner's compositional processes; unfortunately the study is marred not only by careless transcriptions but also by a selective presentation of evidence that is less than

---

[8] See ills 100 and 101 in *Wagner: A Documentary Study*, ed. H. Barth, D. Mack and E. Voss, for a reproduction of the last two pages of this draft. Ill. 102 on the facing page is the first draft of the score of *Die Walküre*.

[9] Two pages of the second complete draft of *Siegfried* are reproduced as ills 107 and 167 in *Wagner: A Documentary Study*, ed. H. Barth, D. Mack and E. Voss.

objective. As has been pointed out,[10] the supposed simultaneity of the poetic and musical creative inspirations can often be a superimposition of the scholar's conviction rather than a fact whose proof is yielded by scrupulously scientific analysis.

Two examples may be given of this. First, Westernhagen makes much of a 'unifying genius' that enabled Wagner to bind his leitmotifs not only to each other but also explicitly to the text so that the text and music of any particular passage come into existence solely to complement each other. This theory is knocked on the head by the inconvenient fact that the sketches for *Siegfried*, for example, frequently use a melody conceived independently of the text and elaborate it in conjunction with the text. There are also ideas that were later taken over into *Tristan*; one early sketch for *Siegfried* is actually headed by Wagner: 'Act III or *Tristan*', showing that he was as yet unsure in which work to use the idea.

The second example concerns the so-called 'vision' of La Spezia. It was in an inn there on 5 September 1853, Wagner recounted in *Mein Leben*, that the long-delayed impetus to start the composition of *Rheingold* suddenly came to him as he lay on a couch in a kind of half-sleep.

> I suddenly got the feeling that I was sinking into a strong current of water. Its rushing soon developed into a musical sound as the chord of E flat major, surging incessantly in broken chords; these presented themselves as melodic figurations of increasing motion, but the pure chord of E flat major never altered ... With the sensation that the waves were now flowing high above me I woke with a violent start from my half-sleep. I recognized immediately that the orchestral prelude to *Das Rheingold* had come to me...[11]

A dramatic story, and one that suited Wagner's intended image as a natural genius whose creative ideas issued spontaneously out of the subconscious; no Beethovenian hammering of motifs for him. A pity to spoil the story but the fact is that the evidence, while clinching the

[10] John Deathridge, 'Wagner's Sketches for the "Ring"', *Musical Times*, cxviii (1977), 383–9.

[11] Trans. by Mary Whittall, reproduced from Curt von Westernhagen, *Wagner: A Biography*, I, 181.

matter conclusively in neither direction, tends to suggest that the actual genesis of the *Ring* occurred earlier and rather more prosaically.[12]

Having seen some of the consequences of misreading the evidence, we may take another look at the composition sketches for the insights they afford. To begin with it is clear that Wagner's first continuous setting of the texts was on the whole an impressively fluent affair; large passages were set down in a form that was not to change radically or even at all before the final score. The first complete draft of *Rheingold* was made between 1 November 1853 and 14 January 1854, that is about ten weeks, less ten days' illness — an astonishingly short space of time in view of the new ground that was being broken in terms of word-setting and motifs. On the other hand, contrary to the belief encouraged by generations of Wagner scholars — following Wagner himself — the act of composition was at the same time a painstaking process of self-correction and improvement. Small changes were sometimes made to the text when he came to set it, in the interests of an effective conjunction of words and music — he had not, of course, the sensitivity or artistic integrity of a Hofmannsthal to contend with; however, it was rare for him to make cuts. A confirmation of Wagner's regard for tonal structure can be found in the indications of key, by the appropriate letter of the alphabet, in passages where the tonality over larger periods is unclear.

We shall see later that the recurrence of leitmotifs in the original key is a favourite structural device of Wagner. The sketches reveal that this was no simple matter: they show Wagner sometimes attempting to bring back a motif in the original key but passing up the temptation if the new tonal context is unable to accommodate it. On very rare occasions he names motifs, but not so as to end controversy on the matter for all time: the motif universally associated with the ring itself is called 'world inheritance'. The sketches have a few stage directions, implying that Wagner was conceiving the work in terms of the stage right from the beginning. Finally, Italian tempo markings in the sketches were turned into German in the scores. Westernhagen believes this was not a matter of chauvinism but done in the interests of flexibility: the definitions of the

---

[12] See Deathridge's article cited in note 10 for a full discussion.

Italian terms were for Wagner too rigid. The truth is more likely to be a combination of the two.

In addition to the composition drafts already mentioned, a sketch exists of a musical setting for *Siegfrieds Tod*, made in 1850. The manuscript is in the Library of Congress in Washington and has to date been transcribed three times, by Curt von Westernhagen,[13] Robert Bailey[14] and Werner Breig.[15] The document is important as a guide to Wagner's search for a suitable vehicle for the text of *Siegfrieds Tod* and since part of the sketch (the duet for Brünnhilde and Siegfried) has the same words as the corresponding part of *Götterdämmerung* (Prelude), it enables us to compare two settings of the same words: one by the composer of *Tannhäuser* and *Lohengrin* searching for a new idiom to express the grand ideas he had conceived, the other by the mature composer of *Tristan*, *Die Meistersinger* and three-quarters of the *Ring*.

The most important aspects of this sketch for *Siegfrieds Tod* may briefly be mentioned. First, it is noticeable that similarities between the sketch and the final setting are only incidental. The much vaunted simultaneous conception of words and music was in this case, then, not held sacrosanct, and Wagner later devised a quite new setting for the same words. Second, Wagner's melodic contours were restricted in 1850, with steps of a tone, semitone and 3rd predominating. Later he developed a freer line with frequent leaps of a 6th and 7th, up and down (a practice to be extended yet further in Expressionistic writing of the following century), and generous melismas in which the voice swoops to several notes on a single syllable. Third, the vocal line in the sketch is very much the part on which all attention focuses; later the voice part came to be integrated into the orchestral texture as *primus inter pares*. Fourth, the har-

---

[13] See *Vom Holländer zum Parsifal*, 38–54; 'Die Kompositionsskizze zu "Siegfrieds Tod" aus dem Jahre 1850', *Neue Zeitschrift für Musik*, cxxiv (1963), 178–82; *The Forging of the 'Ring'*, 13–15.

[14] 'Wagner's Musical Sketches for *Siegfrieds Tod*'.

[15] *Studien zur Entstehungsgeschichte von Wagners 'Ring des Nibelungen'*, (diss. U. of Freiburg 1973). A short summary of Breig's study can be found in John Deathridge's article cited in note 10, p. 385.

monic language of the sketch, though advanced, is considerably less daring than that of the final version.[16]

Before leaving this section on the actual process of composition, a word is due on one of the most singular aspects of the *Ring*: the fact that its composition was abandoned for twelve years, during which time two further and strongly contrasting music dramas (both from each other and from the *Ring*) were produced – *Tristan* and *Die Meistersinger*. On 28 June 1857 Wagner wrote to Liszt: 'I have led my young Siegfried to a beautiful forest solitude; there I have left him under the linden tree, and have bade him farewell with heartfelt tears.' (He had broken off work on the first complete draft of Act II of *Siegfried* on the 26th, and on the second complete draft on the 27th.) However, it is not quite the case, as is sometimes said, that he abandoned the composition after continuing to the end of Act II – even less in the middle of Act II with Siegfried resting under the linden tree – and did not take up work on it again until 1869.

In fact what happened is this. Between 13 and 30 July 1857 Siegfried was retrieved from the linden tree and the first complete draft of Act II finished; the second complete draft followed immediately. On 27 September 1864 Wagner took up again the task of making a fair copy of the score of Act I and between 22 December of that year and 2 December 1865 the scoring of Act II was undertaken. Work on Act III began on 1 March 1869, after the fair copy of the Act I and Act II scores had been finished off. So while it is true that the process of composition itself was suspended for twelve years, it is misleading if the impression is given that *Siegfried* was remote from Wagner's mind throughout that period.

Why did Wagner abandon the *Ring* in 1857? There were a number of contributory factors. His publishers, Breitkopf & Härtel, were not expressing much confidence in him in the tangible way that Wagner needed. The Herculean labour of the work was beginning to get him down – he had after all been engaged on it for nine years already – and it was becoming a burden: 'The Nibelungs are beginning to bore me', he told Princess Marie von Sayn-Wittgenstein (19 December 1856). Wagner was also finding that musical ideas for a work on the Tristan subject were welling up inside him and that he was increasingly getting his wires crossed. The themes that were now

---

[16] See Bailey's essay (note 14) for transcription and full discussion.

occurring to him were of a more chromatic nature and sketches from 1857 suggest that already then Wagner was allowing the *Ring* to move more in that direction. However, having found a suitable dramatic subject on which to try out the new chromaticism, he clearly needed to make a break with the *Ring* until such time as he could devote himself to it wholeheartedly. Finally his discovery of Schopenhauer had brought home to him the fact that his philosophy of life in the mid-1850s was radically different from that of 1848; this shift of outlook and its significance for the conclusion of the *Ring*, and indeed for its interpretation, will be considered later in the chapter.

Musico-poetic synthesis

'The ostensible equality of word and tone renders impossible the full effectiveness of either.' So wrote Wagner's adversary Hanslick[17] about the *Ring* when he heard it at Bayreuth in 1876. It was 'an illusion', he said; continuous dialogue belonged to drama, sung melody to opera. In any case, with most singers one couldn't understand what they were singing. Hanslick's view has been repeated with variations many times since then and it is worth looking more closely at exactly how Wagner applied the principles of the musico-poetic synthesis laid down in *Opera and Drama*, and how far he diverged for practical or aesthetic reasons. In so doing we may arrive at conclusions in a less impressionistic way than one does in the theatre, faced more likely than not with poor diction, bad balance and other distractions.

During the course of this process of composition Wagner was also in the throes of articulating his revolutionary ideas on art in the theoretical essays discussed elsewhere, a fact which gave rise to a fascinating interplay of theory and practice. *Opera and Drama* was written, in spite of its inordinate length, in just four months, between October 1850 and February 1851. Its content could not but be influenced by the nature of the poem *Siegfrieds Tod* which he had already written, and yet *Opera and Drama* goes further, so that the theory exerted its own influence on the remaining poems of the *Ring* and indeed on the revision of *Siegfrieds Tod* into *Götterdämmerung*. Furthermore, as we have just seen (p. 200), Wagner had already

[17] Eduard Hanslick, *Vienna's Golden Years of Music: 1850–1900*, 155.

begun to sketch some music before *Opera and Drama* was written.

The musico-poetic synthesis — that is, the blending of melody and the spoken word into a line that liberated music in order to proclaim the drama instead of being constricted in regular patterns and pre-determined forms — is the key to the mature Wagnerian music drama. It was at the centre of Wagner's efforts to create a new kind of artwork, one that would rekindle the glorious flame of former times.

Wagner never regarded himself as a great poet in the traditional sense of the word. In 1844 he had told Karl Gaillard (30 January): 'I really do not pride myself on my abilities as a poet.' Fifteen years later he accepted that on their own his poems must remain 'almost completely incomprehensible' (letter to Mathilde Wesendonck, 15 April 1859): there was, he said, a fundamental distinction between a purely poetic stage play and a poem designed for music. And it is as a poem for music that the text of the *Ring* must be judged.

The verse of *Rheingold* makes much use of alliteration and root syllables; its lines are compact (minor words eliminated) and in irregular rhythms. It is in those respects faithful to the precepts of *Opera and Drama*. Alliteration comes thick and fast; wherever the eye falls on the libretto, alliteration will not be far away. 'Krumm and grau krieche Kröte!' croaks Alberich as he prepares to turn himself into a toad. 'Hör', Wotan, der Harrenden Wort!' declaims Fafner. And yet even when used appropriately as in the first example it often seems to be pure contriving for effect, rather than revealing underlying associations in the text as recommended in *Opera and Drama*. Ultimately, whether one enjoys or is wearied by the merciless onslaught of alliteration is a matter of taste.

A kind of 'musical alliteration' also occurs, as in the downward octave leap associated with the giants Fasolt and Fafner and the task of building Valhalla which they have now completed. It first appears near the beginning of Scene 2:

Ex. 22

It is next to be found at Freia's words 'Vom Felsen drüben drohte mir

Fasolt' (From yonder rocks Fasolt threatened me) and again at Fasolt's 'Was sagst du?' (What are you saying?). Donner and Loge each have the phrase to the same words:

Ex. 23

Fa - solt und Faf - ner

and there are two further references in the score. Musical alliteration such as this needs to be distinguished both from leitmotif, which in its strict form as a motif of reminiscence becomes the property of the orchestra once it has arisen out of the musico-poetic line, and from 'presentiments', which are orchestral in origin. Another type of musical alliteration involves the repetition of a phrase over a much shorter span – perhaps a few bars.

As a general comment on the word-setting in *Rheingold* one might regret that rather too often Wagner's preoccupation with the trees prevents him from doing justice to the landscape: a musical phrase will match the poetry perfectly in shape and accent but fail to make an emotional impact simply because it is not a sufficiently interesting melodic idea. As in *Lohengrin* Wagner's melodic facility tends to get overwhelmed by his determination to make the text meaningful and project it faithfully. In other passages, notably in scenes 2 and 4, there are incongruous reversions to a recitative-like style of writing. These passages occupy the middle ground between the cadential formulas familiar from eighteenth-century opera and the fully evolved mode of Wagnerian declamation.

It is in *Walküre* that the synthesis is found at its most ingenious; here the subtlety of the interaction between verse and music may be said to represent Wagner's intentions to perfection. One extended example (Ex.24) will give some idea of the quicksilver changes that the melodic line undergoes in order to reflect the poetic substance in all its detail.

Ex. 24

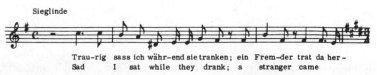

Trau-rig sass ich währ-end sie tranken; ein Frem–der trat da her –
Sad   I   sat while they drank;   a   stranger came

-ein: ein Greis in grauem Ge-wand;   tief
in: an old man dressed in grey;   low

hing ihm der Hut,   der deckt' ihm der Au - gen ei - nes; doch des
hung his hat,   which concealed one of his eyes;   but the

an - dren Strahl, Angst schuf es al - len,   traf die Män - ner sein
flash of the other caused fear in all,   as the men met his

mäch - ti - ges Dräu'n: mir al - lein   weck - te das Au - ge
power - ful glance: in me alone   his eye aroused

süss seh - nen-den Harm, Trä-nen und Trost__ zu - gleich.
sweet yearning sorrow, tears   and consolation together.

Auf mich blickt'er, und blitz-te auf Je - ne,   als ein
On me he looked,   and glared at the others,   as a

Schwert in Hän-den er schwang; das stiess er nun in der
sword in his hands he swung; he thrust it into the

E - sche Stamm, bis zum Heft   haf - tet' es drin:
ash's   trunk,   up to the hilt   it remained there fixed:

'Traurig sass ich' is the end of an eight-bar passage that bears some resemblance to recitative but shows in what a masterly way Wagner now absorbs such declamation into his style. The falling semitone

205

from 'Traurig' to 'sass' and the implied appoggiatura on 'während' suggest Sieglinde's sadness, while the prominence given to 'Frem-der' and the measured tread of the four equally accented beats in that bar announce the entry of the mysterious guest (actually Wotan disguised as the Wanderer, as the Valhalla motif intoned on brass tells us). The three-beat bars of the next passage do not prevent the all-important root syllables from receiving their due accent: 'Greis', '*Gewand*', 'hing', 'Hut', '*Au*gen', with subsidiary accents on '*grau*em', 'tief' and 'deckt' '. The sinister low brim of the guest's hat is depicted in low-lying notes, all on a level, but the melodic line soon hits a peak on 'Strahl' for the flash of fear, and the shape of the phrase 'mächtiges Dräu'n' seems to mirror the raising and dropping of eyebrows in the 'powerful threat' of the glance. The lingering, drooping line 'mir allein weckte das Auge süss sehnenden Harm' is pregnant with sweet sorrow and ends with a yearning rising 4th; all the root syllables are properly accented. 'Tränen' receives a tearful appoggiatura. Then as the narrative tells of the Wanderer's startling gesture in thrusting the sword into the tree, the melodic line becomes more active: 'Auf mich blickt' er'. The arpeggio figure at 'als ein Schwert in Händen er schwang' imitates the swinging of the sword, and the final two lines rising to a climactic top G reflect the mounting excitement both of the spectators and of Sieglinde as she relives the incident.

This is Wagner's musico-poetic synthesis at its finest: a text rich in emotional content is set, with no unnatural word stresses, to a melodic line that registers every nuance while remaining musically interesting in its own right. *Walküre*, especially Act I, is packed with passages like this. It was while Wagner was making his composition sketches for *Walküre* that he encountered the philosophy of Schopenhauer and it may well have been his reading of *Die Welt als Wille und Vorstellung* that was responsible for the slight shift away from absolute equality of poetry and music discernible in Acts II and III of *Walküre*. As we saw earlier (pp. 55–6) Schopenhauer held that music alone was an articulation of what he called the 'will' or noumenon. Because of this direct line of communication, music was capable of expressing the innermost essence of things; it was thus more penetrating than and superior to all the other forms of art.

In 1854 such a glorification of music clearly struck a sym-pathetic chord in Wagner despite his previous theory that all the arts should combine equally to produce the unified dramatic artwork.

Wagner's changing perspective on the subject may be traced as follows. From *Der fliegende Holländer* through *Tannhäuser* and *Lohengrin* to *Rheingold* he had gradually given more emphasis to the drama side of the equation. The furthest point had been reached with *The Artwork of the Future*, in which allowance was even made for occasional spoken dialogue. But with *Opera and Drama* music begins to reassert itself again, and now Schopenhauer's influence provided the intellectual reinforcement for a growing inclination to elevate music.

The musico-poetic synthesis as it features in *Siegfried* and *Götterdämmerung* may next be briefly considered with some observations about the different nature of the styles before and after the twelve-year break. *Siegfried*, although the third to be set to music, was the first poem to be written after the theoretical works of 1849–51. Wagner had not yet acquired the mastery of the new style of verse that marks *Walküre*; there is much alliteration, to be sure, but of a generalized sort, not highlighting parallels of meaning; the free rhythm of lines and high proportion of root syllables conform to *Opera and Drama*. In *Götterdämmerung* there are many fine passages of musico-poetic synthesis, but there is also a tendency towards quick-fire exchanges, a form of dialogue taken over from *Die Meistersinger* (and ultimately from Greek drama) but modified in accordance with the elevated tone of *Götterdämmerung*. The poem features many alliterative parallelisms, but interestingly Wagner refrained from enhancing them when he came to make his musical setting years later. A prominent characteristic of the line in *Siegfried* Act III and *Götterdämmerung* is the degree to which it is ornamented with extraneous little figurations. The following example, with its triplets and appoggiaturas decorating the melismas (i.e. several notes sung to one syllable) on 'Lehren' and 'un-belehret', is chosen at random:

Ex. 25

Nicht zür - ne, wenn dein Leh — ren mich un –be–leh - ret liess.

It will be remembered that in *Opera and Drama* Wagner stated expressly that more than one voice should not sound together, although he did leave himself a loophole. In *Rheingold* that rule is followed: there is no concerted singing except for that of the Rhinemaidens, who may be considered as a single unit. The same is true of *Walküre*, with the comparable exception of the Valkyries. Even Siegmund and Sieglinde at the height of their ecstatic scene together do not sing in ensemble (there are, of course, single beats of overlapping here and there). At the climax of the final duet in *Siegfried* (Act III) Siegfried and Brünnhilde break into concerted singing, but this would seem to fall into Wagner's safety-net since it occurs 'at the peak of lyrical effusion . . . in a communal expression of feeling', and neither is merely providing harmonic support for the other. In *Götterdämmerung*, however, it is a different story: in Act II first the chorus of vassals and then the final trio of the 'conspirators' (Brünnhilde, Gunther and Hagen) represent a complete abandonment of *Opera and Drama* principles – as George Bernard Shaw saw it, a sell-out to traditional opera. In a sense he was right, but the effect in the theatre is anything but bathetic. Wagner's re-integration of existing elements was justified by the new poetic demands of *Götterdämmerung*.

Leitmotif

One of the chief structural features of the *Ring*, and the one that exerted the most influence on post-Wagnerian works of art – both musical and non-musical – is the system of leitmotifs. Hans von Wolzogen gathered together as many of the leitmotifs as he could trace, gave them a name and published the result in the first thematic guide to the *Ring*.[18] From that time on, a veritable industry has developed, devoted to explaining the *Ring* and its motifs. No attempt will be made here to provide that kind of 'guide'. Instead some general observations will be made about Wagner's use of leitmotif, particularly in relation to *Opera and Drama*, and then a single set of transformations will be examined in order to see how Wagner put the technique to expressive effect. The purpose of relating Wagner's art in practice to his theories is not to point an accusing finger at any discrepancies (though it will not do any harm to dispel some of the

---

[18] *Führer durch die Musik zu Richard Wagner's Festspiel 'Der Ring des Nibelungen': Ein thematischer Leitfaden von Hans von Wolzogen* (Leipzig n.d.) The guide first appeared in 1876; the precise title varied from edition to edition. See Bibliography for Eng. trans.

confusion that still exists on this matter) but to use his professed intentions to throw light on the work's structural unity.

Wagner said in *Opera and Drama* that motifs of reminiscence (i.e. leitmotifs) were only to occur when the expressive content of the melodic verse falls to a point where it becomes the intonation of ordinary speech; the function of motifs was to supplement the emotional expression. Conversely, when the intensity of the melodic verse increases, the orchestra reverts to its harmonic role. As far as this declaration of intent is concerned, almost the exact reverse is the case in the actual music dramas. Many of the most highly charged outbursts of the characters are accompanied by motifs of reminiscence, and passages of lower intensity (such as the recitative-like exchanges of scenes 2 and 4 of *Rheingold*) tend to have fewer, not more, motifs.

Any study of Wagner's musico-poetic synthesis – and this one is no exception – is indebted to the thorough and perceptive analysis of Jack Stein in *Richard Wagner & the Synthesis of the Arts*, which shows precisely how the text–music relationship changed from early to late Wagner. Stein has examined the scores very closely indeed alongside the theoretical works. On the question of leitmotifs, he notes that very few in the *Ring* actually conform to the *Opera and Drama* prescription that motifs must originate in the musico-poetic line before being taken over by the orchestra; in *Rheingold* about half, considerably fewer in *Walküre* and *Siegfried*, and almost none in *Tristan*.

Another departure from *Opera and Drama* concerns gestures: they are not always underlined musically in the prescribed method. Many are, of course, and by a variety of colourful means: at Hunding's entry (*Walküre* Act 1, scene 2) the actions of Sieglinde starting, listening and opening the door are all depicted by the orchestra. But in other cases Wagner's artistic judgment overruled his theory and he refrained.

An important difference between the music composed after the twelve-year break (*Siegfried* Act III and *Götterdämmerung*) and the earlier parts of the *Ring* concerns the nature of the leitmotifs. Where the earlier motifs tended to be short and pithy (e.g. Ex.29) – the proper meaning of 'motif' – the later ones are expansive themes which impart a marvellous lyrical sweep to the music (e.g. Ex.26). Furthermore, in spite of numerous powerfully suggestive recurrences of musical ideas, there is in *Siegfried* Act III and *Götterdämmerung*,

Ex. 26

according to Stein, 'only one example of a motif of reminiscence in the *Opera and Drama* sense, the Penalty motif' (allied to the Ring motif and first sung by Gunther to the words 'Bricht ein Bruder den Bund' in the swearing of blood-brotherhood).

Many charges have been levelled at Wagner concerning his supposed carelessness in the use of leitmotif. More often than not it is attributable to a commentator's mindless expectation or artistic myopia. It is complained, for example, that the Valhalla motif is subsequently applied to Wotan himself, or that the Ring or Sword or Spear motif is sounded for no apparent reason – in other words, the object has not been mentioned specifically in the text. It is perfectly true that the associations conjured up by certain leitmotifs shift as the drama progresses. It is also true that the Sword motif, to take one example, often appears without being demanded by the text, and that equally it is often missing when the sword *is* mentioned. To expect Wagner to flag his music drama with leitmotifs as though it were some kind of semaphore, so that the situation can be followed with minimum expenditure of brainpower and imagination, is to choke an artist's creative expression.

Generations of commentators have contributed to this confused state of affairs by their well-meaning motif-naming guides. As soon as one gives a leitmotif the title 'resignation', 'futility' or 'ambition', one is circumscribing the composer's emotional range. It is danger-ous to subject leitmotifs to these limitations, even if some of the labels are appropriate, because the dramatic conditions that call forth a motif are rarely uncomplicated; they are subtle complexes of psychological impulses, and an identical psychological situation will never occur. The gaining of knowledge and experience prevents any precise repetition.

To make matters worse, the significance of some leitmotifs has been misread from the beginning. An egregious example is the motif which has always been labelled the Flight motif; it is the second part of the melody (*a* in Ex. 27) heard in *Rheingold* as Freia enters in agitation followed swiftly by the giants:

Ex. 27

In spite of possible connotations of flight here and in the Prelude to Act II of *Walküre*, the motif is, as Deryck Cooke has shown,[19] actually the main love theme of the tetralogy.

Looking finally at the way motifs are combined in the *Ring*, it is worth pointing out a difference between earlier and later methods. In *Rheingold*, *Walküre* and the first two acts of *Siegfried*, motifs are brought together and superimposed on reasonably strict musico-poetic grounds; that is to say, in spite of the obtuseness of cynical commentators, most people have little difficulty in hearing or working out with the help of the score what is going on at any one point. But it is otherwise in Act III of *Siegfried* and *Götterdämmerung*. Here there is such a riot of motifs and they are combined in such bewildering and breathtaking profusion and with such contrapuntal virtuosity that it is clear that the *Opera and Drama* principles have been abandoned. Again Wagner seems to be anticipating the Expressionist scores (e.g. Schoenberg's *Erwartung*) in which textural density reflects extreme psychological conflict. The Prelude to Act III of *Siegfried* immediately gives notice of the new approach: it is a masterly deployment of no fewer than nine motifs. Throughout these later scores the texture is much denser, more closely worked. Motifs are continually being played off against one another: it is not usual to have more than two sounding simultaneously, but no sooner has one pair made its presence felt than another cuts in. One motif is not allowed to finish before another jostles for attention, and the ear is besieged with motivic interplay. Ex. 28, from which the vocal line has been omitted, is from Act II, scene 4 of *Götterdämmerung*;

[19] *I Saw the World End*, 48–64. Tragically, Deryck Cooke's death occurred before he could reach the musical aspect of his highly important study, but enough of the book was completed to put it in the essential reading category. Cooke blames Wolzogen for the Flight motif label, but in fact it had already been used several years earlier by Gottlieb Federlein in a commentary on *Das Rheingold* published in *Musikalisches Wochenblatt* in 1871.

Siegfried is telling how he obtained the ring and the rest of the hoard after slaying the dragon.

Ex. 28

The following motifs are heard (and repeated) in combination or quick succession: *a* ring; *b* dragon; *c* Rhinemaidens' cry; *d* not a true motif but an idea associated with Alberich watching over the treasure; *e* Fafner. Motivic combinations of this sort are not fluently contrapuntal in the traditional, academic sense; rather, the motifs are pressed together to make a musico-dramatic point – the laws of counterpoint keep up as best they can.

In his 1879 essay *On the Application of Music to Drama*, Wagner offered a hint as to how his music dramas might be analysed, along the lines of motivic transformation. There was an essential distinction, he said, between dramatic and symphonic methods of developing motifs. His transformations were generated according to dramatic imperatives; as such they would, he said, be incomprehensible in a symphonic structure. After quoting Ex.29, he went on: 'Much might be learned from a closer examination of the repeated appearances of the simple Rhinemaidens' motif quoted, so long as it is traced through all the fluctuations of passion throughout the four-part drama, up to Hagen's Watchsong in the first act of *Götterdämmerung* . . .' The last part of this section is precisely that: an examination of the reappearances of that motif as modified by the fluctuations of passion throughout the drama.

The first thing to note about this motif is that there are two forms: a major version (Ex.29) and a minor version (Ex.30):

Ex. 29

Rhein - gold!

Ex. 30

We - he! ach we - he!

Ex. 30 actually occurs first but because of the prominence given to Ex.29 it is probably more appropriate to regard that as the source, as apparently did Wagner (it is prefigured, moreover, in the first two notes of the work's vocal line). The minor version is heard in an agitated figure preceding Freia's entry and both are present in Loge's motif (Ex.31): a neat image of the ambivalent trickster. In Loge's narration of the theft of the gold the ecstatic cry of the Rhinemaidens

Ex. 31

(Ex.29) is transformed into a sombre lament descriptive of the maidens mourning their loss:

Ex. 32

The key is a dark C sharp minor rather than the bright open C major, and the first chord has changed from a thrilling dominant 9th to an ominous diminished 7th; interestingly, the top note of the first chord remains A, but what happens underneath it gives it a quite different colouring. In the descent to Nibelheim the falling semitone reiterates Alberich's grasping greed and frustration, and then appears as a clear statement of a motif alternatively labelled as 'Servitude' or 'Evil':

Ex. 33

There are half a dozen recurrences of Ex.33 in *Rheingold*, all associated with fear, panic or despair experienced by Mime, Alberich or the other Nibelungs. One variant in particular should be quoted as it is specially identified with the power of the ring:

Ex. 34

Ex.34 reappears (at the same pitch) at the climax to the Prelude to Act III of *Siegfried*. The Rhinemaidens' cry (Ex.29) occurs again in the fourth scene of *Rheingold* in a subdued D flat, when Loge suggests that Wotan return the gold to them. It makes only the briefest of appearances in *Walküre* – a measure of the loss of innocence – until the closing pages where in a gently rocking E major transformation it accompanies Wotan's laying Brünnhilde to sleep. It is not the Rhinegold that is recalled here in this evocation of nature but the waters of the Rhine.

In *Siegfried*, Ex. 29 occurs in the Riddle Scene (Act I, scene 2) when the Wanderer alludes to the Rhinegold (Wagner here uses the motif as an alternative to the actual gold motif – see Ex. 37*b*) and less appropriately in a polyphony of motifs associated with Siegfried, the woodbird and the fire, when the Wanderer tries to bar his way to Brünnhilde's rock (Act III, scene 2). Ex.29 also appears in its original C major in a telling stroke of dramatic irony when Alberich confidently asserts that the ring will eventually return to him, its master (Act 2, scene 3), only to be contradicted by the horns intoning the motif and reminding who are the true guardians.

Ex. 33 features much in Act I of *Siegfried* as Mime complains about his forced labour. In *Götterdämmerung* it makes countless appearances, always to indicate servitude, resentment, danger, fear, or plain evil. It is taken over by Hagen and becomes his watchword:

Ex. 35

Hoi - ho!

The entire score of *Götterdämmerung* is suffused with this two-note falling-semitone motif; it appears in all kinds of combinations and always casts a baleful shadow, so sinister and unambiguous is its sound.

The transformation that Wagner mentioned in Hagen's Watchsong (*Götterdämmerung* Act I, scene 2) is by no means its last appearance but it is so poignant a version of the original Rhinemaidens' cry (Ex. 29) that it is worth quoting:

Ex.36

The dissonance, best analysed as a diminished 7th with an appoggiatura F that does not resolve until the following chord, resounds through the score of the whole tetralogy, connecting back to the original Rhinemaidens' cry of joy (Ex.29).

Meanwhile Ex.29 hardly makes itself heard in *Götterdämmerung* as the minor variants take precedence. Significantly it does not appear for a long time in Siegfried's scene with the Rhinemaidens (Act III, scene 1), since they are bemoaning the loss of the gold, but suddenly, as Siegfried invites them to ask of him what they will, the Rhinegold motif rings out (Ex. 37*a*), once again in the original key of C, even though a few bars earlier we were in D:

Ex.37

However, the D in the dominant 9th of the original has become a D sharp and this chromatic alteration gives the motif a plangent, mournful quality. Here, also, it is combined with the true gold motif (*b*) as though to reinforce the urgency of the Rhinemaidens' plea.

Ex. 38

The last important appearance of either motif – major or minoɪ – is in Brünnhilde's peroration. As Brünnhilde bids Wotan rest for ever, 'Ruhe, ruhe, du Gott!', the orchestra brings together several central motifs – the curse, the Rhinemaidens' cry, Valhalla, 'the need of the gods', Erda, the twilight of the gods, Wotan's frustration – into a sublimely beautiful and noble resolution (see Ex. 38). Here Ex. 29 itself is restored to its original dominant 9th, but instead of the brilliance of C major it sounds in a rich, velvety D flat major, the key in which the work is soon to end. Evil is exorcized in this glorious cadence and the falling semitone motif appears no more.

Thus we have traced all the transformations of the Rhine-maidens' cry, 'through all the fluctuations of passion throughout the four-part drama'. Minor key variants (falling semitone) outnumber major key variants (falling tone) by three to one, and we have seen how the falling semitone in particular is woven into the fabric of the tetralogy, always with negative, evil associations.

We have been looking at only one family of motifs; there are many families, and transformations and cross-relationships pro-liferate in abundance. Wagner was right to consider the dramatic transformation of motifs to be one of his greatest achievements.

Tonality and structure

Before looking at Wagner's form in its broadest context, it may be helpful to examine how his 'associative' use of tonality in the *Ring* differs from that in his earlier works. It was mentioned in the chapters on *Tannhäuser* and *Lohengrin* how characters or ideas were associated there with particular keys. But in the *Ring*, motifs associated with individual characters are not tied to specific tonal-ities: they are transposed in accordance with the requirements of the music drama. For example, whereas Lohengrin was associated with the tonality of A major, it is impossible to identify Brünnhilde or Alberich with any single key. Part of the reason is that there are too many leading characters in the *Ring* to apply such a scheme with any consistency.

Some motifs do have a specific tonal association: the curse with B minor, the Tarnhelm with B minor, Valhalla with D flat major (later also E major), the sword with C major (later also D major). By no means every sounding of these motifs is in the 'correct' key but it is remarkable how time and again Wagner steers the music round to a certain key to accommodate one of these motifs. The modulations always sound effortless and unforced; we are not conscious of skilful manoeuvring. Moreover, the tonality of a large-scale unit may be determined by such a harmonic switch: as Siegfried appears in Gunther's form (*Götterdämmerung* Act I, scene 3) the Tarnhelm motif establishes B minor, the key in which the scene and the act will end.

Groups of characters are also identified with a particular tonality: the Valkyries with B minor, the Nibelungs with B flat minor. In all four scenes in the *Ring* that feature the Nibelungs and their racial characteristics B flat minor is predominant and may even be regarded as the tonic key: *Rheingold* scene 3, the Nibelheim scene; the opening scene of *Siegfried*, in which Mime the Nibelung smith hammers at the anvil; *Siegfried* Act II, scene 3, the Mime/Alberich confrontation; *Götterdämmerung* Act II, scene 1, where Alberich appears to the sleeping Hagen.

The all-too-neat symmetries of Lorenz's analyses were discussed in chapter 10, but it should be pointed out that the reaction against Lorenz has led to a tendency to dismiss even valid tonal structures in Wagner's music. It is necessary to identify both the points at which tonality functions in something like the traditional way and those at which some other structural method is at work, for example motivic transformation. A discussion of any of the individual structural aspects of Wagner's music dramas – such as tonality or motif – may or may not be enlightening, but a more comprehensive analysis must also take into account matters such as orchestration, tempo, period and phrase structure, the visual action on stage, the dramatic structure of the text and its division in dialogue.[20]

It is a fact crucial to the understanding of Wagnerian form that his music does not fall into rigid sections definable as an arch or a *Bar*: rather it is in a state of constant flux, a kaleidoscopic chain of shifting patterns. Wagner draws on many traditional forms, among them aria (ABA), strophic song (repeated stanzas with or without refrain), rondo (ABACA) and variation. But he rarely allows the

---

[20] A painstaking analysis of this sort can cover only a small portion of the work at a time and would therefore not be appropriate here. See Anthony Newcomb, 'The Birth of Music out of the Spirit of Drama', for three examples of the method.

form to remain static or 'closed' as in a conventional aria: instead he is constantly manipulating it and changing it into something else. Siegmund's 'Winterstürme' (*Walküre* Act I), for example, begins like a conventional aria with a twenty-bar A section, followed by what appears to be a B section in a contrasting key; but after only nine bars of the B section, themes associated with the love of Siegmund and Sieglinde burst in and we are swept off in a different direction. Act I of *Siegfried* contains a number of identifiable 'songs': Mime's Starling Song 'Als zullendes Kind' and 'Jammernd verlangen Junge' and Siegfried's 'Es sangen die Vöglein' in scene 1; the Forging Song in scene 3, for instance. But none of them is allowed to settle in a pre-ordained Classical mould. The form is broken up by some kind of thematic development, or the appearance of a significant leitmotif, or odd bars of orchestral material. Variants abound; rarely does the same thing happen twice over. Always Wagner is covering his traces. Conventional forms are continually embarked upon and abandoned, beginnings and endings coalesce in the total structure, ambiguity reigns supreme. All this may be summarized in the phrase for the technique which Wagner himself considered to be at the core of his music dramas, the secret of his musical form: the art of transition.

Orchestration

In order to allow himself the maximum flexibility for tone-painting and delineation of character and mood, Wagner expanded his orchestral forces in the *Ring* to an unprecedented scale. He specified quadruple woodwind (for example, 3 clarinets and 1 bass clarinet where *Tannhäuser* and *Lohengrin* called for only three players) and expanded his brass section so that it could divide into four independent families: 8 horns, of which 4 periodically have to switch to provide a family of Wagner tubas; 3 trumpets and a bass trumpet; 3 trombones and a contrabass trombone. Trumpets are the obvious instruments to give out Wagner's numerous fanfare-like motifs, such as those of the Rhinegold and the Sword. The latter often appears on the bass trumpet, an instrument which, according to Walter Piston, is in Wagner's hands 'to all intents and purposes a valve trombone. It is played by trombonists, using the trombone mouthpiece.'[21] The

21 *Orchestration* (London 1955), 263.

bass trumpet was Wagner's own addition to the orchestra and it was constructed specially for the *Ring* according to his specifications. Richard Strauss and Stravinsky are among later composers to have used it. The function in the *Ring* of the contrabass trombone (an instrument rescued from obscurity by Wagner) is to provide a bass for an independent trombone family – conventionally it is the tuba that underpins the trombones. The contrabass trombone has occasionally been used by other composers (Strauss in *Elektra*, and Schoenberg in *Gurrelieder* are two examples) but not often, because the physical demands on the player are considerable. The three usual trombones (two tenor, one bass) are 'liberated' by Wagner, in the sense that he makes melodic demands of them, not just harmonic: they often give out the motifs of Wotan's Spear and the Curse. The celebrated Wagner tubas (again made specially for the *Ring* but this time based on instruments Wagner had seen in the Paris workshop of Adolphe Sax) are actually closer to horns than tubas: they have horn mouthpieces and are played by the 5th–8th members of the horn section. Introduced by Wagner in order to furnish a separate brass family (2 tenor, 2 bass, underpinned by a contrabass tuba) of distinctive tone colour, and bridging the gap between horns and trombones, their rich, round, solemn sound can be heard at the announcement of the Valhalla theme (*Rheingold*, beginning of scene 2) and of Hunding (*Walküre*, Act I, scene 2). Again later composers occasionally took them up, notably Bruckner in his 7th, 8th and 9th symphonies and Strauss in *Elektra*. Wagner tubas (also called 'Bayreuth tubas' or in German 'Waldhorntuben') can cause headaches over intonation in performance.

Such an expansion of the capacities of the brass department was of immense historical significance: the full melodic potential of each brass instrument was realized and the range of possibilities infinitely extended. Moreover, Wagner handled these forces with such mastery – in the blending and grouping of instruments, in tonal balance – that he showed the way to a richer orchestral vocabulary altogether. With the other departments he was no less imaginative. There are countless instrumental solos in the *Ring* – more than anywhere else in Wagner's oeuvre – often consisting of just a bar or two, and time and again we are made aware of how the choice of instrument is an intrinsic part of the enactment of the drama.

This can be seen not only with the more obviously expressive instruments such as the oboe, clarinet or bassoon, but also with the strings. Wagner's prescribed body of strings – 16 first violins, 16 seconds, 12 violas, 12 cellos, 8 double basses – was not quite without precedent in size, but was certainly much larger than the forces available in most opera houses, and even concert halls, of the time. By the first half of the nineteenth century the size of the orchestra had hardly increased since the eighteenth: the orchestra of the Opéra-Comique in Paris is recorded as playing Auber and Boieldieu in 1839 with a string band of roughly half the above strength,[22] and Rossini, Donizetti and Verdi would often have heard their operas given by an orchestra of such a size. Wagner exploited this large body of strings by dividing it into many parts and creating intricate webs of figuration; two marvellous examples in *Rheingold* are the first appearance of the gold under the waters and Donner's 'Heda! Hedo!' A similar technique is used in the Ride of the Valkyries and the Magic Fire music at the end of *Walküre* where a characteristic Wagnerian effect is achieved by swirling figuration on the whole orchestra providing an accompaniment for a broad tune on the brass, in unison and octaves.

With these massively expanded orchestral forces, Wagner had at his disposal a family of instruments for every tone colour. Thus characters, ideas and scenes could be portrayed in whatever depth he chose, as he was able to switch at will from a single instrument to a family or to any combination within or across the orchestra's departments. The corresponding increase in the volume of sound, so tirelessly commented on by contemporary cartoonists, was purely incidental: Wagner's purpose was to create an orchestra sufficiently flexible to give expression to his complex dramatic conceptions.

Interpretations

Ever since the *Ring* was first performed explanations of its 'meaning' have been offered. So vast is its scope, so universal its significance that the *Ring* has been found to have 101 explanations. None of these, whether of commentator or theatrical producer, can be regarded as definitive; a work as multi-faceted as this may be illumin-

[22] See Table 1 under the article 'Orchestra' in the *New Grove* (vol. 13, p. 690) which helpfully juxtaposes characteristic orchestra sizes of all periods. That article and 'Orchestration' are both well worth reading for Wagner's contribution to the development of the art.

ated in one or more of its aspects by a single interpretation, even a partial one, but ultimately its essence will always elude attempts to constrain it. No such interpretation is therefore hazarded here. But it may be helpful to take a look at some of the central interpretations that have been put forward, to consider what Wagner himself had to say on the subject, and to draw some broad conclusions.

George Bernard Shaw, in *The Perfect Wagnerite*, saw the *Ring* up to *Götterdämmerung* as an allegory in which such qualities as kingship, godhead and state law are personified. It is a social and political interpretation with Shaw giving full rein to his socialist and anti-clerical beliefs. Alberich is the plutocrat, the exploitative capitalist. Threatened by his 'whip of starvation' the enslaved Nibelung workers create wealth with their labour only to find that it makes their master more powerful and intensifies their servitude. Lovelessness and greed gave rise to the sordidness of the capitalist system; Siegfried is the naive anarchist hero who will overturn religion, law and order to free humanity from its fetters. Anarchism was in fact denounced by Shaw; he believed that the state was a necessary vehicle to secure a society ordered in the interests of the whole populace. He was a Fabian and essentially a reforming rather than a revolutionary socialist; it is therefore inaccurate to refer to his ideas as 'Marxist'.

For Shaw the allegory collapsed after the second act of *Siegfried*; in *Götterdämmerung* music drama 'degenerated' into opera, and political philosophy gave way to the idea of the 'love panacea', which was 'a romantic nostrum for all human ills'. Shaw's explanation for Wagner's change of heart was his disillusioning experiences during the process of composition. The Siegfrieds of 1848 had turned out to be hopeless political failures, while the Wotans and Alberichs had flourished. Alberich had won back the ring, married into the best Valhalla families with it and instead of plotting to annihilate Wotan and Loge, used them to organize society for him and bolster his power. Alberich had become a pillar of the establishment and by 1876 was even on his way to becoming a model philanthropic employer. Heroes, heroines and revolutionary solutions had thus given way to an appreciation of 'political realities'.

Shaw's interpretation has often been dismissed far too readily. Wagner has been fought over and embraced by both the left and right wings of the political spectrum; more usually he has been identified with the latter. Yet his writings and letters of the time, together with

Cosima's Diaries, show that the *Ring* was indeed embarked upon in an access of socialist fervour; as time passed, however, his own increasingly elevated status in society conspired with other factors to dampen that zeal. Nor, as Shaw pointed out, was there much encouragement for those who favoured radical social changes in the 1860s and 1870s.

Bayreuth and those associated with it have traditionally, on the whole, preferred to play down the revolutionary aspects of the *Ring*. When, in 1976, the French producer Patrice Chéreau celebrated the centenary of the Bayreuth Festival with a *Ring* that echoed Bernard Shaw's political allegory, the old guard was scandalized. Chéreau's staging was set explicitly against a modern industrialized background: hydro-electric dam, pit-wheels, Victorian morning dress and the tuxedo of twentieth-century bourgeois society – all depicted a technological age familiar both to Wagner's audience and to ourselves. Thus the *Ring* was consciously demythologized in order to show the brutalizing struggle for power and status in a context that was more immediately relevant for a present-day audience. At the end a crowd assembled to watch the burning Valhalla – symbol of materialism and privilege. Then they turned to look into the audience: the creation of a new society founded on love is a task for us.

Another 'revolutionary' element in Chéreau's production was the importance attached to gesture, posture, facial expression and movement. Much hostility was aroused at the resulting theatricality – a stark contrast to the static productions with which we are all too familiar – yet as we have seen Wagner himself set much store by these aspects of the drama.

A very different interpretation was put forward in the 1960s by Robert Donington, one that analysed the *Ring* in terms of Jungian psychology.[23] Here the mythological elements – dragons, bear, heroes, world ash tree – come into their own as archetypal symbols, while the characters and their motivations are seen as constituents of the psyche: ego, persona, shadow, anima, animus. The wilful dominance of the ego, represented by Wotan and his spear, has to be overcome in the wider interests of the whole personality; the *Ring* is the story of the struggle to work through unconscious mother-

[23] *Wagner's 'Ring' and its Symbols: The Music and the Myth.*

longings and other obstructions in order to uncover and achieve the underlying purpose of the self.

Such an interpretation is able to do full justice to aspects such as the incest in *Walküre*, and it is particularly valuable for its insights into the light and dark sides of every character – Wagner rarely presents unadulterated good or evil. Jungian psychology revels in ambivalence: nothing is what it seems, any situation is likely to have a fundamental ambiguity. Alberich's terrible renunciation of love has also the positive side that it is an overcoming of infantile fantasies, while death is always losing its sting because it is sure at the same time to prefigure a transformation. Though the *Ring* is rich enough to sustain that kind of treatment, there is a danger that an act will be robbed thereby of its immediate significance: the search for symbolic meanings latent in the *Ring* must never be allowed to diminish the pity and terror we are intended to experience in the theatre – for example at the catastrophe of Siegfried's murder. Within its own terms – that is those of Jungian psychology – Donington's exposition is convincing and charged with insight. It is also possible to feel that at times it is constricting, even distorting, the *Ring*. Nevertheless, no one should deny him- or herself the rewarding experience of reading this book.

Each of the approaches so far mentioned regards the *Ring* in a broadly optimistic way. But there is a strong case to be made, calling on Wagner himself as witness, for a pessimistic interpretation. Because the composition stretched over a period of time in which Wagner's philosophical outlook was changing – as was the world around him – the work encompasses divergent convictions. Indeed, his struggle to find the right conclusion is reflected in the fact that at least six variant endings were tried, of which we will look at the most important.

The original 1848 poem, *Siegfrieds Tod*, contained in Brünnhilde's final address to Wotan the following words: 'Nur Einer herrsche: Allvater! Herrlicher du!' (Let one alone rule: father of all! You, glorious god!) Thus while humanity was to be freed, the old regime was to survive in the shape of one person only – Wotan. (Perhaps this may be seen as an artistic parallel to Wagner's Vaterlandsverein speech of 1848 in which he had mooted a republic led by one enlightened monarch.) These words were scrapped and in 1852 the text was altered so that Wotan too perished in the burning of Valhalla; the following lines were also added:

Nicht Gut, nicht Gold,	Not wealth, not gold,
noch göttliche Pracht;	nor godly splendour;
nicht Haus, nicht Hof,	not house, not court,
noch herrischer Prunk; ...	nor overbearing pomp; ...

selig in Lust und Leid	blessed in joy and sorrow
lässt – die Liebe nur sein. –	only love may be. –

The influence of Feuerbach is evident here, particularly in the elevation of love above possessions, above everything. But Wagner was not happy with the 'Feuerbach ending', as it has come to be known, and in 1856 produced his 'Schopenhauer ending':

Führ' ich nun nicht mehr	Were I no longer to fare
Nach Walhalls Feste,	to Valhalla's fortress,
wiss't ihr, wohin ich fahre?	do you know whither I would fare?
Aus Wunschheim zieh' ich fort,	I depart from the home of desire,
Wahnheim flieh' ich auf immer;	I flee for ever from the home of delus
des ew'gen Werdens	the open gates
off'ne Thore	of eternal becoming
schliess' ich hinter mir zu:	I close behind me:
nach dem wunsch- und wahnlos	to the holiest chosen land,
heiligstem Wahlland,	free from desire and delusion,
der Welt-Wanderung Ziel,	the goal of world-wandering,
von Wiedergeburt erlös't,	redeemed from rebirth,
zieht nun die Wissende hin.	the enlightened one now goes.
Alles Ew'gen	The blessed end
sel'ges Ende,	of all things eternal,
wiss't ihr, wie ich's gewann?	do you know how I attained it?
Trauernder Liebe	Grieving love's
tiefstes Leiden	deepest suffering
schloss die Augen mir auf:	opened my eyes:
enden sah ich die Welt. –	I saw the world end. –

According to Schopenhauer's deeply pessimistic outlook, human desires are intrinsically evil and the will to live is reprehensible; life is but a round of inescapable suffering and pleasure merely the temporary abolition of pain. The only solution lies in denial of the will, in extinction oi Nirvana – the Buddhist state of cessation of individual existence. It was discussed earlier (p. 206) how Wagner's attitude towards music was influenced by his reading in 1854 of *Die Welt als Wille und Vorstellung*; now it becomes clear that Schopenhauer's pessimism also rang true for Wagner at this time. Several letters of the preceding years reveal Wagner brooding on death, even suicide; shackled by exile and a broken marriage he was bitterly disillusioned about the possibility of social and artistic reform, and was desperately lacking money and loving care. Those who argue that such circumstances cast a shadow over the whole conception of the *Ring* justifiably point to such remarks by Wagner about love as a 'fundamentally devastating' force,[24] or his reference to the theme of the *Ring* as 'death through love's suffering'.[25]

In the Schopenhauer ending quoted above – 'Führ' ich nun nicht mehr' – Brünnhilde, the 'enlightened one', sees herself as redeemed from the endless cycle of suffering and rebirth; made wise by the 'deepest suffering of grieving love' she enters the state of non-being. Wagner changed the ending yet again after this, but not because he rejected the sentiments of the Schopenhauer ending. Both that and the Feuerbach ending were included by him as footnotes in the final printed edition of the text of *Götterdämmerung*, together with a note to the effect that he preferred the Schopenhauer ending but that he now realized that the meaning of the lines was better expressed in the music. It was Cosima who had suggested dropping those lines in order not to overload the drama.

The one element common to all these intepretations of the *Ring* is the one that is surely central to any understanding of the work: the lust for power and the compromises and alliances we are forced to make in our lives threaten our capacity for true, selfless love – the love that Wagner believed found its complete expression in the sexual act. Whether love is seen ultimately as a positive or destructive force, and whether the *Ring* is perceived as optimistic or pessimistic, revolutionary or conservative, is for each listener to decide for him or herself. No single interpretation has an exclusive claim to authenticity.

[24] Letter to August Röckel, 23 August 1856.

[25] *Epilogischer Bericht*, Sämtliche Schriften, vi, 268: 'der Tod durch Liebesnot'. Stewart Spencer in ' "Zieh hin! Ich kann dich nicht halten!" ', *Wagner*, ii (1981), 98–120, argues the 'pessimistic case' convincingly. (The above trans. of the 'Schopenhauer ending' is taken from that article.) Carl Dahlhaus' discussion of the ending to *Götterdämmerung* in *Richard Wagner: Werk und Wirkung*, 97–116, is not yet translated but is covered in Roger Hollinrake's 'Carl Dahlhaus and the *Ring*', *Wagner* 1976, ed. S. Spencer, 68–82. Ernest Newman also gives a full historical account in the *Life*, ii, esp. 325–62.

17

Tristan und Isolde

The welling up of ideas for a setting of the Tristan story, and the increasing confusion in Wagner's mind as to which work his inspirations belonged to, were only part of the reason that he abandoned *Siegfried* in order to write *Tristan und Isolde*. Other pressing factors were a dire need for ready cash and the opportunity again to make contact with the musical public, who had heard no new work of his since Liszt had put on *Lohengrin* at Weimar in 1850. His *Tristan* would be a simple work, he told Liszt, one that would prove attractive to the provincial theatres and bring in some money. It was to be thoroughly practicable, requiring only a modest staging, and – he confidently told his publisher – it would only take a year to write.

That *Tristan und Isolde* turned out to be not just a masterpiece but a milestone in the history of music, that it took two years to write and another six to get onto the stage because of the formidable difficulties facing the musicians, is proof enough that there was more to its conception than a hankering for receipts and recognition. In the first half of the 1850s Wagner sank into a state of deep depression. He had seen the revolution fail, and with it disappear the possibilities of social and theatrical reform; he was in exile from his native land; his marriage was crumbling and his wife quite out of sympathy with the *Ring* enterprise; illness (possibly psychosomatic), including skin and bowel disorders, periodically added to his misery. His letters from these years speak of his 'indescribably worthless existence' (to Liszt, 9 November 1852), his realization that for him 'there is no more joy in life' (to Julie Ritter, 7 August 1852), and even of suicidal tendencies. He longed to love and to be loved. More than that, as he later related to Mathilde Wesendonck (12 October 1858), he sought an object for his yearning, a single sympathetic woman who would embrace him and shelter him from the cruel blows of the world. Mathilde was indeed to be that object. Their relationship was intimate, but as was suggested earlier, probably stopped short of the sexual act. Consummation would have shattered the dream and made it impossible to write *Tristan und Isolde*, the ultimate glorification of love. 'As I have never in my life tasted the true joy of love, I will raise a monument to this loveliest of all dreams, in which from first to last this love shall for once be satisfied utterly', he told Liszt (16 December 1854), describing the idea for *Tristan*. In dramatizing the circumstances of his life and his hunger for love, Wagner made himself and Mathilde into the characters of Tristan and Isolde; the strength of their passion leads them to defy society's conventions and to long for death as the only way of being united. Otto Wesendonck is played by King Marke to whom Tristan, the loyal knight and nephew, is taking Isolde as bride and queen; Marke, like Wesendonck, personifies the barrier between the lovers and is called on to exercise the virtue of self-sacrifice.

And yet it is not enough to say that *Tristan und Isolde* is the dramatization of events from Wagner's life, or that it is their artistic counterpart. Nor is it adequate to regard the work as *simply* the ultimate glorification of love. It is also an idealization of love; that is to say, it goes beyond Wagner's experience, beyond our experience and enters a metaphysical realm. This is surely what Wagner meant when he later said that the composition of *Tristan* had been 'divorced from experience and reality' and when he dismissed as 'quite ridiculous' the German Emperor's remark: 'How deeply Wagner must have been in love at that time'. Similarly, it is not the essential validity of the notion but its superficiality that Wagner was mocking when he told Nietzsche in 1871: 'From the fact that I am now composing nothing but bloodthirstiness one can deduce whether I was in love when I wrote *Tristan*' (Cosima Wagner's Diaries: 28 September 1878 and 5 November 1871).

This should help us to explain the apparent paradox that *Tristan*, on the surface a celebration of unbridled sensuality, a four-and-a-half-hour orgy of self-indulgence, could come into being at precisely the time that its creator was responding to the self-abnegatory ideals of Schopenhauer and to the Buddhist concept of renunciation (his prose sketch for a drama based on a Buddhist legend, *Die Sieger*, dates from 1856). Schopenhauer's ethic was a severe one: human feelings and desires are inherently evil, and suffering, the unavoidable condition of life, is perpetuated by the sexual act, which is therefore in itself an act tainted by evil and guilt. But Wagner went only part of the way with Schopenhauer: he believed that his own contribution was to show how the pathway to the pacification of the 'will to live' lay through love, and specifically the sexual love between a man and a woman. He set out to inform Schopenhauer of his view (in a letter which was neither completed nor sent), according to which there lies 'in our natural tendency towards sexual love a path of salvation which itself leads to self-knowledge and self-denial of the will'. With the concept of salvation, or redemption, we are reminded of *Der fliegende Holländer, Tannhäuser* and *Lohengrin* and indeed there is a connection if we regard redemption (as perhaps we may) as a process of enlightenment, of self-discovery and self-fulfilment.[1] Moreover, Schopenhauer's belief in the essential worthlessness and nullity of human existence, his advocacy of renunciation of the 'will to live' as the only liberation from the endless round of suffering – all this is expressed in *Tristan und Isolde*. The salvation sought by the lovers consists in the shedding of their separate phenomenal forms (i.e. themselves as they appear to the outer world) and the merging of their identities in the realm of the single, undifferentiated noumenon (see pp. 55–6 for 'phenomenon' and 'noumenon'). This is the meaning of their yearning for the oblivion of death and it is also what underlies the work's imagery: 'day' is shunned because it represents the outer material world of phenomena; 'night' is welcomed because it is the domain of inner consciousness, the noumenal, the ultimate 'reality'. Thus there is no actual paradox in the concurrence of *Tristan* and Wagner's discovery of Schopenhauer. On the contrary, it can be viewed as the most intensely Schopenhauerian of all his works.

Sources

It is difficult for us in the twentieth century to appreciate the development of a cult in the Middle Ages. In our day a best-selling romance has achieved its definitive form at the time of publication; by the time of the first literary form of the Tristan and Isolde legend in the twelfth century, the story was already centuries old. Scholarly opinion now generally holds that the origin of the legend is Celtic (though a Cornish origin has also been postulated); certainly the name 'Tristan' is derived from the primitive Celtic 'Drostanos'. The

---

[1] In this connection and for further penetrating discussion of *Tristan*, see Michael Tanner's essay 'The Total Work of Art', in *The Wagner Companion*, ed. P. Burbidge and R. Sutton, esp. 178–91.

tradition seems to have migrated from sixth-century Scotland to the Celtic regions of Wales and from there, via Cornwall, to Norman Britain in the first half of the twelfth century. From there it was transmitted to France and Germany, gathering accretions from the common fund of storytelling on the way. Such was the popularity of the story that it inspired countless retellings in poem and song, and portrayals in picture and tapestry.

The version which Wagner chose as the basis for his drama was that by the German poet Gottfried von Strassburg, who was active during the first twenty years of the thirteenth century. As usual he weeded out all the elements for which he had no use and compressed events and characters in order to tighten the structure (for example, the single figure of Melot, Tristan's former friend who deals him the fatal blow, was moulded from three separate characters in Gottfried).[2] But there is a difference between this refashioning of source material and that of his less mature operas: whereas the process in *Tannhäuser* was one of splicing together disparate elements, in *Tristan* it is much more of a distillation. Each act has one central dramatic happening — Tristan and Isolde's drinking of the love-potion, the entry of king and courtiers surprising the lovers, and Isolde's arrival — around which it revolves, and the rest of the action is confined to a very few events. There are only five main characters and again everything is focused on the two key ones: even Marke, Brangäne and Kurwenal are relegated to the sidelines.

Wagner took more than just the story-line from Gottfried. Also reflected in his poem are Gottfried's vocabulary and rhetorical style, the idea of love causing suffering as well as joy, and the rival claims of love and honour.[3] Most surprising of all is to find there the very 'Wagnerian' concept of two bodies, two identities merged: 'We are one body and one life', Gottfried's Isolde tells Tristan. And a few lines later: 'Tristan and Isolde, you and I / we shall both for ever remain / one and undivided.'[4]

[2] The chapter in Newman's *Wagner Nights* has much more information on Wagner's sources and his adaptation of them.

[3] The concept of 'honour' is also central to the works of the seventeenth-century Spanish dramatist Calderón, which Wagner was reading during the composition of *Tristan*.

[4] See S.D. Spencer, ' "Tristan und Isolde": Gottfried and Wagner', *Wagner*, old series, 48 (1976), 7–12. Also ' "Tristan und Isolde": the development of the legend', *Wagner*, old series, 47 (1976), 6–10.

But the parallels should not be seen out of perspective. For all the echoes, Wagner needed to divest the story of its medieval courtly trappings. His characters had to be made convincing dramatically (though they are scarcely fully-rounded) and had to be motivated by forces which were meaningful to a nineteenth-century audience.

Composition

Although he had become acquainted with the Tristan legend in his Dresden years – the period in which, incidentally, the seeds of all the mature music dramas were sown – it was not until the converging, in the mid-1850s, of all the factors mentioned earlier, that inspiration for the work came. Wagner conceived the idea of writing a piece on the Tristan subject probably in the autumn of 1854, shortly after the devastating impact of his introduction to Schopenhauer, but the earliest dated sketches are from 19 December 1856, at which point he was working on Act I of *Siegfried*. Two fragments are elaborated, of which the first was a setting of the words 'Sink' hernieder Nacht der Liebe,/ nimm mich auf in deinen Schoss'. These lines turned up subsequently (slightly altered) in the poem, in the love scene of the second act, as did the melody to which they are set – but independently of each other. The fragment is worked out with chromatic counterpoints and sequential developments, throwing up other ideas that were also to be used in *Tristan*, but the eventual setting of these words was to a different tune altogether. In this case at least, words and music were not indissolubly linked from the start.[5]

Wagner began his prose scenario the following summer, on 20 August 1857, and the poem was completed on 18 September. Like *Siegfried* – but unlike all the other music dramas – each act was drafted and elaborated, in sequence, the full score being reached before the next act was embarked on in sketch. Indeed, since his publishers, Breitkopf & Härtel, were as anxious as Wagner to have a new work ready for public consumption, and since the composition was taking rather longer than Wagner's original estimate of a year,

[5] See Robert Bailey, 'The Method of Composition', in *The Wagner Companion*, ed. P. Burbidge and R. Sutton, esp. 308–26.

the score was actually engraved one act at a time – corroboration of Wagner's astonishing ability to envisage a whole work in his head even before the musical setting had been sketched.

Musico-poetic synthesis

Wagner's later definition of a music drama, coined retrospectively in the light of the experience of *Tristan* and *Die Meistersinger*, was 'deeds of music made visible',[6] and in terms of the relationship between music and text, *Tristan*, as compared with the *Ring*, does indeed demonstrate a marked shift in favour of the former. For long passages of the Act II duet, in particular, it is doubtful whether we are intended to appreciate the subtleties of musico-poetic synthesis as described in *Opera and Drama*. The high proportion of long-held notes, the overlapping and simultaneous declamation of Tristan and Isolde, the overwhelming impact of the orchestra all ensure that the words are frequently inaudible. Nevertheless there are elsewhere many fine examples of *Opera and Drama*-type synthesis, especially in Isolde's Act I narrative and in Tristan's demented Act III monologue:

Ex. 39

schloss,   riss mit dem Schwert sie wieder   los;   das
pain;   then did she o – pen them a –   gain;   yet

Schwert dann   a – ber   liess   sie   sin – ken;
dropped her   wea – pon   and   re –   lent – ed;

Tristan's second phrase in Ex.39 is a sequential variant of the first, as befits the sense of the words. Then the melodic line sinks chromatically, and finally drops a fifth, as the memory of Isolde lowering the sword is recalled.

Every element of *Tristan*, poetical and musical, is geared to the generation and intensification of tension – the tension of promised but evaded fulfilment. To this end the verse is yet richer and more compressed than the *Ring*. Like the *Ring* it is highly alliterative, but in *Tristan* there is also rhyme and assonance – the latter being the reiteration of corresponding vowel sounds, as in 'Dir nicht eigen,/ einzig mein,/ mit-leidest du,/ wenn ich leide'. Rhyme had been eschewed in *Opera and Drama* on the grounds that verse which drew the ear's attention continually to the ends of lines is not capable of communicating with the feelings. However, the rhyme in *Tristan* is quite different. It is not just tacked on as an appendage: the rhyming words are generally the focal centre of the line, for example:

ohne Bangen	without fears
süss Verlangen;	sweet longing;
ohne Wehen	without anguish
hehr Vergehen;	sublime dying;

and as befits the euphonious, essentially musical second act, there is more than twice as much rhyme there than in the first act.

That the sound of the verse is acquiring more importance, even at the expense of its meaning, is further evidenced by the treatment of vowels. There is continual use of vowel extension (where a vowel is set to a single long note) and melisma (a vowel set to a series of different notes), with the result that the sense of the words is frequently lost. It is important to grasp the difference between this and typical pre-Wagnerian verse-setting, in which the meaning of words was not expressed intrinsically by the shape and rhythm of the melodic line. In passages like Brangäne's Watchsong and elsewhere in the central Act II love duet we have come through and, as it were, out of the other side of the musico-poetic synthesis of *Opera and Drama*: words have been absorbed into music and have created an intensified line that is itself integrated closely into the orchestral fabric.

Leitmotif

Another break with *Opera and Drama* principles is seen in Wagner's use of leitmotif in *Tristan*. In this work motifs are less specific, less concrete than in the *Ring*; the rapt, metaphysical world of *Tristan* has no place for motifs symbolizing a sword or a spear. Even more than in the *Ring* it is inadvisable to try to tie these motifs to a particular object or state of mind. The descending chromatic motif that opens the work has been as prolifically labelled as any: 'Tristan', 'Tristan's suffering', 'grief', 'the confession'. The fact is that the motif embodies all these ideas and more; at some points in the drama it is more closely identified with one idea and at others with another. Moreover, it is a close relative of at least four other definable motifs (of which one is quoted in the orchestral part of Ex. 39); all undergo thematic development in the course of the drama and at times they become indistinguishable.

Several key motifs are given their initial statement in the Prelude[7] and that should have warned against encumbering them with labels too eagerly, because the Prelude was composed first (cf. *Lohengrin*, where Wagner followed normal precedent by composing the Prelude last), at which point verse and motifs were not yet fused. But the truth is that in *Tristan* Wagner has virtually abandoned the idea that leitmotifs should originate in the musico-poetic line. A few still do, but neither they nor those originating in the orchestra are treated as motifs of reminiscence – rather as themes for deployment and metamorphosis in a large-scale structure. Two motifs have established a specific association that is unarguable: the motifs of death (Ex.40) and day (Ex.41):

Ex. 40

Ex. 41

and the former is the only one in the whole drama which acts at all like a motif of reminiscence, in that the sense of the original words is

---

[7] The closing stage of *Tristan* (from Isolde's 'Mild und leise') are known, perhaps irreversibly, as the 'Liebestod', but Wagner referred to this passage as Isolde's 'Transfiguration' (*Verklärung*) and the Prelude as the 'Liebestod' (see Sämtliche Schriften, xii, 347 and letter to Mathilde Wesendonck of 10 April 1860). 'Transfiguration' is a more precise term for the closing passage than 'Liebestod' but I do not see any great harm in continuing to use the latter. Nor was Wagner consistent in his term for the Prelude: he also calls it variously 'Vorspiel' or 'Einleitung'.

explicitly recalled on subsequent appearances: 'Death-devoted head! Death-devoted heart!' A new kind of motif, then, has been evolved for *Tristan*. It is less specific conceptually, more plastic, more adaptable, more conducive to symphonic development. And it is an integral part of the harmonic and instrumental style: the melodic line of Ex.40 is a product of the chromatic progression A flat—A, not vice versa, and the harmonic switch is reinforced by a change from woodwind to brass – a telling stroke that is repeated on future appearances of the motif. Verse, motifs, harmonic idiom and instrumentation are all interdependent: one cannot be conceived without the others.

Tonal relations

The characteristic idiom of *Tristan* is extreme chromaticism of both line and harmony. The work is still essentially tonal over the longer span, but in its shorter units there are powerful agents operating in a new way. Extravagant chromaticism not only epitomizes the lovers' unassuageable yearning, the passion striving for but never in this life attaining fulfilment; it is also the perfect vehicle for the air of decadence that hangs over the work like a thick pall. The harmonic language appropriate to this is one which emphasizes dissonances and suspensions, a continuous texture of dominant 7ths and 9ths, augmented 6ths, appoggiaturas and so on, all heightened by chromatic alteration.[8] Tristan and Isolde are perilously near the edge of sanity and their obsessive, neurotic absorption in themselves and each other is expressed in the vocabulary of clinging chromaticism. Conversely the temporal values of society represented by Marke and Melot are often reflected in 'wholesome' diatonicism. The merest mention of honour, loyalty or feudal rights provokes a spate of common triads. Marke's Act II monologue is also predominantly diatonic and other instances from that act of the diatonic representation of the worlds of king and courtiers are the triadic calls of the hunting horns at the beginning and the sudden return to reality at the end after Melot draws his sword. The character of Kurwenal who,

[8] Strictly speaking, 'chromatic alteration' is not an appropriate term here, since the diatonic chords of which these chromaticisms might have been considered derivations have been absorbed into a chromatic flux to the point where they can no longer be called derivations.

though Tristan's retainer, is stolid and down-to-earth, is likewise mirrored in his four-square diatonic music.

Ex. 42

Wer Korn - walls Kron' und Eng - lands Erb' an Ir - lands Maid ver - macht,

Even in the fervid chromatic world of Tristan and Isolde, the idiom periodically relaxes, as the tension is eased, into something more stable. The central 'O sink' hernieder' duet and Brangäne's Watchsong (both Act II) still have chromatic colouring but the harmonies are basically diatonic and often moving at the indolent rate of one harmony per bar. However, in all this the underlying tonal structure of the work never completely disappears from view and frequently makes its presence felt in a direct way, by means of traditional tonic/dominant relationships. The last stages of the main climax of the Act II duet (immediately before the lovers are discovered *in flagrante delicto*) are nothing more than a chromatic embellishment of a huge perfect cadence (Ic—V7—I) – in the event, of course, interrupted.

As prevalent in the *Tristan* score as chromaticism is the device of the sequence. Indeed, the two are used in conjunction as a further means of intensification: a phrase is repeated a semitone higher and then a semitone higher again, screwing up the tension. Innumerable kinds of sequential variation are found in *Tristan*. In Ex.39 the phrase heard in the orchestra in the first two bars is repeated sequentially a major third higher and then a major 3rd higher still, but its tail is modified so that it continues to fall chromatically (to match the sense of the musico-poetic line) instead of rising expectantly for another repetition. Ex.39 also demonstrates a further refinement of sequential technique. The vocal line joins the orchestra on the second note but continues on after the orchestral phrase has finished, bridging the gap to the next cycle of the sequence. The second vocal phrase, 'riss mit dem Schwert sie wieder los', is a variant of the first but again it bridges the gap to the next cycle. It is therefore a kind of double sequence and shows Wagner deploying a traditional device in a new, individual way – one tailored to his musical and dramatic needs.

One of the most powerful elements in the stretching of tonality in *Tristan* is the tonally ambiguous chord of the $\frac{6}{4}$, or second inversion. An example of its very frequent use here is underneath the first two notes of Isolde's Transfiguration;[9] the unsettling effect is a result not only of the rapid modulations but also of the unstable bass which denies the longed-for sense of fulfilment. The diminished 7th is used by Wagner in *Tristan* both in the traditional way, with tremolando, for its dramatic effect (as in the passage following the rude intrusion of Marke and Melot) and in a disruptive way, exploiting the tonal uncertainty of the chord. The chord of the dominant 7th is ubiquitous, and if the score of *Tristan* is opened at random, several examples will immediately be apparent of a dominant 7th that has not been allowed to resolve. Again musical idiom and poetic significance are one, for the unresolved dominant 7th is both an important factor in the dislocation of tonality and a potent symbol of unfulfilled passion. Almost as prevalent are interrupted cadences, which likewise symbolize the unattainable.

A further assault on the tonal system is made by use of the mediant (or submediant) relationship, in place of the Classical dominant. Third-related progressions are everywhere present in *Tristan*: they echo the states of passive acceptance and sensual gratification, just as the dominant traditionally represented order, discipline and logical development. The harmonies of the first two bars of Isolde's Transfiguration illustrate the point perfectly: A flat—E flat—C flat—B flat.

[9] See note 7.

Ex. 43

The dominant 7th on E flat fails to resolve onto the traditional tonic, A flat, instead sidling into the flattened mediant, C flat. The Transfiguration and the whole work are shortly to end in B (the enharmonic equivalent of C flat) and so this mediant relationship can be seen to be an epitome of the larger structure.

Lorenz's contention that the tonal centre of *Tristan* is E major[10] must be rejected, not only because this requires him to regard the work as beginning, somewhat quaintly, in the subdominant and ending in the dominant, but also because it is inconceivable that even the most highly trained ear hears in *Tristan* a single unifying tonality – least of all E major. But what the ear *can* detect is a series of relationships of keys a third apart. Thus C, which is associated with day, is a third away from A flat, the key of the great 'Liebesnacht' duet of Act II and also from E, the key of Tristan's 'vision' in his Act III delirium. This particular circle of thirds is important for Act III, while elsewhere one may contrast the F major of the faithful Kurwenal with the D minor of the faithless Melot, and the relationship between A flat and B (C flat) has already been mentioned.

The unity of *Tristan*, then, is not achieved by a central tonal force which generates subsidiary, related tonalities; rather it consists in a complex of inter-related tonalities, often a major or minor third apart, which compels us to abandon traditional assumptions about tonal centres. Another unifying device is the celebrated 'Tristan chord', the first chord to be heard in the work and one of the most pregnant – as well as one of the most discussed – in the history of music (see the first chord of Ex.44). Analysts still agonize over the parsing of that chord, but we seem to be no nearer a solution when it

10 *Das Geheimnis der Form bei Richard Wagner*, Band II, esp. 173–80.

may be necessary to regard the opening tonality of the work as D sharp minor in order to explain it. The precise nomenclature of the 'Tristan chord' is perhaps less important than the observation that it contains a superimposition of perfect and augmented 4ths, the traditional poles of the tonal system. The perfect 4th and 5th have always provided the backbone of tonality, whereas the augmented 4th, or tritone (the 'diabolus in musica' in the medieval era), has generally been regarded as the agent of tonal anarchy and dissolution. Together with the rising and falling chromatic lines in bars 1–3, that chord encapsulates the basic material – or at least symbolizes its essence – of the whole work. The opening phrase of the work is repeated twice, each time a third higher, so that the 'Tristan chord' appears immediately three times; furthermore, the three chords stand in a special relationship to each other:

Ex. 44

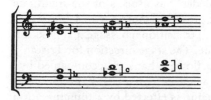

The lower of the 4ths of the first chord (b) becomes the upper of the second (though with a changed accidental) and the lower of the second becomes the upper of the third. The pitches are preserved once again when these chords are opened out melodically in Isolde's Transfiguration:

Ex. 45

Other examples of the melodic use of the '*Tristan* chord' could be given,[11] and the chord itself appears, always with the original pitch preserved, many times throughout the work, constantly injecting a further element of intensity.

In musical terms, therefore, the last section of the work is not only a recapitulation of 'So stürben wir' from the Act II duet; it is also the final transformation of the material compressed into the first chord of the work – another reason why 'Transfiguration' is perhaps a preferable term to 'Liebestod'. Transformation – the repetition or recollection of material in a heightened form – was in the later dramas a matter of cardinal importance to Wagner.

The other process central to Wagner's music dramas, but especially *Tristan*, is what he referred to as the 'art of transition' (letter to Mathilde Wesendonck, 29 October 1859). By this means, he said, violently contrasting moods could be bridged, and every change could appear to be inevitable. The score abounds in masterly transitions serving these purposes; one example must suffice here. The Act II duet 'O sink' hernieder' has aspects of the traditional operatic duet and would seem a great deal more out on a limb were it not for the skilful (and ravishing) transitional passage that links it to the animated preceding dialogue. The stage direction for Tristan to lead Isolde tenderly down to a flowery bank is accompanied by a gradual reduction in tension, achieved dynamically, harmonically and rhythmically. The diminuendo is effected by a thinning out of the orchestral texture, with solo viola and harp creating an aura of intimacy. The rhythm – previously a sturdy 2/2 – becomes more flexible, with gentle syncopations first in the melodic line, then in the bass, all evoking a mood of hushed expectancy which is enhanced by changing instrumental colours. Meanwhile out of the tonal flux of the previous duet the tonality of A flat gradually establishes itself: the bass line descends slowly from the F of the '*Tristan* chord' on 'wahr' through a whole octave to E flat, where it becomes a dominant pedal. The violas pick up the gentle syncopations from the bass line and they rise through the string section until a rich texture is produced by all the strings divided and with mutes. At last the long-heralded entry of Tristan occurs, 'O sink' hernieder', but even this apparently new melody is not a total surprise because it has been foreshadowed

---

[11] See Rudolph Reti, *The Thematic Process in Music* (New York 1951), 336–43.

shortly before, at Tristan's words 'da erdämmerte mild erhab'ner Macht'.

For all Wagner's avoidance of sharp contrasts, *Tristan* was a shocking experience for his contemporaries, even for the most avant garde of them. And that is only to be expected, for *Tristan* largely deserves its reputation as the seminal work in the emancipation of harmony from the Classical tonal system. It was to be another half a century before the twelve notes of the chromatic scale were to be treated as co-equals, but *Tristan*, perhaps more than any other piece of music, symbolized the end of one era and looked forward to the birth of another.

18

Die Meistersinger von Nürnberg

The sadness and bitterness with which Wagner had launched himself into the composition of *Tristan* had not left him by the 1860s. On the contrary, his letters reveal another low point in his life: avoiding painful contact with the outside world but as a result feeling miserably isolated; anxious about getting *Tristan* on the stage; short of money and afflicted by bladder complaints. And yet *Die Meistersinger* is a radiant, life-affirming work – evidence that the inter-relation of factors in the life–art equation is more complex than is allowed by a simple juxtaposition of the two. Wagner himself thought that the composition of *Die Meistersinger* would exorcize his suffering and reconcile him to the world: 'This work should lead me through the portals of calm resignation into the new, last stage of my life in which I might hope for consolation and healing for the pains and sorrows of the past' (letter to Editha von Rhaden, 14 September 1863).

One of the key words of *Die Meistersinger* is 'Wahn', best translated as 'illusion', but also containing the ideas of madness, folly, fancy. Wagner had come to believe that all human endeavour was underpinned by illusion and futility, and the notion of *Wahn* is fully discussed in his 1864 essay *On State and Religion*. Offered there is also a more positive conception of illusion: art is a 'noble illusion', one that may be joyfully embraced by the person who is aware of the world's true essence. Wagner was by no means the first creative artist to hail art as illusion.

In Act III of *Die Meistersinger*, Hans Sachs tells Walther: 'Believe me, man's truest illusion is disclosed to him in dreams: the whole art of poetry and verse is nothing but the true interpretation of dreams.' Wagner had always been fascinated by dreams: they had often occurred and served a dramatic function in his earlier works. On reading Schopenhauer he readily became a convert to the view that creativity originated in the dream-world: dreams and illusions led to enlightenment and revelation of the highest truth. Thus it is that Walther conceives his prize-winning entry in a dream.

244

Walther von Stolzing is the young knight who arrives as a stranger in Nuremberg, but who hopes to become a Master, to win the song-contest and with it the hand of Pogner's daughter Eva. Walther, the unconventional artist, the natural genius, has no time for the arid rules and conventions of the Masters. He eventually wins the contest and Eva by subjecting his spontaneous, dream-inspired lyrical effusion to the beneficent discipline of the sympathetic Sachs. His rival, the town clerk Beckmesser, who had been the most critical of the newcomer, makes a public fool of himself by stealing Walther's song for the contest and mangling it to ludicrous effect.

The central theme of *Die Meistersinger* may therefore be considered to be the lesson Sachs teaches Walther: even the inspiration of genius must be regulated by form. To the extent that Wagner's music had long since broken all the rules, defying the critics and challenging audiences, one may say that the composer identified himself with Walther. But of course he realized better than anybody the necessity of formal structure, even if throughout his adult life he had gone out of his way to ensure that the technical aspects of his compositional process remained hidden. Art must conceal art; everything must appear spontaneous and inevitable. Too many commentators have fallen into the trap of supposing that his works were indeed created like Walther's Prize Song: conceived in a dream, and set down fully fashioned with only minor adjustments to be made.

Die Meistersinger is the only one of Wagner's mature music dramas to have a precise designation of historical time and place: mid-sixteenth-century Nuremberg. Hans Sachs himself was a poet and playwright of renown: his famous ode 'The Wittenberg Nightingale', in honour of Luther, the herald of the Reformation, is sung by the chorus at the end of Act III in acclamation of the poet. The mastersingers' guilds came into being in the fourteenth century, mostly in the southern German imperial cities, for the composition and performance of Meisterlieder. Their members were artisans of the lower and middle classes who also belonged to the craft guilds which effectively restricted the practice of each trade to guild members. Both species of guild adhered rigidly to rules and regulations, the better to exclude unwanted outsiders; the mastersingers' guilds looked back to the art of the minnesingers as their heritage and had little sympathy for the modern, progressive ideas represented by Walther von Stolzing.

Sources

When Wagner made his first prose draft for the work in Marienbad, in July 1845, he was basing much of his background on Georg Gottfried Gervinus's *Geschichte der poetischen National-Literatur der Deutschen* of 1835–42 (History of the Poetic National Literature of the Germans). His main idea at this stage was to achieve a comic effect by playing off the rule-book pedantry of the mastersingers – personified by 'the Marker', who noted breaches in the rules – against the less affected artistic instincts of the People, championed by Sachs. This first draft dates from the time of Wagner's dissatisfaction with the principles and standards of musical life in Dresden, a dissatisfaction reflected in the desire of the 'young man' – not yet called Walther – to challenge the 'archaic' practices of the mastersingers' guild. The love element is present but not yet integrated with the themes of creativity and artistic reform.[1] *Die Meistersinger* was conceived by Wagner as a comic antidote to *Tannhäuser*, rather like the relationship between tragedy and satyr play in Greek drama.

Other volumes which we may assume Wagner was familiar with, since they were in his library at Dresden, are Jacob Grimm's *Über den altdeutschen Meistergesang*, 1811 (On the Old German Meisterlieder), Johann Gustav Büsching's edition of Hans Sachs' plays, 1816–19, and Friedrich Furchau's life of Sachs, 1820. A particularly rich source for him in the making of the second and third prose drafts was Johann Christoph Wagenseil's Nuremberg Chronicle of 1697, which contained copious information on the ancient crafts and guilds and on other aspects of Nuremberg. Wagner was especially interested in its detailed appendix (in German, unlike the bulk of the book which Wagenseil wrote in Latin) entitled 'Book of the Mastersingers' Most Gracious Art; its Origin, Practice, Utility and Rules'. He made full notes from this appendix, about the rules of the *Tabulatur* governing the form of a song (read out by Kothner in the opera), the different rhyme and versification schemes, the various errors commonly made, and the names of twelve 'old Nuremberg masters' which he took over almost intact; all this information was

---

[1] For a full discussion of all three prose drafts in relation to the final poem, see Richard Turner, 'Wagner's *Die Meistersinger von Nürnberg*: the conceptual growth of an opera', in *Wagner 1976*, ed. S. Spencer; reprinted in *Wagner*, iii (1982), 2–16. See also Robert M. Rayner, *Wagner and 'Die Meistersinger'*, where a translation of the first draft is reproduced.

subsequently printed by Wagner in his collected writings, at the end of the second draft.[2] Other motifs were woven in from different stories of the time, such as E.T.A. Hoffmann's *Meister Martin der Küfner und seine Gesellen* (Master Martin, the Cooper, and his Journeymen), which is set in sixteenth-century Nuremberg and centres around a competition with a daughter as prize.

Composition

In November 1861 the idea for the Prelude came to him (according to Wagner) on a train journey from Venice to Vienna. Soon after his arrival, Peter Cornelius provided him with a copy of Wagenseil's book, obtained from the Imperial Library in Vienna, and the second prose draft was written down probably between 14 and 16 November. A slightly revised, third prose draft was prepared on the 18th for the publisher Schott. In these drafts 'the Marker' became 'Hanslich' – a malicious and scarcely veiled identification with his celebrated critical adversary, Eduard Hanslick. Wagner wisely replaced the name with an appropriate-sounding one from Wagenseil's list, Sixtus Beckmesser, but when he read the poem to an invited audience including Hanslick in Vienna on 23 November 1862, the critic, aware that he was being immortalized as a buffoon, not unreasonably took offence and left the room in disgust. Wagner had begun the poem at the end of December 1861 and settled down in Biebrich, near Wiesbaden, to begin the musical composition in March 1862. A series of delays meant that he did not complete the full score until October 1867.

Musico-poetic synthesis

For much of the work's length the orchestra is the chief arena of musical and dramatic interest in *Die Meistersinger*, providing a rich, seamless texture of ideas. Occasionally the focus shifts to the vocal line, especially at points where it is consolidated into a structure of more regular periods, for example Walther's 'Am stillen Herd' in Act I, or his Prize Song. Motifs are combined and transformed with the dexterity that is by now customary. Often, too, the rigid guidelines of *Opera and Drama* seem remote: sometimes the first appearance of a

---

[2] *Sämtliche Schriften*, xi, 371–8.

motif is the signal for an extended quasi-symphonic development of that motif, accommodating the requirements of the poem in a general rather than a specific way, until a new idea is called into play.

It has been pointed out that in his combining of themes in *Die Meistersinger*, Wagner is following the principle of 'fixed improvisation' that he was to set down just a few years after finishing the opera in his 1871 essay *On the Destiny of Opera*. His theory was that the improvisatory element in acting could be harnessed to the essential improvisatory ingredient in musical composition: a composer's genius could make these permanent in a 'fixed improvisation'. Wagner presents this as a restatement of *Opera and Drama*; in reality, the freedom it allows the composer to develop ideas at will represents a considerable slackening of the reins. *Die Meistersinger* is the creative embodiment of these new principles, as yet unformulated on paper, and Sachs's 'Wahn' monologue is an excellent example of this free improvisation at work.

The musical line to which the verse is set is a remarkable contrast to that of the *Ring* or even that of the recent *Tristan*. The most unexpected thing about it is the high proportion of recitative-like setting: the line darts about in semiquavers – just as in an *opera buffa* recitative – and the orchestra even punctuates at times with the orthodox cadences. But the baldness of the recitative is more often than not masked by the orchestra, whose sustained chords and continuous texture bridge the gaps between the groups of notes declaimed by the voice. The musical interest of these recitatives is surprisingly scanty but is simply another symptom of the directing of attention to the orchestra. This is the chief difference between these recitative-like passages and those of *Lohengrin*, where the orchestra had not yet assumed the role of commentator on the dramatic action.

If Wagner had left behind some of the more rigorous precepts of *Opera and Drama* he was nevertheless in little danger of reverting wholesale to the style of conventional opera. It was surely with the confidence of this knowledge that he was able to call *Die Meistersinger* an 'opera' (*Grosse komische Oper*) and the work is an intriguing blend of old and new. In the first place the Prelude (called *Vorspiel* in the score) is, in effect, a return to the overture form of *Tannhäuser* or the *Holländer*, where the main themes are expounded and developed; this is quite a different concept from the single-mood preparations for the drama that open *Lohengrin*, *Tristan* and all four parts of the *Ring*. The culmination of the *Meistersinger* Prelude is a

combination of three themes – not the most felicitous of contrapuntal textures but one that works in its own poetic terms, because
the combination epitomizes the central issue of the opera: a
rapprochement of the ideals of the masters and of Walther.

Formal structure

Given that the story revolves around the creation of a mastersong
(consisting of two identical *Stollen* and a contrasting *Abgesang*:
AAB) it was perhaps inevitable that Lorenz would find the whole
work to be dominated by the *Bar*-form.[3] As with all Wagner's
mature music dramas an adequate analysis of his formal structures
has to go deeper than that, but it is certainly interesting to look at
some of the ways he uses *Bar*-form in *Meistersinger*.

Walther's try-out for his Prize Song in Sachs' workshop (Act III,
scenes 2 and 4) is a fairly complex structure – as indeed Meisterlieder
sometimes were. It is in three parts, of which the last is not supplied
by Walther until scene 4, when he reappears in the workshop and is
struck by the significance of his vision – the union of art and love.
The three parts are identical (AAA) and each breaks down into a
Bar-form (AAB) of its own. The larger structure is therefore not a
true *Bar*-form as it is AAA rather than AAB. That it has sometimes
been taken to be so is probably owing to Wagner's misunderstanding
or misapplication of the term. After Walther has sung his first three
stanzas – *Stollen, Stollen* and *Abgesang* — Sachs says: 'That I call an
Abgesang! Look how the whole *Bar* worked! Now do me a
second *Bar* to fix the first in mind.' The German mastersingers did
not use '*Bar*' like this to mean one part of a tripartite structure, but in
any case, as pointed out, the three parts of Walther's song here do not
add up to a *Bar*-form because they are identical.

For Walther's prizewinning performance in the meadow (scene
5) Wagner could not have him repeat all this *in extenso*: coming
within the same act, the repetition would be too much to take in the
theatre, and as Cosima observed to King Ludwig the intimate sentiments expressed in Sachs' workshop were hardly appropriate to the
festival atmosphere in the meadow. His solution was to reduce the

---

[3] *Das Geheimnis der Form bei Richard Wagner*, Band III. See also *Wagner*,
iv (1983), 9–13 for a trans. of the article by Lorenz that appeared in the
Bayreuther Festspielführer for 1925, pp. 131–5.

song to a single *Bar*-form of three stanzas (AAB) but with each stanza expanded; in addition, the second stanza now has an element of surprise as it makes an unexpected and heartwarming plunge into the remote key of B major (the song is in C). Such a modulation would certainly not have had the approval of the masters; indeed, the whole song is in many details now further from the traditional rules than the original dry run (or Morning Dream Song, as it is sometimes called), but the masters are presumably swept away by Walther's artistic integrity and impassioned delivery.

Bar-form is also present in Walther's Trial Song in Act I (' "Fanget an!" So rief der Lenz in den Wald'), the song he sings as he makes his first attempt at entry to the guild of mastersingers. It is, however, so complex a *Bar*-form – $A^1B^1A^2B^2C$ (each *Stollen* falling into two parts) – that it is scarcely surprising that Beckmesser fails to recognize it as such. He interrupts after A^2, clearly labouring under the misapprehension (an understandable one) that Walther's song was in ternary form (ABA). The illusion only becomes evident when Walther is allowed to continue. Though the orchestral motifs have to be taken into account, Beckmesser's criticism of the song may itself be regarded as a *Bar*-form. It is an appropriate touch, but surely an indication of Wagner's sense of humour rather than an element in a consistent overall formal plan.

Shortly before the Trial Song, Wagner seems to be playing with *Bar*-form again in 'Am stillen Herd', which Walther sings in response to a question about his teacher. 'Am stillen Herd' is an AAB structure but it is a mockery of *Bar*-form. B is supposed to be related to A but varied: this variation is so florid that no one is able to contradict Beckmesser's opinion that it is but a 'deluge of words'.

All of these numbers are typical of *Die Meistersinger* in that the score is full of self-contained songs, ensembles of main characters, choruses of massed onlookers, even processions, marches and dances such as, a decade before, Wagner had relegated to the lowest regions of the Inferno. It is not the case that Wagner is trying here to return to the principles of grand opera; rather that he has found a way of integrating these elements into his music drama. The skill with which he deploys the forms is the best evidence of that. The first stanza of 'Am stillen Herd' is a series of one- and two-bar phrases; indetectably, by means of frequent little pauses, Wagner manages to avoid a regular sixteen-bar period. The stanza, actually consisting of seventeen bars, converts periodicity into 'unending melody'.

With the Prize Song Wagner was not merely integrating an old-fashioned number into his music drama: he was, with the supreme confidence of his maturity, making it the focal centre of his work. As we have seen, he adapted and compressed the *Bar*-form of the original Morning Dream Song in order to create something dramatically appropriate. But he was also setting himself the task of finding an inspiration that would indeed crown the proceedings and quash all opposition. Few would dispute that the Prize Song admirably fits the bill.

The celebrated and exquisite quintet (Act III, scene 4) is often cited as an example of Wagner's back-sliding in *Die Meistersinger*. In fact, it is integrated into the score in a particularly subtle way. It is given a remote tonality, G flat major, that is a tritone away from the C major of the preceding music and of the following scene 5 (which is reached through a series of modulations launched by turning G flat into its enharmonic equivalent of F sharp). The quintet is in this way elevated onto another plane – a condition reinforced by its (at first) new thematic material and its scoring – so that an old-fashioned operatic form is not so much utilized as sublimated.

Tonal relations

The most obvious contrast between *Die Meistersinger* and its predecessor *Tristan und Isolde* lies in the nature of the harmonic language. Whereas *Tristan* was the apotheosis of chromaticism, *Die Meistersinger* is firmly rooted in diatonicism. The Prelude, opening with a solid affirmation of C major – as forthright as the opening of *Tristan* was elusive – gives immediate notice of the new work's diatonic orientation. But there are also unexpected sidesteps, such as that eight bars before the key change to E major: a dominant preparation is resolved onto the submediant. The effect is not to be compared with the symbolically frustrated non-resolutions of *Tristan*; rather it initiates a crossing-over from the world of civic pomp and external reality to the inner world of love and artistic creativity.

The following E flat section, depicting the jauntiness of the apprentices, invokes a contrapuntal texture (Baroque rather than sixteenth-century, but never mind) of a quite different kind from that prevalent in *Tristan*. In the latter work, polyphony created by individual chromatic lines had dictated its own harmony; in the apprentices' music the counterpoint arises out of and is anchored to a secure harmonic foundation. Archaism and modernity exist side-by-side in *Die Meistersinger*, both in terms of the plot and of the music. Secondary triads are favoured, giving a traditional, almost modal flavour at times. But if this challenge to the tonic-dominant hierarchy is a musical metaphor for the work's nostalgic retrospection, it is at the same time a means of rejuvenating tonality: the old enhances the new. Moreover, as Dahlhaus has noted,[4] dissonance, the emblem of modernity, is ever-present but often without the chromatic intensification that characterized *Tristan*.

Historical and political background

An intrinsic element of *Die Meistersinger*, and one which turned out to have devastating repercussions, is the work's nationalist sentiments. The setting of Nuremberg – its narrow streets, a workshop and the festival meadow – is the first point of significance. The scenery of old German towns made a direct appeal to the German Romantic imagination: it represented an escape from the harsh world of industry and commerce to an idyllic, fairytale world of the past – a daydream which has always had a particularly strong attraction for many Germans. Wagner's depiction of medieval Nuremberg was thus a symbolic celebration of German art and life.

At the same time the setting of the imperial free city of Nuremberg had a symbolic significance: the autonomy of these states had long been an inspiration and example to the *Bürger* class in their struggle for power against the feudal forces. Furthermore the 1860s, the decade in which text and music of *Die Meistersinger* were written, was a time of momentous importance for the German people, a time of deep uncertainty, of hope and despair. The rise of heavy industry produced, between 1848 and 1873, a rapid expansion of the economy; many, though not all, Germans enjoyed a period of prosperity which in turn fed a burgeoning sense of national prestige. The momentum for the unification of Germany became unstoppable. Chauvinism, insularity and xenophobia were the besetting attitudes of the era, and the movement towards national unity began to be seen as less a struggle for democratic, constitutional government than as the necessity for asserting German values and culture over those of other races.

[4] *Richard Wagner's Music Dramas*, esp. 72–5.

This was the atmosphere that inspired Wagner's 1865 essay *What is German?* In that essay he salutes the German spirit as the quest for the beautiful and the noble, rather than the profitable and the superficial. The German spirit, he argues, has the capacity to absorb alien elements but the princely rulers squandered the opportunity and the Jews have stepped into the breach, taking over German culture in order to exploit it. Germany is in mortal peril; it is insufficient to safeguard its frontiers and its people if the German spirit itself is allowed to be extinguished. Germans must awaken and protect themselves.

It should be noted that the tone is defensive rather than aggressive: 'The German does not conquer, but neither does he allow himself to be attacked.' Even while observing that aggressors traditionally cloak their instincts in a defensive guise, an objective reading of *What is German?* is bound to conclude that this is not the voice of imperial aggrandizement but of social and artistic concern, concern albeit tinged with a sense of desperation and paranoia.

Were it not for Wagner's artistic predilection for non-particularity, *Die Meistersinger* might have been much more explicit. The one passage where a character does come very close to stepping outside the drama and making a more or less political appeal to the audience is the final part of Sachs' closing address to the people. At one point Wagner had thought of ending the work with Walther's winning of Eva, precisely because the address seemed to him to be extraneous to the drama. Cosima, uncharacteristically, urged him to retain the passage, and Wagner – equally uncharacteristically – yielded to her judgment. Sachs' address ends:

> Beware! Evil tricks threaten us.
> If the German people and Empire should one day disintegrate
> Under a false, French [*wälsch*] rule[5]
> Soon no prince will understand his people any more,
> And French vapours with French baubles
> They will implant in our German land;
> What is German and true no one would know any more,
> Unless it lives on in the honour of German masters.
>   Therefore I say to you:
> Honour your German masters.

[5] *Wälsch* is properly less specific than 'French'; it could be translated by 'Romance' or 'Latin', i.e. Italian, French, Spanish etc. However, there is no doubt which nation Wagner has in mind in these lines.

> Then you will call up good spirits!
> And if you favour their endeavours,
> Even if the Holy Roman Empire
> Should vanish in mist
> For us would yet remain
> Holy German art!

The Nazis had only to give the screw a sharp turn to read this as a ringing declaration of German superiority and of willingness to defend true Aryan virtues. (Indeed, they were obliged to do that, because they were inclined to see the attitude Wagner expressed here as 'defeatist'.) When *Die Meistersinger* was given in Bayreuth in 1924, the first festival to be held after the war, Sachs' address was acknowledged by the audience rising to its feet; at the end of the performance the national anthem was sung and shouts of 'Heil' were also reported. *Die Meistersinger* had been taken up from the early years of the Second Reich as the ideal festival opera for patriotic occasions such as parades, commemorations and consecrations. In the Third Reich the work became almost obligatory to celebrate important events, including the party congress.

Embarrassment over Sachs' address today is often the result of misunderstanding; nevertheless it is not without foundation. The passage is not a call to arms but an affirmation that even foreign domination cannot obliterate the German spirit so long as it resides in the art of the old masters and they are respected. It is clearly a warning to Germany in the 1860s, but it is also a prophecy in the mouth of Hans Sachs: after Sachs' death, German culture was to be threatened by the nadir of the nation's fortunes in the Thirty Years' War (1618–48), and then by absolutist rule and Napoleonic domination. Yet the German spirit survives, Wagner is saying, and will survive even the challenges of the present and future, so long as the nation's cultural heritage is honoured. Moreover, the idea is far from an individual quirk of Wagner's: it was common currency in nineteenth-century Germany. One of many similar statements that could be quoted is a poetic fragment of Schiller, whose phraseology bears a striking affinity: 'Separated from the political, the German has established for himself his own worth, and even if the Empire were to be destroyed, German excellence would remain undisputed.'[6]

---

[6] Poem fragment *Deutsche Grösse* (1797), Sämtliche Werke, ed. G. Fricke and H. Göpfert, 4th edn (Munich 1965), i, p. 473.

Wagner was not responsible for German nationalism; but he reflected it, focused it and gave it such resonant expression that it sparked the imagination of future generations.

The situation has been confused further for English-speaking people because of the coercive overtones of the line 'Honour your German masters' ('Ehrt eure deutschen Meister'). However, the German word for 'master', in the sense of 'overlord', is *Herr*; *Meister* is used only in the sense of a master of a craft. The line might properly be paraphrased, therefore, as 'Honour your German craftsmen' or 'Honour your nation's artists'.[7]

The notion of a culture being under threat from foreign elements may seem unduly insular and alarmist to us today, but it was one that exercised the minds of German intellectuals right through the nineteenth century. Wagner's hatred of the French was as vitriolic as that of the Jews, yet it is not an issue of central concern in *Die Meistersinger*. As he was to do in *Parsifal*, he expunges political extremism from his work of art, making it instead a discourse on the value of art and the manner of its creation: the regulation of genius by formal discipline. Given the work's ideological background, coupled with the vigorous, affirmative nature of the music, it is hardly surprising that it made such an appeal to the National Socialists and that they found it such an ideal vehicle for their propaganda. There is ironic justice in the fact that the Nazis' enthusiasm for *Die Meistersinger* has brought Wagner notoriety for sentiments whose explicit expression he had been on the point of suppressing from the work.

[7] Wagner was well aware of Grimm's derivation of 'deutsch' from the Middle High German 'diet' (nation, people) and of his assertion that it is akin to 'deutlich' (i.e. clear, intelligible to ordinary people), a usage for which Grimm cites the poetry of Sachs himself as evidence.

19

Parsifal

Sources

Wagner had long since sensed the appropriateness of the *Parsifal* subject for the crowning of his career as a music dramatist; indeed, he had made the acquaintance of the material as early as his period in Dresden. As described in chapter 15, it was in the summer of 1845, while he was taking a water cure at Marienbad, that he read Wolfram von Eschenbach's Parzivâl and Titurel poems, in versions by Simrock and San-Marte. Parzival's name duly turned up in Lohengrin's Narration: the knight reveals that his father is Parzival, Lord of the Grail. At one point Wagner had considered bringing Parzival to Tristan's sick-bed, identifying in his mind the suffering of Tristan with that of Amfortas.

The epic poem *Parzivâl*[1] by Wolfram von Eschenbach (*c.* 1170– *c.*1220) was his main source; written during the early years of the thirteenth century, it came just a few years after Crétien de Troyes had left unfinished his *Li Contes del Graal*, which Wagner also read.[2] Crétien conceived of the Grail as a dish, but for Wolfram it was a stone with miraculous powers: it supplied food and drink for the knights who possessed it; it kept them eternally young; and it had the power to sustain for a week the life of anyone who gazed on it. Wolfram did not identify the Grail with either the chalice used by Christ at the Last Supper or the vessel in which Joseph of Arimathea caught the blood of Jesus as he hung on the Cross; these associations were made for the first time in the early years of the thirteenth century by the Burgundian poet Robert de Boron and the first of the anonymous poets to continue Crétien's story.

---

[1] Wagner retained Wolfram's spelling until March 1877, at which point also the prose draft was versified.

[2] See Stewart Spencer, ' "Parzivâl" and "Parsifal" ', *Wagner*, ii (1981), 2–20, for a highly informative discussion of the medieval background, especially Wolfram's poem.

The quest for the Grail proved to be one of the most popular tales of all time, both in poetry and prose, the hero being variously named Gawain, Perceval, Lancelot and Galahad. But Wolfram was indisputably Wagner's chief source in spite of his subsequent belittling of Wolfram's abilities as a poet and his characteristic attempt to distance himself: 'I could just as well have been influenced by my nurse's bedtime story,'[3] he told Cosima.

Wagner's compression of a wide range of sources, containing both Christian and pagan elements, was once again masterly.[4] It involved placing the sphere of the Grail (Monsalvat, in the northern mountains of Spain) alongside the domain of Klingsor, the sorcerer whose aim is to ensnare and destroy the knights of the Grail, so that Klingsor wounds Amfortas with the sacred spear of Longinus itself (Longinus' spear, which pierced the side of Christ on the Cross, was not identified with Parzival's spear by Wolfram, nor by Wagner in his prose draft – only in the final poem). And again, characters from the various sources are eliminated and amalgamated in the customary way: Kundry, for example, is a conflation of several of Wolfram's characters into one, admittedly schizophrenic, figure; Amfortas has connections with, among others, the pagan mythical figure of the Fisher King, an incurably sick ruler, whose waste land of a kingdom mirrors his own ailment. Wagner has also changed the very nature of the Grail community. In Wolfram it was open to both sexes and although normally its members were required to forswear the joys of love, the maidens could travel abroad and marry, and the knights when sent on special missions to help those in distress were able to marry and have children. Wagner's Grail brotherhood, on the other hand, is exclusively male and seems ill-endowed with the qualities of goodness and love which it was their calling to spread abroad.

In addition to its Christian and pagan elements, Wagner's poem incorporates Buddhist and Schopenhauerian ideas, with intentions and consequences which will be discussed later in the chapter. The story, briefly, is the development of the innocent, ignorant young man Parsifal from his inability to understand the suffering of

[3] Cosima Wagner's Diaries, 17 June 1881.

[4] For a more detailed discussion of the sources and Wagner's manipulation of them see the *Parsifal* chapter in Newman's *Wagner Nights*, and chap. 1, 'The sources', of Lucy Beckett's *Parsifal*.

Amfortas, the fallen guardian of the Grail, to his assumption of the role of redeemer – of Amfortas and the whole Grail brotherhood. It is Kundry's kiss that awakens him to the reality of suffering, but it is only after many years of wandering that he finally achieves the state of enlightenment that enables him to redeem both the community and himself.

Composition and first performances

The first sketch for *Parsifal* was made in 1857, in circumstances described in chapter 6. It is now lost. Wagner next made a prose draft in Munich in 1865 and a second in 1877 which is mostly written in dialogue form. Shortly afterwards (14 March – 19 April 1877) the poem was written and the composition followed in what was now Wagner's habitual fashion: two drafts were made, the first (in pencil) primarily a setting of the text, and the second (in ink) primarily a working out of the accompaniment. He alternated between one draft and the other, thus minimizing the gap between the word-setting and the elaboration of the score. These two processes, which took place between August 1877 and April 1879, disposed of the most taxing part of the composition; he orchestrated the Prelude in 1878 (first version) and then it remained only to make his full score of the body of the work, which he did between August 1879 and January 1882.

Rehearsals took place in July 1882 and the first performances were given in the Festspielhaus on the 26th and 28th for members of the Society of Patrons, followed by fourteen further performances in July and August. Copious documentation exists on the rehearsals and performances regarding Wagner's wishes on all aspects, such as interpretation of the score, staging and characterization.[5]

In order to signify a new kind of drama, Wagner called *Parsifal* a *Bühnenweihfestspiel*. 'Sacred stage festival play' is probably the best English equivalent but that does not take account of the other sense of the German word *weihen*, namely to 'consecrate' or 'dedicate'. Wagner specifically announced that he was using *Parsifal* to consecrate the Festspielhaus in much the same way as the Church's festivals were celebrated with feasts. And so 'stage consecration festival play' is also a suitable translation.

The special relationship between *Parsifal* and the Bayreuth

[5] See *Sämtliche Werke*, ed. Carl Dahlhaus, xxx, pp. 139–229.

Festspielhaus was enshrined in a thirty-year embargo on the work's performance outside Bayreuth. King Ludwig had the work put on privately in Munich in the years after Wagner's death and it was also seen by members of the Wagner Society in Amsterdam in 1905. The latter staging was criticized by the Bayreuth circle, but the greatest opprobrium was reserved for the management of the Metropolitan Opera and the singers who performed it in New York in 1903. For Europeans there were only limited opportunities to see the work until the embargo expired in 1913, though concert performances were given, including one in London under Joseph Barnby in 1884.

Musico-poetic synthesis

The verse of *Parsifal* is some of Wagner's freest, ranging from sonorous, measured lines to short, violently expressive ones, such as Kundry's anguished opening of the second act: 'Ach! – Ach! / Tiefe Nacht – / Wahnsinn! – Oh! – Wut! – ' About one third of the lines are rhymed, but there is much freedom of metre. Alliteration has all but disappeared. The self-conscious archaisms of the *Ring* and other texts are to a considerable extent abandoned and there is a palpable move in the direction of clarity of thought and refinement of utterance. Even recitative-like declamation occurs occasionally, for example in Gurnemanz's Act I narrative.

A vestige of the *Opera and Drama* principles remains in the word-setting, but Wagner gives himself a free hand to intensify the melodic line or not, as he wishes. As far as leitmotifs are concerned, all the motifs in *Parsifal*, with one exception, originate in the orchestra rather than in the musico-poetic line.[6] They are not, therefore, true motifs of reminiscence. Indeed, even their attachment to various characters, objects and concepts is lacking in consistency. The theme with which the work opens is usually known as the motif of the Last Supper (see Ex. 46), but its appearances are not restricted to the mention of that celebration. The group of rising quavers in its fourth bar is often called the Spear motif, but the spear is also accompanied by quite different music. Motifs are deployed with sufficient consistency to enable the listener to make some sort of identification, but Wagner is clearly less concerned to achieve a scrupulous concordance of text and motifs than with their cumu-

[6] See Jack Stein, *Richard Wagner & the Synthesis of the Arts*, 210.

Ex. 46

lative dramatic effect. This may perhaps be explained by the fact that the entire score could be said to flow thematically from the opening motif, Ex. 46.

The one exceptional use of a true motif of reminiscence is that heard to the words 'Durch Mitleid wissend, der reine Tor', which expresses one of the basic themes of the work: the idea of the pure fool made wise by compassion is specifically recalled on each occurrence of the motif. Even this, however, does not make an orthodox first appearance, because it is anticipated by Gurnemanz in his exchange with the two knights early in Act I.

Such contradictions of *Opera and Drama* principles by no means indicate a falling-off in Wagner's compositional powers. On the contrary his self-liberation from formulas and pre-ordained rules is symptomatic of an increasing inclination towards clarification, a distillation of essence. Wagner had a lifelong compulsion to communicate; in his final masterpiece, the urgency of his message is matched by total assurance of technique.

Tonal relations

This clarification is reflected in stretches of uncomplicated tonal harmony, but these exist side-by-side with passages whose harmonic language is one of extreme ambiguity. The modes of diatonicism and chromaticism are once again counterposed, but the relationship of the two is more equivocal than in *Tristan* or *Die Meistersinger*. The realm of the Grail, sanctified and ritualized, is represented by diatonicism (heard in its purest form in the Prelude, for example, and in the Grail scene at the end of Act I). The realm of the evil sorcerer Klingsor is represented by chromaticism, its shifting, dissolute qualities a potent metaphor for spiritual degeneration. But between these two basic categories there are many cross-currents. Dahlhaus, for instance, points out that the use of chromaticism for both Klingsor's kingdom and Amfortas' suffering makes 'a connection between deception and suffering'.[7] It is instructive, too, to compare the opening melodic phrases of the first two acts. They have a very similar outline, both rising through a whole octave, but the opening of Act I (the Grail, see Ex.46) is based on a common chord and shares its stability, whereas that of Act II (Klingsor's magic castle) immediately introduces a disruptive tritone:

Ex. 47

This chromatic transmutation of a diatonic theme is typical, for in Wagner's music diatonicism is always on the verge of dissolution, and there is a greater propensity for diatonicism to yield to chromaticism than vice versa.[8] The climax of Kundry's Act II seduction of Parsifal – her kiss – might be given as another example. In the eleven orchestral bars before Parsifal's cry of 'Amfortas!' part of the Last Supper motif is gradually revealed in an unfamiliar chromatic context, by a clever twist of the tail of the theme associated with sorcery:

Ex. 48

---

[7] *Richard Wagner's Music Dramas*, 151.

[8] This point is made by Arnold Whittall on p.64 of his invaluable chapter on the music of *Parsifal*; see L. Beckett, *Parsifal*, 61–86.

Several bars later, at 'Jammervollster!', as Parsifal is still recoiling from Kundry's seduction, there is a chromatic modification of the Last Supper motif, and a little later, as Kundry recounts her act of blasphemy ('Ich sah Ihn'), the motif is heard in a highly unstable chromatic context.

Another aspect of *Parsifal*'s tonal ambiguity is seen in the way Wagner confirms, or appears to confirm, a particular key by a cadential resolution even though that key may be at odds with the tonal context. Amfortas' first paragraph, for example, has a strong inclination towards B flat major — much of it is underpinned by a dominant pedal anticipating a cadence on B flat. But the paragraph resolves at 'Die Schmerzensnacht wird helle' (The night of pain grows light) in a decisive cadence on G flat major. Amfortas' hope of imminent release from suffering is, this suggests, illusory. But there is also a more fundamental significance that it is an incidental rather than a primary key that is emphasized with a perfect cadence: uncertainty is elevated to a structural principle.

Further ambiguity surrounds the work's central polarity of the tonalities of A flat major and D (major and minor). This turns out to be less a Manichean struggle between two opposing and irreconcilable forces — as occurs with the same two keys, for example, in Elgar's First Symphony — than an integration of two complementary spheres, two sides of a coin, which have to be brought into resolution. Such a reading is first suggested by the powerful conclusion of Gurnemanz's Narration, where at 'Durch hell erschauter Wortezeichen Male' (Through luminously beheld signs of words) the sphere of D flat and its dominant A flat is juxtaposed with, and transformed into by an enharmonic modulation, the sphere of A and D. The final resolution of the two spheres occurs at the end of the work, in a series of progressions that reach a climax at the words 'Enthüllet den Gral, öffnet den Schrein!' (Uncover the Grail, open the shrine!). The sensation produced by the modulation on these words — that of expectation fulfilled — is one of the great moments of *Parsifal*.

At one notable point in the score, the chords of A flat and D seem to be compressed into one. It is during the Good Friday music in Act III, a context of unequivocal D major when at the words 'Ihn selbst am Kreuze' (Him on the Cross) the '*Tristan* chord' suddenly sounds, superimposing the notes of A flat and E flat (notated as G sharp and D sharp). One of the several other appearances of the '*Tristan* chord', after Kundry's 'sein Blick!', as she describes in Act II the fateful moment of her mockery of Christ, likewise brings the religious and the sexual into close proximity. Redemption has also its erotic aspect.

The tritone that makes up the other half of the 'Tristan chord' (F—B) and the tritone that is inherent in the A flat/D relationship are once again agents of dissolution, undermining tonal stability. Augmented triads, for example that around which Amfortas' motif is built, work to similar effect. But on a larger scale the most significant challenge to the hierarchical structure based on tonic/dominant polarity is posed by the predilection for tonal relationships founded on keys a third apart. Act I ends in C major, which is a third away from the opening A flat. C major is established as a primary key by its assertion, in comparatively untrammelled diatonic form, in the Hall of the Grail: the knights open their hymn 'Zum letzten Liebesmahle' (At the last love-feast) with it. It thus achieves a stable form which allows it to vie with A flat as the key likely to end the act.

Relationships based on 3rds rather than 5ths again predominate in Act II. Exceptionally for Wagner this act begins and ends in the same key: B minor. In between the outer pillars of B minor there are three main tonal areas: E flat (appearing with Parsifal), A flat (the flowermaidens) and G (Kundry's attempted seduction). These keys, however, provide merely a framework for passages of much less clearly defined tonality and, especially in the sorcery music of Klingsor and Kundry, much chromaticism. It should also be mentioned that the hierarchy of the Classical tonal system is undermined melodically as well as harmonically. Augmented triads (as in Amfortas' motif) and melodic configurations based on the diminished 7th (much of the sorcery music) both tend to divide the octave into equal, symmetrical parts (with gaps of a minor 3rd) as opposed to the unequal divisions (perfect 4th and 5th) demanded by the tonic/dominant relationship.

To conclude this section on the tonal relations of Parsifal, it should be made clear that neither A flat (the key in which the work begins and ends) nor any other key can be regarded as any kind of 'tonal centre', around which the other primary tonalities revolve. Rather the scheme should be seen as an evolutionary process. Changing dramatic situations and developments of character result in a tonal continuum that veers between diatonicism and chromaticism, stable and unstable tonality, motivic and non-motivic passages. Motifs are continually subjected to development and transformation, and forms are not of the old-fashioned periodic type but irregular, incomplete, hybrid – frequently starting out according to one model and becoming something else. Structure in *Parsifal* thus depends not on a single immobile centre of gravity but on an active, evolving series of events.

Orchestration

Wagner's orchestration in *Parsifal* differs from that of his earlier music dramas in a number of revealing ways. In *Die Meistersinger* he had made an effort to ensure that the performance would be a practical proposition by slimming down the orchestration to double wind: two flutes (plus piccolo and very occasionally a third flute), two oboes (no cor anglais), two clarinets (no bass clarinet) and two bassoons. *Tristan* had called for triple wind and now in *Parsifal* he reverts to quadruple woodwind, as for the *Ring*; however, he does not return completely to the enormous forces of the *Ring*, because there are four horns rather than eight (no Wagner tubas) and as in both *Tristan* and *Die Meistersinger* the bass trumpet and contrabass trombone are discarded.

In terms of the technique of scoring, *Parsifal* and *Tristan* are radically divergent. In the latter, the constant state of flux is partly a product of the orchestration: strands of melodic line pass from one instrument to another; beginnings and endings of phrases are disguised by overlapping instruments; woodwind and horns insinuate themselves into the texture rather than draw attention to themselves; the brass emerge and vanish with similar discretion, their movements often masked by artful crescendos and diminuendos. Such a subtle interweaving of lines both within and between departments of the orchestra may be contrasted with the relatively block-like scoring of the less mature *Holländer*, *Tannhäuser* and *Lohengrin*.

In *Parsifal* Wagner in a sense reverted to his former style of scoring, but it has now attained a refinement and a sensuousness unsurpassed by anything else in his oeuvre. Instrumental groups are heard as distinct entities; often they are explicitly set off against each other in antiphonal style. The difference in appearance on the printed page of the scores of *Tristan* and *Parsifal* reflects the contrasting techniques in a striking manner: where that of *Tristan* is fragmentary and interlocking, that of *Parsifal* is vertically and hierarchically ordered. The ritualistic conception of the work dictates the stateliness and formality of its scoring, though, as might be expected, this is the case chiefly in Acts I and III – the absence of ritual in Act II results in considerably less vertical grouping. The type of motifs used in the respective works is another factor: where those of *Tristan* are mostly elusive and interweave horizontally, those of *Parsifal* are, except for the music of Klingsor and Kundry, invested with the dignity of ritual and call for chordal treatment.

Interpretations

The 'meaning' of *Parsifal* can best be approached through some of the key characters. Perhaps the most complex is Kundry, who is not only a composite of several characters from the medieval sources, but who also owes her identity to the transmigration of souls: her incarnations have included the Nordic Gundryggia, and Herodias, who was responsible for the death of John the Baptist. Like Ahasuerus and the Flying Dutchman she has committed the sin of blasphemy – she laughed in the face of Christ; now, like them a Wandering Jew figure, she is condemned to roam through the centuries. She can only be released from this fate if a man is strong enough to resist her allurements; her cruel sentence means that she has continually to seduce men and suffer torture as they finally give in. Her only wish is for extinction, to be freed from the wheel of life; this is eventually made possible by Parsifal's self-restraint and compassion. Inevitably, therefore, the drama ends without a representative of the female of the species: dramatic necessity caused Wagner to compress several characters into one, and any resolution other than extinction would be unsatisfactory. But this leaves a nagging doubt: does not the all-male community at the end have an unhealthy, misogynistic ring? Much depends on how one views Parsifal's repulsion of Kundry; as will shortly be suggested, it is a more complex matter than at first appears. But it is also worth remembering that Wagner identified himself with the Wandering Jew, whose purging and even whose 'annihilation' were both desirable and necessary.

Amfortas also seeks to die, but he cannot be allowed to, for death would not bring him redemption or true penitence, and therefore no release from the cycle of suffering. He performs his duty of uncovering the Grail reluctantly but (at first) conscientiously. He knows that the revealed Grail will prolong his life for another period and renew his agony, but he knows also that he is bound to do his duty as Keeper of the Grail: it will sustain his knights and it will bring

265

him into painful but longed-for contact with his Saviour. Kundry and Amfortas both vacillate between the extremes of chastening remorse and voluptuous self-indulgence. They both fail to find a satisfactory synthesis of the two and like Tannhäuser they inflict suffering on themselves by lurching from one extreme to the other.

Amfortas was originally altruistic; he received his wound when he went to deal with the sorcery that was ensnaring his knights. But he has long since, like Kundry, been caught in a web of selfish, egoistic desires. Parsifal is able to be the redeemer in the first place because he is innocent, untainted by deceit, in the second because he achieves wisdom through suffering and is able thereby to transcend the limitations of his personality. Redemption can thus once again be seen as a painful process of self-enlightenment. Once he has attained the goal, the enlightened one, Parsifal, is able to liberate others.

An essential concept here is that of *Mitleid*, usually translated as 'pity' or 'compassion'; in his writings, Wagner also uses the form *Mitleiden*, which makes a little clearer the vital sense of 'suffering together with'. Wagner's empathy with Buddhist thought and with the allied philosophy of Schopenhauer is nowhere more apparent than in *Parsifal*, for all its Christian symbolism. Schopenhauer is indirectly referred to in a key passage in *Religion and Art* (1880) which brings us to the essence of *Parsifal*. The divine sphere, says Wagner, where suffering is no longer possible [cf. Nirvana] can only be reached through the spirit of self-denial, and the attainment of this self-knowledge can finally be brought about only by compassion born of suffering.

> If we take this great thought of our philosopher [Schopenhauer] as guide to the inexorable metaphysical problem of the purpose of the human race, we shall have to acknowledge that what we have termed the decline of the race, as known to us by its historical deeds, is really the stern school of Suffering which the Will imposed on its blind self for sake of gaining sight, – somewhat in the sense of the power 'that ever willeth ill, and ever doeth good.'[9]

Kundry's kiss is the catalyst that awakens Parsifal to the reality of suffering. He does not merely pity Amfortas: he suffers with him, and in that moment of destiny he begins to acquire the self-knowledge that he has hitherto lacked. It is the beginning of his liberation from

[9] Trans. by W. Ashton Ellis. The closing quotation is from Goethe's *Faust*, part 1.

self-centredness. He is learning that his actions cannot stand in isolation: they affect others – even a refusal to act can harm others. The gaining of true understanding is a matter of throwing off the shackles of the ego by which we are all bound.

It is often a cause of anxiety that Wagner appears, in *Parsifal*, to be suggesting that chastity is a necessary virtue, that Parsifal's spurning of Kundry and her expiring are indicative of an old man at last renouncing and repudiating sexuality. But the significance of the seduction scene lies not in a rejection of sexuality. What Kundry is offering is something closer to lust: irresponsible, uncaring – one of the extremes between which she is continually vacillating. Moreover, her motive is to free herself thereby from her curse, in order to achieve the blissful state of non-being. She imposes a severe test on Parsifal, one she wishes him both to pass and to fail. Parsifal, for his part, is sufficiently attuned to the process of self-enlightenment to respond correctly to her falsely posed test. But his spontaneous fellow-suffering with Amfortas still needs to be properly channelled: a lesson he will learn during the tribulations of his wandering, and which will be represented on Good Friday by a recognition of the significance of the ultimate act of fellow-suffering – that of Christ. Thus it becomes clear that self-denial is not a question of chastity but acceptance of moral responsibility.

Is *Parsifal* a religious work, and if so how does this square with Wagner's own convictions? It has been claimed that *Parsifal* is an essentially Christian drama,[10] an argument that can be maintained by pointing to the centrality of the Grail, representing the Christian profession of atonement through Christ's blood, celebrated at the Last Supper, and representing also God's promise of eternal life and his presence among men and women. The argument can be supported, too, by the clear evidence for Wagner's acceptance of the doctrine of the Incarnation – another fundamental dogma of Christianity, whereby the divine took on human form. There are also numerous comments by Wagner in letters and writings from the last two decades of his life which seem to reinforce such a view. Some of the most explicit are among those addressed to King Ludwig – which may, however, make us suspicious of their sincerity. 'It seems to me',

10 Lucy Beckett argues the case persuasively in the final chapter, 'A proposed interpretation', of her *Parsifal*, 129–49. Chapter 5, 'Reactions and critical assessments', offers a stimulating résumé of all the major interpretations from 1882 on.

he wrote, 'as though I have been inspired to undertake this work in order to sustain for the world its inherent, most profound mystery – the truest Christian faith; indeed, to awaken this faith anew.'[11]

On the other side it can be argued that Wagner was primarily interested in the myths and symbols of religion, and that far from accepting the Church's dogmas he inveighed bitterly against many of them. (One of the glories of Wagner, as we have seen, is that like the Bible itself he can be quoted in support of most arguments.) His aim, according to this reasoning, was to use the superior powers of art to express the deepest significance of religion through its own mythic symbols. As Wagner puts it at the beginning of *Religion and Art*:

> One could say that at the point where religion becomes artificial it is for art to preserve the essence of religion by grasping the symbolic value of its mythic symbols, which the former would have us believe in their literal sense, so that the deep, hidden truth in them might be revealed by their ideal representation.

The value of religion, therefore, was to be found not in a fundamental acceptance of its tenets, but in a presentation in symbolic form of its universal spiritual truths. *Parsifal*'s Christian imagery in any case stands at a further remove by being ritualized: the Last Supper, for example, is not re-enacted in the Grail scenes so much as recalled – like a vision summoned from the recesses of the psyche.[12]

Other writers, too, have taken the view that *Parsifal* is less a religious work than a work *about* religion. Regarding it as a study of 'the psychopathology of religious belief in artistic terms',[13] it is perfectly possible to respond to the work's central moral dilemmas from an agnostic or atheistic position. Thus, in the Good Friday scene, Wagner draws our attention away from the image of Christ on the Cross and towards nature and redeemed humanity.

A less savoury aspect of *Parsifal* that should neither be overlooked nor exaggerated out of proportion is the fact that it was

[11] *König Ludwig II. und Richard Wagner: Briefwechsel*, ed. O. Strobel, iii (Karlsruhe 1936), 21.

[12] Dahlhaus' introductory essay 'Richard Wagner: *Parsifal*' interestingly discusses the music from this point of view.

[13] Michael Tanner, 'The Total Work of Art', in *The Wagner Companion*, ed. P. Burbidge and R. Sutton, 209. The essay has many valuable insights into *Parsifal*.

composed at the period in Wagner's life when his views on 'racial purity' were finding their most extreme and strident expression. In the series of essays from his last years, sometimes known as the 'regeneration writings', a number of ideas are propounded at considerable length: blatant racist ideology partly derived from Gobineau's views on miscegenation; unabashed anti-semitism in by now familiar tirades; the role of religion and of Christ the Redeemer in a process of regeneration. The essays concerned are: *Modern*, *Public and Popularity*, *Shall we hope?*, *Religion and Art*, *What use is this Knowledge?*, *Know Thyself* and *Heroism and Christianity*.

More detailed résumés are given in chapter 8; here the salient themes may be extracted. The degeneration of the human race has come about through its departure from its natural food. People have slaughtered animals and spilt blood to get their food; and the substitution of an animal for a vegetable diet has led to a change in the fundamental substance of the body and to corrupted blood; this in turn has caused the degeneration. Regeneration must be based on a return to a vegetable diet and it must be rooted in the soil of a true religion. Christ's blood was pure – the highest possible development of the human species; by partaking of the blood of Jesus, in the sacrament of the Eucharist, the very lowest races might be raised to the most godly purity. Wagner also floats the concept of the Aryan Jesus: for him such a saviour cannot be reconciled with the Jewish God of the Old Testament.

Wagner's letters of the time, and Cosima's Diaries, show that his racist ideas could achieve an even uglier form when he was not inhibited by the constraints imposed by publication. The Jews are likened to a swarm of flies in a wound on a horse; on another occasion Cosima records that 'He makes a drastic joke to the effect that all Jews should be burned at a performance of *Nathan*.' Other races equally fall victim to the conviction of innate white superiority: 'A human being who is born black, urged towards the heights, becomes white and at the same time a different creature.'[14]

This is the ideological background against which *Parsifal* was written, and seen in this light many aspects of it take on a dubious significance: the partaking of Christ's blood – evidently for the

---

[14] Cosima Wagner's Diaries, 9 February 1882, 18 December 1881 and 16 October 1882. Wagner particularly disliked Lessing's *Nathan der Weise*, a play that preached tolerance towards Jews.

purpose of purging impure racial elements; the exclusive élite of the Grail brotherhood; even the adherence to a new creed based on faith, hope and the love that springs from fellow-suffering, rather than on Old Testament principles.[15] It must not be forgotten that the sketch of *Parsifal*, which prefigures all this, dates from 1865 – thirteen years before the first of the 'regeneration writings'. But as so often with Wagner, the artistic conception came first: he simply needed to argue out his ideas in literary form before crystallizing them in an artistic one.

Much of the stifling atmosphere of secretiveness and segregation that characterized the Bayreuth circle at Wahnfried in the last two decades of the nineteenth century and into the twentieth revolved around the imagery and ideology of *Parsifal*. 'Grail Brotherhood' was a favourite expression, and Cosima even spoke of the possibility of a 'Bayreuth freemasonry'. At the end of his introduction to the first edition of *Bayreuther Blätter* (1877), Wagner used the words 'unter uns!' (among ourselves!) as a sort of motto, pledging thereby that the first performance of *Parsifal* would be only for members of the Society of Patrons; 'unter uns' and 'unsere Sache' (our affair, or 'mission') developed into catchwords at Wahnfried, reflecting a mentality that thrived on secret bonds and societies. Wagner's own outlook in the late essays is pacifist, but after his death a militant undercurrent became apparent in phrases like 'soldier of Bayreuth Idealism', applied to Bernhard Förster in his obituary notice in *Bayreuther Blätter*. The embargo on performances of *Parsifal* other than in the Festspielhaus was of course partly a product of this determination to make Bayreuth a spiritual centre, the shrine of a new religion.[16]

What, then, are we to make of *Parsifal*? We have seen that in it Wagner incorporated pagan elements from the earlier medieval sources; Christian virtues implanted in the later medieval sources; Schopenhauerian–Buddhist concepts such as renunciation of the

[15] Hartmut Zelinsky develops these ideas in his controversial 'Die "feuerkur" des Richard Wagner oder die "neue religion" der "Erlösung" durch "Vernichtung" '. There is much of interest in this article, but in order to prove that the whole of Wagner's mature life was devoted to the propagation of a creed of destruction and regeneration, Zelinsky is obliged to resort to manipulation of his sources.

[16] The whole process is discussed alongside a breathtaking range of documents covering many different aspects of the Second and Third Reichs in Zelinsky's *Richard Wagner: ein deutsches Thema*.

will, extinction, and learning through suffering; and finally ideas of regeneration and racial purity. Any of the last three can be claimed for an interpretation of *Parsifal* and there is abundant evidence to support each of these claims. The letter quoted above in which Wagner spoke to Ludwig of his 'mission' to rekindle the spirit of Christianity might seem to clinch the argument for a Christian interpretation, but the Schopenhauerian ideas and vocabulary cannot be magicked away. Similarly, one could point to innumerable connections between *Parsifal* and the late essays (and contemporary letters and diaries). Some are quite explicit, as at the end of *Shall we hope?*, in which Wagner has been discussing the prospects of a renewal of the German spirit: 'That I myself have not yet abandoned hope I affirm in that I was recently able to complete the music for my *Parsifal*.' But how is one to reconcile the poisonous notion of racial purity with the Christian spirit of tolerance and forgiveness? And why is there not a single expression of anti-semitism to be found in *Parsifal*?

The answer to these questions is simple. Wagner chose not to tie *Parsifal* to any particular creed or ideology; it harbours all these diverse and sometimes conflicting perceptions, just as Wagner's writings and conversations were peppered with widely diverging ideas. In private and public life he was never reluctant to express his views, if perhaps with more passion than clarity. In his works of art, he was as eclectic about philosophies of life as he was about literary sources: taking from each exactly what he required, he clothed it in richly allusive, symbolic terms, caring little for the ensuing contradictions.

To read *Parsifal* as an exclusively Christian or exclusively Buddhist allegory, or to see it only as the artistic counterpart of the late writings, is grievously to diminish the work.[17] Coming to grips with *Parsifal* entails accepting that its fabric is riven with inconsistencies; only by facing up to that fact are we likely to penetrate to its essence.[18]

[17] This is the error made by both Zelinsky and Robert Gutman. In both cases, valid insights are vitiated by an unwillingness to take into account the full richness of the work.

[18] I firmly believe, however, that a staging of the work can fruitfully concentrate on single aspects. Productions that attempt to be either neutral or 'definitive' are rarely as rewarding as those that inspire reappraisal of the whole by illumination of the part.

20

Other instrumental and vocal works

The essence of Wagner's achievement is to be found in his operas and music dramas; these are the works in which he made his unique contribution to the course of music history and by which he will continue to be remembered. But he also essayed compositions in many other genres, some of which are of sufficient quality to merit performance, and others of which can most productively be viewed for the light they throw on Wagner the man and artist. The works selected for discussion below include all those normally encountered; all have been published[1] and recorded.[2]

Wagner's tendency in later life was to dismiss his early compositions as either mere academic exercises or as inconsequential juvenile effusions. At the time, he regarded them very differently. His interests in the early 1830s lay not in opera and the theatre, but in the Classical orchestral repertory and especially the symphonies of Beethoven. His ambition was to master the Classical forms for himself and the closeness in these early works to procedures and even themes of Beethoven, Mozart, Mendelssohn and others is evidence of the thoroughness with which he had studied those composers. *Mein Leben* describes many of these youthful works and the circumstances that brought them into being, but it is not a reliable guide to models and influences, for reasons that will be discussed in this chapter. There are, in addition, a number of instrumental and vocal works scattered throughout Wagner's creative life. These were all occasioned by specific events or inspired by particular people who came within his orbit.

Orchestral

Wagner's Symphony in C major – his only completed work in that

[1] See Appendices B and D for further details.

[2] Though not all the recordings are easily accessible.

genre – was written in 1832. Its assured handling of the form immediately gives the lie to the notion of Wagner's dilettantism – a view of his approach to musical composition that was encouraged by Wagner himself. *Mein Leben* is at pains to play down the significance of his instruction under Müller and Weinlig, in order to foster the impression of a naturally gifted, self-taught genius who simply chose to channel his talents into music. But we now know something that *Mein Leben* does not tell us: the studies with Müller lasted the best part of three years (1828–31), and they must have been taken rather more seriously than Wagner would have us believe, for him to be in a position to imitate his models as successfully as he did the following year in the C major Symphony.[3]

Beethoven was the chief model for this work and from the opening hammer-blows on there are Beethovenian hallmarks in abundance. The second movement, Andante ma non troppo, contains some very close thematic parallels to the slow movements of Beethoven's Fifth and Seventh Symphonies; indeed, looking back at the work half a century later Wagner said his Andante would not have seen the light of day had it not been for those other two slow movements.[4] He also mentions the 'Eroica' as important to him in this context and certainly there are echoes, conscious or unconscious, of all those odd-numbered symphonies of Beethoven. In the Finale it is Mozart's K551, the 'Jupiter', in the same key, that comes to mind. Perhaps this was the product of the lapidary note under 1828 in the Red Pocketbook: 'Get to know Mozart'.

For all the Beethovenian gestures, Wagner's symphonic technique should not be identified with that of his exemplar. This is not the place for an analytical comparison of the two composers' procedures, but it should be noted that it was largely Wagner's dissatisfaction with the Beethovenian technique of fragmentary development, and his realization that it was not suitable for his own purposes, that led him ultimately to turn away from abstract instrumental forms to fashion a new genre, the music drama, in which

---

[3] John Deathridge's article 'Wagner und sein erster Lehrmeister' discusses the importance to Wagner of his studies with Müller and reproduces a revealing and previously unpublished letter from Wagner to Müller.

[4] *Bericht über die Wiederaufführung eines Jugendwerkes*, Sämtliche Schriften, x, 314.

quasi-symphonic processes could be pressed into the service of a dramatic conception.[5]

Shortly before the C major Symphony Wagner had written an overture to accompany a performance of Ernst Raupach's play *König Enzio* in the Royal Saxon Court Theatre in Leipzig. Again the forceful repetitions and emphatic cadences are reminiscent of Beethoven; the former, at least, were to become a distinctive Wagnerian fingerprint. Some more incidental music was written two years later for a performance of the play *Columbus* by Wagner's friend Theodore Apel. Wagner was instrumental in having the play put on at the theatre in Magdeburg; of the music he wrote for it, only the overture survives. The *Columbus* Overture, like Apel's play, celebrated the great navigator's heroic voyage of discovery and the opening up of a new continent. It is an amateurish piece of music, inferior to the Symphony in respect of the banality of much of its material and the uncertainty of its motivation. Yet there is some interesting pictorialism in the swirling waves and the vision of the promised land – the latter atmospheric effect is achieved by three pairs of trumpets playing what Wagner described as a fata Morgana theme. The six trumpets eventually combine in a triumphant conclusion to the work. The model for the *Columbus* Overture would seem to have been not Beethoven, but Mendelssohn. The alternation of sections, each distinguished in tempo, theme and instrumentation, is a feature of Mendelssohn's overtures, and Wagner almost certainly took the idea of the trumpet fanfare (representing a similar vision) from *Calm Sea and Prosperous Voyage*, at the same time recklessly expanding Mendelssohn's third trumpet into a massive 4 horns, 6 trumpets, 3 trombones and tuba.[6]

In 1836 Wagner gave belated expression to his sympathy for the Poles in their unsuccessful struggle against the Russians in 1831. He

[5] There is much of interest on the interaction of Wagner and Beethoven in Egon Voss, *Richard Wagner und die Instrumentalmusik* and Klaus Kropfinger, *Wagner und Beethoven*. The latter is an exhaustive study of the subject; the C major Symphony's thematic parallels with Beethoven and the differing approaches to symphonic development are discussed (with copious music examples) on pp. 193–7, 207–11 and 216.

[6] See Egon Voss, *op. cit.*, 58–61. Wagner conducted *Calm Sea and Prosperous Voyage* in Magdeburg on 13 January 1835; the score of *Columbus* was completed in the same month.

had been closely drawn to the plight of the refugees, whom he had encountered personally in Leipzig, and his *Polonia* Overture brings in Polish references, allusions which impart a flavour rather than being fully integrated. The piece has great vitality, veering constantly between feverish agitation and melancholy.

The following year he wrote another overture informed by nationalist sentiment, this time based on *Rule Britannia*; like *Polonia* it is a heavily orchestrated work, the youthful composer's exuberance being expressed in the augmented wind (including serpent), brass (including ophicleide) and percussion departments. Wagner was by no means ashamed of this overture; indeed, he sent it to the Philharmonic Society in London in the hope of a performance. He was unsuccessful, but worse still, when the score was sent back to him in Paris a few years later, he was unable to pay the postage and *Rule Britannia* returned again to England.[7]

Yet another piece in this style was planned – a Napoleon overture; in fact, Wagner regarded *Polonia*, *Rule Britannia* and *Napoléon* as a sort of trilogy. In this work he 'intended to depict his hero in all his glory up to the Russian campaign, from then on in his decadence'. He claimed later that the idea had petered out because he could not bring himself to use the gong for the climactic stroke, being unsure whether it was 'permissible' in orchestral music.[8] He may not have known that Gossec had used the gong in his Funeral Music for Mirabeau as long ago as 1791, but he must have been aware of its operatic use as it appears both in Bellini's *Norma* and in Meyerbeer's *Robert le Diable*, two works he had been involved in rehearsing.

Wagner's subsequent dismissal of the Napoleon project, as of the other executed works from the 1830s, distracts our attention – as was the object – from the seriousness with which he took them at the time. With the *Faust* Overture Wagner entered a new phase; it is the first of his instrumental works to have gained anything like a regular place in concert programmes today and the composer continued in later life to consider it a significant work, one worthy of revision. The original intention was to write a *Faust* symphony; indeed Wagner went as far as to write down a Gretchen melody for the second

---

[7] The autograph score is not lost, as sometimes stated; it is now in the British Library, Loan MS 77, Part 49. See reproduction as ill. 4 in this book.

[8] Cosima's *Wagner's Diaries*, 12 July 1869.

movement. But within days of completing the score, he was describing it to Meyerbeer (18 January 1840) as an 'overture to Faust', no doubt on the supposition that it would stand a better chance of performance as an independent composition than as the first part of an incomplete work.[9]

Wagner's account of the genesis of this work in *Mein Leben* is somewhat idealized. He describes there how the rehearsals of Beethoven's Ninth that he heard under Habeneck revealed to him for the first time the full glory of that symphony, and how the experience inspired him to compose something that would give him a similar feeling of satisfaction. To take the second point first, the designations of the instruments in French[10] indicate that the work was written not purely for personal satisfaction but in the hope of performance or publication in Paris. But more importantly there is good reason to think that the work was directly inspired not by Beethoven's Ninth but by Berlioz's dramatic symphony *Roméo et Juliette*. The rehearsals of the Ninth that Wagner heard probably took place in the early months of 1840 rather than in October or November 1839[11] and since the *Faust* Overture was sketched in December 1839 and completed on 12 January 1840, we should clearly look somewhere else for a primary inspiration. Berlioz's *Roméo et Juliette*, on the other hand, was given its first performance on 24 November 1839 in Paris and Wagner attended on either that evening or that of its second performance on 1 December. He was deeply impressed by the work and the criticisms of Berlioz expressed in *Mein Leben* may well have been intended, at least in part, to disguise a debt. For Wagner's later autobiographical account is determined to put the revelation of Beethoven at the centre of his Paris experience, as though to establish the pedigree of all the subsequent operas and music dramas. From that time, Wagner seems to be telling us, he was a mature and, above all, a German composer.

[9] The reproduction of the first page of the autograph in *Wagner: A Documentary Study*, ed. H. Barth, D. Mack and E. Voss (ill. 36) shows how the blank heading was replaced first by 'Overture', in red ink, with the words 'to Goethe's *Faust*, Part 1' added subsequently in black. Other changes in red are also shown.

[10] See autograph score (previous note).

[11] See Egon Voss, *Richard Wagner und die Instrumentalmusik*, 70–71.

(It may be noted, however, that the work is not linked with Beethoven's Ninth in either the *Autobiographical Sketch* of 1843 or *A Communication to my Friends* of 1851.)

There are certainly reminiscences of Beethoven in the *Faust* Overture, most notably of *Coriolan* in the much-repeated quaver figure first heard in the cello in bar 3, and of the Ninth in the striding dotted theme:

Ex. 49

Wagner: *Faust* Overture, bars 63–4

Beethoven: Symphony no. 9,
1st movement, bars 17–19

But Wagner's themes are by this time of a quite different kind from Beethoven's. For Wagner a theme was imbued with expressive content of its own, and often prompted by a pictorial or dramatic impulse; the opening theme of the *Faust* Overture, for example, embodies Faust's questing spirit:

Ex. 50

For Beethoven, on the other hand, a theme was primarily a cell for development: raw material as opposed to Wagner's ready-fashioned artefact.

Nor can there be much doubt that Berlioz's *Roméo et Juliette* opened up to him, as it was to do to a whole generation of composers, the possibilities for a new kind of choral symphony. For Wagner, struggling to reconcile his fundamentally literary inspirations with the traditional form of the abstract symphony, this revolutionary accommodation must have given him new heart, and he too chose a literary classic on which to base his new work. It is curiously something of a vehicle for the trying out of compositional techniques that were to be brought to perfection in the music dramas. Partly for that reason Wagner subjected the work to a series of changes, until it reached its final form in the version published in 1855.

Another piece influenced by Berlioz is the *Trauermusik*, written in 1844 to accompany the torchlight procession in which Weber's remains were carried through the streets of Dresden, having been transferred from London. The Berlioz model this time was the *Grande symphonie funèbre et triomphale* written for a wind band of two hundred players. Wagner's piece, scored for a mere seventy-five wind instruments and six muffled drums, was based, in homage to Weber, on two themes from *Euryanthe*, one from the overture and the other Euryanthe's cavatina 'Hier dicht am Quell'.

Solemn processions and state pageantry continued to elicit music from Wagner in his mature years, though the ritual instinct was unquestionably satisfied more profoundly in the Hall of the Grail than in the group of three marches that were written to mark various occasions of note. The first, the *Huldigungsmarsch* (March of Homage), was composed to celebrate the birthday of King Ludwig on 25 August 1864, though the first performance had to be postponed until 5 October. Scored originally for a full military band, the march was subsequently arranged for a large orchestra with strings by Joachim Raff.[12] Judged on its own terms, as a military march, the *Huldigungsmarsch* is an unconventional but successful and attractive work. It abandons the usual March and Trio formula in favour of a single extended march section, framed by an introduction of a partially chromatic and more characteristic nature that recurs at the end. The main section itself, though four-square and abounding in martial rhythms, has an elegant, graceful tune for its principal theme which undergoes a considerable amount of development in the

---

[12] On 11 February 1865 Wagner offered Schott the 'Young King of Bavaria's March', saying that a capable bandmaster would be able to arrange it for a smaller military band, and that he himself was already engaged in an arrangement of it for an ordinary orchestra with strings.

Wagnerian manner with much use of sequential repetition and chromaticism.

A rather less attractive piece is the *Kaisermarsch*, written in 1871 to cater for the mood of jingoism that gripped Germany following the proclamation of the Second Reich and the defeat of the French. A choral finale for unison male voices expresses these sentiments in verse that is not of the highest poetic order; the words are sometimes omitted. The Hohenzollerns' staunch Protestantism is reflected in the use of Luther's *Ein' feste Burg*. The *Kaisermarsch* is by turns discursive and bombastic, and it is difficult to see why Wagner should have regarded it as 'probably the nicest [*die hübscheste*] of my instrumental compositions'.[13] Much of it lacks a sense of direction and thematic ideas are often repeated sequentially with an insistence which while typical of the composer is far less convincing than in the music dramas. The fundamental problem is that march tunes, which are essentially four-square and of a folk-like simplicity, are not amenable to motivic development or transformation.

Labouring under the same difficulty is the third of these marches, the *Grosser Festmarsch*, or *Centennial March*, written in 1876 to celebrate the centenary of the USA's declaration of independence. The piece, unusually, was the result of a commission and even without Wagner's own admission that during its composition he could think only of the 5000 dollars he had demanded for it,[14] it might easily be surmised from the empty rhetorical gestures that his heart was not in it.

At the opposite extreme stands the *Siegfried Idyll*, both Wagner's most popular instrumental work and his most intimate. The introspective quality derived from the circumstances of its composition in 1870. At last safely ensconced at Tribschen with wife and children, and finding a security he had so long lacked, Wagner gave expression to his blissful state of mind in a piece that looked back to the birth of his son Siegfried and the composition of *Siegfried* Act III the previous year. Cosima's birthday in 1870 (she was actually born on 24 December but always celebrated her birthday on the 25th) was marked with one of the extravagant gestures in which the Wagners

---

[13] Cosima Wagner's Diaries, 9 February 1881.

[14] *ibid.*, 14 February 1876.

were to revel: a small orchestra of thirteen players, secretly rehearsed by Hans Richter (who learnt the trumpet specially for the occasion), assembled on the staircase and serenaded Cosima with the first performance of the Idyll. The title-page of the autograph bore the following esoteric inscription: '*Tribschen Idyll* with Fidi-Birdsong and Orange Sunrise, presented as a symphonic birthday greeting to his Cosima by her Richard, 1870.' (Fidi was their pet-name for Siegfried; the 'Orange Sunrise' refers to what Wagner assumed was nature's own tribute to his first son – 'an incredibly beautiful, fiery glow' caused by the blazing of the sun on the orange wallpaper in the bedroom.[15])

The personal associations of the Idyll for Wagner and Cosima caused Wagner to indulge in some myth-making that has misled scholars and other writers for decades. When composing Act III of *Siegfried* he spoke of certain themes, including that to 'Ewig war ich, ewig bin ich' – which is also the main theme of the Idyll – as dating from the 'Starnberg days'.[16] Later he referred to this theme as the one 'which had come to him in Starnberg (when we were living there together), and which he had promised me as a quartet'.[17] Ernest Newman drew the not unreasonable conclusion that a 'Starnberg Quartet' had been planned by Wagner using this theme[18] and Gerald Abraham went as far as to make and publish a reconstruction of this quartet movement.[19] However, the hypothesis collapses in the light of the information that the 'Ewig war ich' theme was not conceived by Wagner until 14 November 1864, at which time he was no longer together with Cosima at Starnberg, but alone in Munich. Furthermore, the theme was worked out sometimes in five or six parts, suggesting that it was from the start intended not as a quartet, but for *Siegfried*. No evidence survives of a quartet composed in Starnberg, but it is quite possible that Wagner did indeed intend to commemorate that summer of 1864 – when they found bliss together for the

---

15   *ibid.*, 6 June 1869.

16   *ibid.*, 19 May 1869.

17   *ibid.*, 30 January 1871.

18   *The Life of Richard Wagner*, iii, pp. 271ff.

19   Oxford University Press 1947. See also Gerald Abraham, 'Wagner's String Quartet. An Essay in Musical Speculation', *Musical Times*, lxxxvi (1945), 233f.

first time – with a chamber work, and that he even jotted down ideas for it. It seems likely, then, that it was merely Wagner's fertile imagination that brought together the promised Starnberg quartet and the *Siegfried Idyll*, his most intimate expression of love for Cosima.[20]

So deeply had the couple come to identify the Idyll as a personal testament that it was only with great reluctance that it was sent, out of financial necessity, to the publisher: 'the secret treasure is to become public property', wrote Cosima in her diary (19 November 1877). And yet, in spite of the pastoral pedal-points and cast of the melodies, it was at the same time a token of Wagner's symphonic ambition, for up to the end of his life he continued to talk – seriously – about turning again to symphonies.[21] The symphonic impulse behind the *Siegfried Idyll* is seen both in the inscription quoted earlier – 'presented as a symphonic birthday greeting' – and in the structure of the work itself. It is in a modified sonata form, of which the subsidiary material is represented by the lullaby 'Sleep, baby, sleep', noted down in the Brown Book on New Year's Eve 1868, and in which new thematic ideas are given out in place of an orthodox development.

Piano

Wagner's works for piano fall into two groups: those from his student years and those written for and dedicated to particular individuals at different points in his life. The first group, all composed in Leipzig in 1831 and 1832, consists of sonatas in B flat and A, a Fantasia, and a Polonaise for four hands. According to Wagner's account in *Mein Leben* the B flat Sonata was the result of his teacher Weinlig's instruction to write a piano sonata which 'should be constructed on the most insipid harmonic and thematic principles, as a model for which he recommended one of the most childlike sonatas of Pleyel.' Such a prototype by Pleyel has never been

---

[20] See Egon Voss, *op. cit.*, 96–9 for a fuller account of the evidence and for a discussion and transcription (p. 183) of a theme which is a more probable candidate for such a quartet.

[21] See Egon Voss, *op. cit.*, for a thorough survey of Wagner's instrumental works in the context of his symphonic ambition.

found and in fact there are better reasons for supposing that the model was Beethoven and/or Mozart.[22] In later life Wagner belittled and disowned the B flat Sonata with uncustomary vigour. It seems likely that he was attempting to emulate his idol but knew he had fallen far short; Pleyel, a name associated with banal, superficial music, would then have been a suitable façade to slip behind. Whatever its model, the piece is thematically inventive and both geniality and vivacity are sustained to the end. The name given to the A major Sonata, the Grosse Sonate, proclaims its more ambitious intentions. There is less doubt that Beethoven is the model here, though probably several works rather than a single one. The opening motif, two A's and a G sharp in the rhythm ♫|♩ , is a characteristically Beethovenian figure and it recurs again and again turning the movement in new directions, often cheating expectation by appearing *piano* or in imitation.[23] The slow movement, Adagio molto, e assai espressivo, in the relative minor with a 12/16 time signature, sustains a long-drawn bel canto line over sombre low-pitched chords in the bass; the Adagio sostenuto of Beethoven's 'Hammerklavier' Sonata op. 106 does not seem far away, nor does the Adagio, ma non troppo (also in 12/16) of the same composer's Sonata in A flat op. 110. A cadenza-like Maestoso passage of nine bars introduces the full-length finale. Between bars 7 and 8 of the Maestoso, a fugue of forty-one bars was struck out of the autograph manuscript by Wagner himself. This three-part fugue, on an attractive subject, follows all the rules, but Wagner presumably realized that it was more successful as the working out of an academic exercise than as a movement of a piano sonata.[24]

[22] R. Breithaupt, 'Richard Wagners Klaviermusik', and Otto Daube, *'Ich schreibe keine Symphonien mehr'*, both mention Mozart. Dahlhaus, in his edition in the Sämtliche Werke, xix (Piano Works), p. viii, and Voss, *op. cit.*, 120–21, both assert that Beethoven was the true model. Kropfinger, however (*Wagner und Beethoven*, 219), argues for Pleyel, also on stylistic grounds.

[23] Klaus Kropfinger, *op. cit.*, esp. 219, discusses the divergencies of Beethoven's procedures with Wagner's here.

[24] The fugue is reproduced on p. 115 of Dahlhaus's edition and along with the complete sonata in Daube, *op. cit.*, 230–57. It is also incorporated into the performance recorded by Martin Galling on Turnabout TV 34654S.

The much less conventional Fantasia sprang from Wagner's attempt, with Weinlig's encouragement, to express himself more freely than in the B flat Sonata. It abounds in unshapely phrases, abrupt rhythms, and frequent stops and starts, as the young composer revels in his newly-found, if short-lived freedom. A brooding atmosphere is evoked, largely by means of a persistent threatening motif that rises and falls through a minor third – a curious pre-echo of the figure that haunts Tannhäuser's Narration. And, indeed, whereas both the B flat and A major sonatas are written in a genuinely pianistic idiom, the Fantasia is quite clearly feeling its way towards vocal expression, albeit in the manner of Bellini and the bel canto school. Once again there are also echoes of Beethoven.

The second group of Wagner's piano pieces consists of albumleaves short compositions dedicated to someone to whom a composer wishes to show gratitude or affection and presented to them in a folio or album. The first of these, described as a 'song without words', the province of Mendelssohn, of course, was written for Kietz in 1840. The *Züricher Vielliebchen-Walzer* was addressed to Marie Luckemeyer, Mathilde Wesendonck's sister, who visited Wagner at Zurich in 1854. A pair of albumleaves, both from 1861, were written as expressions of gratitude: *In das Album der Fürstin M.* to Princess Metternich, who had helped to secure the performance of *Tannhäuser* in Paris; and *Ankunft bei den schwarzen Schwänen* (Arrival at the House of the Black Swans) to Countess Pourtalès. To the Count and Countess Wagner owed his stay in a guesthouse belonging to the Prussian Embassy in Paris; the 'black swans' graced an ornamental pond in the garden. The *Ankunft* is the more characteristic of the two pieces; the atmosphere is redolent of *Tristan und Isolde* (the Act III Prelude at the beginning, for example), though it is 'Sei mir gegrüsst' from Elisabeth's Hall of Song aria in *Tannhäuser* that emerges in a magical transformation to the major.

Wagner's last albumleaf was written for Betty Schott, the wife of his publisher, in 1875. Something of Wagner's later style is reflected in its comparative freedom and variety of rhythm, and in its uninhibited harmonic changes, but it is an unassuming piece that makes no great claims for itself. From 1853 date two pieces both dedicated to Mathilde Wesendonck – the first musical compositions to be written since the completion of *Lohengrin* in 1848. The Polka, a mere twenty-three bars in length, is an almost unique example of frivolity in Wagner's oeuvre; that adolescent exuberance that would send him scurrying up a tree even in his adulthood is well attested by his friends, but it is never allowed to break into his serious compositions.

The Album Sonata,[25] written immediately after the Polka, is by far the most substantial of this dedicatory group of works. It is in one movement, not an integration of several movements into one (as in Liszt's B minor Sonata), but a single sonata form movement. Very few works of consequence appeared in this form in the nineteenth century; the most notable are Moscheles' op.49, Liszt's 'Dante' Sonata and Joachim Raff's op. 129. There is, in the animated semi-quavers of the Album Sonata's development, a hint of a multi-movement structure, but it is essentially a movement in Classical sonata form. In the exposition three thematic ideas are given out in the tonic, A flat major, and four subsidiary ones beginning in the mediant, C major. The cohesion of the movement is considerably enhanced by the fact that the rhythmic figure ♩♪ is contained in six of these themes. In contrast to the conventional use of sonata form in the earlier two sonatas discussed, the Album Sonata has a recapitula-tion in which the order of the subjects is reversed, so that the main theme of the work is the last to appear back in the home key. It has been suggested that this sonata is the composer's last attempt to come to terms with the central symphonic formal structure; Wagner, with his symphonic ambitions and essentially literary/dramatic inspiration, had always encountered problems in that quarter and he perhaps felt that some sort of reconciliation needed to be made before he embarked on the *Ring*.[26]

Songs

Of Wagner's works for solo voice and piano, the Seven Pieces for Goethe's *Faust* were written at the beginning of 1831, several months before the lessons with Weinlig began, and are therefore

[25] The title in the first printed edition of 1878 was *Eine Sonate für das Album von Frau M.W.* The autograph is entitled *Sonate für Mathilde Wesendonk* [sic].

[26] See Klaus Kropfinger, *op. cit*, 222 (also 206, 216–17 and 220–21). See also E. Voss, *op. cit*. For more information, in English, on all the piano works, see Barry Millington, 'Wagner's works for piano', in *Wagner 1976*, ed. S. Spencer, 30–38, and on the sonatas, W.S. Newman, *The Sonata Since Beethoven*, 378–88.

among the first pieces that he wrote. Since four overtures, three sonatas and a string quartet have been lost, the *Faust* songs are also some of his earliest pieces to survive. They were written for solo voices (some with chorus) and a piano accompaniment. The latter is mostly of a rudimentary kind, but in the last piece, *Melodrama*, it comes into its own, providing a dramatic backdrop (with much tremolo) against which the text is spoken by the singer.

Most of Wagner's other songs were composed during his time in Paris (1839–42). His planned conquest of the world's operatic capital had turned out to be more problematic than he had expected, and several of the songs he wrote at this time came about as the result of an unsuccessful attempt to interest the leading singers of the day. *Dors, mon enfant*, *Mignonne* and *L'attente* were published in Paris in 1840 as 'Trois Mélodies' and they each have charm as well as a certain individuality – without leaving the distinctive stamp of a great composer. *Adieux de Marie Stuart* is very different. Pierre-Jean de Béranger's poem about the tearful farewell from France of Mary Queen of Scots is made the subject of a magniloquent setting in which some rather vulgar grand operatic gestures remind us that Wagner was in the middle of composing *Rienzi*. On the words 'patrie' and 'Marie' the melodic line sweeps down through a whole octave; later on flourishes become even more extravagant. Nevertheless, given with panache and conviction the song has a certain high-flown dignity.

Les deux grenadiers is a setting of a French translation of Heine's poem describing the return from Moscow of two defeated soldiers. The appearance of the *Marseillaise* at the end, as one soldier fantasizes about his resurrection from the grave to defend the Emperor, is in accord with Heine's Napoleonic sympathies. Schumann used the same device when he made his own setting of *Die beiden Grenadiere* a few months later, but that composer's ironic five-bar postlude for the piano has no parallel in Wagner. Wagner had the song published at his own expense the same year by Schlesinger; the title page was adorned with a poignant lithograph by Kietz.

The best known of his songs for solo voice, and undoubtedly the finest, are the Wesendonck Lieder,[27] a group of five songs to texts by

[27] Published under the title *Fünf Gedichte für eine Frauenstimme.*

Mathilde Wesendonck. Two of them are called 'studies for *Tristan und Isolde*': *Im Treibhaus* ('In the Conservatory'), which pre-echoes the bleak Prelude to Act III, and *Träume* ('Dreams'), which looks forward to the Act II duet; *Träume* also became known through an arrangement for solo violin and orchestra. Mathilde Wesendonck's poems have generally been criticized for their banality and mimicking of earlier poets and philosophers; certainly they provide evidence of her ability to absorb completely Wagner's language and outlook – an ability which equipped her perfectly for her role as Wagner's muse. The published order of the songs – that in which they are now usually given – is *Der Engel, Stehe Still!, Im Treibhaus, Schmerzen, Träume*. The first four were orchestrated by Felix Mottl, *Träume* by Wagner himself.

Choral

Two of Wagner's works for ensemble voices should be mentioned: *Das Liebesmahl der Apostel* (The Love-Feast of the Apostles) and the *Kinder-Katechismus*. The first came about when Wagner was Hofkapellmeister in Dresden. In January 1843 he had accepted the conductorship of a male-voice choral society in the city, the Dresden Liedertafel, whose leading light – a Professor Löwe – was planning a gala performance in which all the male choral societies in Saxony would participate. Wagner was delegated to write for the occasion a piece for male voices only, lasting about half an hour. Thus an element of monotony was programmed in from the start. Wagner was aware of that danger in writing for such forces and it came naturally to him to look for a way of injecting some drama. The result was a 'biblical scene' depicting the events at Pentecost at which the Holy Ghost descended on the Apostles – a happening marked in the piece by the long-awaited introduction of the orchestra. *Das Liebesmahl der Apostel* is a little over half an hour long and the male voices remain unaccompanied for nearly twenty-five minutes until 'Welch' Brausen erfüllt die Luft?' (What rushing fills the air?) gives the signal for whispering tremolando strings to enter low down, soon followed by a unison figure declaimed on brass, bassoons and cellos.

The piece has some delicate effects, such as the reverentially hushed 'Preis seinem Namen!' (Praise to his name!) and some dramatic ones, for example the imploring outburst 'Allmächt'ger Vater' (Almighty Father) by the full choir. In the *a cappella* section

Wagner attempted to achieve more variety of timbre by dividing his forces into three choirs, of which 'the first choir is to be less strong than the second and third'. These separate choruses alternate and combine in an effective manner but it must be admitted that the problem of monotony has not been solved entirely satisfactorily.

Much depends, also, on the quality of the performance. Wagner's disappointment at the 'comparatively feeble effect' (*Mein Leben*) produced at the first performance, in the Frauenkirche, Dresden, on 6 July 1843 (at which he had 1200 singers and an orchestra of 100), was undoubtedly partly a result of the amateur participants. In a performance in which the unaccompanied section is technically secure, the delayed appearance of the orchestra can be a telling dramatic stroke.

The full title of the other piece is *Kinder-Katechismus zu Kosel's Geburtstag* (A Children's Catechism for Kosel's Birthday). 'Kosel' or 'Cosel', one of Wagner's pet-names for Cosima, was derived from the verb *kosen* (to caress), a word which is also at the root of this little song for four high voices and piano. The verse, by Wagner himself, of course, is in question-and-answer form (hence the 'catechism'); it is a word play on the roses that bloom in May and the *Kose* that blooms at Christmastime, a juxtaposition that led Cosima to call it the 'Kose-und Rosenlied'. The *Kinder-Katechismus* was sung outside her bedroom as a birthday gift on 25 December 1873 by her four daughters (perhaps also son); Siegfried then recited the poem to her at her bedside. The following December Wagner made a new version for children's voices and small orchestra; at the end, in a postlude, he incorporated the so-called 'Redemption' motif from *Götter-dämmerung*, whose score he had completed a month before. Charming or cloyingly sentimental, according to taste, the *Kinder-Katechismus* encapsulates all the qualities that were held in highest regard at Wahnfried: love, devotion, fidelity and adoration.

Appendix A

Calendar

Year	Age	Life	Contemporary Events
1813		Wilhelm Richard Wagner born 22 May in Leipzig. Carl Friedrich Wagner dies, 23 Nov.	Napoleon defeated at Leipzig, Oct, in the Battle of the Nations. Verdi born, 9/10 Oct; Alkan born, 30 Nov; Auber aged 32; Beethoven 42; Bellini 11; Berlioz 9; Boieldieu 37; Cherubini 52; Chopin 3; Donizetti 15; Halévy 13; Liszt 1; Lortzing 11; Marschner 17; Méhul 49; Mendelssohn 4; Meyerbeer 21; Rossini 21; Schubert 16; Schumann 2; Spohr 29; Weber 26.
1814	1	Johanna Wagner marries Ludwig Geyer, 28 Aug.	Congress of Vienna, Sept 1814–June 1815, creating German Confederation in 1815.
1820	7	Enters care of Pastor Christian Wetzel at Possendorf; piano lessons.	
1821	8	Geyer dies, 30 Sept.	Premiere of Weber's *Der Freischütz*, 18 June, Berlin.
1822	9	Enters Dresden Kreuzschule, 2 Dec, as Richard Geyer.	Franck born, 10 Dec.
1824	11		Premiere of Beethoven's Ninth Symphony, 7 May, Vienna. Smetana born, 2 Mar; Bruckner born, 4 Sept; Cornelius born, 24 Dec.
1826	13	Family moves to Prague, but Wagner remains in Dresden. Displays enthusiasm for Greek.	Weber (39) dies, 5 June.
1827	14	Visits his Uncle Adolf in Leipzig; leaves school in Dresden to rejoin family now back in Leipzig.	Beethoven (56) dies, 26 Mar.
1828	15	Enters Nicolaischule, 21 Jan; now called Richard Wagner. Completes grisly tragedy called *Leubald*.	Premiere of Marschner's *Der Vampyr*, 29 Mar, Leipzig. Schubert (31) dies, 19 Nov.

Year	Age	Life	Contemporary Events
		Studies Logier's manual *Thorough-Bass*. Harmony lessons, at first secret, with Müller (autumn).	
1829	16	First compositions: two sonatas and string quartet (all lost).	Berlioz publishes *Huit scènes de Faust*. Premiere of Rossini's *Guillaume Tell*, 3 Aug, Paris. Gossec (95) dies, 16 Feb.
1830	17	Easter, leaves Nicolaischule. Violin lessons. Piano transcription of Beethoven's Ninth. Writes three overtures (lost).	July Revolution in Paris inspires unrest elsewhere in Europe, including Leipzig. Premiere of Bellini's *I Capuleti e i Montecchi*, 11 Mar, Venice, and of Berlioz's *Symphonie fantastique*, 5 Dec, Paris.
1831	18	Writes Seven Pieces for Goethe's *Faust* for voice and piano. Attends Leipzig University. Lessons with Weinlig, for whom he writes several piano pieces.	Premiere of Meyerbeer's *Robert le Diable*, 21 Nov, Paris, and of Bellini's *Norma*, 26 Dec, Milan.
1832	19	C major Symphony written and performed. Brief infatuation with Count Pachta's daughter Jenny. Sketches *Die Hochzeit* text, Oct/Nov, but abandons composition of music in new year.	Goethe (82) dies in Weimar; *Faust*, part 2, published posthumously.
1833	20	Joins brother Albert in Würzburg and becomes chorus master at theatre there, Jan. Text and music for *Die Feen*.	Premiere of Marschner's *Hans Heiling*, 24 May, Berlin. Brahms born, 7 May; Borodin born, 12 Nov.
1834	21	Comes under the influence of Laube and Young Germany. Publication, June, of *German Opera*, Wagner's first critical essay. Holiday in Bohemia, June; *Das Liebesverbot* begun. Becomes musical director of Bethmann's theatre company, July. Meets Minna Planer. Début as opera conductor with *Don Giovanni*, Aug.	Wilhelmine Schröder-Devrient makes guest appearance in Leipzig as Romeo in Bellini's *I Capuleti e i Montecchi*, Mar. Boieldieu (58) dies, 8 Oct.
1835	22	Music for Apel's play *Columbus*. Schröder-Devrient performs with him. Begins notes in Red	Writings of Young Germany banned; Laube imprisoned. First German railway (Nuremberg–

Pocketbook, Aug, for future autobiography.

1836   23 *Das Liebesverbot* given in Magdeburg, 29 Mar, under Wagner. Bankruptcy of Bethmann company. Minna takes acting post in Königsberg. They marry, 24 Nov.

1837   24 Appointed musical director at Königsberg Theatre, 1 Apr. Minna leaves him; he pursues her. Begins text of *Rienzi*. Musical director in Riga.

1838   25 Begins music of *Rienzi*, 7 Aug. First of series of six concerts, 15 Nov, in which Wagner conducts Beethoven Symphonies nos 3–8, as well as works by Mozart, Weber, Cherubini, Mendelssohn and himself.

1839   26 Secret retreat from Riga with Minna; destination Paris. Stormy voyage on board *Thetis* bound for London. Received by Meyerbeer at Boulogne. Arrives Paris 17 Sept; writes aria for *Norma* and several French songs. Meets Heinrich Heine. Conceives symphony on *Faust* theme, Dec, probably under influence of Berlioz's *Roméo et Juliette*; work later becomes *Faust Overture*.

1840   27 Work continues on *Rienzi*. Prose sketch of *Der fliegende Holländer* sent to Scribe, 6 May, and to Meyerbeer, June. Meanwhile writes three numbers for *Holländer*. Undertakes work for Schlesinger: arrangements, novellas and essays. Meets Liszt

Fürth). Mendelssohn assumes conductorship of Leipzig Gewandhaus orchestra. Premiere of Halévy's *La juive*, 23 Feb, Paris. Saint-Saëns born, 9 Oct; Bellini (33) dies, 23 Sept. Premiere of Meyerbeer's *Les Huguenots*, 29 Feb, Paris, and of Mendelssohn's *St Paul*, 22 May, Düsseldorf.

Balakirev born, 2 Jan; Field (54) dies, 23 Jan.

Bruch born, 6 Jan; Bizet born, 25 Oct.

First performances of Berlioz's dramatic symphony *Roméo et Juliette*, 24 Nov and 1 Dec. Musorgsky born, 21 Mar; Paer (67) dies, 3 May.

Berlioz's *Grande symphonie funèbre et triomphale* for 200 wind players given at 10th anniversary of the 1830 Revolution, 28 July. Proudhon's *De la propriété* published in Paris. Tchaikovsky born, 7 May; Paganini (57) dies, 27 May.

Year	Age	Life	Contemporary Events
		briefly. Financial position desperate but probably not imprisoned for debt.	
1841	28	*Holländer* text written, May, followed by rest of music, July–Nov. First signs of resentment towards Meyerbeer. Continuing disillusionment with Paris.	Feuerbach's *Das Wesen des Christentums* published. Weber's *Der Freischütz* performed at Paris Opéra with Berlioz's recitatives. Premiere of Halévy's *Le guitarrero* and *La reine de Chypre*, Paris. Chabrier born, 18 Jan; Dvořák born, 8 Sept.
1842	29	With Minna, leaves Paris, 7 Apr, making for Dresden, where *Rienzi* is to be performed. Negotiations over *Holländer* in Berlin. Holiday in Teplitz, June; *Tannhäuser* sketches. Premiere of *Rienzi*, 20 Oct, under Reissiger; immense success.	Liszt takes post as director of music at ducal court in Weimar (full time from 1848). Verdi scores first success with *Nabucco*. Massenet born, 12 May; Cherubini (81) dies, 15 Mar.
1843	30	Premiere of *Holländer*, 2 Jan, also in Dresden. Publishes *Autobiographical Sketch*, Feb. Appointed Kapellmeister (with Reissiger) at King of Saxony's court in Dresden, 2 Feb. Writes and conducts, 6 July, *Das Liebesmahl der Apostel*. Begins music of *Tannhäuser*. Builds up library.	Berlioz's treatise on instrumentation published. Grieg born, 15 June.
1844	31	Publishing venture with Meser. After supporting campaign to have Weber's remains transferred, Wagner writes *Trauermusik* for 75 wind instruments and 6 muffled drums for a torchlight procession; delivers oration at graveside.	Nietzsche born, 15 Oct; Rimsky-Korsakov born, 18 Mar.
1845	32	Completes *Tannhäuser* score, 13 Apr. With Minna, dog and parrot to Marienbad, 3 July, to take waters. Absorbs himself in Parzival and Lohengrin legends. Prose drafts for *Die Meistersinger*, 16 July, and *Lohengrin*, 3 Aug. Premiere of *Tannhäuser*, 19 Oct, Dresden, under Wagner.	Friedrich Engels' *The Condition of the Working Class in England* published in Leipzig. Fauré born, 12 May.

Wagner

Year	Age	Life	Contemporary Events
1846	33	Submits report *Concerning the Royal Orchestra*, 2 Mar. Conducts Beethoven's Ninth at traditional Palm Sunday concert, 5 Apr.	Premiere of Mendelssohn's *Elijah*, 26 Aug, Birmingham.
1847	34	Conducts his own revised version of Gluck's *Iphigénie en Aulide*, 22 Feb. Work on *Lohengrin*. Reads several Greek plays in translation, including *Oresteia* trilogy. *Rienzi* in Berlin.	Mendelssohn (38) dies, 4 Nov.
1848	35	Mother dies, 9 Jan. Arranges Palestrina's Stabat Mater; conducts Bach motet and Classical symphonies. Completes score of *Lohengrin*, 28 Apr. Submits *Plan for the Organization of a German National Theatre*, May. Delivers speech and publishes text, June, on relation of monarchy to republicanism. Through his assistant Röckel, he meets Bakunin, the Russian anarchist. *Ring* project begins to crystallize.	Communist Manifesto published, Feb. Uprisings in Paris, Feb, Vienna and Berlin, Mar. Frankfurt Parliament assembles, 18 May. Duparc born, 21 Jan; Parry born, 27 Feb; Donizetti (50) dies, 8 Apr.
1849	36	Scenario for *Jesus von Nazareth*. Further contributions to Röckel's *Volksblätter*, including poem *Need [Die Not]* and the socialist rhetoric of *The Revolution*. Participates in insurrection, reporting on troop movements; apparently involved in manufacture of hand-grenades. Narrowly escapes arrest; sheltered by Liszt at Weimar, May, but flees to Switzerland. Remains in exile until 1861. *Art and Revolution*, July, *The Artwork of the Future*, Nov.	Friedrich Wilhelm IV of Prussia spurns offer of crown from Frankfurt Parliament, 3 Apr, Friedrich August II of Saxony rejects and violates Frankfurt constitution. Provisional government defeated by Prussian troops. Premiere of Meyerbeer's *Le prophète*, 16 Apr, Paris. Heinrich Laube becomes director of Burgtheater, Vienna. Chopin (39) dies, 17 Oct.
1850	37	Prose draft for projected three-act opera, *Wieland der Schmied*. Annual allowance of 3000 francs proposed by Julie Ritter and Jessie Laussot. Affair with latter, Mar.–May, in Bordeaux; 'elopement' thwarted	

Year	Age	Life	Contemporary Events
		by husband. Returns to Zurich and Minna. Musical sketches for *Siegfrieds Tod* (later *Götterdämmerung*). Publishes *Jewishness in Music*, Aug. Premiere of *Lohengrin* in Weimar, 28 Aug, under Liszt. Writes *Opera and Drama* (finished 10 Jan, 1851).	
1851	38	Sketches *Der junge Siegfried* (later *Siegfried*) in May, then writes poem, June. *A Communication to my Friends*, July–Aug. Allowance of 800 Talers received from Julie Ritter (autumn) until 1859. Wagner, still hoping for revolution, starting in France, initially refuses to acknowledge 1852.	Coup d'état of Louis-Napoleon, 2 Dec, heralds repression of progressive forces and proclamation of Second Empire in France. Premiere of Verdi's *Rigoletto* 11 Mar, Venice. D' Indy born, 27 Mar; Lortzing (49) dies, 21 Jan; Spontini (76) dies, 24 Jan.
1852	39	Introduced to Otto and Mathilde Wesendonck, Feb, and later to Georg Herwegh and François and Eliza Wille. Conducts *Holländer* in revised version in Zurich. Contemplates suicide. Poems of *Walküre*, 1 July, and *Rheingold*, 3 Nov, completed.	Stanford born, 30 Sept.
1853	40	Fifty copies of complete *Ring* poem published; recited to an invited audience in Zurich, Feb. Moves with Minna into larger apartment, 15 Apr. Conducts three concerts of excerpts from his earlier works, May. Writes piano sonata for Mathilde Wesendonck. Trip to Italy; inspiration for music of *Rheingold*, supposedly in 'vision' at La Spezia. Meets Cosima.	Premiere of Verdi's *Il trovatore* and *La traviata*. Liszt's Sonata in B minor. Gobineau's *Essai sur l'inégalité des races humaines* (1853–5).
1854	41	Minna's heart condition deteriorates. Marital relationship at low ebb. Begins composition of *Walküre*, 28 June. Love for Mathilde Wesendonck; Otto settles his debts of 10,000 francs.	Premiere of Liszt's *Les Préludes*, *Orpheus* and *Mazeppa* in Weimar. Janáček born, 3 July; Humperdinck born, 1 Sept.

Year	Age	Life	Contemporary Events
		Reads Schopenhauer (autumn). Conceives *Tristan*.	
1855	42	Revises work now entitled *Faust Overture*, Jan. Conducts Philharmonic season in London, Mar–June; savaged by press. Makes closer acquaintance of Berlioz, also conducting in London. Frequent attacks of erysipelas.	Gustav Freytag's popular novel *Soll und Haben* published, embodying the anti-semitic stereotype. Chausson born, 20 Jan.
1856	43	Finishes score of *Walküre*, 23 Mar. Contrite plea to King Johann of Saxony, 16 May, rejected. On same day, prose sketch for projected Buddhist opera: *Die Sieger*. New, 'Schopenhauer' ending for the *Ring* (summer); later rejected. Becomes intimately acquainted with Liszt's symphonic poems. Begins composition of *Siegfried*, Sep. First musical sketches for *Tristan*, 19 Dec.	Schumann (46) dies, 29 July.
1857	44	Occupies the Asyl, adjoining the Wesendoncks' villa, with Minna, Apr. Conceives *Parsifal*, May. Breaks off composition of *Siegfried* at end of Act II, 9 Aug. Hans von Bülow and his bride Cosima stay with the Wagners on their honeymoon, Sept. Passion for Mathilde Wesendonck reciprocated; he works on *Tristan* and sets five of Mathilde's poems to music.	Premieres of Liszt's *Faust* and *Dante* Symphonies. Leoncavallo born, 8 Mar; Elgar born, 2 June. Glinka (52) dies, 15 Feb.
1858	45	Atmosphere on Green Hill necessitates Wagner's decampment to Paris, 14 Jan. Berlioz reads him *Les Troyens*. Back in Zurich, Minna intercepts 'Morning Confession' letter to Mathilde, 7 Apr; resulting jealous scenes eventually force Wagner to leave the Asyl for good, 17 Aug. Travels with Karl Ritter to Venice,	Premiere of Offenbach's *Orphée aux enfers*, 21 Oct, Paris. Puccini born, 23 Dec.

Year	Age	Life	Contemporary Events
		where he continues to work on Act II of *Tristan*.	
1859	46	Suffers from bad health and police harassment in Venice. Completes Act III of *Tristan* in Lucerne, 6 Aug. Revisits Wesendoncks in Zurich; Otto buys copyright in *Ring* scores.	Spohr (75) dies, 22 Oct.
1860	47	Minna rejoins him in Paris. Conducts three concerts of his music there, Jan/Feb. Schott obtains rights in *Rheingold*. Partial amnesty (Saxony still excluded).	Wolf born, 13 Mar; Albéniz born, 29 May; Charpentier born, 25 June; Mahler born, 7 July; MacDowell born, 18 Dec.
1861	48	Staging of revised version of *Tannhäuser* at Opéra, Mar, is a fiasco: a political demonstration by the Jockey Club causes an historic scandal. Looked after by Seraphine Mauro in Dr Standhartner's house in Vienna. Embarks on *Die Meistersinger*, Nov.	Berlioz's *Les Troyens* accepted by Paris Opéra. Marschner (66) dies, 14 Dec.
1862	49	With Minna in Biebrich: 'ten days in hell'. Attracted to both Mathilde Maier and Friederike Meyer. Visited by the Bülows. Last meeting with Minna, in Dresden, Nov. The critic Hanslick, caricatured in Beckmesser, storms out of reading of *Die Meistersinger* poem, 23 Nov.	Otto von Bismarck made minister-president of Prussia (later chancellor). Premiere of Verdi's *La forza del destino*, 10 Nov, St Petersburg. Delius born, 29 Jan; Debussy born, 22 Aug; Halévy (62) dies, 17 Mar.
1863	50	Concerts in Vienna, Prague, St Petersburg and Moscow, Jan–Apr. Lavish furnishing of new apartment in Penzing, near Vienna, May. Concerts in Budapest, Prague, Karlsruhe, Breslau, Vienna.	Mascagni born, 7 Dec.
1864	51	Eighteen-year-old Ludwig II becomes King of Bavaria, 10 Mar. He pays off Wagner's debts and houses him near the royal castle Schloss Berg, overlooking Lake Starnberg, near Munich. Cosima	Austria and Prussia at war with Denmark. *La belle Hélène* launches the period of Offenbach's greatest success. R. Strauss born, 11 June; Meyerbeer (72) dies, 2 May.

Year	Age	Life	Contemporary Events
		von Bülow arrives at Starnberg with two daughters, June; union with Wagner consummated. King provides spacious house for Wagner in Munich and generous annual stipend; he summons Semper to design a festival theatre for the *Ring* in Munich.	
1865	52	Wagner suffers first ill-treatment by courtiers and press, Feb. His and Cosima's first child, Isolde, born. 10 Apr. Premiere of *Tristan* under Bülow, 10 June. Dictation of *Mein Leben* begins, 17 July. Ludwig compelled to banish Wagner from Bavaria, Dec.	Nielsen born, 9 June; Glazunov born, 10 Aug; Dukas born, 1 Oct; Sibelius born, 8 Dec.
1866	53	Minna dies in Dresden. Cosima joins Wagner in Geneva. They decide to make the house Tribschen, on Lake Lucerne, their home. Deception of Ludwig in 'Volksbote affair'. Malvina Schnorr, unheeded as the bearer of messages from the spirit world, denounces Wagner's liaison with Cosima to the king.	Austro-Prussian War; Bavaria sides with Austria. Busoni born, 1 Apr; Satie born, 17 May.
1867	54	Eva born, 17 Feb. Bülow appointed Court Kapellmeister to Ludwig and director of proposed music school. Hans Richter made répétiteur at Court Theatre, Munich.	Premiere of Verdi's *Don Carlos*, 11 Mar, Paris. Granados born, 27 July.
1868	55	Festival theatre plans abandoned. Premiere of *Die Meistersinger* in Court Theatre under Bülow, 21 June. Cosima frequently at Tribschen. *Luthers Hochzeit* project. With Cosima in Italy, after which Cosima moves into Tribschen with Isolde and Eva, 16 Nov. Ludwig officially informed. Meets Nietzsche.	Berwald (71) dies, 3 Apr; Rossini (76) dies, 13 Nov.
1869	56	Resumes composition of *Ring*. Reprinting of *Jewishness in Music*	Nietzsche appointed Professor of Classical Philology at Basle

Year	Age	Life	Contemporary Events
		with new preface complaining of alleged persecution by Jews. Siegfried born, 6 June; Nietzsche present at Tribschen and visits frequently thereafter. *Das Rheingold* performed in Munich, 22 Sept, despite Wagner's strenuous efforts to prevent it. Reads *Parsifal* sketch to Nietzsche (Christmas).	University. Emancipation of Jew enshrined in law passed in Nort German Confederation, July. Roussel born, 5 Apr; Dargomïzhsky (55) dies, 17 Jan Berlioz (65) dies, 8 Mar; Loewe (72) dies, 20 Apr.
870	57	Bayreuth considered as venue for festival. *Die Walküre* performed in Munich, 26 June. Legal dissolution of Bülows' marriage, July. Wagner and Cosima marry, 25 Aug. Writes essay *Beethoven* and the comedy *Eine Kapitulation. Siegfried Idyll* written for Cosima's birthday.	Franco-Prussian War, July–2 Sep
871	58	Finishes score of *Siegfried* and writes *Kaisermarsch*. Wagners visit Bayreuth and decide on new building, Apr. Town council offer free site, Nov.	Second German Empire established and Wilhelm I proclaimed Kaiser, 18 Jan. Capitulation of Paris to the Germans, 28 Jan. Auber (89) die 12/13 May.
872	59	Sites for Wahnfried and Festspielhaus selected. Society of Patrons of the Bayreuth Festival established. Laying of foundation stone, 22 May. Tour undertaken to scout for singers, Nov.	Nietzsche's *Die Geburt der Tragödie* published. Skryabin born, 6 Jan; Vaughan Williams born, 12 Oct.
873	60	Sends Bismarck his report on the laying of the foundation stone of the Festspielhaus, including his nationalistic speech; the overture is not heeded.	Great economic crash, followed b depression lasting from 1874 to 1895. Reger born, 19 Mar; Rakhmaninov born, 1 Apr.
874	61	After despairing of financial help from either Ludwig or the Reich, Wagner receives positive response from former, 25 Jan; loan of 100,000 Talers follows. Wagners move to new home, 28 Apr, and call it 'Wahnfried'. Score of *Ring* finally completed, 21 Nov.	Schoenberg born, 13 Sept; Ives born, 20 Oct; Schmidt born, 22 Dec; Cornelius (49) dies, 26 Oc
875	62	Concerts in Vienna, Budapest and	Premiere of Bizet's *Carmen*, 3 N

Year	Age	Life	Contemporary Events
		Berlin. Preliminary rehearsals for *Ring*.	Paris. Ravel born, 7 Mar; Bizet (36) dies, 3 June.
1876	63	Rehearsals followed by three cycles of the *Ring* under Richter beginning 13 Aug. Luminaries and admirers attend from all over Europe. Nietzsche present but leaves before end of festival in severe physical pain; he and Wagner meet for the last time in Sorrento, Oct. Deficit of 148,000 Marks.	Premiere of Brahms' Symphony no. 1, 4 Nov. Falla born, 23 Nov.
1877	64	In an attempt to reduce the deficit, Wagner and Richter undertake a series of concerts in the Royal Albert Hall, London; profits only marginal. Considers emigration to the USA. Writes libretto for *Parsifal* and begins music, Sept.	Edison invents phonograph. Premiere of Bruckner's Symphony no. 3, dedicated to Wagner, 16 Dec.
1878	65	First issue of *Bayreuther Blätter*, under editorship of Hans von Wolzogen, Jan. 'Affair' with Judith Gautier, conducted since festival of 1876, brought to an end by Cosima, Feb. Agreement with Ludwig whereby King's right to produce Wagner's works is confirmed in exchange for a 10 per cent royalty which is set against the debt, 31 Mar. Wagner begins series of notoriously reactionary essays concerned with 'racial purity'; *Modern* and *Public and Popularity* are the first.	Anti-Socialist laws renewed at intervals until 1890; Bismarck's repressive measures effectively drive Socialism underground for twelve years.
1879	66	Supports campaign against vivisection. Leaves Bayreuth with family for Italy, 31 Dec.	Bridge born, 26 Feb.
1880	67	Paul von Joukovsky, future stage designer for *Parsifal*, stays with Wagners at Villa d'Angri, Naples. He sketches two settings to be incorporated into scenery of *Parsifal*. *Religion and Art* continues theme of 'regeneration	Bloch born, 24 July; Offenbach (61) dies, 5 Oct.

Year	Age	Life	Contemporary Events

of mankind'. Conducts *Parsifal* Prelude for Ludwig; last meeting with him, Nov. Returns to Bayreuth.

1881 68 Count Gobineau in Bayreuth. Wagner reads and applauds the racist Aryan ideology expounded in his *Essai sur l'inégalité des races humaines*. Wagner's *Heroism and Christianity*, Aug–Sept, expresses the more optimistic view that redemption from corrupting influences is possible through the agency of Christ's blood. Suffers chest pains, not diagnosed as heart condition.

Premiere of Offenbach's *Les contes d'Hoffmann*, 10 Feb, Paris. Bartók born, 25 Mar; Musorgsky (42) dies, 28 Mar.

1882 69 Finishes score of *Parsifal* in Italy. Portrait sketched by Renoir, 15 Jan. Cardiac spasms continue; first major heart attack, Mar. Bayreuth scholarship fund set up. Premiere of *Parsifal* under Hermann Levi, 26 July. Departure for Venice, Sept; Wagner spends remaining days of his life with his family in the Palazzo Vendramin.

Stravinsky born, 17 June. Szymanowski born, 6 Oct; Kodály born, 16 Dec.

1883 70 Begins essay *On the Feminine in the Human*, Feb. After a furious row with Cosima during the morning, apparently over the flowermaiden Carrie Pringle, he suffers final fatal heart attack on 13 Feb; dies some time after 3 o'clock in Cosima's arms. Coffin conveyed to Bayreuth where, after a procession through the town, the burial takes place privately in the garden of Wahnfried, 18 Feb.

Bax born, 8 Nov; Webern born, 3 Dec. Bartók aged 1; Brahms 49; Bruckner 58; Busoni 16; Debussy 20; Elgar 25; Fauré 37; Granados 15; Janáček 28; Mahler 22; Puccini 24; Rakhmaninov 9; Ravel 7; Rimsky-Korsakov 38; Satie 16; Schoenberg 8; Sibelius 17; R. Strauss 18; Tchaikovsky 42; Vaughan Williams 10; Verdi 69; Wolf 22.

Appendix B
List of works

I OPERAS, MUSIC DRAMAS

Composition dates include all chief drafts and execution of fair copy of score but not preliminary sketches and jottings. Oblique stroke indicates uncertain dating.

Die Feen, Romantic opera in 3 acts, after Carlo Gozzi's *La donna serpente*.
Text: Jan.–Feb. 1833.
Composition: 20 Feb.–6 Jan. 1834. Rev. spring 1834.
Premiere: Königliches Hof- und Nationaltheater, Munich, 29 June 1888.

Das Liebesverbot, oder Die Novize von Palermo, grand comic opera in 2 acts, after Shakespeare's *Measure for Measure*.
Text: June 1834 (prose sketch); poem begun 12 Aug.
Composition: Jan. 1835–early 1836.
Premiere: Stadttheater, Magdeburg, 29 Mar. 1836.

Rienzi, der Letzte der Tribunen, grand tragic opera in 5 acts, after Edward Bulwer-Lytton's *Rienzi, the Last of the Tribunes*.
Text: June/July 1837–5/6 Aug. 1838.
Composition: 7 Aug. 1838–19 Nov. 1840. Rev. 1843–4, 1847.
Premiere: Königlich Sächsisches Hoftheater, Dresden, 20 Oct. 1842.

Der fliegende Holländer, Romantic opera in 3 acts (orig. 1 act), after Heinrich Heine's *Aus den Memoiren des Herren von Schnabelewopski*.
Text: May 1840–May 1841.
Composition: Begun May–July 1840; score completed Nov. 1841. Rev. 1846, 1852, 1860.
Premiere: Königlich Sächsisches Hoftheater, Dresen, 2 Jan. 1843.

Tannhäuser und der Sängerkrieg auf Wartburg, grand Romantic opera in 3 acts.
Text: 28 June 1842–Apr. 1843.
Composition: 19 July 1843–13 Apr. 1845. Rev. 1845, 1847, 1851, 1860–61, 1865, 1875.
Premiere: Königlich Sächsisches Hoftheater, Dresden, 19 Oct. 1845.

Lohengrin, Romantic opera in 3 acts.
Text: July/Aug. 1845–27 Nov. 1845.

Composition: May 1846–28 Apr. 1848.

Premiere: Grossherzogliches Hof-Theater, Weimar, 28 Aug. 1850.

Der Ring des Nibelungen, a stage festival play for 3 days and a preliminary evening: 1st prose draft, 4 Oct. 1848, published as *Der Nibelungen-Mythus. Als entwurf zu einem Drama.*

Das Rheingold, preliminary evening, 4 scenes.

Text: Oct./Nov. 1851–3 Nov. 1852.

Composition: 1 Nov. 1853–26 Sept. 1854.

Premiere: Königliches Hof- und Nationaltheater, Munich, 22 Sept. 1869.

Die Walküre, first day, 3 acts.

Text: Nov./Dec. 1851–1 July 1852.

Composition: 28 June 1854–23 Mar. 1856.

Premiere: Königliches Hof- und Nationaltheater, Munich, 26 June 1870.

Siegfried, second day, 3 acts.

Text: May 1851–24 June 1851 (rev. before 15 Dec. 1852; 1856).

Original title: *Der junge Siegfried.*

Composition: Before 22 Sept. 1856–1869 (except last few pages of score completed 5 Feb. 1871).

Premiere: Festspielhaus, Bayreuth, 16 Aug. 1876.

Götterdämmerung, third day, prologue and 3 acts.

Text: Oct. 1848–28 Nov. 1848 (rev. late 1848/early 1849 and Dec. 1852).

Original title: *Siegfrieds Tod.*

Composition: 2 Oct. 1869–21 Nov. 1874.

Premiere: Festspielhaus, Bayreuth, 17 Aug. 1876.

Tristan und Isolde, 3 acts.

Text: 20 Aug.–18 Sep. 1857.

Composition: 1 Oct. 1857–6 Aug. 1859.

Premiere: Königliches Hof- und Nationaltheater, Munich, 10 June 1865.

Die Meistersinger von Nürnberg, 3 acts.

Text: 1st prose draft July 1845; 2nd prose draft ?14–16 Nov. 1861; 3rd prose draft 18 Nov. 1861; poem Dec. 1861–Jan. 1862.

Composition: Mar. 1862–Oct. 1867.

Premiere: Königliches Hof – und Nationaltheater, Munich, 21 June 1868.

Parsifal, a sacred stage festival play in 3 acts.

Text: 1st prose sketch Apr. 1857; prose draft 27–30 Aug. 1865; poem completed 19 Apr. 1877.

Composition: Aug. 1877–13 Jan. 1882.

Premiere: Festspielhaus, Bayreuth, 26 July 1882.

II PROJECTED OR UNFINISHED DRAMATIC WORKS

Leubald, tragedy in 5 acts, 1826–8.
Pastoral opera modelled on Goethe's *Die Laune des Verliebten* (only a scene for 3 female voices and a tenor aria written; lost), ?early 1830.
Die Hochzeit, opera in 3 acts (poem lost; of music, only introduction, chorus and septet were written), Oct./Nov. 1832–1 Mar. 1833.
Die hohe Braut, oder Bianca und Giuseppe, grand opera in 4 acts (5 in original prose sketches), 1836, 1842. Finally set by Johann Kittl.
Männerlist grösser als Frauenlist, oder Die glückliche Bärenfamilie, comic opera in 2 acts (composition unfinished; music lost), summer 1838.
Die Sarazenin, opera in 5 acts (prose draft), 1841, 1843.
Die Bergwerke zu Falun, opera in 3 acts (prose draft), draft dated 5 Mar. 1842.
Friedrich I., ?opera in 5 acts (prose sketches), Oct. 1846, 1848.
Jesus von Nazareth, ?opera in 5 acts (prose draft), Jan.–Apr. 1849.
Achilleus, ?opera in 3 acts (prose sketches), early 1849, Feb.–July 1850.
Wieland der Schmied, heroic opera in 3 acts (prose drafts), Dec. 1849–Mar. 1850.
Die Sieger, opera in ?3 acts (prose sketch), May 1856.
Luthers Hochzeit, drama (prose sketches), Aug. 1868.
Lustspiel in 1 Akt (prose draft), dated 1 Sept. 1868.
Eine Kapitulation: Lustspiel in antiker Manier (drama), Nov. 1870. Setting undertaken by Hans Richter.

III ORCHESTRAL

Overture in B flat ('Drum-beat Overture'), summer 1830 (lost).
Political Overture, Sept. 1830 (prob. frag; lost).
Orchestral work in E minor, prob. 1830 (frag; possibly to be identified with the lost Overture to Schiller's *Die braut von Messina*).
Overture in C (in 6/8 time), end 1830 (lost).
Overture in E flat, early 1831 (frag; lost).
Overture in D minor (Concert Overture no. 1), summer/autumn 1831.
Overture in E minor and incidental music to Ernst Raupach's play *König Enzio*, winter 1831–2 (overture only survives).
Entr'actes tragiques, no. 1 in D, no. 2 in C minor, early 1832.
Concert Overture no. 2 in C, Mar. 1832.
Symphony in C. Apr.–June 1832
Symphony in E, Aug. 1834 (frag; lost).
Overture in E flat and incidental music to Theodor Apel's play *Columbus*, Dec. 1834–Jan. 1835 (overture only survives).
Polonia Overture in C, May–July 1836.

Incidental music to J. Singer's play *Die letzte Heidenverschwörung in Preussen*, Feb. 1837 (frag).

Rule Britannia Overture in D, Mar. 1837.

A *Faust* Overture, D minor (originally planned as 1st movt of a *Faust* Symphony), Dec. 1839–Jan. 1840; rev. 1855.

Trauermusik, on motifs from Weber's *Euryanthe*, for wind band, Nov. 1844.

Huldigungsmarsch, E flat, for military band, Aug. 1864 (arr. J. Raff for large orch. with strings).

Romeo und Julie (frag of a projected orch work), Apr.–May 1868.

Siegfried Idyll, small orch, Oct.–Dec. 1870.

Kaisermarsch, B flat, with choral finale for male voices, Jan.–Mar.1871.

Grosser Festmarsch (Centennial March), Jan.–Mar. 1876.

Various symphonies and overtures were planned and/or sketched in 1846–7 and during the 1870s and 1880s.

IV CHORAL

Dein ist das Reich, vocal fugue, autumn 1831/winter 1831–2.

New Year's Cantata, incidental music (overture and 4 numbers) for Wilhelm Schmale's *Beim Antritt des neuen Jahres*, Dec. 1834.

Nicolay, anthem for the birthday of Tsar Nicholas, for soloist (tenor or soprano), chorus and orch, autumn 1837.

Gesang am Grabe, winter 1838–9 (lost).

Descendons, descendons, chorus for the vaudeville *La descente de la courtille* by Marion Dumersan and Dupeuty, Jan. 1841.

Der Tag erscheint, chorus for ceremony of unveiling of the monument to Friedrich August I, male voices unacc. or with brass, May 1843.

Das Liebesmahl der Apostel, biblical scene for male voices and orch, Apr.–June 1843.

Gruss seiner Treuen an Friedrich August den Geliebten ('Im treuen Sachsenland'), choral greeting to king on return from England, male voices and wind (also arr. for baritone and piano), July 1844.

An Webers Grabe ('Hebt an den Sang'), chorus for ceremony at reburial of Weber's remains, male voices unacc., Nov. 1844.

Wahlspruch für die deutsche Feuerwehr, motto for the German fire brigade, male voices unacc., Nov. 1869.

Kinder-Katechismus zu Kosel's Geburtstag, children's voices with piano (1st version, Dec. 1873) or orch (2nd version, Dec. 1874).

Willkommen in Wahnfried, du heil'ger Christ, children's voices, Dec. 1877.

Ihr Kinder, geschwinde, geschwinde, 'antique choral song', children's voices, Dec. 1880 (performed by the Wagners' children on 25 Dec. 1880 for Cosima's birthday).

V CHAMBER

String quartet in D, autumn 1829 (lost).
The Adagio for Clarinet and String Quintet formerly attributed to Wagner is in fact by Heinrich Joseph Baermann (1784–1847), belonging to his Clarinet Quintet, op. 23.

VI SOLO VOICE AND ORCHESTRA

Aria, 1829 (lost; possibly for voice and piano).
Aria, soprano and orch. ?early 1830 (lost).
Scene and aria, soprano and orch, 1832 (lost).
'Doch jetzt wohin ich blicke', new allegro section (words by Wagner) for Aubry's aria 'Wie ein schöner Frühlingsmorgen' in Marschner's *Der Vampyr*, tenor, Sept. 1833.
'Sanfte Wehmut will sich regen', bass aria for K. Blum's Singspiel *Marie, Max und Michel*, Aug. 1837.
Bass aria for J. Weigl's opera *Die Schweizerfamilie*, Dec. 1837 (lost).
'Norma il predisse, o Druidi', aria for Bellini's *Norma*, bass solo with male chorus, Sept./Oct. 1839.

VII SOLO VOICE AND PIANO

Songs (drafts), 1828–30.
Seven pieces for Goethe's *Faust*, songs for solo voices (some with chorus) and piano, beginning of 1831.
Glockentöne (also entitled *Abendglocken*), setting of poem by T. Apel, Oct. 1832 (lost).
Der Tannenbaum (text Georg Scheurlin), autumn 1838.
Dors mon enfant, (poet unknown), autumn 1839.
Extase (Victor Hugo), frag, autumn 1839.
Attente (Hugo), autumn 1839.
La tombe dit à la rose (Hugo), frag, autumn 1839.
Mignonne (P. de Ronsard), autumn 1839.
Soupir (Jean Reboul), autumn 1839.
Les deux grenadiers (Heinrich Heine), Dec. 1839/Jan. 1840.
Adieux de Marie Stuart (Pierre-Jean de Béranger), Mar. 1840.
Five songs for a female voice (Wesendonck Lieder), poems by Mathilde Wesendonck. Pubd order, with dates of completion: *Der Engel* (30 Nov. 1857); *Stehe still!* (22 Feb. 1858); *Im Treibhaus* (1 May 1858); *Schmerzen* (19 Dec. 1857); *Träume* (5 Dec. 1857, also arr. by Wagner for solo violin and small orch, mid-Dec. 1857). Second version of all 5 songs, beginning Oct. 1858.

Es ist bestimmt in Gottes Rat (draft), early 1858.
Schlaf, Kindchen, schlafe, lullaby, theme used also in *Siegfried Idyll*, end Dec. 1868.
Der Worte viele sind gemacht, song for Louis Kraft, Apr. 1871.

VIII PIANO

Sonata in D minor, summer 1829 (lost).
Sonata in F minor, autumn 1829 (lost).
Sonata in B flat (four hands), beginning 1831; a subsequent orchestration of it is lost.
Sonata in B flat, op. 1, autumn 1831.
Fantasie in F sharp minor, op. 3, autumn 1831.
Polonaise in D (four hands), op. 2, end 1831/beginning 1832. The 4-handed arr. is a revised, improved version of a 2-handed original.
Sonata in A (Grosse Sonate), op. 4, beginning 1832.
Albumblatt (Lied ohne Worte), E major (autograph untitled), end 1840.
Polka, G, May 1853.
Eine Sonate für das Album von Frau M[athilde] W[esendonck], A flat, June 1853.
Züricher Vielliebchen-Walzer, E flat, May 1854.
Theme, A flat (incorrectly known as the 'Porazzi Theme'), 1858, 1881 (the 'Porazzi Theme', marked 'Adagio', dates from Mar. 1882).
In das Album der Fürstin M[etternich], C, June 1861.
Ankunft bei den schwarzen Schwänen, A flat, July 1861.
Albumblatt (dedicated to Frau Betty Schott), E flat, Jan. 1875.

IX EDITIONS, ARRANGEMENTS

Beethoven, Symphony no. 9, for piano, 1830–31.
Haydn, Symphony no. 103 in E flat, for piano, 1831 (lost).
Bellini, cavatina from *Il pirata*, orchn from piano score, 1833 (lost).
Bellini, *Norma*, retouching of orchn, 1837.
Rossini, 'Li marinari' from *Les soirées musicales*, orchn of piano acc., 1838.
Meyerbeer, *Robert le Diable*, harp part of cavatina transcribed for strings, 1838.
Weber, hunting chorus from *Euryanthe*, reorch, 1839.
Various composers, suites for the *cornet à pistons* (operatic excerpts), 1840 (lost).
Donizetti, *La favorite* and Halévy, *La reine de Chypre*: vocal scores and various arrs., 1840–2. Halévy, *Le Guitarrero*, various arrs., 1841.
Herz, *Grande fantaisie sur 'La romanesca'*, arr. piano duet, 1841.
Auber, *Zanetta*, arrs. for string quartet, 1842.
Spontini, *La vestale*, retouching of orchn, 1844.

Wagner

Gluck, *Iphigénie en Aulide*, rev. version, 1846/7.
Palestrina, Stabat Mater, rev. version, 1848.
Mozart, *Don Giovanni*, rev. version, 1850 (lost).
Gluck, *Iphigénie en Aulide*, concert ending for overture, 1854.
Johann Strauss the Younger, *Wine, Women and Song* waltz, directions for instrumentation, 1875.

Appendix C
Personalia

Anders, Gottfried Engelbert (1795–1866). A man of aristocratic origins (original surname unknown) who chose to conceal them by calling himself Anders ('Otherwise'). From 1833 an employee of the Bibliothèque Royale in Paris; also a contributor to Schlesinger's *Gazette musicale*. Close friend of Wagner in his Paris years.

Apel, Theodor (1811–67). Studied law but turned to writing poetry and drama. As young men he and Wagner went on holiday together in Bohemia, exploring the delights of hedonism; *Das Liebesverbot* was the result.

Bakunin, Mikhail (1814–76). Russian anarchist who, arriving in Dresden in 1849, was one of the leading figures of the May uprising. He met Wagner through Röckel, and they enjoyed prolonged conversations together on politics and art (Bakunin himself had compositional ambitions). Bakunin's nihilism prevented him from embracing Wagner's proposed artistic reforms, but they were united in their enthusiasm for Beethoven's Ninth.

Berlioz, Hector (1803–69). The leading French composer of his age. For all his debt to Classicism, he was in many ways the Romantic artist *par excellence*, not least in the extra-musical inspiration of much of his work and in his unconventional life style. He was also an irrepressible idealist and his intolerance of mediocrity is wittily and pungently expressed in his *Memoirs*. During his lifetime he was commonly ignored or denigrated; full recognition of his genius came only in the present century. His outlook and experiences offer many parallels with Wagner; each recognized the fact, though their differences stood in the way of a long-lasting or intimate relationship.

Bülow, Hans (Guido) von (1830–94). German conductor and pianist. As a young man he associated himself with the New German school, studying the piano under Liszt and putting himself at Wagner's disposal. He took up the conductorship of the Munich Court Opera in 1864, conducting the premieres of *Tristan* and *Die Meistersinger*. His first wife, Cosima, divorced him and married Wagner after a protracted and socially embarrassing liaison. Bülow also idolized Wagner and continued to do so. As musical director at the court of Meiningen (1880–5) he brought the orchestra there wide renown.

Cornelius, (Carl August) Peter (1824–74). German composer remembered now primarily for his Lieder and the opera *Der Barbier von Bagdad*. He became a member first of Liszt's circle in Weimar (from 1852) and subsequently of Wagner's (from 1861) and throughout his career was engaged in a struggle to assert his independence as a composer, while acknowledging the influence and superior talents of his mentors.

Dietsch, (Pierre-) Louis (-Philippe) (1808–65). French conductor and composer, mostly of sacred works in a traditional style. Wagner claimed that Dietsch's opera *Le Vaisseau fantôme*, staged at the Paris Opéra in November 1842, used a libretto based on his own scenario for *Der fliegende Holländer*. In fact, Dietsch's librettists Foucher and Révoil drew primarily not on Wagner but on Captain Marryatt's *The Phantom Ship* and to a lesser extent on Heine, as well as probably Fenimore Cooper (*The Red Rover*), the tales of Wilhelm Hauff and various poems. From Walter Scott's novel *The Pirate* they took several names and other details. Dietsch made another fateful appearance in Wagner's life when he presided over the *Tannhäuser* fiasco in Paris in 1861.

Dorn, Heinrich Ludwig Egmont (1804–92). German composer, conductor and writer. His path crossed with Wagner's first in Leipzig and then in Riga, where they were initially friends. Dorn's forthright reviews of Wagner's music and the circumstances in which the former succeeded the latter as musical director in Riga drew them irreconcilably apart. Dorn went on to take appointments in Cologne and at the Berlin Opera. As a composer he was best known for his humorous Lieder, though his operas included one on the Nibelungen saga (1854).

Gautier, Judith (1845–1917). French author and writer on music; daughter of the poet Théophile Gautier. Both she and her husband Catulle Mendès (m. 1866) were ardent Wagnerians. They visited the Wagners at Tribschen in 1869 (with Villiers de l'Isle-Adam) and again in 1870 (with Villiers, Saint-Saëns, Duparc and others). Wagner's liaison with Judith began at the first *Ring* festival in 1876 and was brought to an end by Cosima in February 1878.

Gobineau, Count Joseph-Arthur de (1816–82). French diplomat, novelist and historian. The elegance and subtlety of his literary works, notably some first-rate short stories, have generally been eclipsed by the essay for which he is chiefly remembered: *Essai sur l'inégalité des races humaines* (1853–5). In it Gobineau attributes the supposed degeneration of the human species to miscegenation, pessimistically asserting that some degree of interbreeding is necessary for the continuation of civilization. Wagner's more optimistic belief that redemption was possible through Christ's blood differentiates his outlook from Gobineau's. Nevertheless, he was deeply impressed and also influenced by the *Essai*, as were the anti-semites associated with Wahnfried after Wagner's death. Nazi ideologists were also indebted to Gobineau, though they were obliged to purge his theory of its defeatism.

Hanslick, Eduard (1825–1904). German writer on music and aesthetics. The most eminent music critic of his time, Hanslick admired Wagner's early scores and his long, favourable analysis of *Tannhäuser* (1846) elicited a friendly response from the composer. However, Hanslick's reverence for tradition, and his unshakeable conviction that content in music is inseparable from and governed by form led him to side with Brahms and the champions of absolute music against Wagner, Liszt and other members of the New German school, who were advocating such notions as music drama and programme music. Hanslick was not, as the Wagner camp claimed, motivated chiefly by malice, in spite of Wagner's cruel caricature of him as Sixtus Beckmesser (originally called Veit Hanslich). His aesthetic outlook, though deeply conservative and narrow in its horizons, was expressed with consistency and in a manner that is temperate in comparison with Wagner's cruder detractors.

Heine, Heinrich (1797–1856). German writer and poet. As one of the inspirational figures of Young Germany, Heine may be said to have made an indirect contribution to the conception of *Das Liebesverbot*. But greater debts date from after their meeting in Paris: Wagner drew on stories by Heine for *Der fliegende Holländer* and *Tannhäuser*. Less often observed is the fact that Heine's fragmentary *Elementargeister* (Elemental spirits) of 1837 prefigures much of the mythical world of the *Ring*: giants and dwarfs, Valkyries, Siegfried, and gnomes called Nibelungs who mine precious metals in the earth and wear little caps called *Tarnkappen* which make them invisible.

Herwegh, Georg (1817–75). German poet and political activist. He emigrated to Switzerland in 1839 to escape military service, and after returning to Germany was then expelled for writing a pamphlet directed against the King of Prussia. He was active in the 1848–9 uprisings in France and in the 1850s his house in Zurich sheltered many political refugees. It was Herwegh who in 1854 introduced Wagner to Schopenhauer's *Die Welt als Wille und Vorstellung*.

Joukovsky, Paul von (1845–1912). Russian painter who designed the sets and costumes for the first production of *Parsifal* in 1882. After visiting Wagner in January 1880 at the Villa d'Angri, Naples, Joukovsky abandoned his friend the novelist Henry James to live with the Wagners. Until the end of Wagner's life Joukovsky was regarded as a member of the family.

Kietz, Ernst Benedikt (1815–92). German painter who moved to Paris in order to pursue his art studies. One of Wagner's bosom companions during the years of his Paris tribulations (1839–42). He was always very close to Wagner and Minna, who both treated him, with his childlike disposition, as a younger member of the family; indeed, in 1858 (when Kietz was 43) they offered to 'adopt' him.

Laube, Heinrich (1806–84). German writer and critic. A leading member of Young Germany, he was hounded by the authorities and his writings banned. As editor of the *Zeitung für die elegante Welt* he was responsible for publishing some of Wagner's earliest essays. From 1840 he was a theatre critic in Leipzig; subsequently he was director of the Vienna Burgtheater (1849–67), Leipzig Stadttheater (1869–71) and Vienna Stadttheater (from 1872).

Laussot, Jessie (born *c.* 1829). Of English birth (*née* Taylor) she married the Bordeaux wine merchant Eugène Laussot. With Julie Ritter she proposed to provide Wagner with an annual allowance of 3000 francs. Her affair with Wagner came to an abrupt end when her husband was apprised of their plan for an oriental elopement. After living apart from her husband in Florence she finally married the essayist Karl Hillebrand.

Lehrs, Samuel (1806–43). German philologist resident in Paris, where he was one of Wagner's close friends. As well as furnishing Wagner with background material on the Tannhäuser and Lohengrin legends, Lehrs probably introduced him to such thinkers as Proudhon and Feuerbach. Like Wagner he suffered real hardship in Paris and it was that poverty that was responsible for his early death, which occurred shortly after Wagner had left for Dresden.

Levi, Hermann (1839–1900). German conductor. After appointments at Saarbrücken, Mannheim, Rotterdam and Karlsruhe he became Court Kapellmeister in Munich (1872–90). One of the finest conductors of his time he soon came to Wagner's attention and was highly esteemed by him. Feeling that Levi's Jewishness made him inappropriate as the conductor of *Parsifal*, Wagner tried first to secure an alternative and then to persuade Levi to undergo baptism (unsuccessfully, though Levi himself, a classic example of Jewish self-hatred, had considered the possibility some time before). Levi did conduct the premiere of *Parsifal* in 1882 as well as performances in several seasons subsequent to Wagner's death.

Liszt, Franz (1811–86). Hungarian composer and pianist. His long friendship with Wagner began in earnest after Liszt helped him escape from Germany in 1849. Their correspondence, sustained throughout Wagner's exile, reveals a sincere, deep-rooted relationship based on mutual admiration and understanding; the rift caused by Wagner's liaison with Liszt's daughter Cosima was eventually healed. Wagner was indebted to Liszt for various aspects of his harmonic idiom and even for specific melodic inspirations.

Meyerbeer, Giacomo (1791–1864). German composer who became the leading figure in French grand opera after 1831. Born into a wealthy Jewish merchant family in Berlin, he conquered Paris with *Robert le Diable* (1831), following it with the immensely successful *Les Huguenots* (1836) and two other works of the same five-act grand opera pattern. The relationship of Meyerbeer to Wagner has many complicating ramifications, but in essence it exhibits the ugliest aspects of the latter's ingratitude, jealousy and anti-semitism.

Nietzsche, Friedrich (1844–1900). German philosopher. From the time of his first visit to Tribschen in 1869, shortly after being made Professor of Classical Philology at Basle University, Nietzsche was a regular visitor at the Wagners' house. In these years he revelled in the 'insidiously' seductive quality of Wagner's music and actively espoused his cause. With the deeply ambiguous essay *Richard Wagner in Bayreuth* (1875–6) Nietzsche began to register his disquiet, and he left before the end of the first Bayreuth

Festival with severe headaches. His later essays contain many bitter references to what he regarded as Wagner's betrayal and his espousal of the 'philosophy of pessimism'.

Porges, Heinrich (1837–1900). German writer on music. Co-editor of the *Neue Zeitschrift für Musik* from 1863, editor of the *Süddeutsche Presse* from 1867; also a music critic, conductor and teacher. He first came within Wagner's orbit when he was instrumental in arranging a successful concert for him in Prague in 1863. From then on he was a valued member of the circle and in 1872 he was entrusted with a special commission: to record for posterity all the details of the performance and interpretation of the *Ring* at the first Bayreuth Festival (1876). Porges' faithful account is now available in a modern English translation.

Pusinelli, Anton (1815–78). Wagner's family doctor in Dresden and life-long friend. In addition to giving Wagner financial assistance and supporting him in his publishing venture of 1844, Pusinelli was often entrusted with commissions of a delicate nature.

Reissiger, Karl Gottlieb (1798–1859). German composer, conductor and teacher. He was Kapellmeister at the Dresden court from 1828 until his death. Initially he was responsible for making the Dresden Opera the finest in Germany, but later in his tenure his enthusiasm seems to have waned; certainly he was content to let his co-Kapellmeister, Wagner, undertake the more onerous duties. Reissiger's compositions are in the Kapellmeister tradition: well crafted but lacking distinction. They include eight operas, the popular melodrama *Yelva*, songs, chamber and church music.

Richter, Hans (1843–1916). Austro-Hungarian conductor. After studying the violin, horn and theory at the Vienna Conservatory, he played horn at the Kärntnertor Theater (1862–6) and was recommended to Wagner by the theatre's conductor. For Wagner he copied scores and learnt the trumpet specially to play in the intimate premiere of the *Siegfried Idyll* at Tribschen. Meanwhile his career was progressing: he was chief conductor at the National Theatre, Pest (1871–5), and was appointed to the Vienna Court Opera in 1875. The honour of conducting the first *Ring* cycle at Bayreuth (1876) fell to him, and subsequently he shared the rostrum with Wagner for a fund-raising festival in the Albert Hall, London. He became an established figure in English musical life, retaining the conductorship of the Hallé Orchestra from 1897 to 1911, as well as conducting the premiere of Elgar's *Enigma Variations, Dream of Gerontius* and First Symphony.

Ritter, Karl (1830–91). Son of Julie Ritter (benefactress of Wagner) and her husband Karl, Germans who had settled in Russia. The sons Karl and Alexander (later a composer and violinist who also entered Wagner's circle) were born in Narva (Estonia) and after the father's death the family moved to Dresden, where Karl encountered Wagner and his music. He was a loyal 'disciple', following him into exile in Switzerland and accompanying him to Venice in 1858 after the crisis of the Wesendonck affair.

Röckel, August (1814–76). German conductor and composer. Trained by his father Joseph, a singer, he became a répétiteur for his travelling company, before studying in Vienna and Paris, where he was assistant to Rossini. His appointment as assistant conductor at Dresden brought him into contact with Wagner. They became involved together in revolutionary activities and Röckel edited the *Volksblätter*, to which Wagner contributed (and briefly edited in Röckel's absence). Röckel survived a death sentence but was imprisoned for thirteen years (1849–62), a fact to which we owe an important series of letters from Wagner.

Schnorr von Carolsfeld, Ludwig (1836–65). German tenor. Son of the painter Julius Schnorr von Carolsfeld. Settling in Dresden in 1860 with his bride Malvina, he took such roles as Tannhäuser and Lohengrin, and, after Wagner's return from exile, studied with him the role of Tristan. Malvina took Isolde, and together they performed in the premiere in Munich in 1865. Schnorr's death shortly after deprived Wagner of both a valued friend and his favourite tenor.

Schopenhauer, Arthur (1788–1860). German philosopher. His major work, *Die Welt als Wille und Vorstellung* (published 1818, though dated 1819), was universally ignored until 1853, when an article in an English periodical brought it to light. Wagner read it in the autumn of 1854 and was profoundly influenced both by Schopenhauer's aesthetic (in which music was given pride of place) and by his philosophy of pessimism. To a certain extent the book was an eloquent formulation of ideas already held by Wagner; nevertheless, its impact on the *Ring* and the other late music dramas was decisive.

Schröder-Devrient, Wilhelmine (1804–60). German soprano. One of the leading sopranos of the day; renowned as a singing actress, she impressed all by the intensity and conviction of her dramatic portrayals. In 1822 she took the role of Leonore in *Fidelio*, an assumption that was to bring her immense success. In the same year she first sang in Dresden, with which opera she was to be associated for a quarter of a century. Wagner had previously been overwhelmed by her performances in Leipzig (though *Mein Leben* incorrectly attributes a momentous decision about his career to her portrayal of Leonore; no such performance of *Fidelio* took place in Leipzig in 1829). In Dresden she created the roles of Adriano (*Rienzi*), Senta and Venus, but by the 1840s her voice was declining, and both her figure (in trouser roles) and a proneness to mannerism occasioned adverse comment.

Semper, Gottfried (1803–79). German architect. Builder of the Court Theatre in Dresden, he was one of Wagner's closest friends there. They participated together in the uprising of 1849, Semper taking responsibility for the construction of barricades. Fleeing from arrest, he lived first in London and then in Zurich where he taught and renewed his acquaintance with Wagner. In 1864 Ludwig summoned him to Munich to build a festival theatre there, but the project never proceeded beyond the design stage.

Tausig, Carl (1841–71). Polish pianist and composer. One of the most talented of Liszt's first pupils, his technical mastery and consummate musicianship astonished all who heard him, but his dynamic, impulsive manner at the keyboard attracted criticism as well as praise. In May 1858 Liszt sent him, at the age of sixteen, to Wagner in Zurich, who delighted in his uninhibited playing and personality. In 1871 he took charge of the scheme of patrons' certificates to subsidize the Bayreuth Festival, but within months he was dead – a victim of typhus at the age of twenty-nine.

Uhlig, Theodor (1822–53). German violinist, theorist, critic and composer. He became a member of the Court orchestra in Dresden in 1841 and although originally opposed to Wagner he became one of his closest friends and staunchest advocates. Because of his empathy with Wagner on aesthetic and political matters, the correspondence they sustained in the early years of Wagner's exile is of primary interest and importance. So revealing was it that Cosima later found it prudent to censor passages on publication.

Wesendonck, Mathilde (née Luckemeyer) (1828–1902). German poet and author. She and her husband Otto arrived in Zurich in 1851 and made Wagner's acquaintance the following year. The sexual relationship that developed between Wagner and Mathilde may or may not have been consummated; in any case her role was seen by both as essentially that of muse. Wagner claimed that she provided the inspiration for *Tristan*, which is to some extent a dramatization of the triangular relationship formed by Wagner and the Wesendoncks. Five of Mathilde's poems were set by Wagner (the *Wesendonck Lieder*).

Wesendonck, Otto (1815–96). German businessman. Having made his fortune as a partner in a firm of New York silk importers, Wesendonck was in a position to offer Wagner generous financial assistance during the first part of his exile in Zurich. Indeed, he became his chief benefactor of the period, though he drew the line at his wife, and Wagner was eventually obliged to leave the little house Otto had placed at his disposal.

Wolzogen, Hans (Paul), Baron von (1848–1938). German writer on music. He moved to Bayreuth in October 1877 in order to edit the newly-founded periodical *Bayreuther Blätter* in liaison with Wagner; the first edition appeared at the beginning of the following year. The journal soon established itself as the mouthpiece of Wahnfried, and after Wagner's death Wolzogen became one of the chief guardians of the 'Holy Grail' of Bayreuth. He remained editor of the *Bayreuther Blätter* for sixty years, until his death, when it was discontinued. Wolzogen's other main claim to fame is his series of 'thematic guides' to the *Ring* and other works. His identification and labelling of the various leitmotifs provided the basis for scores of similar guides produced over the next century.

Appendix D
Select bibliography

I MUSICAL WORKS

Richard Wagners Werke, ed. Michael Balling (Leipzig 1912–29; repr. New York 1972). Only 10 vols appeared; none conforms to the demands of a critical edition.

Sämtliche Werke, gen. eds. Carl Dahlhaus and Egon Voss (Mainz 1970–). Planned in 31 vols, this is a critical edition of all the works based on the most authentic sources.

Die Musikdramen (Hamburg 1971; Munich 1978). Texts of the music dramas, with an introduction by Joachim Kaiser.

Verzeichnis der musikalischen Werke Richard Wagners und ihrer Quellen, J. Deathridge, M. Geck and E. Voss (Mainz 1986). A complete index, with commentaries, of Wagner's musical works and of all their traceable sources.

II WRITINGS BY WAGNER

Gesammelte Schriften und Dichtungen, 10 vols (Leipzig 1871–83). The first edition of Collected Works, prepared under Wagner's own supervision. 4th edn (Leipzig 1907) repr. Hildesheim 1976.

Sämtliche Schriften und Dichtungen, Volks-Ausgabe, 16 vols (Leipzig, n.d.). The most complete edition available.

Mein Leben, ed. Martin Gregor-Dellin (Munich 1963, 2/1976). First authentic edition.

III DIARIES/NOTEBOOKS

Die Rote Brieftasche, in *Sämtliche Briefe*, ed. G. Strobel and W. Wolf, i (1967), 79–92. Wagner's Red Pocketbook, containing brief biographical notes for the years 1813 to 1839.

Das Braune Buch: Tagebuchaufzeichnungen 1865 bis 1882, ed. Joachim Bergfeld (Zurich and Freiburg im Breisgau 1975).

Cosima Wagner: Die Tagebücher 1869—1883, 2 vols, ed. Martin Gregor-Dellin and Dietrich Mack (Munich 1976–7).

IV SOURCES AVAILABLE IN ENGLISH TRANSLATION

Richard Wagner's Prose Works, ed. and trans. W.A. Ellis, 8 vols (London 1892–9).

My Life, trans. of 1976 edn by Andrew Gray, ed. Mary Whittall (Cambridge 1983).

The Diary of Richard Wagner 1865—1882: The Brown Book, trans. by George Bird of above edn (London 1980).

Cosima Wagner's Diaries, trans. by Geoffrey Skelton of above edn, 2 vols (London 1978–80).

Selections of prose writings:

Goldman, Albert and Sprinchorn, Evert (eds): *Wagner on Music and Drama: A Compendium of Richard Wagner's Prose Works* (New York 1964, repr. 1977).

Jacobs, Robert (ed.): *Three Wagner Essays*, trans. by R. Jacobs of '*Music of the Future*', *On Conducting* and *On Performing Beethoven's Ninth Symphony* (London 1979).

Jacobs, Robert and Skelton, Geoffrey (ed. and trans.): *Wagner Writes from Paris . . . Stories, Essays and Articles by the Young Composer* (London 1973).

Osborne, Charles (ed.): *Richard Wagner: Stories and Essays* (London 1973).

V LETTERS

In German:

A complete edition of Wagner's 10,000 surviving letters, based on the most reliable sources and scrupulously edited and annotated, is in progress: *Sämtliche Briefe*, ed. G. Strobel and W. Wolf (Leipzig 1967–). Four of the projected 15 volumes have appeared to date (1984) and the present editors are Werner Wolf and Hans-Joachim Bauer.

A selection of 206 letters, *Richard Wagner: Briefe*, ed. Hanjo Kesting, is published by Piper Verlag (Munich and Zurich 1983).

Beginning in the years following Wagner's death, and initially under the supervision of Cosima Wagner, the majority of his letters were published grouped according to the recipients, as follows:

   Theodor Apel (Leipzig 1910)
   Bayreuth letters, 1871–1883 (Berlin and Leipzig 1907)
   Bayreuth artists (second vol. of 'Bayreuth letters') (Berlin and Leipzig 1908)
   Hans von Bülow (Jena 1916)
   Family letters, 1832–1874 (Berlin 1907)
   Richard Fricke (Dresden 1906)
   Friends and contemporaries (Berlin and Leipzig 1909)
   Judith Gautier (Zurich and Leipzig [1936])

Bertha Goldwag ('eine Putzmacherin') (Vienna 1906)
Emil Heckel (Berlin 1899)
Franz Liszt [includes Liszt's letters to Wagner] (Leipzig 1887)
Ludwig II, 5 vols (Karlsruhe 1936–9)
Mathilde Maier (Leipzig [1930])
Malwida von Meysenbug (Basle 1956)
Albert Niemann (Berlin 1924)
Friedrich Nietzsche (Munich 1915)
Wagner's publishers, 2 vols (Mainz 1911)
Ferdinand Praeger (Bayreuth [1894])
Hans Richter (Vienna and Leipzig 1924)
Julie Ritter (Munich 1920)
August Röckel (Leipzig 1894)
Theodor Uhlig, Wilhelm Fischer and Ferdinand Heine (Leipzig 1888)
Johanna and Franziska Wagner (Berlin 1927)
Minna Wagner, 2 vols (Berlin and Leipzig 1908)
Mathilde Wesendonck (Berlin 1904)
Otto Wesendonck (Charlottenburg 1898; new enlarged edn. Berlin 1905)
Eliza Wille [with her reminiscences and annotations] (Berlin 1894)

Other important collections are:
Richard Wagners Briefe nach Zeitfolge und Inhalt (Leipzig 1905; repr. Niederwalluf bei Wiesbaden 1971) [an index of 3143 of Wagner's letters arranged chronologically, with a résumé of their contents and quotation of selected extracts]
Richard Wagners Gesammelte Briefe, ed. J. Kapp and E. Kastner, 2 vols (Leipzig 1914)
Richard Wagners Briefe, selected and annotated by Wilhelm Altmann, 2 vols (Leipzig [1933])
Briefe: Die Sammlung Burrell, ed. John N. Burk (Frankfurt am Main 1953)

In English translation:
A critical edition of some 500 of Wagner's letters is in preparation (ed. Stewart Spencer and Barry Millington). Meanwhile, the two chief sources of translated correspondence are:
Letters of Richard Wagner. Selected and ed. by Wilhelm Altmann (trans. M.M. Bozman), 2 vols (London and Toronto 1927)
Letters of Richard Wagner: The Burrell Collection. Ed. with notes by John N. Burk (London 1951)

Other collections in English include the following:
The Story of Bayreuth as told in the Bayreuth Letters of Richard Wagner. Trans. and ed. Caroline V. Kerr (London [1912])
Richard Wagner's Letters to his Dresden Friends, Theodor Uhlig, Wilhelm Fischer, and Ferdinand Heine. Trans. J.S. Shedlock (London 1890)

Family Letters of Richard Wagner. Trans. and ed. W.A. Ellis (London 1911)

Letters of Richard Wagner to Emil Heckel [*with reminiscences of Wagner by Emil Heckel*]: *With a brief account of the Bayreuth festivals.* Trans. W.A. Ellis (London 1899)

Correspondence of Wagner and Liszt. Trans. F. Hueffer (rev. edn London 1897; repr. New York 1973)

The Nietzsche–Wagner Correspondence. Ed. E. Foerster-Nietzsche, trans. C.V. Kerr (London [1922])

The Letters of Richard Wagner to Anton Pusinelli [with letters of Pusinelli]. Trans. and ed. Elbert Lenrow (New York 1932)

Richard Wagner's Letters to August Roeckel. Trans. E.C. Sellar. With an introductory essay by H.S. Chamberlain (Bristol [1897])

Richard to Minna Wagner: Letters to his First Wife. Trans. and ed. W.A. Ellis, 2 vols (London, 1909)

Richard Wagner to Mathilde Wesendonck. Trans. and ed. W.A. Ellis (London 1905)

Richard Wagner: Letters to Wesendonck et al. Trans. W.A. Ellis (London 1899)

Previously unpublished letters to and from Wagner appear in *Wagner*, iii (1982), 98–123 [concerning Wagner's visit to London in 1855]; iv (1983), 98–114 and v (1984), 2–20 [various letters and drafts held by the British Library].

VI BOOKS AND ARTICLES

English translations of foreign-language works are given where available.

Abraham, Gerald. *A Hundred Years of Music* (London 1938, 4/1974)
—— *Slavonic and Romantic Music* [esp. chap. 'Wagner's Second Thoughts'] (London 1968)
Adorno, Theodor. *In Search of Wagner* (Eng. trans.) (London 1981)
—— 'Wagner, Nietzsche and Hitler' [review of Newman's *Life*, vol. iv], *Kenyon Review*, ix (1947), 155–62
Amerongen, Martin van. *Wagner: A case history* (Eng. trans.) (London 1983)
Bailey, Robert. 'The Structure of the *Ring* and its Evolution', *19th Century Music*, i (1977–8), 48–61
—— 'Wagner's Musical Structures for *Siegfrieds Tod*', in *Studies in Music History: Essays for Oliver Strunk*, ed. Harold Powers (Princeton, New Jersey, 1968), 459–94
Barth, Herbert, Mack, Dietrich and Voss, Egon (eds). *Wagner: A Documentary Study* (Eng. trans.) (London 1975)
Bauer, Oswald Georg. *Richard Wagner: The Stage Designs and Productions from the Premières to the Present* (Eng. trans.) (New York 1983)

Becker, Heinz. 'Giacomo Meyerbeer: On the Occasion of the Centenary of his Death', Leo Baeck Institute, Year Book IX (London 1964), 178–201

Beckett, Lucy. *Richard Wagner: 'Parsifal'* (Cambridge 1981)

Bekker, Paul. *Richard Wagner: His Life in his Work* (Eng. trans.) (London 1931)

Biddiss, Michael D. *Father of Racist Ideology: the Social and Political Thought of Count Gobineau* (London 1970)

—— 'The founder of Aryan racism' [on Gobineau], *Times Higher Education Supplement*, 8 Oct 1982, p. 11

Blunt, Wilfrid. *The Dream King: Ludwig II of Bavaria* (London 1970)

Borchmeyer, Dieter. *Das Theater Richard Wagners: Idee – Dichtung – Wirkung* (Stuttgart 1982)

Branscombe, Peter. 'Wagner as Poet', in *Richard Wagner: The Ring* (trans. Andrew Porter) (London 1976), pp. xxix-xl

Breithaupt, R. 'Richard Wagners Klaviermusik', *Die Musik*, iii (1903–4), 108–34

Brinkmann, Reinhold. ' "Drei der Fragen stell' ich mir frei". Zur Wanderer-Szene im 1. Akt von Wagners "Siegfried" ', *Jahrbuch des Staatlichen Instituts für Musikforschung Preussischer Kulturbesitz* (Berlin 1972), 120–62

Brod, Max. 'Some Comments on the Relationship between Wagner and Meyerbeer', Leo Baeck Institute, Year Book IX (London 1964), 202–5

Burbidge, Peter, and Sutton, Richard (eds). *The Wagner Companion* (London 1979)

Burrell, Mary. *Richard Wagner: His Life & Works from 1813 to 1834* ([London] 1898)

Carnegy, Patrick. 'Damming the Rhine' [review of H. Mayer's *Richard Wagner in Bayreuth*], *TLS*, 10 June 1977, 707–8

Chancellor, John. *Wagner* (London 1978)

Coleman, Alexander. 'Calderón/Schopenhauer/Wagner: The Story of a Misunderstanding', *The Musical Quarterly*, lxix (1983), 227–43

Conrad, Herbert. 'Absturz aus Klingsors Zaubergarten: Ein biographischer Beitrag zu den letzten Lebensjahren Richard Wagners', *Fränkischer Heimatbote* (monthly suppl. to *Nordbayerischer Kurier*), II. Jahrgang (1978), no. 8

Cook, Peter. *A Memoir of Bayreuth 1876* ('related by Carl Emil Doepler including illustrations of his costume designs for the first production of the "Ring" ') (London 1979)

Cooke, Deryck. *I Saw the World End: A study of Wagner's 'Ring'* (London 1979)

Culshaw, John. *Reflections on Wagner's 'Ring'* (New York and London 1976)

Dahlhaus, Carl. *Between Romanticism and Modernism: Four Studies in the Music of the Later Nineteenth Century* (Eng. trans.) (Berkeley and Los Angeles, California, and London 1980)

—— (ed.) *Das Drama Richard Wagners als musikalisches Kunstwerk* (Regensburg 1970)

—— 'Richard Wagner: *Parsifal*', essay (in Ger. and Fr. only) in booklet accompanying Decca's Solti recording (1972) of *Parsifal* (Decca SET 550–54), 2 and 18

—— (ed.) *Richard Wagner: Werk und Wirkung* (Regensburg 1971)

—— *Richard Wagner's Music Dramas* (Eng. trans.) (Cambridge 1979)

—— *Wagner's Aesthetics* [selection of Wagner's writings with introductory essays] (Eng. trans.) (Bayreuth 1972)

—— *Wagners Konzeption des musikalischen Dramas* (Regensburg 1971)

Daube, Otto. '*Ich schreibe keine Symphonien mehr': Richard Wagners Lehrjahre nach den erhaltenen Dokumenten* (Cologne 1960)

Deathridge, John. 'The Nomenclature of Wagner's Sketches', *Proceedings of the Royal Musical Association*, ci (1974–5), 75–83

—— 'Wagner und sein erster Lehrmeister', Bayerische Staatsoper, Munich, (*Meistersinger* Programmheft 1979), 71–5

—— *Wagner's 'Rienzi': A reappraisal based on a study of the sketches and drafts* (Oxford 1977)

DiGaetani, John Louis (ed.) *Penetrating Wagner's Ring: An Anthology* (Rutherford, New Jersey, and London 1978)

—— *Richard Wagner and the Modern British Novel* (Rutherford, New Jersey, and London 1978)

Donington, Robert. *Wagner's 'Ring' and its Symbols: The Music and the Myth* (London 1963)

Ellis, William Ashton, *Life of Richard Wagner*, 6 vols (London 1900–08) [vols i–iii are a trans. of C.F. Glasenapp's biography]

Ewans, Michael. *Wagner and Aeschylus: The 'Ring' and the 'Oresteia'* (London 1982)

Fischer-Dieskau, Dietrich. *Wagner and Nietzsche* (Eng. trans.) (London 1978)

Furness, Raymond. *Wagner and Literature* (Manchester 1982)

Gal, Hans. *Richard Wagner* (Eng. trans.) (London 1976)

Garten, H.F. *Wagner the Dramatist* (London 1977)

Gay, Peter. *Freud, Jews and Other Germans: Masters and Victims in Modernist Culture* (New York 1978; Oxford 1979), esp. chap. IV: 'Hermann Levi: A Study in Service and Self-Hatred', 189–230, which originally appeared as 'Hermann Levi and the Cult of Wagner', *TLS*, 11 April 1975, 402–4

Geck, Martin. *Die Bildnisse Richard Wagners* (Munich 1970)

Glasenapp, Carl Friedrich. *Das Leben Richard Wagners* (Leipzig 3/1894–1911 (rev., enlarged edn; for Eng. trans. see under Ellis, W.A.))

Glass, Frank W. *The Fertilizing Seed: Wagner's Concept of the Poetic Intent* (Ann Arbor 1983)

Gregor-Dellin, Martin. *Richard Wagner: His Life, His Work, His Century* (Eng. trans., abridged) (London 1983)

—— *Wagner-Chronik: Daten zu Leben und Werk* (Munich 1972)

Gutman, Robert. *Richard Wagner: The Man, His Mind, and His Music* (London 1968)

Hanslick, Eduard. *The Beautiful in Music* (Eng. trans.) (New York 1957)

—— *Vienna's Golden Years of Music: 1850–1900* (Eng. trans.) (New York 1969)

Hartford, Robert. *Bayreuth: the Early Years. An Account of the Early Decades of the Wagner Festival as seen by the Celebrated Visitors & Participants* (London 1980)

Hollingdale, R.J. *Nietzsche: The Man and His Philosophy* (London 1965)

Hollingrake, Roger. *Nietzsche, Wagner, and the philosophy of pessimism* (London 1982)

Holloway, Robin. *Debussy and Wagner* (London 1979)

John, Nicholas (ed.). Opera Guides 6 (*Tristan*), 12 (*Holländer*), 19 (*Meistersinger*), 21 (*Walküre*), plus forthcoming volumes (London 1980–)

Karbaum, Michael. *Studien zur Geschichte der Bayreuther Festspiele (1876–1976)* (Regensburg 1976)

Kerman, Joseph. 'Opera as Symphonic Poem', chap. 7 in *Opera as Drama* (New York 1956)

Kropfinger, Klaus. *Wagner und Beethoven: Untersuchungen zur Beethoven-Rezeption Richard Wagners* (Regensburg 1975)

Kubizek, August. *Young Hitler: the Story of our Friendship* (Eng. trans.) (London 1954)

Kurth, Ernst. *Romantische Harmonik und ihre Krise in Wagners 'Tristan'* (Berne and Leipzig 1920, 2/1923)

Laudon, Robert T. *Sources of the Wagnerian Synthesis: A Study of the Franco-German Tradition in 19th-Century Opera* (Munich and Salzburg 1979)

Lippert, Woldemar. *Wagner in Exile: 1849–62* (Eng. trans.) (London 1930)

Lloyd-Jones, Hugh, 'Wagner and the Greeks', *TLS*, 9 January 1976, pp. 37–9; repr. in *Blood for the Ghosts* (London 1982)

Lorenz, Alfred. *Das Geheimnis der Form bei Richard Wagner*, i: *Der musikalische Aufbau des Bühnenfestspieles Der Ring des Nibelungen* (Berlin 1924, repr. 1966); ii: *Der musikalische Aufbau von Richard Wagners 'Tristan und Isolde'* (Berlin 1926, repr. 1966); iii: *Der musikalische Aufbau von Richard Wagners 'Die Meistersinger von Nürnberg'* (Berlin 1930, repr. 1966); iv: *Der musikalische Aufbau von Richard Wagners 'Parsifal'* (Berlin 1933, repr. 1966)

Low, Alfred D. *Jews in the Eyes of the Germans: From the Enlightenment to Imperial Germany* (Philadelphia 1979)

McCreless, Patrick. *Wagner's Siegfried: Its Drama, History, and Music* (Ann Arbor 1982)

Machlin, Paul S. 'A Sketch for the "Dutchman" ', *Musical Times*, cxvii (1976), 727–9

—— 'Wagner, Durand and "The Flying Dutchman": the 1852 Revisions of the Overture', *Music & Letters*, lv (1974), 410–28

Mack, Dietrich (ed.) *Theaterarbeit an Wagners Ring* (Munich 1978)

Magee, Bryan. *Aspects of Wagner* (London 1968, rev. 2/1972)

—— *The Philosophy of Schopenhauer* (Oxford 1983)

Mann, Thomas. 'Sufferings and Greatness of Richard Wagner', in *Essays of Three Decades*, trans. H.T. Lowe-Porter (London [1947]). Collection also contains essays 'Richard Wagner and the *Ring*' (1937) and 'Schopenhauer' (1938)

Marek, George R. *Cosima Wagner* (New York 1981; London 1983)

Martin, Stoddard. *Wagner to 'The Waste Land': A Study of the Relationship of Wagner to English Literature* (London and Basingstoke 1982)

Mayer, Hans. *Richard Wagner in Bayreuth: 1876–1976* (Eng. trans.) (London 1976)

Mosse, George L. *Germans and Jews: The Right, the Left, and the Search for a 'Third Force' in Pre-Nazi Germany* (New York 1970)

Murray, David R. 'Major Analytical Approaches to Wagner's Musical Style: A Critique', *Music Review*, xxxix (1978), 211–22

Neumann, Angelo. *Personal Recollections of Wagner* (Eng. trans.) (London 1909)

Newcomb, Anthony. 'The Birth of Music out of the Spirit of Drama: An Essay in Wagnerian Formal Analysis', *19th Century Music*, v (1981–2), 38–66

Newman, Ernest. *The Life of Richard Wagner*, 4 vols (London 1933–47; repr. 1976)

—— *Wagner as Man and Artist* (London 2/1924)

—— *Wagner Nights* (London 1949)

Newman, William S. *The Sonata Since Beethoven* (Chapel Hill 1969)

Poliakov, Léon. *The History of Anti-Semitism: vol. III From Voltaire to Wagner* (Eng. trans.) (London 1975)

Porges, Heinrich. *Wagner Rehearsing the 'Ring': An Eye-Witness Account of the Stage Rehearsals of the First Bayreuth Festival* (Eng. trans.) (Cambridge 1983)

Porter, Andrew (trans.). *Richard Wagner: 'The Ring'* (London 1976)

Prieberg, Fred K. *Musik im NS-Staat* (Frankfurt am Main 1982)

Rayner, Robert M. *Wagner and 'Die Meistersinger'* (London 1940)

Reeser, Edward. 'Die literarischen Grundlagen des "Fliegenden Holländer" ', Bayreuth Festival Programme for *Der fliegende Holländer*, 1959, pp. 47–54

Sessa, Anne Dzamba. *Richard Wagner and the English* (Rutherford, New Jersey, and London 1979)

Shaw, George Bernard. *The Perfect Wagnerite: A Commentary on the Niblung's Ring* (New York 1967; repr. of 4/1923)

Skelton, Geoffrey. *Richard and Cosima Wagner: Biography of a Marriage* (London 1982)

—— *Wagner at Bayreuth: Experiment and Tradition* (London and New York rev. edn 1976)

—— *Wieland Wagner: the Positive Sceptic* (London 1971)

Spencer, Stewart (ed.). *Wagner*, the periodical of the Wagner Society, London. New series (1980–), lodged in the British Library, Senate House Library, and the Central Music Library, Westminster.

Wagner

—— (ed.). *Wagner 1976: A celebration of the Bayreuth Festival* (Wagner Society, London, 1976)

Spiel, Hilde, 'Living with a Genius. On the Marriage of Cosima and Richard Wagner', Bayreuth Festival Programme, vol. vii (*Götterdämmerung*), 1978, pp. 22–7

Stein, Jack M. *Richard Wagner & the Synthesis of the Arts* (Detroit 1960; repr. 1973)

Strobel, Otto. *Richard Wagner: Skizzen und Entwürfe zur Ring-Dichtung* (Munich 1930)

Strohm, Reinhard. 'On the History of the Opera "Tannhäuser" ', Bayreuth Festival Programme, vol. iii (*Tannhäuser*), 1978, pp. 21–9

—— ' "Rienzi" and Authenticity', *Musical Times*, cxvii (1976), 725

Taylor, Ronald. *Richard Wagner: His Life, Art and Thought* (London 1979)

Thomson, Joan L. 'Giacomo Meyerbeer: the Jew and his Relationship with Richard Wagner', *Musica Judaica*, i (1975–6), no. 1, pp. 54–86

Turing, Penelope. *New Bayreuth* (London 1969)

Vetter, Isolde. *'Der fliegende Holländer' von Richard Wagner: Entstehung, Bearbeitung, Überlieferung* (diss. Technical University, Berlin 1982; publication in prep.)

—— 'The "Ahasverus of the Oceans" – Musically Unredeemed? The Flying Dutchman and its Revisions', Bayreuth Festival Programme, vol. ii (*Der fliegende Holländer*), 1979, pp. 27–33

Viereck, Peter. *Metapolitics: The Roots of the Nazi Mind* (New York 1961; rev. and enlarged edn of *Metapolitics: From the Romantics to Hitler*, New York 1941). See esp. chaps 5 and 6, pp. 90–143, and the Letter from Thomas Mann 'To the Editor of *Common Sense*', repr. on pp. 356–63.

Voss, Egon. *Die Dirigenten der Bayreuther Festspiele* (Regensburg 1976)

—— 'Once again: the secret of form in Wagner's works' [critique of Lorenz], *Wagner*, iv (1983), 66–79. Eng. trans. of article that appeared in *Theaterarbeit an Wagners Ring*, ed. D. Mack (Munich 1978), 251–67

—— *Richard Wagner: Dokumentarbiographie* (Mainz and Munich 1982) [rev. and extended edn of Barth, Mack and Voss (eds), 1975]

—— *Richard Wagner und die Instrumentalmusik: Wagners symphonischer Ehrgeiz* (Wilhelmshaven 1977)

—— *Studien zur Instrumentation Richard Wagners* (Regensburg 1970)

Wagner, the periodical of the Wagner Society; see under S. Spencer.

Wagner, Wolf-Siegfried. *The Wagner Family Albums* (Eng. trans.) (London 1976)

Wapnewski, Peter. *Der traurige Gott: Richard Wagner in seinen Helden* (Munich 1978)

Watson, Derek. *Richard Wagner: A Biography* (London 1979)

Westernhagen, Curt von. *Richard Wagners Dresdener Bibliothek 1842–1849* (Wiesbaden 1966)

—— *The forging of the 'Ring': Richard Wagner's composition sketches for 'Der Ring des Nibelungen'* (Eng. trans.) (Cambridge 1976)

—— *Vom Holländer zum Parsifal: Neue Wagner-Studien* (Zurich 1962)

—— *Wagner: A Biography*, 2 vols (Eng. trans.) (Cambridge 1978)

—— 'Wagner's Last Day', *Musical Times*, cxx (1979), 395–7

Whittall, Arnold. 'The music', chap. in L. Beckett, *Richard Wagner: 'Parsifal'* (Cambridge 1981)

—— 'The Music: A Commentary', in *The Mastersingers of Nuremberg*, Opera Guide 19, ed. Nicholas John (London 1983), 15–26

—— *Wagner in Transition* (in prep.)

—— 'Wagner's Music Dramas', *New Oxford History of Music*, ed. G. Abraham, ix (*Romanticism*) (forthcoming)

Wolzogen, H. von. *Guide through the music of R. Wagner's 'The Ring of the Nibelung'* (Eng. trans.) (London and Leipzig 1882). [The guide first appeared in 1876, after which the title of both German and English versions varied from edition to edition.]

Zelinsky, Hartmut. 'Die "feuerkur" des Richard Wagner oder die "neue religion" der "Erlösung" durch "Vernichtung" ', *Musik-Konzepte 5: Richard Wagner: wie antisemitisch darf ein Künstler sein?* (Munich 1978)

—— *Richard Wagner: ein deutsches Thema: Eine Dokumentation zur Wirkungsgeschichte Richard Wagners* (Vienna 3/1983)

Zuckerman, Elliott. *The First Hundred Years of Wagner's Tristan* (New York and London 1964)

Important publications since 1984 include:

Bailey, Robert (ed.) *Prelude and Transfiguration from 'Tristan and Isolde'* (Norton Critical Scores) (New York and London 1985)

Bloch, Ernst. *Essays on the Philosophy of Music* (Eng. trans.) (Cambridge 1985), esp. 'Paradoxes and the Pastorale in Wagner's Music', 146–82

Deathridge, John, and Dahlhaus, Carl. *Wagner* (The *New Grove* Composer Biography Series) (London and New York 1984)

Dennison, Peter (ed.) *The Richard Wagner Centenary in Australia* (Adelaide 1985)

Katz, Jacob. *The Darker Side of Genius: Richard Wagner's Anti-Semitism* (Eng. trans.) (Hanover, New Hampshire, and London 1986)

Large, David C., and Weber, William. *Wagnerism in European Culture and Politics* (Ithaca, New York, and London 1984)

Mann, Thomas. *Pro and Contra Wagner* [Eng. trans. of Mann's writings on Wagner] (London 1985)

Appendix E   The stages of Wagner's composition

The issues raised by Wagner's changing method of composition are discussed in chapters 10–19 (see esp. pp. 124–5, 170, 182–3, and 196–7). The following table is based on the nomenclature adopted for the *Verzeichnis der musikalischen Werke Richard Wagners und ihrer Quellen* by J. Deathridge, M. Geck and E. Voss (Mainz 1985).

Early operas	sketches	complete draft		fair copy of full score
Tannhäuser	sketches for individual sections	(fragmentary) complete draft (i.e. survives in fragmentary form)	complete draft	fair copy of full score
Lohengrin	first complete draft	second complete draft		fair copy of full score
Rheingold	complete draft	full score (draft)		fair copy of full score
Walküre	complete draft	full score		fair copy of full score
Siegfried (Acts I/II) and *Tristan* (Prelude to Act I)	first complete draft	second complete draft	full score	fair copy of full score
Tristan (remainder) and *Meistersinger* (Act I)	first complete draft	second complete draft		fair copy of full score
Meistersinger (Acts II/III), *Siegfried* (Act III), *Götterdämmerung* and *Parsifal*	first complete draft	second complete draft (short score)		fair copy of full score

Index

Index

About the Author

Barry Millington has written widely for newspapers and periodicals, including *The Times* and *The Musical Times*. He is now at work (with Stewart Spencer) on a selection of Wagner's letters in translation.